JOURNAL FOR THE STUDY OF THE PSEUDEPIGRAPHA
SUPPLEMENT SERIES
44

Editors
Lester L. Grabbe
James H. Charlesworth

Editorial Board
Randall D. Chesnutt, Philip R. Davies, Jan Willem van Henten,
Judith M. Lieu, Steven Mason, James R. Mueller, Loren T.
Stuckenbruck, James C. VanderKam

The Antichrist Theme in the Intertestamental Period

G.W. Lorein

T&T CLARK INTERNATIONAL
A Continuum imprint
LONDON • NEW YORK

Copyright © 2003 T&T Clark International
A Continuum imprint

Published by T&T Clark International
The Tower Building, 11 York Road, London SE1 7NX
15 East 26th Street, Suite 1703, New York, NY 10010

www.tandtclark.com

All rights reserved. No part of this publication may be reproduced or transmitted in any form or by any means, electronic or mechanical, including photocopying, recording or any information storage or retrieval system, without permission in writing from the publishers.

British Library Cataloguing-in-Publication Data
A catalogue record for this book is available from the British Library

Library of Congress Cataloging-in-Publication Data
A catalogue record for this book is available from the Library of Congress

Typeset by CA Typesetting, Sheffield
Printed on acid-free paper in Great Britain by MPG Books Ltd, Bodmin, Cornwall

ISBN 0-8264-6653-2 (hardback)
     0-5670-8300-4 (paperback)

CONTENTS

Preface vii
Abbreviations ix

Chapter 1
INTRODUCTION 1
  1. A Survey of the Antichrist in the Intertestamental Period 1
  2. The Antichrist in the New Testament and in the Writings of the Church Fathers 26
  3. The Antichrist in the Old Testament 30

Chapter 2
THE ANTICHRIST IN THE APOCRYPHA AND PSEUDEPIGRAPHA 43
  1. Introduction 43
  2. Psalm 152 44
  3. Sirach: Laus Patrum 46
  4. *Sibylline Oracles*, Book 3, Oldest Parts 49
  5. Judith 57
  6. 2 Maccabees 65
  7. 1 Maccabees 77
  8. *3 Maccabees* 83
  9. *Psalms of Solomon* 89
  10. *Testaments of the Twelve Patriarchs* 106
  11. *Sibylline Oracles*, Book 3, Old Additions 125
  12. *Treatise of Shem* 129
  13. *Assumption of Moses* 133
  14. *2 Enoch* 142

Chapter 3
THE ANTICHRIST IN THE QUMRAN WRITINGS 148
  1. Introduction 148
  2. *Pseudo-Ezekiel* 150
  3. *Wiles of the Wicked Woman* 153

	4. *Damascus Document*	163
	5. *Testimonia*	179
	6. *Hymns*	186
	7. *Nahum Pesher*	192
	8. *Habakkuk Pesher*	197
	9. *War Scroll*	205
	10. *Pseudo-Moses*	217

Chapter 4
THE ANTICHRIST IN THE INTERTESTAMENTAL PERIOD 219
   1. Theme Development 219
   2. Comparisons with Other Figures 233
   3. Evaluation of the Views of Other Researchers 236
   4. Final Conclusions 241

Bibliography 244
Index of References 267
Index of Authors 278

PREFACE

It has been a number of years since my wife and I were sitting in Professor A.S. van der Woude's study, and he suggested that since I had written a Licentiate's thesis on the figure of Antioch IV Epiphanes in Jewish apocalyptic sources, I might as well look at the theme of the Antichrist in the intertestamental period. However, the *word* 'Antichrist' does not appear in writings of that period and I soon found that it was vitally important to give a clear description of the *theme*. It seemed best to do this on the basis of the earliest possible texts in which the word Antichrist has a clearly distinguishable meaning, that is, the texts of the Church Fathers. From these I made a definition of the theme of the Antichrist and then looked at whether the theme occurs in the writings of the intertestamental period, even though the word itself does not. The results of my research are set out in this work. I found the research interesting and I hope that the reader will agree. Although it meant focusing on the same subject for several years, it was good to delve into the intertestamental period and its writings—the Jewish non-protocanonical, non-epigraphical writings in which Christian influence is impossible—as they form such an important background to the study of both the Old and the New Testament.

The first version of this research was presented at the University of Groningen on 19 June 1997; my promoters were Professor A.S. van der Woude and Professor A. Schoors. I am very grateful to both of them. Professor Van der Woude has since passed away (Oosterlittens, 16 October 1927–Groningen, 18 November 2000). May the number of references to his writings serve as a homage to him.

For this newer version of my research I have attempted to include any truly new viewpoints dating from 1997 and later, at times as recent as the year 2000. I wish to express my thanks to the late Professor A.-M. Denis (Fulham, 16 October 1915–Hermalle-sous-Argenteau, 15 November 1999) and to Professor J.H. Charlesworth for allowing me to publish in this series. I want to thank Dr A. Hilhorst and Professor J.C. de Moor for their encouragement, and Marjolein Turner-Prins MITI for her translation. I would also like to thank my wife Erika; my work has taken up a lot of her time. I hope that this work may be of use to other researchers and that she will be pleased as well.

Leuven, December 2001

ABBREVIATIONS

Bibliographical

AB	Anchor Bible
ad loc(c).	at the place(s) discussed
AGJU	Arbeiten zur Geschichte des antiken Judentums und des Urchristentums
ALGHJ	Arbeiten zur Literatur und Geschichte des hellenistischen Judentums
ANRW	Hildegard Temporini and Wolfgang Haase (eds.), *Aufstieg und Niedergang der römischen Welt: Geschichte und Kultur Roms im Spiegel der neueren Forschung* (Berlin: W. de Gruyter, 1972–)
ANTJ	Arbeiten zum Neuen Testament und Judentum
AOAT	Alter Orient und Altes Testament
APOT	R.H. Charles (ed.), *Apocrypha and Pseudepigrapha of the Old Testament in English* (2 vols.; Oxford: Clarendon Press, 1913)
ArOr	*Archiv orientální*
ATANT	Abhandlungen zur Theologie des Alten und Neuen Testaments
ATDan	Acta Theologica Danica
BASOR	*Bulletin of the American Schools of Oriental Research*
BDR	Friedrich Blass, Albert Debrunner and Friedrich Rehkopf, *Grammatik des neutestamentlichen Griechisch* (Göttingen: Vandenhoeck & Ruprecht, 16th edn, 1984 [and other editions])
BEATAJ	Beiträge zur Erforschung des Alten Testaments und des antiken Judentums
BETL	Bibliotheca ephemeridum theologicarum lovaniensium
BJRL	*Bulletin of the John Rylands University Library of Manchester*
BSOAS	*Bulletin of the School of Oriental and African Studies*
BZNW	Beihefte zur *ZNW*
CAH	Cambridge Ancient History
CAT	Commentaire de l'Ancien Testament
CBQ	*Catholic Biblical Quarterly*
CBQMS	*Catholic Biblical Quarterly*, Monograph Series
CChr	Corpus Christianorum
CNT	Commentaire du Nouveau Testament
ConBOT	Coniectanea biblica, Old Testament

corr. edn	corrected edition
CRAIBL	*Comptes rendus de l'Académie des inscriptions et belles-lettres*
CRINT	Compendia rerum iudaicarum ad Novum Testamentum
DJD	Discoveries in the Judaean Desert
DSD	*Dead Sea Discoveries*
DTT	*Dansk teologisk tidsskrift*
EBib	Etudes bibliques
EKKNT	Evangelisch-Katholischer Kommentar zum Neuen Testament
ETL	*Ephemerides theologicae lovanienses*
fr(r).	fragment(s)
FRLANT	Forschungen zur Religion und Literatur des Alten und Neuen Testaments
GCS	Griechische christliche Schriftsteller
HNT	Handbuch zum Neuen Testament
HO	Handbuch der Orientalistik
HSM	Harvard Semitic Monographs
HSS	Harvard Semitic Studies
HTR	*Harvard Theological Review*
IBP	Institut Biblique Pontifical
ICC	International Critical Commentary
IOS	*Israel Oriental Studies*
JAOS	*Journal of the American Oriental Society*
JBL	*Journal of Biblical Literature*
JJS	*Journal of Jewish Studies*
JQR	*Jewish Quarterly Review*
JSHRZ	Jüdische Schriften aus hellenistisch-römischer Zeit
JSJ	*Journal for the Study of Judaism in the Persian, Hellenistic and Roman Period*
JSJSup	JSJ Supplement Series
JSNTSup	*Journal for the Study of the New Testament*, Supplement Series
JSOTSup	*Journal for the Study of the Old Testament*, Supplement Series
JSP	*Journal for the Study of the Pseudepigrapha*
JSPSup	*Journal for the Study of the Pseudepigrapha*, Supplement Series
KAT	Kommentar zum Alten Testament
KEK	Kritisch-exegetischer Kommentar über das Neue Testament
LCL	Loeb Classical Library
LD	Lectio divina
LLAVT	E. Vogt, *Lexicon linguae Aramaicae Veteris Testamenti documentis antiquis illustratum* (Roma: Pontifical Institutum Biblicum, 1971)
LSJ	H.G. Liddell, Robert Scott and H. Stuart Jones, *Greek–English Lexicon* (Oxford: Clarendon Press, 9th edn, 1968)

Abbreviations

*LTK*²	J. Höfer, K. Rahner and M. Buchberger, *Lexikon für Theologie und Kirche* (Freiburg: Herder, 2nd edn, 1957–68)
Mem.	Memorial
Mus	*Le Muséon*
NedTTs	*Nederlands Theologisch Tijdschrift*
NICNT	New International Commentary on the New Testament
NICOT	New International Commentary on the Old Testament
NTOA	Novum Testamentum et orbis antiquus
NTS	*New Testament Studies*
NumenSup	Numen Supplement Series
OBO	Orbis biblicus et orientalis
*OCD*²	N.G.L. Hammond and H.H. Scullard (eds.), *Oxford Classical Dictionary* (Oxford: Clarendon Press, 2nd edn, 1970)
Or	*Orientalia*
OTL	Old Testament Library
OTP	James Charlesworth (ed.), *Old Testament Pseudepigrapha*
OTS	*Oudtestamentische Studiën*
PEQ	*Palestine Exploration Quarterly*
PGL	G.W.H. Lampe, *Patristic Greek Lexicon* (Oxford: Clarendon Press, 1961)
PIB	Pontificium Institutum Biblicum
PVTG	Pseudepigrapha Veteris Testamenti graece
PW	August Friedrich von Pauly and Georg Wissowa (eds.), *Real-Encyclopädie der classischen Altertumswissenschaft* (Stuttgart: Metzler, 1894–)
RB	*Revue Biblique*
REJ	*Revue des études juives*
RevQ	*Revue de Qumran*
*RGG*²	H. Gunkel and L. Zscharnack (eds.), *Religion in Geschichte und Gegenwart* (Tübingen: Mohr, 2nd edn, 1927–32)
RHPR	*Revue d'histoire et de philosophie religieuses*
RHR	*Revue de l'histoire des religions*
RTL	*Revue théologique de Louvain*
SacEr	*Sacris erudiri*
SB	Sources bibliques
SBLDS	SBL Dissertation Series
SBLEJL	SBL Early Judaism and Its Literature
SBLMS	SBL Monograph Series
SBLSCS	SBL Septuagint and Cognate Studies
SBM	Stuttgarter biblische Monographien
SBT	Studies in Biblical Theology
ScEs	*Science et esprit*
ScrHier	Scripta Hierosolymitana
s.d.	no date
Sem	*Semitica*

SJLA	Studies in Judaism in Late Antiquity
SJOT	*Scandinavian Journal of the Old Testament*
SPB	Studia post-biblica
SSN	Studia Semitica Neerlandica
ST	*Studia Theologica*
STDJ	Studies on the Texts of the Desert of Judah
SUNT	Studien zur Umwelt des Neuen Testaments
s.v./s.vv.	under the words
SVTP	Studia in Veteris Testamenti pseudepigrapha
TS	*Theological Studies*
TLZ	*Theologische Literaturzeitung*
TRu	*Theologische Rundschau*
TTZ	*Trierer theologische Zeitschrift*
TU	Texte und Untersuchungen
TWNT	Gerhard Kittel and Gerhard Friedrich (eds.), *Theologisches Wörterbuch zum Neuen Testament* (11 vols.; Stuttgart, W. Kohlhammer, 1932–79)
TOTC	Tyndale Old Testament Commentaries
TZ	*Theologische Zeitschrift*
VT	*Vetus Testamentum*
VTSup	*Vetus Testamentum*, Supplements
WBC	Word Biblical Commentary
WUNT	Wissenschaftliche Untersuchungen zum Neuen Testament
ZAW	*Zeitschrift für die alttestamentliche Wissenschaft*
ZNW	*Zeitschrift für die neutestamentliche Wissenschaft*

Philological

acc.	accusative
act.	active voice
adv.	adverb
aor.	aorist
Aram.	Aramaic
Arm.	Armenian
cj.	conjecture
conj.	conjunctive; conjunction
fem.	feminine
fut.	future
fut. s.	future simple
Gr.	Greek
Gr. acc.	accusative of limitation
Hebr.	Hebrew
imperf. (cons.)	imperfect (consecutive)
ind.	indicative
ind. juss.	indirect jussive

inf. abs.	infinitive absolute
lit.	literally
m.	masculine
med.	middle voice
MS(S)	manuscript(s)
opt.	optative
perf. (cons.)	perfect (consecutive)
pl.	plural
prep.	preposition
ptc.	participle
sg.	singular
st. abs.	absolute state
st. cstr.	construct state
subst.	substantive
suff.	suffix
Syr.	Syriac
trans.	translation
v.l.	variant reading
v. app. crit.	see the critical apparatus

Textual

א	Codex Sinaiticus
α'	Aquila
θ'	Theodotion
σ'	Symmachus
LXX	Septuagint
MT	Masoretic Text
NT	New Testament
SamP	Samaritan Pentateuch
Tg.	*Targum*

Apocrypha

1 Macc.	1 Maccabees
2 Macc.	2 Maccabees
Jdt.	Judith
Sir.	Sirach

Other early Jewish and Christian Literature

Asc. Isa.	*Ascension of Isaiah*
Ass. Mos.	*Assumption of Moses*

Patristic

Ep. Polyc.	*Epistle of Polycarp*

Pseudepigrapha
2 Bar.	*2 Baruch*
3 Macc.	*3 Maccabees*
4 Macc.	*4 Maccabees*
Jub.	*Jubilees*
Pss. Sol.	*Psalms of Solomon*
Sib. Or.	*Sibylline Oracles*
T. XII Patr.	*Testaments of the Twelve Patriarchs*
T. Ash.	*Testament of Asher*
T. Benj.	*Testament of Benjamin*
T. Dan	*Testament of Dan*
T. Gad	*Testament of Gad*
T. Iss.	*Testament of Issachar*
T. Jud.	*Testament of Judah*
T. Levi	*Testament of Levi*
T. Naph.	*Testament of Naphtali*
T. Sim.	*Testament of Simeon*
T. Zeb.	*Testament of Zebulun*
Tr. Shem	*Treatise of Shem*

Qumran
1Q2 iii 4	From the first cave, the second fragment, third column, line 4
1QH	The large scroll of *Hymns* from the first cave
1QM	*War Scroll*
1QpHab	*Habakkuk Pesher* from the first cave
1QS	*Rule of the Community*
4QpPs	*Psalms Pesher* from the fourth cave
4QSam[a]	4Q51 (first scroll of the biblical book of Samuel from the 4th cave)
4QTest	4Q175 (*Testimonia*)
4QWWW	4Q184 (*Wiles of the Wicked Woman*)
CD	*Damascus Document*
CšD	*Songs of David* from the *Genizah* of Cairo
M	*War Scroll*
PAM	photograph of the Palestine Archaeological Museum
Test.	4Q175 (*Testimonia*)

Chapter 1

INTRODUCTION

1. *A Survey of the Antichrist in the Intertestamental Period*

a. *Introduction*
Although there has never been a time in which no attention was paid to the Antichrist figure, scholarly research into this subject—especially research focusing on the intertestamental period—is of recent date. It was the *religionsgeschichtliche* (History of Religions) School, with its interest in this period, as well as Bousset's book,[1] that has turned the spotlight on this issue. Another advantage of choosing the *religionsgeschichtliche* School as our starting point is that it is the oldest 'modern' school of research that still holds influence in the area of exegesis.[2]

After discussing the *religionsgeschichtliche* School we will look at several other researchers. Of course we need to be selective, since not all explorations into the subject of the Antichrist in New Testament commentaries can be included in this historical overview. We will focus on the important works of Charles and Rigaux, and on some of the lines of thought that have arisen as a result of the discovery of the Qumran writings.

The most recent researchers are also included in this historical overview.[3]

b. *Religionsgeschichte*
The *religionsgeschichtliche* School came into being at the eve of the twentieth century, at the theological faculty of Göttingen, in an attempt to study New Testament theology—and especially New Testament apocalyptic—in

---

1. W. Bousset, *Der Antichrist* (Göttingen: Vandenhoeck & Ruprecht, 1895).
2. For an overview covering the period from the Middle Ages to *zeitgeschichtliche* exegesis, see M.J. van der Westhuizen, *De Antichrist in het Nieuwe Testament* (Amsterdam: Van Bottenburg, 1916), pp. 9-41.
3. For a *comparison* between the results of these researchers and the author's, see Chapter 4.

the extra-biblical context from which its terms historically originated. The school used the norms and methods prevailing in classical philology and orientalistics, mainly looking for the 'historical' aspect in the areas of culture and religion—which explains its name.[4] It thus arrived at Hellenism and the many cultures of the ancient Near East, including Egypt, while focusing on the beliefs of the common people.[5] This method was later also applied to the Old Testament, thereby bringing to an end the *zeitgeschichtliche* method, which Gunkel[6] considered impossible in most places.[7] The only positive aspect of the *zeitgeschichtliche* method, Gunkel thought, was its breaking away from the ecclesiastical interpretation.[8]

Eissfeldt mentions the following founders of the *religionsgeschichtliche* School: W. Bousset, A. Eichhorn,[9] H. Gunkel and W. Wrede.[10] Eissfeldt believes that E. Troeltsch[11] and J. Weiss[12] also belong to the first genera-

---

4. G. Lüdemann and M. Schröder, *Die Religionsgeschichtliche Schule in Göttingen* (Göttingen: Vandenhoeck & Ruprecht, 1987), p. 7. A.F. Verheule, *Wilhelm Bousset: Leben und Werk. Ein theologiegeschichtlicher Versuch* (Amsterdam: Bolland, 1973), pp. 74, 281.

5. Verheule, *Bousset*, pp. 65 (quoting Bousset, *Antichrist*, p. 2), 301. Cf. Eissfeldt, 'Religionsgeschichtliche Schule', RGG^2, IV, cols. 1898–1905 (1900): During the last 30 years of the nineteenth century, historians started to put the main emphasis on the masses rather than on important figures.

6. H. Gunkel, *Schöpfung und Chaos in Urzeit und Endzeit. Eine religionsgeschichtliche Untersuchung über Gen 1 und Ap Joh 12* (Göttingen: Vandenhoeck & Ruprecht, 1895), p. 233. However, Bousset pays more attention to the *Zeitgeschichte*: see n. 32 below.

7. The name of Renan (1823–92) deserves special mention here. See A. Bertholet, 'Renan', RGG^2, IV, cols. 1983-84.

8. Gunkel, *Schöpfung und Chaos*, p. 233. One could say that the ecclesiastical explanation for the present looked at the author's present (1st century CE), and the *religionsgeschichtliche* explanation to the past.

9. 1856–1926. See Lüdemann and Schröder, *Die Religionsgeschichtliche Schule*, pp. 63-66; H. Mulert, 'Eichhorn', RGG^2, II, col. 46. This and further references will be to the RGG's 2nd edition, since this edition is closest to the people concerned.

10. 1859–1906. See Lüdemann and Schröder, *Die Religionsgeschichtliche Schule*, pp. 90-108; A. Meyer, 'Wrede', RGG^2, V, col. 2025.

11. 1865–1923. See Lüdemann and Schröder, *Die Religionsgeschichtliche Schule*, pp. 81-87; K. Bornhausen, 'Troeltsch', RGG^2, V, cols. 1284-87.

12. 1863–1914. See Lüdemann and Schröder, *Die Religionsgeschichtliche Schule*, pp. 88-89; A. Meyer, 'Weiss', RGG^2, V, col. 1811; B. Lannert, *Die Wiederentdeckung der neutestamentlichen Eschatologie durch Johannes Weiss* (Tübingen: Francke, 1989). This school of thought according to Eissfeldt, 'Religionsgeschichtliche Schule', cols.

tion. Of course the members of this core group were themselves influenced by others, but they independently developed into a new school. Systematic theologian A. Ritschl[13] and the dogmatics historian A. von Harnack[14] may be regarded as 'forerunners' or rather as influencing predecessors, as well as B. Duhm,[15] P.A. de Lagarde[16] and J. Wellhausen,[17] who were all orientalists, or Old Testament specialists, or both.[18]

The big breakthrough of the *religionsgeschichtliche* School came in 1895, when H. Gunkel's *Schöpfung und Chaos* was published.[19] It contains all the typical characteristics of the *religionsgeschichtliche* School, including its weaknesses. From this moment the School experienced great success, which has undoubtedly contributed to the establishment of a chair in religious studies and religious history. From 1904, for instance, there were six full professors per theological faculty.

1898-99; he includes H. Gressmann and S. Mowinckel (about whom see N.A. Dahl, 'Sigmund Mowinckel: Historian of Religion and Theologian', *SJOT* [2.]2 [1988], pp. 8-22 [esp. 9-11]) in the second generation; cf. Lüdemann and Schröder, *Die Religionsgeschichtliche Schule*, p. 15, and Verheule, *Bousset*, p. 314. I would also include R. Reitzenstein with the older authors who became well-known mainly for their *religionsgeschichtliche* work. The reason he was not included in Eissfeldt's list is probably that he was a classicist, not a theologian (Verheule, *Bousset*, p. 374; cf. Eissfeldt's definition ['Religionsgeschichtliche Schule', col. 1898]: 'eine Gruppe gleichgerichteter und gleichgesinnter theologischer [!] Forscher'.)

13. 1822–1889. See H. Stephan, 'Ritschl', *RGG*², IV, cols. 2043-46. For Ritschlianism, see Verheule, *Bousset*, pp. 271-78. Ritschl was not really a 'forerunner': Eissfeldt, 'Religionsgeschichtliche Schule', col. 1899, claims it was a reactionary movement *against* Ritschl.

14. 1851–1930. See H. Freiherr von Soden, 'Von Harnack', *RGG*², II, cols. 1633-36; W. Döbertin, *Adolf von Harnack: Theologe, Pädagoge, Wissenschaftspolitiker* (European University Studies, 23.258; Frankfurt: Lang, 1985).

15. 1847–1928. See H. Gunkel, 'Duhm', *RGG*², I, cols. 2043-44.

16. 1827–1891. See E. Littmann, 'De Lagarde', *RGG*², III, cols. 1452-53.

17. 1844–1918. See H. Gunkel, 'Wellhausen', *RGG*², V, cols. 1820-22.

18. Lüdemann and Schröder, *Die Religionsgeschichtliche Schule*, pp. 13, 25-31; Verheule, *Bousset*, pp. 11, 276, 281, 298.

19. Eissfeldt, 'Religionsgeschichtliche Schule', col. 1902; Verheule, *Bousset*, p. 65; W. Klatt, *Hermann Gunkel: Zu seiner Theologie der Religionsgeschichte und zur Entstehung der formgeschichtlichen Methode* (FRLANT, 100; Göttingen: Vandenhoeck & Ruprecht, 1969), p. 77. This was also the year Bousset's *Der Antichrist* was published, but he had skimmed through the draft version of *Schöpfung und Chaos* (Verheule, *Bousset*, p. 66).

Wilhelm Bousset has been called the head of the school by his biographer Verheule.[20] Although this is not completely true, he was one of its most important representatives, especially on the subject of the Antichrist. We will therefore delve a little deeper into his life and method.

Johann Franz Wilhelm Bousset was born on 3 September 1865 in Lübeck, the eldest son of clergyman Johann Hermann Bousset and his wife Auguste. The family were descendants of Patrician Huguenots who had fled to Germany from France.[21] His studies took him to several German universities, but he spent most of his time in Göttingen, where he was heavily influenced by Ritschl.[22] After his clerical exams he decided to pursue an academic career, and returned to Göttingen. Not all obstacles in his career were successfully overcome, but in 1890 he received his first permission to teach—*venia legendi*—on New Testament exegesis. In 1895 he even received payment for this.[23] Shortly afterwards[24] his work *Der Antichrist in der Überlieferung des Judentums, des neuen Testaments und der alten Kirche: Ein Beitrag zur Auslegung der Apokalypse* was published. In 1896 he became extraordinary professor. From 1915 he was full professor in Giessen,[25] where he died 8 March 1920.

Der Antichrist is a very wide collection of everything that was written about the Antichrist during the first centuries CE and BCE. Bousset assumes that what was said in later times may largely be projected back into the intertestamental period, because in those times thought developed so slowly, or rather was so stable, that there were no differences between ideas from the intertestamental period and the traditions found with the

---

20. Verheule, *Bousset*, p. 352.
21. Verheule, *Bousset*, p. 5; Lüdemann and Schröder, *Die Religionsgeschichtliche Schule*, p. 55.
22. Verheule, *Bousset*, p. 11; Lüdemann and Schröder, *Die Religionsgeschichtliche Schule*, p. 55.
23. Around the turn of the century, a career at a German university meant financial hardship—apart from the academic obstacles they had to overcome, people needed considerable financial resources to reach the function of full professor. Full professors were paid well (Lüdemann and Schröder, *Die Religionsgeschichtliche Schule*, pp. 143-46).
24. The preface dates from June 1895 (Bousset). Salary payment dates from 25 April 1895 (Lüdemann and Schröder, *Die Religionsgeschichtliche Schule*, p. 55).
25. Lüdemann and Schröder, *Die Religionsgeschichtliche Schule*, pp. 55-56. By German standards, Bousset changed universities very little during his career (cf. the other biographies in the survey).

Church Fathers.[26] Bousset also assumes that through oral tradition the Church Fathers still had access to materials originating directly from the intertestamental period,[27] and that the 'classical' form of the Antichrist myth, as found in the book of Revelation, is an eschatologization and personification of a myth that was originally a creation myth. This idea is essentially in agreement with Gunkel.[28] Unlike Gunkel, however, Bousset looks for the origin of this myth in Iran rather than Babylon.[29] According to him, Gog and Magog are closely related to the image of the Antichrist,[30] and the development from dragon myth to Antichrist myth took place relatively late.[31] The writer of Revelation, however, did not just *repeat* old traditions, he *assimilated* them to make them useful for his own message.[32]

In view of the assumed stability it is not surprising that Bousset's collection contains mostly late Christian writings, while we are more interested in what actually happened during the intertestamental period. Bousset too often *reconstructs* from certain sources what might have existed in the old times.[33]

He also assumes that Belial in the New Testament[34] is synonymous with the Antichrist, and that the Belial mentioned in other texts[35] is an interme-

---

26. This stability axiom did not originate with Bousset, but with Gunkel (J. Ernst, *Die eschatologischen Gegenspieler in den Schriften des Neuen Testaments* [Biblische Untersuchungen, 3; Regensburg: Pustet, 1967], p. 278).

27. Verheule, *Bousset*, p. 69. Cf. Bousset, *Antichrist*, pp. 14-15, 18-19.

28. Verheule, *Bousset*, p. 70. Cf. Bousset, *Antichrist*, pp. 62-93.

29. Verheule, *Bousset*, pp. 70-71; F. König, *Zarathustras Jenseitsvorstellungen und das Alte Testament* (Wien: Herder, 1964), p. 12; M. Boyce, 'On the Antiquity of Zoroastrian Apocalyptic', *BSOAS* 47 (1984), pp. 57-75 (73). This does not happen very much in his work of 1895, in which Bousset, *Antichrist*, p. 4, warns against overconfidence on this point. However, see pp. 408-10, 435-36.

30. Bousset, *Antichrist*, pp. 128-29.

31. Bousset, *Antichrist*, p. 122 ('Um die Zeit des neuen Testaments'); *idem*, *Die Offenbarung Johannis* (KEK; Göttingen: Vandenhoeck & Ruprecht, 5th edn, 1896), p. 385 n. 1 (probably the end of the Maccabean era). The two concepts can be reconciled if both are taken quite generally.

32. Verheule, *Bousset*, pp. 66-67, 74-76, 84-85. Cf. Bousset, *Antichrist*, p. 3, where he stresses the 'traditionsmässige', and p. 6, where he stresses their assimilation ('Auch dann, wenn der Apokalyptiker traditionsmässig feststehendes Material herübernimmt, thut er dies vielfach doch nicht ganz grundlos. Er denkt dabei dann doch an seine Zeit und ihre Vorgänge').

33. E.g. Bousset, *Antichrist*, p. 62.

34. Bousset, *Antichrist*, pp. 86, 99: 2 Cor. 6.15.

35. Bousset, *Antichrist*, pp. 99-101: in *T. Dan.*, *Sib. Or.* 3; *Asc. Isa.*

diate between the protological dragon and the eschatological Antichrist. In later times Judaism developed the Antichrist figure even further under the name of Armillus, taken from Romulus, thus showing their hatred towards Rome, which was then Christian.[36]

The definition that Bousset attributes to the term 'Antichrist' is naturally closely related to his method. His method, in which he uses texts from all ages and places, leads to a very complex Antichrist image. Actually, he never really defines the Antichrist, so we will have to collect elements from several places. Strictly speaking, these elements are applicable to many different figures, but Bousset combines them under the common heading of 'Antichrist'.

Problematic at this point is the relationship between the Antichrist and Satan. Is the Antichrist identical to Satan, or is he only a servant? This is often difficult to determine.[37] According to Bousset, the Antichrist is the incarnation of Satan, but in a human form.[38] He does state, however, that the early Church was not united on this subject.[39] Beliar, who is at least the *forerunner* of the Antichrist, is either an evil spirit, or Satan himself.[40] The complete figure is presented in more than one form in the book of Revelation—'der Drache, das Tier, der Pseudoprophet'—whereby the source of the image, as well as two different elaborations of it, feature in the form of three different figures. The old Antichrist function is found mostly in the Pseudoprophet, the helper of the first beast.[41] It is clear that the Antichrist contains several different elements, stemming from one root: he is both a God-hating tyrant and a false messiah.[42]

We may conclude that Bousset has worked very thoroughly, although now, a century later, improvements on details may be possible. The big problem however, is that he assumes that thinking in the first centuries CE

36. Bousset, *Antichrist*, pp. 66, 123. Actually even in the book of Revelation: *idem, Offenbarung Johannis* (1896), p. 432.

37. C. Fontinoy, 'Les noms du Diable et leur étymologie', *Acta Iranica* 23 (1984), pp. 157-70 (157): '...on ne voit pas toujours clairement la différence entre les noms portés par le Diable lui-même et ceux qui l'ont été par certains de ses subordonnés.'

38. Bousset, *Antichrist*, pp. 80, 93; *idem, Die Offenbarung Johannis* (KEK; Göttingen: Vandenhoeck & Ruprecht, 6th edn, 1906), p. 329.

39. Bousset, *Antichrist*, pp. 88-89.

40. Bousset, *Antichrist*, pp. 100, 115; *Offenbarung Johannis* (1896), p. 385 n. 1.

41. Bousset, *Antichrist*, pp. 121-24; *Offenbarung Johannis* (1896), p. 432; *Offenbarung Johannis* (1906), p. 378.

42. Bousset, *Offenbarung Johannis* (1896), p. 383; *Offenbarung Johannis* (1906), pp. 327-28, 378.

1. *Introduction* 7

and BCE was so static, that it is possible to draw conclusions on the thinking of the whole intertestamental period by looking merely at very late literature. This 'stability axiom' is unacceptable. Another problem is that, strictly speaking, he does not arrive at a definition of the term 'Antichrist' for the intertestamental period.[43]

Hermann Gunkel (1862–1932)[44] assumes that the origin of ideas about the Antichrist may be sought in Babylon wherever there is a striking analogy that cannot be explained from the Jewish internal context, and where interdependence is also probable for other reasons.[45] He does, however, feel free to work with hypotheses, and refers to the example of literary criticism.[46] According to Gunkel, the evolution from Protology to Eschatology took place as follows: The main theme of the *Enuma Elish* is death and resurrection in nature.[47] This is cyclical, which means that the things that happened in the past will happen again in the future. In Israel, this Babylonian primeval myth was often applied to actual situations (which changed all the time), in order to picture the approaching end of some enemy. Later, starting with a great prophet, people no longer interpreted these passages *zeitgeschichtlich* (in the context of its time), but eschatologically, that is, in order to give a picture of the approaching end of the world. The myth started a new life, no longer as a picture of the very first beginning, but of the very end. For example, the number 666 in Revelation has evolved from the number of תהום קדמוניה, the primeval monster Tiamat. Later 'users'

---

43. J. Geffcken, 'Die Sage vom Antichrist', *Preussische Jahrbücher* 102 (49. Jahrgang; 1900), pp. 385-99, claims to build on Bousset's work (p. 385), but he writes mainly about Nero (pp. 389-94) and Simon Magus (pp. 392-93).

44. Lüdemann and Schröder, *Die Religionsgeschichtliche Schule*, pp. 66-67; G. Wallis, 'Hermann Gunkel. Zum 100. Geburtstag am 23. Mai 1962', in *idem* (ed.), *Mein Freund hatte einen Weinberg, Aufsätze und Vorträge zum Alten Testament* (BEATAJ, 23; Frankfurt: Peter Lang, 1994), pp. 241-53 (242-43).

45. Verheule, *Bousset*, p. 357.

46. Gunkel, *Schöpfung und Chaos*, p. vi: 'Auf dem Gebiete der Literarkritik reconstruiert jedermann; und auf dem der Religionsgeschichte sollte das verboten sein?'

47. R. Labat, *Le poème babylonien de la création* (Paris: Adrien-Maisonneuve, 1935), p. 68. Cf. A.T. Nikolainen, *Der Auferstehungsglauben in der Bibel und ihrer Umwelt*. I. *Religionsgeschichtlicher Teil* (Annales academiae scientiarum Fennicae, B 49.3; Helsinki: Academia scientiarum Fennica, 1944), p. 60, and W. Paulus, 'Marduk Urtyp Christi?' (*Or*, 29; Rome: PIB, 1928), p. 44. However, J. Bottéro, *Mythes et rites de Babylonie* (Geneva: Slatkine–Champion, 1985), pp. 157-61, claims that the main theme is power.

did not necessarily know the original meaning.[48] The evidence for the position that the final idea definitely evolved from this early myth, is that in the biblical texts the fight with a pre-existing monster is also followed by creation.[49] Gunkel is surprised by the striking similarity between the original Babylonian primeval myth and the Israelite adapted version, although the 'adaptors' removed the names of the gods.

Gunkel clearly sees a link between the Babylonian creation myth and the Antichrist. But which Antichrist does he have in mind? What is Gunkel's definition of the Antichrist? His exegesis of Daniel shows that the author had based characteristics of the animals on Tiamat.[50] Tiamat is neither a goddess nor a human; therefore the Antichrist is not divine—this seems evident—but neither is he human—and this is important. However, much more cannot be concluded. 'The mountains brought forth a mouse', is Hepp's evaluation.[51] We should also remember that Gunkel sees Marduk as a type of Christ.

Since Gunkel's statements on the Antichrist are quite vague, we will now have to discuss his general approach, that is, his vision on the link between the biblical and the Babylonian images.

Gunkel's approach has already been criticized by his contemporaries. At this stage, we will not discuss Wellhausen's criticism of Gunkel. Wellhausen thinks that the place of origin of non-Jewish elements is not relevant and that Gunkel has therefore wasted his time.[52] This position actually criticizes the approach of the *religionsgeschichtliche* School in general and not Gunkel's specifically.

Bousset gives some general criticism in his 1896 commentary: he thinks Gunkel's position is too hypothetical.[53] He also thinks that the author of the book of Revelation is too serious to be playing number games.[54]

---

48. Gunkel, *Schöpfung und Chaos*, pp. 89-90, 111, 334-35, 369-70; p. 89: 'So beginnt die prophetische Verwendung des Mythus apokalyptische Deutung zu werden'; pp. 89, 328, mention Isa. 27.1; 30.7; Ezek. 29; 32; Ps. 68.31; 74; 87.4 as well as the basic text of Dan. 7. (Only the proto-canonical texts mentioned are referred to here.)

49. Gunkel, *Schöpfung und Chaos*, pp. 114, 292; Klatt, *Gunkel*, pp. 74-75; H.F.W. Saggs, *The Encounter with the Divine in Mesopotamia and Israel* (Jordan Lectures 1976; London: Athlone Press, 1978), p. 54.

50. Gunkel, *Schöpfung und Chaos*, pp. 332-33.

51. V. Hepp, *De Antichrist* (Kampen: Kok, 1st edn, 1919), p. 32.

52. Verheule, *Bousset*, pp. 353-54.

53. Bousset, *Offenbarung Johannis* (1896), pp. 408-10.

54. Bousset, *Offenbarung Johannis* (1896), pp. 435-36.

1. Introduction

One may conclude that Gunkel's surprise about the great similarity between the Babylonian primeval myth and its Israelite adaptation is unjustified: it was—at least partly—the logical consequence of his presuppositions. The fact that Gunkel sees references to the Babylonian chaos myth in so many Old Testament passages[55] also speaks against him: *Nihil probat qui nimium probat*. Saggs doubts whether Gunkel has successfully shown that there is an actual link between the fight with a pre-existent monster on the one hand and creation on the other, or—even less likely—that the Old Testament ever refers to pre-existing monsters.[56] Widengren remarks that Tiamat has been conquered once and for all in the beginning, and that Babylonian mythology is no longer expecting an eschatological fight in which the evil powers have to be conquered.[57] Gunkel does not claim this, however.[58] He views the evolution from Protology to Eschatology as an internal Jewish development. Another of Widengren's objections to Gunkel's view that Tiamat models the Antichrist, is that Tiamat does not represent or lead evil powers, sin or sickness in the human world.[59]

There is also the question of the time in which the influence of Babylonian mythology on Israel's religion would have taken place. Lagrange remarks that inclusion of this thinking is definitely impossible after the restoration during the time of Kores, because no more ideas were accepted that would affect the greatness of Israel's God.[60] Gunkel himself, however, places this inclusion earlier, during the Israelites' entry into Canaan, which —he claims—had by then been under Babylonian influence for centuries.[61]

Gunkel claims that the 'three and a half times' (Dan. 7.25) cannot be interpreted *zeitgeschichtlich,* and are not the writer's own finding, but must be a traditional element. 'In the myth the reign of chaos will [!] have lasted so long.'[62] In other words: Gunkel reconstructs the myth himself, from

---

55. Gunkel, *Schöpfung und Chaos*, p. 328.
56. Saggs, *Encounter with the Divine*, pp. 54, 59-61.
57. G. Widengren, *Religionsphänomenologie* (Berlin: W. de Gruyter, 1969), p. 140.
58. Some other Babylonists may well claim this.
59. Widengren, *Religionsphänomenologie*, pp. 141-42.
60. M.-J. Lagrange, *Le Judaïsme avant Jésus-Christ* (Ebib; Paris: Gabalda, 2nd edn, 1931), pp. 409, 414.
61. Gunkel, *Schöpfung und Chaos*, p. 168. He refuses to date the take-over any earlier, because that would force us 'den sicheren Boden zu verlassen' (p. 168). At other times he seems to have fewer qualms about leaving safe ground. (Cf. n. 46 above.)
62. 'Im Mythus wird [!] so lange die Herrschaft des Chaos gedauert haben'. Gunkel, *Schöpfung und Chaos*, p. 330. Cf. pp. 267-68, where he explains it cannot be *zeitgeschichtlich*. In Daniel's days, the end was still future. On pp. 390-91 he claims that

Dan. 7! The conclusion that the beast splits into four beasts, corresponding to the four kingdoms,[63] can be based only on Dan. 7 and in no way agrees with the data known from Babylonian mythology.

Finally, another 'detail': Marduk as a type of Christ.[64] Marduk took part in creation, just like Christ, but unlike Jesus Christ he is definitely not a redeemer of people, only of gods. Marduk was definitely not human, but Christ was incarnate. Christ fulfilled Old Testament prophecies, but did not perform the Babylonian New Year's festival rites. Christ will return as a judge at the end of times, but the same is not said of Marduk.[65]

We must therefore conclude that Gunkel's theory is too weak, at least in his view of the Antichrist. This can definitely be linked to the absence of a definition—he does not offer a well-defined description of the Antichrist. We must also conclude that his theory does not meet his own requirements: there is a striking analogy, but it is one that he has put in by himself;[66] he did not prove that the fact can not be explained from a Jewish internal context. Other reasons for assuming interdependency probably rests on an—insufficiently founded—assumption about Babylonian influence on the Israelites as they entered Canaan.[67]

Moriz Friedländer (1814–1919) follows in the footsteps of Gunkel and Bousset.[68] He claims that the Minim were not Jewish Christians, but an antinomic sect of pre-Christian origin, comparable to the Gnostics.[69] The

the 'three and a half times' are the period of Tiamat's reign, i.e., the time between Christmas and Easter—three months and an intercalary month.

63. Gunkel, *Schöpfung und Chaos*, p. 332.

64. According to R. Reitzenstein, *Die hellenistischen Mysterienreligionen nach ihren Grundgedanken und Nachwirkungen* (Leipzig: Tübner, 3rd edn, 1927), p. 219, Marduk could actually be an illustration of the Antichrist, because in one Manichean apocalypse he is depicted as a kind of Antimithras, i.e., someone who claims to be Mithras and demands to be worshipped as a Saviour. Reitzenstein does not elaborate on this—at least not here.

65. Paulus, *Marduk Urtyp Christi?*, pp. 62-66; the fact that Gunkel, *Schöpfung und Chaos*, p. 386 n. 4, equates Marduk with the Son of Man is of course an interesting thought.

66. Cf. R.H. Charles, *A Critical and Exegetical Commentary on the Revelation of St. John*, I (ICC; Edinburgh: T. & T. Clark, 1920), pp. 307, 311.

67. M. Friedländer, 'L'Anti-Messie', *REJ* 38 (1899), pp. 14-37, and more extensively *Der Antichrist in den vorchristlichen jüdischen Quellen* (Göttingen: Vandenhoeck & Ruprecht, 1901).

68. Friedländer, 'L'Anti-Messie', p. 17.

69. Friedländer, 'L'Anti-Messie', pp. 14-15, 19, 21; cf. *Antichrist*, pp. 1-129.

Antichrist, then, is the incarnation of this apostasy, as is Beliar.[70] This sect would have been in conflict with the majority of Jews and with the Christians.[71]

However, Friedländer labels all supernatural beings who rebel against God, including Satan, as Antichrists.[72] His theory on the Minuth has never been proven, and his definition is quite general. In spite of the titles of his works, Friedländer actually devotes little space to the Antichrist, and has very little influence on the study of the subject.

c. *R.H. Charles*

Now that we have looked at the *religionsgeschichtliche* School, let us take a look at the UK and Ireland. Their exegetes are often more cautious and less outspoken than their German and Scandinavian colleagues,[73] even though there is some German influence.[74] Robert Henry Charles (1855–1931)[75] is the most outstanding.[76] We will restrict our research to him.

---

70. Friedländer, 'L'Anti-Messie', pp. 14-17, 19-20; cf. *Antichrist*, pp. 118-44.

71. Friedländer, 'L'Anti-Messie', p. 24. He also pays a lot of attention to Dan ('L'Anti-Messie', pp. 24-30; cf. *Antichrist*, pp. 114-74).

72. Friedländer, 'L'Anti-Messie', pp. 15, 34-37; cf. *Antichrist*, pp. 144-74.

73. F. König, *Zarathustras Jenseitsvorstellungen*, p. 34.

74. Charles himself became interested in the Pseudepigrapha when he was in Germany to recover from a nervous breakdown, in 1890–91: see G.W. Buchanan, 'Introduction', in R.H. Charles, *Eschatology: The Doctrine of a Future Life in Israel, in Judaism, and in Christianity. A Critical History* (New York: Schocken Books, 3rd edn, 1963), pp. vii-xxx (vii n. 2 [p. xxiv]).

75. 'Obituary. Archdeacon Charles. A Great Apocalyptic Scholar', *The Times* (2 February 1931); J. Schmid, 'Charles', *LTK*^{2}, II, cols. 1030-1331; F.C. Burkitt, 'Robert Henry Charles. 1855–1931', *Proceedings of the British Academy* 17 (1931), pp. 437-45; T.W. Manson, 'Charles, Robert Henry', in L.G.W. Legg (ed.), *The Dictionary of National Biography 1931–1940* (London: Oxford University Press–Cumberlege, 1949), pp. 169-70.

76. Other British apocalypsists are H.H. Rowley and D.S. Russell. J.H. Charlesworth, 'A History of Pseudepigrapha Research: The Re-emerging Importance of the Pseudepigrapha', *ANRW*, II 19.1, pp. 54-88 (57-63), sees 1713–1850 as the first and preliminary phase, 1851–1913 with Migne, Dillmann and Charles as the second phase, and 1914–1969 as the third phase. Apparently not much happened during the third phase, and anyone checking the literature on the Sibylline Oracles, for instance, will immediately notice this. Charlesworth attributes it (p. 61) to: (1) material circumstances, e.g., the Great War, which also marked the end of the *Religionsgeschichtliche* School (cf. W.G. Kümmel, *Das Neue Testament: Geschichte der Erforschung seiner Probleme* (Freiburg: Alber, 1958), p. 417), and forced theologians to turn their thoughts

Not everybody is happy with the method Charles used. He is said to have made too much use of the *lectio difficilior* rule, which made the text unintelligible in places.[77] However, even after Charlesworth's work, *The Old Testament Pseudepigrapha*, Charles's publication *Apocrypha and Pseudepigrapha of the Old Testament* remains useful and important. In his other works he is reputed to assume a clarity and consistency in describing Judaism during the first centuries CE and BCE, which is greater than the texts allow for.[78]

But we do Charles a disservice by beginning with these two critical remarks. In general he uses a very broad method. In *Studies in the Apocalypse* Charles describes the methods that have been used throughout history in the exegesis of the book of Revelation.[79] He applies many of them in his commentary: the Contemporary-Historical Method, the Eschatological Method, Chiliastic Interpretation, the Literary-Critical Method, the Traditional-Historical Method, the Religious-Historical Method, the Philosophical Method, the Psychological Method and—as his own main contribution—the Philological Method.[80] Since he uses a combination of methods, his work generally does not contain the typical German one-sided approaches. However, his approach leads to a possible combination of the weaknesses of the different methods.

Charles writes specifically on this subject several times. He makes a detailed sketch of how he thinks the data on Beliar, Nero and the Antichrist

back to day-to-day practical issues (e.g. see Barth's theology); (2) a contempt for historicism, which could be explained by elements of the above; and (3) the cyclical pattern of all scientific research. Charlesworth, 'Pseudepigrapha Research', p. 64, actually writes: 'among a stellar group of Germans..., Charles stands as the single most significant figure in the history of scholarly research on the Pseudepigrapha'.

77. A. Caquot (ed.), *La littérature intertestamentaire* (Paris: PUF, 1985), p. 8.

78. J.H. Charlesworth, 'The Significance of the New Edition of the Old Testament Pseudepigrapha', in A. Caquot (ed.), *La littérature intertestamentaire* (Paris: PUF, 1985), pp. 22, 25 n. 1. (I share Charles's beliefs on progressive revelation.) Burkitt, 'Charles', p. 443. Cf. Manson, 'Charles', p. 170: 'He could never be completely at home in the world of the Apocalyptists. And this made it impossible for him to achieve that perfect understanding which demands sympathy as well as knowledge.'

79. R.H. Charles, *Studies in the Apocalypse* (Edinburgh: T. & T. Clark, 1913), pp. 1-49. Here we also note Charles's Chiliasm, e.g., p. 31: '...the possibilities of a right interpretation of ch. xx. was denied [to Protestant continental scholars], since in the Augsburg and Helvetic Confessions, Chiliastic views were condemned as heretical. Since no such veto existed in England...this fragment of the right interpretation was in the main preserved' (cf. *idem*, *Revelation*, I, p. clxxxiv).

80. Charles, *Revelation*, I, pp. clxxxiii-clxxxvii.

have come together in the Antichrist figure.[81] This, he believes, happened between CE 88 and 90. His reconstruction of the development of the Antichrist theme[82] is as follows:

The idea of the Antichrist as '*a god-opposing being of human origin*' originated from the figure of Antiochus IV Epiphanes, as sketched in the book of Daniel. This idea was further developed through inclusion of some of Pompey's characteristics. In this new form, the Antichrist was not superhuman and not Jewish. However, there was also a collective Antichrist, the tradition of whom played a part in the current edition of Rev. 13.11-14, 16-17. Apart from this tradition of a human opponent there is another tradition, that of Beliar as a satanic spirit. A third tradition originated from the figure of Nero. The Roman emperor did not really die,[83] but found refuge in the East, and was to return from there as *Nero redivivus*, at the head of Parthian troops. This tradition had already been included in Hellenistic Judaism in CE 80, and also formed the basis of the image of the beast in Rev. 17.12-17.[84]

Charles finds the Antichrist figure again in CE 50, in Paul's second epistle to the Thessalonians, under the name of ψευδοπροφήτης, and merged with the figure of Beliar into one figure named ὁ ἄνθρωπος τῆς ἀνωμίας. Thus an image is created of the Antichrist as a 'God-opposing man armed with miraculous or Satanic powers', or possibly even a fully satanic being. This phase, Charles claims, can also be found in the beast from the abyss in Rev. 11.7, in the second beast of Rev. 13.11-17 and in the false prophet in Rev. 16.13, 19.20 and 20.10. The number 666 shows that the Antichrist theme has also been combined with ideas about Nero (Rev. 13.18).[85]

Finally, Charles claims, Beliar was incarnated in Nero as the Antichrist. A first version of this image is found in *Sib. Or.* 3.63-74, the date of which is quite uncertain. The main version of this image already existed in CE 88

---

81. This was first published in R.H. Charles, *The Ascension of Isaiah* (London: A. & C. Black, 1900), pp. li-lxxiii; and again in his commentary on *Revelation*, II, pp. 76-87.

82. We will use the word 'theme' instead of Charles's 'myth', because his term may lead some readers to suspect that any possibility that it contains at least some historical truth has been eliminated from the start.

83. In CE 68, immediately after his death, it was already rumoured that Nero had not really died. He was said to have committed suicide and to then have been cremated. See Charles, *Revelation*, II, p. 80.

84. Charles, *Ascension of Isaiah*, pp. lxvii-lxxiii; *Revelation*, I, p. xcvii; II, pp. 83-86.

85. Charles, *Ascension of Isaiah*, pp. lxi-lxvi; *Revelation*, II, pp. 81-83.

or slightly later. It is this version that is most prevalent in the present form[86] of chs. 13 and 17 in the book of Revelation.[87]

Since Charles dismisses specific influence from elsewhere,[88] what his position boils down to is that the complete Antichrist image—at least from before the influences from rumours about Nero—was based on Old Testament data, historic events from the intertestamental epoch and Jewish internal developments.[89]

In spite of this impressive reconstruction of the Antichrist theme, some questions remain. Charles convincingly demonstrates that the New Testament forms of the Antichrist theme are compound and that the characteristics derived from Beliar and Nero played a secondary role in the construction of the image. But what about the Antichrist himself? Charles states that the idea is ancient, although the term is recent,[90] but then he actually refers to the tradition around Antiochus IV Epiphanes.[91] It would have been better if he had said that the later Antichrist tradition was a composition of three traditions: those around Antiochus IV Epiphanes, Beliar and Nero. He actually uses the word 'Antichrist' in two meanings: that of the *core* of the Antichrist theme—in which the figure of Antiochus IV played an important role, but no identification took place—and in that of the *developed* Antichrist theme. Thus 'Antichrist' in Charles's work often refers to a figure vaguely described, up into in the New Testament and later.

Although Charles is very convincing when he sees various ingredients, he is less convincing when he manages to reconstruct its development and fusion accurately to within a year. Of course it is great to achieve such a reconstruction, but do we really have enough elements at our disposal to be this precise, or is Charles making things up?

Ernst has made some criticisms of Charles's work, but this is not completely justified, since he states that the influence of the Beliar tradition on the Antichrist theme is debatable.[92] However, when reading about Beliar in intertestamental literature, we are regularly confronted with the question

---

86. Charles believes that the book of Revelation was written during the reign of Domitian (81–96 CE), albeit with elements form the reigns of Nero (54–68 CE) and Titus (79–81 CE). Charles, *Revelation*, I, pp. xclii-xcvi.
87. Charles, *Ascension of Isaiah*, pp. lxvii-lxxiii; *Revelation*, I, p. xcvii; II, pp. 83-86.
88. Charles, *Revelation*, I, pp. 307, 310-14.
89. Charles, *Ascension of Isaiah*, pp. lii-lx.
90. Charles, *Revelation*, II, p. 77.
91. Albeit complemented with Pompey, *et al.*
92. Ernst, *Die eschatologischen Gegenspieler*, pp. 292, 294-95.

1. Introduction

whether he could be the Antichrist or not. An identification of the Antichrist and Beliar is therefore debatable, but a certain amount of influence is definitely possible. Charles does not give sufficient evidence for the link with the ψευδοπροφήτης,[93] but of course this does not mean that there is no link at all.

Charles's reference to *Sib. Or.* 3.63-74[94] as evidence for the fusion of the Antichrist, Beliar and Nero elements is weak, as Rigaux and Ernst rightly remark, and this is not only because the date of this passage is uncertain.[95] It is clear that Beliar figures in these lines. But can he be identified with the Antichrist? Fifteenth-century Codex Monacensis 351 says in an introduction that this passage is about the Antichrist. Lanchester says in Charles's well-known collection of translations of Apocrypha that Σεβαστηνῶν (*Sib. Or.* 3.63) could be Samaria, and in that case the Antichrist would be its notorious inhabitant Simon Magus.[96] However, Charles himself does not say this. He believes that Σεβαστηνῶν is the *Augusti* lineage, the Imperial lineage from which also Nero stemmed.[97] Charles definitely needs this explanation, because it is the only way to make Nero feature in these verses! That Σεβαστηνός refers to Samaria is more plausible,[98] which makes Lanchaster's explanation the more obvious of the two. Therefore not all the elements that Charles mentioned can really be found in this part of the *Sibylline Oracles*.

Finally, we can say that Charles's idea to suppose that the Antichrist theme contains various elements that can be traced to various different situations is definitely a good idea, and also that Charles's reasoning shows that the Antichrist figure gets its clearer features only relatively late.

---

93. Charles, *Revelation*, II, p. 80, does refer to vol. I, pp. 342-44, but does not delve deeper.
94. *Sib. Or.* 3.63 starts with ἐκ δὲ Σεβαστηνῶν ἥξει Βελίαρ.
95. Ernst, *Die eschatologischen Gegenspieler*, p. 292. B. Rigaux, *L'Antéchrist et l'Opposition au Royaume Messianique dans l'Ancien et le Nouveau Testament* (Universitas Catholica Lovaniensis. Dissertationes ad gradum magistri in Facultate Theologica consequendum conscriptae, 2.24; Gembloux: Duculot; Paris: Gabalda, 1932), pp. 199-200, 400-401.
96. H.C.O. Lanchester, 'The Sibylline Oracles', in *APOT*, II, pp. 368-406; Geffcken, 'Die Sage vom Antichrist', p. 392, also refers to the link Simon Magus–Antichrist–*Sib. Or.* 3.63.
97. Charles, *Ascension of Isaiah*, p. lxviii; *idem, Revelation*, II, p. 84. Charles keeps open the possibility that it does refer to Samaria.
98. Rigaux, *Antéchrist*, p. 200.

d. B. Rigaux

We will now look at an extensive study on the Antichrist problem, that was written by the Roman Catholic exegete Béda Rigaux (1899–1982), and in which a whole chapter is devoted to the intertestamental period.[99]

Rigaux's magisterial dissertation (1932)[100] is very elaborate, both in number of pages and in subject area. He views the Antichrist as a collective concept and therefore discusses the theme of anti-divine powers throughout the centuries. Rigaux thinks that no influence from outside Israel is needed to explain the rise of this area of thought. He believes that Eschatology as a whole developed from the ancient national religion of Israel and is organically linked to it, and that we therefore need to focus on Israelite data.[101] Under the influence of messianism, especially after it had developed universalistic characteristics, there was a further development of ideas about the Antichrist and the other enemies of God's Kingdom.[102]

According to Rigaux, the idea of the Antichrist was applied to concrete persons like Gog[103] and Antiochus IV Epiphanes. The collective element, however, is primary and the individual secondary, both in terms of chronology and of function (no king without nation).[104] However, we may say that Antiochus IV was of importance: in the book of Daniel his life and death are viewed in eschatological perspective—after his death comes the end of times. Although not one verse in the book of Daniel discusses the Antichrist directly, Daniel apparently saw the Antichrist through the mists of the faraway future. In any case, Antiochus IV's life should not be regarded as a detailed type of the Antichrist.[105]

---

99. J. Ponthot, 'In memoriam Béda Rigaux', *RTL* 13 (1982), pp. 256-60; A. Descamps, 'Le Révérend Père Béda Rigaux', in A. Descamps and A. de Halleux (eds.), *Mélanges bibliques en hommage au R.P. Béda Rigaux* (Gembloux: Duculot, 1970), pp. ix-xxi.

100. His other dissertations, for his licentiate (Master's) and his doctorate, have the same subject: 'L'Antéchrist. Les origines de la tradition chrétienne' (1927; the structure of this work of 178 pages, a large amount for a licentiate's thesis in those days, is generally quite similar to his magisterial thesis; he also had the same supervisor, E. Tobac, until his death when J. Coppens took over) and 'L'homme du péché dans saint Paul' (1928; excerpt published in the 1929 issue of *ETL*; cf. Ponthot, 'Rigaux', p. 256 n. 1).

101. Rigaux, *Antéchrist*, pp. 11-18.
102. Rigaux, *Antéchrist*, p. 5.
103. See Rigaux, *Antéchrist*, pp. 108-34.
104. Rigaux, *Antéchrist*, pp. 168-70, 204.
105. Rigaux, *Antéchrist*, pp. 153-73; see esp. p. 173: 'Daniel doit être regardé

1. Introduction

Rigaux devotes a separate chapter to the Antichrist in the apocryphal apocalypses.[106] Their world differs completely from that of the Old Testament: Rigaux finds no unity of opinions, partly because of the many Christian interpolations in these writings. In the history of the apocalypses originating from Palestine, he distinguishes three periods: the time of the Maccabees, the time after Pompey's seizure of Jerusalem, and the time after the destruction of Jerusalem in CE 70. Around the same time, the *Sibylline Oracles* were written in Egypt. Rigaux views the first period, the Maccabean period, of lesser importance for the development of the theme. In the second period, after 63, more attention was paid to Israel's enemies. The Romans were God's enemies, and Pompey was their leader. In *Sib. Or.* 3[107] we find largely the same ideas as in the writings that originated in the Promised Land: they are mostly about the enemy nations. The third period does not concern our study. Throughout the three periods, the structure of the book of Daniel (in which the collective kept dominating) was elaborated on, but the head of the eschatological enemies became more and more an 'ideal' figure,[108] the Antichrist.

On a higher plane than that of Israel's national enemies,[109] Beliar plays an important role. He features mostly in the *Testaments of the Twelve Patriarchs*.[110] At the end of times, Beliar—this is actually another name for Satan[111]—will wage war against the Messiah like a true Antichrist. *Sibylline Oracles* 3.63-76, dating from later than CE 30, features a figure named

---

comme ayant prophétisé, au sens littéral, l'opposition eschatologique au royaume de Dieu... Si aucun verset de sa révélation ne s'applique immédiatement à l'Antéchrist, c'est bien lui qu'il entrevoyait, comme c'était la figure idéale du Roi-Messie que les chantres de la royauté apercevaient dans la pénombre de l'avenir à travers les images hyperboliques par lesquelles ils exaltaient un roi de leur époque.'

106. 'Les nations, l'Antéchrist et Béliar dans les apocalypses apocryphes', pp. 174-204.

107. Rigaux, *Antéchrist*, p. 190 n. 1, offers several possible dates, but does not choose between them. Rigaux dates this book to the second period.

108. One might conclude (cf. Rigaux, *Antéchrist*, pp. 191-93) that this figure of the end times is gradually influenced by the messianic figure, but Rigaux does not explicitly state this.

109. We should not overestimate the difference (Rigaux, *Antéchrist*, pp. 193-94); as regards to our subject it was only Paul who made a distinction: Satan at the highest level and the Man of lawlessness below him (p. 202).

110. Rigaux, *Antéchrist*, p. 179, dates the *Testament of the Twelve Patriarchs* in his first period, but he knows this date is disputed—see his p. 178 n. 6 (pp. 178-79).

111. This can be deduced from Rigaux, *Antéchrist*, pp. 196-98, but he does not explicitly state this anywhere.

Beliar, who has more human-like characteristics. Although he also mentions arguments against, Rigaux decides that this part is Jewish and that Beliar is a spirit,[112] not a man, and that therefore Beliar must be a superhuman, satanic being in all writings originating from the Jewish sphere of influence.

Ultimately the Christian concept of the Antichrist was made clear in the New Testament.[113] Here too the continuous opposition is largely collective, although no longer national. During the eschatological opposition this collective opposition is realized in an individual: the Antichrist, the Man of Lawlessness, a man acting in the power of Satan.[114] Satan heads the evil spirits, and although Satan remains in overall leadership, the head of the godless people is the Antichrist.[115]

Rigaux starts his discourse with the second part of his work's title, *l'Opposition au Royaume Messianique*. He talks about the opposition in all its forms, but also about messianism, because the ideas about the opposition depend on the ideas about the messiah.[116] The risk of thereby ending up with a rather voluminous work was something Rigaux did not manage to avoid, and it was made even worse by his failure to make choices in several places in the text.[117]

Because Rigaux overrates the collective at the cost of the individual, he directs his study—which is very interesting nonetheless—less often toward the figure of the Antichrist before the New Testament period than the size of his work would suggest. Again we are thus confronted with the problem of defining the term 'Antichrist'.

e. *Research in Connection with the Findings of Qumran*
The discovery, from 1947 onwards, of the writings of the Qumran Community,[118] has yielded new options for many subjects, so that many older

112. Rigaux, *Antéchrist*, pp. 197-201.
113. The second part of Rigaux's dissertation, pp. 205-398, is about the Antichrist in the New Testament.
114. Rigaux, *Antéchrist*, pp. 270, 287, 396-98.
115. Rigaux, *Antéchrist*, pp. 402, 407.
116. Rigaux, *Antéchrist*, pp. ix-xi; e.g. p. x: 'La méthode de nos recherches est simple. Nous suivons l'histoire du peuple élu et du premier siècle chrétien... Nous avons eu à cœur de ne point dresser de cloison étanche entre le point spécial de nos recherches et les autres traditions. L'anti-messianisme répond au messianisme.'
117. See, for instance, nn. 105 and 107 above.
118. H.L. Ginsberg, 'The Hebrew University Scrolls from the Sectarian Cache', *BASOR* 112 (1948), pp. 19-23, and J.P.M. van der Ploeg, *Vondsten in de woestijn van*

1. Introduction

studies have suddenly become obsolete or at least in need of additions. Not only have new texts appeared, but clearly the dating of these Qumranic texts also has repercussions for the dating of other texts.[119]

Even though the term משיח as a proper name for an eschatological figure appears quite late, messianism is much older and was definitely around in Qumran. Van der Woude was the first to thoroughly research the Messianic images in Qumran.[120] The term Ἀντίχριστος or even a Semitic equivalent does definitely not occur. This means that Charlesworth's requirement for the study of messianism, namely, that only texts containing the term 'Anointed' should be studied and no other texts,[121] is definitely not feasible for the study of the Antichrist. Even more than with messianism, the hope that all relevant passages will be studied is uncertain.[122] Yet a number of authors have ventured into theories about the origin of the Antichrist image. Three lines can be distinguished, and all three could have originated in Van der Woude's work,[123] as he speaks about אחד בליעל,[124] with whom the lineage to Belial starts (from 1959). However, no-one positively links Belial to the Antichrist.[125] Van der Woude also discusses Melchizedek and his opponent,[126] with whom the

---

Juda: De rollen van de Dode Zee (Aula, 447; Utrecht: Spectrum, 1957), give a clear impression of the tension that first existed. J.T. Milik, *Dix ans de découvertes dans le désert de Juda* (Paris: Cerf, 1957), pp. 13-22, gives an overview of the discoveries. For a *status quaestionis,* see A.S. van der Woude, 'Fifty Years of Qumran Research', in P.W. Flint and J.C. VanderKam (eds.), *The Dead Sea Scrolls after Fifty Years: A Comprehensive Assessment,* I (Leiden: E.J. Brill, 1998), pp. 1-45.

119. Charlesworth, 'Pseudepigrapha Research', pp. 74-75.

120. A.S. van der Woude, *Die messianischen Vorstellungen der Gemeinde von Qumrân* (SSN, 3; Assen: Van Gorcum, 1957). Cf. J.H. Charlesworth, 'The Concept of the Messiah in the Pseudepigrapha', *ANRW,* II 19.1 (1979), pp. 188-218 (189-90).

121. Charlesworth, 'Concept of the Messiah', p. 195. More open-minded is P. Sacchi, *L'apocalittica giudaica e la sua storia* (Biblioteca di cultura religiosa, 55; Brescia: Paideia, 1990), p. 199.

122. Cf. Charlesworth, 'Concept of the Messiah', p. 197.

123. Historically it may not have happened this way, but it is possible to draw these lines with hindsight.

124. Van der Woude, *Die messianischen Vorstellungen,* p. 121.

125. See H.W. Huppenbauer, 'Belial in den Qumrantexten', *TZ* 15 (1959), pp. 81-89 (81, 86-89); P. von der Osten-Sacken, *Gott und Belial: Traditionsgeschichtliche Untersuchungen zum Dualismus in den Texten aus Qumran* (SUNT, 6; Göttingen: Vandenhoeck & Ruprecht, 1969), pp. 73, 75, 116; J. Duhaime, 'Dualistic Reworking in the Scrolls from Qumran', *CBQ* 49 (1987), pp. 32-56 (56).

126. A.S. van der Woude, 'Melchisedek als himmlische Erlösergestalt in den

lineage to Melchiresha starts (with Flusser, in 1972), and he names the *Testimonia* from the fourth cave in Qumran (4Q175) as one of the oldest sources of the Antichrist figure;[127] this is where the line starts that leads to Simon as a type of the Antichrist (with Burgmann, in 1980).

In 1972, Milik spotted, in two writings from Qumran's fourth cave—namely in the *Testament of Amram* (4Q544; beginning of the second century) and in the *Berachot* (4Q280; first century)—a certain מלכי רשע, who he thinks is undeniably Melchizedek's counterpart.[128] This Melchiresha is the 'chef des mauvais esprits', the 'prince des ténèbres'.[129] This points to a very high position in the spiritual domain, not in the human world. Even Melchizedek should not be interpreted as a human figure, although he is material in a way and at least a creature in the Testament of Amram, in contrast to the *Melchisedek Pesher* from Qumran's eleventh cave (11Q13), who is a hypostasis.[130] The same is true for Melchiresha: he is a created, spiritual being.[131] Milik identifies him with Satan and Belial.[132]

To Flusser (1980), Melchiresha is certainly human. He also believes that even in pre-Christian times ideas about the Antichrist, a human exponent of satanic evil powers, were in existence, and that these must have originated in Jewish apocalyptic circles, including the Qumran Community.[133] According to him, the document that he calls 4QpsDanA[a],[134] is also about

neugefundenen eschatologischen Midraschim aus Qumran-Höhle XI', *OTS* 14 (1965), pp. 354-73 (368-69).

127. Van der Woude, *Die messianischen Vorstellungen*, pp. 121-22. His opinion on the Antichrist (p. 122) is: 'Der Antichrist ist seinem Wesen nach nicht der Satan selber, sondern Organ seines Wirkens in der Endzeit.'

128. J.T. Milik, '4Q Visions de 'Amram et une citation d'Origène', *RB* 79 (1972), pp. 77-97 (78-79); idem, '*Milkî-ṣedeq* et *Milkî-rešaʻ* dans les anciens écrits juifs et chrétiens', *JJS* 23 (1972), pp. 95-144 (95, 129). For the struggle between Melchizedek and an opponent, see Van der Woude, 'Melchisedek', p. 368.

129. Milik, '4Q Visions', p. 85.

130. An image of God working on the earth, in a visible form in which He appears to people: Milik, '*Milkî-ṣedeq*', pp. 125, 139. Van der Woude, 'Melchisedek', p. 369, disagrees.

131 Milik, '*Milkî-ṣedeq*', p. 139.

132. Satan: Milik, '4Q Visions', p. 85; '*Milkî-ṣedeq*', p. 127. Belial: idem, '4Q Visions', p. 86. Idem, '*Milkî-ṣedeq*', pp. 132-37, also discusses ראש as a form derived from מלכי רשע, but here he is taking it too far.

133. D. Flusser, 'The Hubris of the Antichrist in a Fragment from Qumran', *Immanuel* 10 (1980), pp. 31-37 (34-35).

134. Not to be confused with 4QpsDan[a], published by J.T. Milik, ' "Prière de Nabonide" et autres écrits d'un cycle de Daniel', *RB* 63 (1956), pp. 407-15 (411-15).

1. Introduction

the Antichrist, who desires to be viewed as the son of the Most High (בר עליון). This points to his hubris.[135] Flusser applies his thesis to other writings as well, and even includes relatively late writings.[136]

Van der Woude already (1957) viewed the *Testimonia* (4Q175) as 'one of the oldest sources from which the concept of the Antichrist may be demonstrated'.[137] He saw a *Doppelgestalt* (double figure) in it, consisting of the two כלי המס, namely, אחד בליעל and another being which is not identified.[138]

Milik too, in the English edition of his overview of ten years of Qumran (1959),[139] points to the *Testimonia* as a possible parallel for early Christian ideas about the Antichrist.[140]

Burgmann (1914–92)[141] elaborates on this theme in an article published in 1980, and in a book published in 1987. His starting point is the idea that the Qumran Community had a historical, human enemy. Because the Community were God's elected, their arch enemy must also have special qualities. He thus became the model of the eschatological Antichrist.

The text Flusser refers to here is now called 4Q246. The origin of the codes 4Q243 used by G. Vermes, *The Dead Sea Scrolls in English* (London: Penguin Books, 3rd edn, 1987), p. 73, and Dan^{d}209 by Flusser, 'Hubris', p. 31, and *idem*, 'Hystaspes and John of Patmos', in S. Shaked (ed.), *Irano-Judaica* (Jerusalem: Ben Zvi Institute, 1982), pp. 12-75 (75), is unclear.

135. Flusser, 'Hubris', p. 33. Here Flusser deviates from the interpretation by J. Fitzmyer, 'The Contribution of Qumran Aramaic to the Study of the New Testament', in *A Wandering Aramean: Collected Aramaic Essays* (SBLMS, 25; Missoula, MT: Scholars Press, 1979), pp. 85-113 (91-92). G. Strecker, 'Der Antichrist. Zum religionsgeschichtlichen Hintergrund von 1 Joh 2, 18.22; 4, 3 und 2 Joh 7', in T. Baarda, A. Hilhorst, G.P. Luttikhuizen and A.S. van der Woude (eds.), *Text and Testimony* (Festschrift A.F.J. Klijn; Kampen: Kok, 1988), pp. 247-54 (p. 250 n. 4), also refers to 4QTest 23-24 for the theme of arrogance.

136. Flusser, 'Hubris', p. 34 n. 11; see also *idem*, 'Hystaspes', p. 75. See also Strecker, 'Antichrist', pp. 250-52.

137. 'eine der ältesten Quellen, aus denen sich die Vorstellung des Antichristen belegen lässt'. Van der Woude, *Die messianischen Vorstellungen*, p. 122.

138. Van der Woude, *Die messianischen Vorstellungen*, pp. 121-22.

139. J.T. Milik, *Ten Years of Discovery in the Wilderness of Judea* (trans. J. Strugnell; SBT, 26; London: SCM Press, 1959), is not a straightforward translation of *Dix ans de découvertes* (1957; see n. 118 above): see p. 7 in the translation. The passage discussed here does not occur in the French edition.

140. Milik, *Ten Years*, p. 125.

141. Z.J. Kapera, 'Hans Burgmann 1914–1992', in H. Burgmann, *Weitere lösbare Qumranprobleme* (Qumranica Mogilanensia, 9; Cracaw: Enigma, 1992), pp. 167-73.

This development can be found in the *Testimonia*. There was no Old Testament model.[142]

How does Burgmann interpret the *Testimonia* text? After quotations from the Pentateuch about three messianic figures, a fourth is introduced, this one belonging to Belial's camp. He is the Hasmonean Simon (142–134), who had the stronghold of Dok (near Jericho) built by his son-in-law, an Arab, because the latter did not know the curse in Josh. 6.26. Simon's two sons, killed by their brother-in-law because of their father's treacherous act, had become instruments in their father's hands, and thereby instruments of violence: כלי המס. The remaining son, John Hyrcanus, actually the oldest, was not much better and is described in the last lines of the *Testimonia*.[143] Burgmann claims that Simon had incurred the anger, indeed the hatred of the Qumran Community, by gradually manoeuvring the Pharisees away from the Hasidim.[144] Simon's acts can only be explained by viewing him as a human instrument in the hands of the evil one. He is the איש הכזב, the Antichrist.[145] Burgmann claims that a passage in the *Damascus Document* (CD 1.20-21), which shows that this person had political power,[146] confirms that this Simon is the איש הכזב. Simon did have power, but the *Damascus Document* does not mention איש הכזב. The figure has later been linked with Antiochus IV Epiphanes[147] and after that also with Nero and Caligula.[148]

142. H. Burgmann, 'Antichrist–Antimessias: der Makkabäer Simon?', *Judaica* 36 (1980), pp. 152-74 (153-55).

143. Burgmann, 'Makkabäer Simon?', pp. 153-57; idem, *Vorgeschichte und Frühgeschichte der essenischen Gemeinden von Qumrân und Damaskus* (ANTJ, 7; Bern: Peter Lang, 1987), pp. 478-80, 485-86, 500-501. Naturally, the son-in-law, Ptolemy, also tried to kill the oldest son, but he failed (p. 497). For the historical context—and for a different angle on the story—see 1 Macc. 16 and Josephus, *Ant.* 12.228-29, 235, 240-41.

144. Burgmann, 'Makkabäer Simon?', pp. 162-63. The view commonly held is that the Qumran Community detached itself from the Hasidim by becoming more radical.

145. Burgmann, 'Makkabäer Simon?', pp. 156, 161, 164; idem, *Vorgeschichte und Frühgeschichte*, pp. 486-87. According to idem, 'Makkabäer Simon?', p. 157, and *Vorgeschichte und Frühgeschichte*, p. 484, this is confirmed by Ps. 110, which can be read as an acrostic: שמעון איש, if ש is the first letter of v. 1bβ.

146. Burgmann, 'Makkabäer Simon?', p. 164; idem, *Vorgeschichte und Frühgeschichte*, p. 489.

147. Antiochus IV has more than once been mentioned as the person behind איש הכזב. Cf. H.H. Rowley, 'The Internal Dating of the Dead Sea Scrolls', *ETL* 28 (1952), pp. 257-76 (271) (but see also his 'The Teacher of Righteousness and the Dead Sea Scrolls', *BJRL* 40 [1957–58], pp. 114-46 [140]), A. Mertens, *Das Buch Daniel im Lichte*

Burgmann is not the only one who holds to this identification of the father and the two sons. However, it has been remarked that the identification in itself is risky and that it is better to interpret it as purely eschatological).[149] He is not really the only one who regards it as 'the most ancient document for the concept of the Antichrist',[150] but he is the only one who elaborates on the combination, and probably it is too risky.

The study of the theories concerning the origin of the Antichrist image based on Qumran texts continually gives us the impression that we are close to the source. In the Qumran writings, Belial and dualism are both linked to the eschatological fight, but the Antichrist is hardly ever discussed. Melchiresha could easily be identified with the Antichrist, but he is identified much more often with Satan. Finally, Burgmann combines several current theories about the *Testimonia* and the Antichrist and about the historical identification of the איש הכזב, and deduces a very concrete, historical situation from which the Antichrist image apparently originated. Our picture is getting clearer, with Bergmann perhaps even clearer than legitimately possible.

Of course these theories cannot be isolated from the theories dating from the time before the Qumran discoveries, but those were often restricted to footnotes. A complete study has not really been carried out; nobody has yet studied all the sources from this period to find out whether an image of the Antichrist really existed in this period. Before such a study can be successfully conducted, however, a definition should be given of the term 'Antichrist'. Or, specifically for the Qumran situation, we have to ask ourselves whether a superhuman being can be identified with the Antichrist.

f. *G.C. Jenks*
In *The Origins and Early Development of the Antichrist Myth*, the study he wrote in 1991, Jenks assumes that the 'Antichrist myth' is typically Chris-

---

der Texte vom Toten Meer (SBM, 12; Würzburg: Echter Verlag; Stuttgart: KBW, 1971), pp. 77-78, W.H. Brownlee, *The Midrash Pesher of Habakkuk: Text, Translation, Exposition with an Introduction* (SBLMS, 24; Missoula, MT: Scholars Press, 1979), p. 95.

148. Burgmann, *Vorgeschichte und Frühgeschichte*, pp. 492-93.

149. P.R. Callaway, *The History of the Qumran Community: An Investigation* (JSPSup, 3; Sheffield: JSOT Press, 1988), p. 173 n. 1, pp. 179-80, 183. F.M. Cross, *The Ancient Library of Qumran and Modern Biblical Studies* (Garden City, NY: Doubleday, 2nd edn, 1961), pp. 147-49, also has this identification. About the text, see also Chapter 3 Section 3.

150. 'das älteste Dokument für diese Auffassung von…dem Antimessias'. Burgmann, *Vorgeschichte und Frühgeschichte*, p. 487. Cf. Van der Woude, *Die messianischen Vorstellungen*, p. 122.

tian and only received its definitive form in the third century CE, albeit through the convergence of older traditions. This stance totally differs from that of Bousset and Charles, who both assume the presence of the Antichrist theme in intertestamental literature. (For the rest their theories differ significantly.) However, at a later stage Jenks returns to Bousset's stance that there was an oral tradition, which surfaced in written texts much later and then only occasionally. Jenks clearly believes that without Jesus Christ the notion of an Antichrist is not possible. And this evidently makes it difficult to distinguish any Antichrist figure in intertestamental literature. Anyhow, Jenks did search the intertestamental writings for a wide variety of traditions and themes which he assumes all converged into the Antichrist theme.

g. *L.J. Lietaert Peerbolte*

Lietaert Peerbolte's study *The Antecedents of Antichrist: A Traditio-Historical Study of the Earliest Christian Views on Eschatological Opponents* dates from 1996. As the title indicates, the objective of his study is similar to that of Jenks. Lietaert Pierbolte points out that there is no passage that contains all the elements of the image that Jenks reconstructs for the third century Antichrist, and that there is no element which appears in all passages.

Whilst Jenks centres his work around the themes, Lietaert Peerbolte centres the edition of his work around the texts. This method ensures that it is the texts, and not the themes, that receive prominence, and that the possible trap of forcing all writings into a mould determined by a definition is avoided. In his study of the texts, Lietaert Peerbolte focuses on the similarities between them and on the motivations of their authors. He finds the similarities by grouping all eschatological expectations around the person of Jesus Christ. By doing this, he turns all opponents into pseudo-Christs until eventually only one figure is left, the Antichrist, but only from the time of Irenaeus onward. Lietaert Peerbolte's conclusion is very similar to that of Jenks. One wonders how successful he has been in finding an explanation for all similarities between the texts, since he gives no genetic explanation.

Like Jenks, Lietaert Peerbolte mainly focuses on a later phase, namely, the first two centuries of Christendom. A number of elements which he discovers in the first, early Christian part of his research, are followed through into the second, Jewish part. He is clearly more interested in the Apocrypha than in the Qumran Documents, although his study of both groups of writings is mainly limited to his search for traditions.

Lietaert Peerbolte attempts to find the origin of the elements in the immediate Christian or Jewish (or even pagan) context, within the framework of Christian eschatology. He finds them in the Jewish eschatology of the second century BCE and later. The main theme is apparently the 'climax of evil', which the writers thought had arrived in their own days. Lietaert Peerbolte claims that this setting in their own time provides comfort, because it is the necessary step toward the eventual triumph of Jesus Christ. The Antichrist later started a life of his own in Christian eschatology, which opened the door to all sorts of theories on the subject and in the last observations we can distinguish an answer to Lietaert Peerbolte's question about the authors' motivation.

h. *The Problem of Definition*
In the historical overview of studies into the Antichrist in the intertestamental period we have noticed several times that defining 'Antichrist' was difficult or had even been omitted.

Bousset, for example, never gave a definition, but combined many elements into the rather vague collective term 'Antichrist'. Also in Gunkel's work the definition is unclear. Charles originally defined the Antichrist as 'a god-opposing being of human origin', but because of all the postulated fusions with other traditions it is unclear which definition goes with which phase. Apparently the contours of the Antichrist become clear relatively late in history.[151]

To Rigaux, the Antichrist is closely linked, throughout the centuries, to the collective anti-divine power. This position makes the picture less clear again.

After the discovery of the Qumran writings, several new definitions and descriptions arose. In 1957, Van der Woude gave a clear definition: 'According to his essence the Antichrist is not the Satan himself, but instrument of his action during the end time.' He also stated that it actually concerns a *Doppelgestalt* (double figure), that is, the wicked priest and the false prophet.[152] This point of view can be compared to that of Hepp, who also distinguishes two aspects, albeit those of false teacher and persecutor. The Belial figure proves to be unhelpful for defining the Antichrist. The Melchiresha figure is more interesting for our purpose. However, research-

---

151. Charles, *Ascension of Isaiah*, p. liii.
152. 'Der Antichrist ist seinem Wesen nach nicht der Satan selber, sondern Organ seines Wirkens in der Endzeit.' Van der Woude, *Die messianischen Vorstellungen*, p. 122.

ers' opinions differ on the question whether he is spiritual or human, or perhaps could be identified as Satan. According to Burgmann, the Antichrist is a human instrument in the hands of the evil one; the origin of this figure can be found in the concrete actions of Simon the Hasmonean. Although he lays links with the New Testament, he does not specify how we should picture the Antichrist in the present, and even less how we should view him in an eschatological perspective.

Jenks's definition of the Antichrist is closely linked to Jesus Christ. Lietaert Peerbolte refused to give a definiton, and wanted to let the texts speak for themselves. That is a good idea, but we need to know what aspect we want to study in the intertestamental period.

It has now been firmly established that the problem of defining the Antichrist is an ever-recurring problem in the study of this subject. Also, it seems that we have to take into account that the Antichrist is a compound figure. On the grounds of this conclusion it is evident that we need to find a better solution. Within the intertestamental period this is impossible, as the term 'Antichrist' does not occur, even though researchers sometimes seem to overlook this fact. For this reason I shall attempt to base our case on the meaning of the word Ἀντίχριστος in those passages where this word is used for the first time, namely, in the first and the second Epistle of John.

2. *The Antichrist in the New Testament and in the Writings of the Church Fathers*

a. *The Church Fathers*[153]

Our studies in the Epistles of John have led to very little results. Many questions remain and it is still very unclear what the term 'Antichrist' actually means. For this reason, we have to include data from a later period, namely the oldest period of the history of the Church. This is also the first period in which efforts were made to describe the Antichrist in a more systematic way. On the one hand, we wish to limit this research to the writings of the Apostolic Fathers and the Church Fathers, because we wish to find out what was said about the Antichrist in the mainstream of the Church during the early Christian period.[154] On the other hand, we

---

153. For details, see G.W. Lorein, 'The Antichrist in the Fathers and their Exegetical Basis', *SacEr* 42 (2003), pp. 5-60 (35-57).

154. For this reason we will not discuss the New Testament Apocrypha, Gnostic writings, etc.

1. Introduction

wish to limit this research to those texts that shed light on the *essence* of the Antichrist. This should enable us to compose a definition of 'Antichrist' that is both as clear as possible and as early as possible, and to find an answer to some questions. Are there many antichrists throughout the course of history, or will there be only one Antichrist at the end of times? Can he be identified with Satan, or is he a man, albeit with a special relationship to Satan? How can the Antichrist's activities be described? In other words, what characteristics does he have and are these mainly political or mainly religious? Or should we avoid making the distinction altogether? Or is the Antichrist a corporate personality, as some researchers suggest?[155]

The Apostolic Fathers and the Church Fathers do not all agree in their answers to these questions. I would like to suggest the following synthesis.

The data for the Apostolic Fathers are too scanty to make up a separate overview for the first period: Polycarp (*Ep. Polyc.* 7.1) is the only one who used the word ἀντίχριστος and he was unclear in his explanation.

Later, the Antichrist was nearly always presented as a once-and-for-all, eschatological figure who has a close relationship with Satan, but without the two being identical. Firmicus Maternus (*De errore profanarum religionum* 22.4) is the only one who clearly speaks about such an identity, but he does not elaborate on it. Victorinus of Pettau (*Commentarii in Apocalypsin editio Victorini* 12.3b, 7-9) is unclear. Methodically speaking it is slightly dubious to deduce from this that a separate tradition existed that saw the Antichrist as identical with Satan,[156] especially as Firmicus Maternus's theological education was very limited.[157]

The Antichrist is nearly always portrayed as a man, albeit a man who is completely possessed, not by some demon, but by Satan himself.

The writers who discuss antichrists in plural, usually regard them as forerunners of the eschatological Antichrist. Athanasius speaks about the

---

155. E.g. B. Rigaux, *Saint-Paul: Les épîtres aux Thessaloniciens* (Ebib; Paris: Gabalda; Gembloux: Duculot, 1956), p. 278; H.-J. Klauck, *Der erste Johannesbrief* (EKKNT; Zürich: Benziger; Neukirchen–Vluyn: Neukirchener Verlag, 1991), p. 151. Against: Van der Westhuizen, *Antichrist*, p. 74. To F. Vouga, *Die Johannesbriefe* (HNT; Tübingen: Gerd Mohr, 1990), p. 44, this is only a typological singular.

156. Against Bousset, *Antichrist*, pp. 88-91.

157. R. Turcan, *Firmicus Maternus: L'erreur des religions païennes* (Collections des Universités de France...Budé; Paris: Belles Lettres, 1982), pp. 22, 43-44. Neither is his pagan (astrological) work a model of erudition (p. 21; cf. G. Guldentops, 'Iulius Firmicus Maternus, *Mathesis* I 6. Filosofische retoriek tussen Oudheid en Middeleeuwen', *Kleio* 29 [1999–2000], pp. 172-86 [179]).

many antichrists only, but this can be explained by the subject of his writings.[158] Origen stands alone in considering the Antichrist mainly as a principle (*Contra Celsum* 6.45.13-19; *Commentariorum series* XLVII, p. 96 l. 25—p. 97 l. 2), but he supports also the coming of an eschatological Antichrist (*Contra Celsum* 6.46.3).

In my last conclusion I want to discern three different currents, with some chronological sequence; it is unclear whether there is a possible link with the historical development of the statute of Christianity. In a first current, the Church Fathers situated the Antichrist's actions mainly in the area of politics. Here his characteristics were injustice, lawlessness, lack of respect for human lives, tyrannical behaviour, guile, deceit (in this way Irenaeus, *Adversus haereses* 5.25.1; Tertullian, *De praescriptione haereticorum* 4.5; Hippolytus, *De Antichristo* 6, 15, 57). In a second current, that of Jerome and Augustine, there was a combination: the Antichrist's actions were described as both political and religious. Political characteristics were then political deceit, lawlessness, injustice, lack of respect for human lives, tyrannical behaviour. Religious characteristics were: religious deceit, rebellion against God and all religion, presenting himself as god. (In this way Cyril of Jerusalem, Λόγοι κατηχητικοί 15.12; Jerome, *De Antichristo in Danielem* [11.21] [IV] 82-83, [11.31] [IV] 177-178, *Ad Algasiam* 11.8; Chrysostom, *In epistulam II ad Thessalonicenses homilia III* 530A; Augustine, *De civitate Dei* 20.19.30-33, *Enarrationes in Psalmos* 9.27.11.) In a last current[159] the religious field of action dominated, and the Antichrist's characteristics were: presenting himself as god and attempting to lead others into apostasy. (See Theodore of Mopsuestia *In epistulam ad Thessalonicenses II* [2.3-4], p. 51 ll. 2-4, p. 52 ll. 1-3 [2.8], p. 56 l. 13; Theodoret of Cyrrhus, *Interpretatio in quatuordecim epistolas S. Pauli* 664 A-B; John of Damascus, *Expositio fidei* 99.14-15.)

b. *The New Testament*[160]

Although it must be admitted that the Fathers have been systematizing, the elements of the definition we have built up from their writings can also be

---

158. Actually it becomes implicitly clear that he does assume that an Antichrist will come at the end of times as well (cf. *Apologia contra Arianos* 409D2, *Oratio I contra Arianos* 13A10, 25B7 and *Vita Antonii monachi* 69.2). The same applies to Tertullian, who is also rather polemical.

159. Partly overlapping: Augustine and Theodore of Mopsuestia were contemporaries!

160. For details, see Lorein, 'Fathers and their Exegetical Basis', pp. 12-34.

found in the New Testament. This conclusion matches the aporia we found ourselves in after a first reading of the Epistles of John and which actually urged us to study the Fathers.

The man of lawlessness in 2 Thess. 2.1-12 appears to be another description of the named 'Antichrist'. There is no reason why they should be regarded as two different figures or themes. However, the Antichrist has to be differentiated from Belial. Here Bousset and Charles reason incorrectly, because they do not differentiate between the Antichrist and Satan.

By holding John's Epistles against the light of the Patristic concepts, we are able to better interpret the data they contain. It emerges that John pays more attention to the forerunners of the Antichrist, but that he assumes that an eschatological Antichrist is coming.

In the book of Revelation, 'Beast' proves to be the description of 'Antichrist'. In Rev. 13 the two Beasts describe two aspects of the Antichrist, namely, his political and his religious aspect. Also the term 'false prophet' describes an aspect of the Antichrist, namely, the religious aspect. For the book of Revelation, Bousset made the mistake of not differentiating between the Antichrist and Satan, thus arriving at a triple Antichrist.

c. *Conclusion and Definition*[161]

If we do not wish to contrast the New Testament and the Fathers, but rather to find out which direct line can be drawn from the New Testament data to the first processors of those data, we may generally assume one well-defined Antichrist concept both in the New Testament and with the Fathers, although this concept has not been fully and systematically defined in one single writing. In any case, we should avoid the extremes both of being so minimalist that we cannot distinguish our theme anywhere as such, and of being so inclusivist that we see forerunners of our theme everywhere.[162]

The Antichrist is a man who will appear at the end of time, wholly filled with Satan. He will be an arch deceiver, as a tyrant (unjust, murderous) and as a false god (turning himself and others away from all existing religion). Other descriptions of the Antichrist are 'man of lawlessness', 'Beast' and 'false prophet' (the latter only for his religious aspect).

---

161. For details, see Lorein, 'Fathers and their Exegetical Basis', pp. 57-59.

162. Cf. J. Zimmermann, *Messianische Texte aus Qumran: Königliche, priesterliche und prophetische Messiasvorstellungen in den Schriftfunden von Qumran* (WUNT, 2.104; Tübingen: J.C.B. Mohr, 1998), pp. 452-53.

3. *The Antichrist in the Old Testament*

Does the Antichrist theme occur in the Old Testament? It is relatively easy to accept that it might occur in the book of Daniel,[163] but for the other Old Testament books this is not necessarily evident. However, I wish to suggest a number of passages that deserve more research from this angle, and with a clearly defined idea about the Antichrist in mind: the definition with which we ended the previous paragraph.

a. *Deuteronomy 13.1-6*

If anyone in Israel[164] who has visions or dreams, claiming religious authority within the community,[165] leads fellow-Israelites into idolatry,[166] and then announces a sign or miracle that will legitimize him or her and impress the public, and if this announcement comes true (vv. 2-3a), one must not simply conclude that this prophet is reliable. A prophet who advocates idolatry should never be followed (vv. 3b-4a),[167] since God is only permitting this[168] to test Israel's love for Him. He is the one who must be followed and his commandments kept (vv. 4b-5). The false prophet should be killed because he has spoken about God in a deceitful way (v. 6).[169]

This is obviously about a man, or, more precisely, a religious leader. By way of 'idealizing' people could have formed a picture of an archetypal false prophet for themselves, and that picture could have contributed to the

---

163. Cf., e.g., Lorein, 'Fathers and their Exegetical Basis', pp. 6-12.

164. בקרבך does not necessarily imply an Israelite (*pace* C.J. Labuschagne, *Deuteronomium*, II (Prediking van het Oude Testament; Nijkerk: Callenbach, 1990), p. 46).

165. P.C. Craigie, *The Book of Deuteronomy* (NICOT; Grand Rapids: Eerdmans, 1976), pp. 222-23. Cf. Num. 12.6.

166. U. Rütersworden, 'Das Böse in der deuteronomischen Schultheologie', in T. Veijola (ed.), *Das Deuteronomium und seine Querbeziehungen* (Schriften der Finnischen Exegetischen Gesellschaft, 62; Helsinki: Finnische Exegetische Gesellschaft; Göttingen: Vandenhoeck & Ruprecht, 1996), pp. 223-41 (230).

167. Labuschagne, *Deuteronomium*, II, p. 47; Craigie, *Deuteronomy*, pp. 223, 262-63. For a prophet who announces something will happen, but whose prophecy is not fulfilled, see Deut. 18.21-22. H.M. Barstad, 'The Understanding of the Prophets in Deuteronomy', *SJOT* 8 (1994), pp. 236-51 (240), is right in saying that this text is more about the temptation into idolatry than about the question whether a prophecy is fulfilled or not.

168. Craigie, *Deuteronomy*, p. 223.

169. Labuschagne, *Deuteronomium*, II, p. 48.

Antichrist theme.[170] The link with Satan is clear from the idol propaganda.[171] He speaks deceitfully about God and turns the people away from Him.

In this passage about the false prophets, the elements of our Antichrist definition are present. The functional equation of the religious aspect of the Beast, of the False Prophet and of the Antichrist in the book of Revelation is already being prepared here. There are also remarkable links with the Antichrist passage in the First Epistle of John.[172]

b. *1 Samuel 17*
This passage is historical narrative. Whatever one may think of the historical reliability, no single author doubts that 1 Sam. 17 was meant to be a description of a historic event. The fact that we discuss this passage in our study of an eschatological figure can only be accounted for by explaining that David grew into an ideal figure very quickly—the figure of the ideal king, the Messiah. Viewed from this angle it is not so surprising that his greatest opponent, Goliath, also grew into an 'ideal' figure, namely, that of the anti-Messiah, the Antichrist.[173]

Once again, that was not the intention of the original writer. Only in much later literature is the comparison of Goliath with the Antichrist made explicitly.[174] Probably—but this is hypothetical—the concept had long existed, but implicitly.[175]

---

170. It is also notable within this context that we find with P. Buis and J. Leclercq, *Le Deutéronome* (SB; Paris: Gabalda, 1963), p. 111, that this was not practised during the history of Israel; it was even 'un passage à la limite'. Does that also refer to the end times? (One could think of the slaughter of the prophets of Baal on Mount Carmel [1 Kgs 18.40], but the question is whether they had personally tempted others into apostasy and whether they were from Israel.)

171. Buis and Leclercq, *Deutéronome*, pp. 57, 110.

172. G. Sánchez Mielgo, 'Perspectivas eclesiológicas en la primera carta de Juan', *Escritos del Vedat* 4 (1974), pp. 9-64 (15-16, 32, 34).

173. Cf. D. Chilton, *The Days of Vengeance: An Exposition of the Book of Revelation* (Fort Worth: Dominion, 1987), pp. 345-46; C. Brütsch, *Clarté de l'Apocalypse* (Geneva: Labor et Fides, 5th edn, 1966), p. 232.

174. See E. van Staalduine-Sulman, 'The Aramaic Song of the Lamb', in J.C. de Moor and W.G.E. Watson (eds.), *Verse in Ancient Near Eastern Prose* (AOAT, 42; Kevelaer: Butzon & Bercker; Neukirchen–Vluyn: Neukirchener Verlag, 1993, pp. 265-92 (*passim*, esp. 279, 284, 287-89) for a passage from the Tosephta Targum from the first century (pp. 285-87) and p. 291 for other literature.

175. Cf. A. Rofé, 'The Battle of David and Goliath: Folklore, Theology, Eschatol-

We will not enter into the history of the text, even though the widely differing text type of the Codex Vaticanus Septuagint shows that something is wrong.[176] In view of our goal there is no need to explain the parallel traditions in 2 Sam. 21.19 and 1 Chron. 20.5.[177]

In the summer of 1020[178] the Philistines went to war against Israel and pitched their camp at the south side of the Valley of Elah[179] (which was dry), in the part of Judah that borders Philistine area, about 25 kilometres (15 miles) west of Bethlehem.[180] Israel pitched its camp at the other side of the valley (vv. 1-3). The Philistines delegated a fighting champion to provoke the Israelite army:[181] Goliath, a real giant[182] and heavily armed.[183]

---

ogy', in J. Neusner et al. (eds.), *Judaic Perspectives on Ancient Israel* (Philadelphia: Fortress Press, 1987), pp. 117-51 (140-41, 144).

176. Notwithstanding this, the text was once written as a *whole* and has long been *read* as a whole. See also A. van der Kooij, 'The Story of David and Goliath: The Early History of its Text', *ETL* 68 (1992), pp. 118-31; D.W. Gooding, 'An Approach to the Literary and Textual Problems in the David–Goliath Story', in D. Barthélemy, D.W. Gooding, J. Lust and E. Tov, *The Story of David and Goliath: Textual and Literary Criticism, Papers of a Joint Research Venture* (OBO, 73; Göttingen: Vandenhoeck & Ruprecht; Fribourg: Editions Universitaires, 1986), pp. 55-86. Cf. R.W. Klein, *1 Samuel* (WBC; Waco, TX: Word Books, 1983), pp. 173-74 (p. 174: 'The best way to interpret these verses is to note their function in the recension of MT and not in a hypothetical and indeterminable non-MT version'). C.J. Goslinga, *Het eerste boek Samuël* (Commentaar op het Oude Testament; Kampen: Kok, 1968), pp. 322-23 (p. 328, translated quote: 'After all we are only dealing with the text as it has been passed down to us [in which it is extremely difficult to distinguish between that which was part of the 'original' story and that which was not]'). A.H. van Zyl, *I Samuël*, II (Prediking van het Oude Testament; Nijkerk: Callenbach, 1989), pp. 26-27 (p. 26, translated quote: 'The story shows a remarkable coherence,' although it would be unnecessary to note this if there was no discussion about it).

177. See possibly H.-J. Stoebe, *Das erste Buch Samuelis* (KAT; Gütersloh: Gerd Mohn, 1973), pp. 314-15, 319; Van Zyl, *I Samuël*, II, pp. 28-29.

178. Goslinga, *Eerste boek Samuël*, pp. 321, 325; the dating of Samuel and Saul is quite problematic; for Goslinga's view see pp. 51-55.

179. The Wadi es-Sant. See also P.K. McCarter Jr, *I Samuel* (AB; Garden City, NY: Doubleday, 1980), pp. 283, 290; Goslinga, *Eerste boek Samuël*, p. 325.

180. Van Zyl, *I Samuël*, II, p. 28; A. Caquot and P. de Robert, *Les livres de Samuel* (CAT; Geneva: Labor et Fides, 1994), p. 201; McCarter, *I Samuel*, pp. 283, 290. (As regards the location of Efes-Dammin, the text is apparently wrong and the map is right [*contra* Klein, *1 Samuel*, p. 175].)

181. F. Zorell, *Lexicon Hebraicum et Aramaicum Veteris Testamenti* (Rome: PIB, repr., 1968), *s.v.* בֵּין; Goslinga, *Eerste boek Samuël*, p. 325.

182. According to MT, six cubits and a span, that is nearly three metres. For a

1. Introduction

Goliath proposed a single combat between himself and one Israelite, which would determine the result of the war between the Philistines and the Israelites. He assumed—and rightly so (v. 11)—that no-one would be found to combat him (vv. 4-10).

Thus far the depiction of a single lead player. The other, the younger David,[184] was still far removed from the battlefield. Only his three elder brothers were in Saul's army.[185] David had served under Saul, but when Saul went to war, David returned to the sheep (vv. 12-15).[186] By now the war had been continuing for a long time[187] and David's father asked him to take some provisions[188] to his brothers and their commander. He was to ask for a receipt for the services delivered (for tax reasons?)[189] (vv. 16-19).

---

defence of this reading, see Van Zyl, *I Samuël*, II, p. 29, and for the medical side of it, D. Kellermann, 'Die Geschichte von David und Goliath im Lichte der Endokrinologie', *ZAW* 102 (1990), pp. 344-57 (349). Manuscript evidence seems to favour the reading *four* cubits and a span (about two metres), as this occurs both in the Codex Vaticanus of the LXX and in 4QSam^a (for an overview, see E.C. Ulrich Jr, *The Qumran Text of Samuel and Josephus* [HSM, 19; Missoula, MT: Scholars Press, 1978], p. 79). According to McCarter, *I Samuel*, p. 286, this would not mean a rationalisation in the Codex Vaticanus but a writing error in MT, influenced by שש in v. 7. Unfortunately the first numeral in 4Q373 1-2 2 is missing.

183. For weaponry, see N. Bierling, *Giving Goliath his Due: New Archaeological Light on the Philistines* (Grand Rapids: Baker Book House, 1992), pp. 149-50.

184. He had been anointed king in 16.13, but nobody knew. (Did he realise it himself?)

185. This was still a people's army, not a standing army.

186. According to Klein, *1 Samuel*, p. 177, the editor introduced David as a commuter between town (working in the palace) and countryside (after-hours work in the agrarian sector). According to Van Zyl, *I Samuël*, II, p. 30 n. 76 (p. 165), Saul wanted David to be permanently available, but it is possible that Saul had no need for psychiatric care during wartime. According to Goslinga, *Eerste boek Samuël*, pp. 329-30, David only had to be present in the palace when Saul had problems, but he lived nearby so that he could come quickly if needed. However, the distance is 15 kilometres (10 miles)—and that twice, unless they worked with smoke signals. This is problematic.

187. ארבעים יום should not be taken literally according to Van Zyl, *I Samuël*, II, pp. 30-31. Cf. H. Jagersma, '"…Veertig dagen en veertig nachten…"', *NedTTs* 28 (1974), pp. 1-15.

188. For food, see Stoebe, *Das erste Buch Samuelis*, p. 323; Van Zyl, *I Samuël*, II, p. 31.

189. Goslinga, *Eerste boek Samuël*, p. 331, and Stoebe, *Das erste Buch Samuelis*, p. 323, say that this refers to a sign of life from his brothers; against this pleads the fact that Jesse would have believed his son without obtaining written proof. Van Zyl, *I Samuël*, II, p. 31, mentions this objection with the food transport, but it also applies

David left early the next day, crossing the Valley of Elah,[190] and arrived at the camp, where the chariots were placed in a circle to form a defending wall,[191] right at the time the army of Israel left its night quarters for work.[192] David left his luggage in the camp and so witnessed the daily goings on (vv. 20-24). David interpreted the insult to Israel as an insult to the living God, and found out what reward was promised to the person who beat Goliath: great wealth, the king's daughter and exemption from taxes and duties for his family.[193] His oldest brother was not pleased with his interest.[194] King Saul was notified and he sent for David (vv. 25-31). David promised to fight Goliath. Saul doubted at first, but when David argued that with God's help his experience with Goliath would be the same as with lion and bear,[195] Saul even equipped him with his heavy coat of armour. David was not used to this,[196] and preferred to go out carrying only his sling[197] and five smooth stones (vv. 32-40).

here. The receipt only makes sense if it was to be handed over to a third party. A 'receipt for tax reasons' may be an anachronism, but it is clear that the people who stayed at home must have had a part in the war too (cf. T.R. Hobbs, *A Time for War: A Study of Warfare in the Old Testament* [Old Testament Studies, 3; Wilmington, DE: Michael Glazier, 1989], pp. 56, 80-81), and so the possibility that a receipt was required for these purposes cannot be excluded.

190. Van Zyl, *I Samuël*, II, pp. 28, 31-32.
191. Goslinga, *Eerste boek Samuël*, p. 332.
192. David had left early, but the distance from his home to the army camps was about 15 miles. This leads us to suspect that because of the boredom at that time, the daily entertainment only started quite late. The army did not move very much (A. Wénin, 'David roi, de Goliath à Bethsabée. La figure de David dans les livres de Samuel', in L. Desrousseaux and J. Vermeylen [eds.], *Figures de David à travers la Bible*: *XVIIe congrès de l'ACFEB* [LD, 177; Paris: Cerf, 1999], pp. 75-112 [84-85]).
193. McCarter, *I Samuel*, p. 304. N.P. Lemche, "חפשי in 1 Sam. XVII 25', *VT* 24 (1974), pp. 373-74 (374), pleads for the interpretation that the winner's family would become the king's clients, but not enough is known about this. For David's motivation, see Wénin, 'David roi', pp. 103-107, 111.
194. See Van Zyl, *I Samuël*, II, pp. 33-34; Goslinga, *Eerste boek Samuël*, pp. 334-35. Wénin, 'David roi', p. 82.
195. For the animals, see Goslinga, *Eerste boek Samuël*, pp. 336-37. For the comparison of Goliath with a beast, see Wénin, 'David roi', pp. 84, 86 n. 21.
196. This does not contradict what has been said about the fights with wild animals. Walking around in a coat of armour is quite awkward. Stoebe, *Das erste Buch Samuelis*, p. 337, points out that coats of armour were not a normal part of military outfits. Van Zyl, *I Samuël*, II, p. 36, opts for a different solution (and also explains this theologically): David could not walk in Saul's coat of armour because of the difference in their physical build. (Saul was a head taller than all the others.) Does this fit in with

1. *Introduction*

Then followed the confrontation. When Goliath finally saw his opponent,[198] he noted that he had expected someone quite different and wished his undersized[199] enemy a terrible end. David too spoke of the enormous contrast between the two fighters.[200] Goliath trusted in his weapons, but David came in the name of the Lord of Hosts,[201] whom Goliath had insulted. Everyone should know that God was going to give the victory (vv. 41-47).[202] The actual fight was extremely short. Goliath slowly approached David; David ran—therefore having greater speed—and took a roundabout route[203] towards Goliath. He grabbed a stone from his bag and let fly at Goliath, who was deeply wounded in his forehead,[204] apparently just underneath the rim of his helmet (vv. 48-49). Goliath was stunned but not dead, and he only died when David beheaded him with his own sword (vv. 50-51a). The Philistines fled and the Israelites forced them back into their own territory (vv. 51b-53). David deposited Goliath's head and his weapons in Jerusalem (v. 54).[205]

---

the meaning of נסה? Possibly, if we translate this word with 'being accustomed to'. Of course David was not accustomed to Saul's large armour. However, see also Goslinga, *Eerste boek Samuël*, pp. 337-38.

197. Van Zyl, *I Samuël*, II, p. 37, and R. de Vaux, *Les institutions de l'Ancien Testament. II. Institutions militaires. Institutions religieuses* (Paris: Cerf, 1960), pp. 53-54. Both describe how the sling works.

198. Kellermann, 'Endokrinologie', pp. 355-56.

199. Not only small, but young as well (cf. Caquot and de Robert, *Livres de Samuel*, p. 209).

200. Stoebe, *Das erste Buch Samuelis*, p. 337.

201. The author is right in using this name of God here.

202. This does not exclude the use of weapons or tricks (cf. Stoebe, *Das erste Buch Samuelis*, p. 337; Goslinga, *Eerste boek Samuël*, p. 338). According to McCarter, *I Samuel*, p. 294, this is the theological core of this passage. Cf. Caquot and de Robert, *Livres de Samuel*, p. 213. There is disagreement about the meaning of קהל. If this only refers to the army of Israel, no distinction should be made between the 'army' (according to McCarter, *I Samuel*, p. 294) and 'a religious council', as in Israel each military meeting also had a religious dimension. If this is about *both* halves of the audience, however, about the Israelites and the Philistines, then we have to choose the very neutral meaning ('all those gathered here'). (Cf. Goslinga, *Eerste boek Samuël*, p. 341.)

203. Kellermann, 'Endokrinologie', pp. 356-57. Different: A. van der Lingen, *David en Saul in I Samuel 16–II Samuel 5: Verhalen in politiek en religie* (dissertation, Groningen; The Hague: Boekencentrum, 1983), p. 16: Goliath struggled to stay upright.

204. Goslinga, *Eerste boek Samuël*, p. 341.

205. Several solutions have been suggested for the problem that Jerusalem was not yet in David's power. McCarter, *I Samuel*, p. 294, calls it an anachronism. J.G.

Finally the account looks back on the phase of the fight and the time immediately afterwards. This shows Saul's amazement and his need to gather intelligence.[206] David answered the question immediately after coming back from the combat; he had not even found the time to put Goliath's head down (vv. 55-58).

Now that we have an overview of this chapter and its problems, we will find out how similar the image of Goliath is to that of the Antichrist. I have already pointed out that this similarity has been elaborated on in ancient days by a number of writers. Modern commentators who take note of its textual history point out that we should also take into account the symbolic element of this story.[207] In order to study this problem in more detail, we will have to use the definition that has been developed before.

Goliath was a man (albeit a tall one), as is the Antichrist, and he was a Philistine,[208] a hereditary enemy of the old people of the Covenant. But he was not necessarily wholly filled with Satan. We have not yet seen any compelling reason to read this account in an eschatological light.

Nowhere is Goliath shown to be a deceiver. We can only say that the Philistines acted deceptively by fleeing after David's triumph rather than submitting to Israel in compliance with Goliath's words in v. 9, but Goliath was already dead by then. Goliath did tyrannize the Israelites, however, and in this way influenced the mood of the people. His threats against David (v. 44) appear to be murderous, but David used the same terminology (v. 46). In the religious area David concluded that Goliath defied the armies of the living God (v. 26b) and further on the story tells us that Goliath cursed David by his gods (v. 43b). This way of speaking about Goliath reminds us of a false prophet or perhaps in this context of an anti-prophet.[209] Furthermore, everything in Goliath's attitude points at

---

Baldwin, *1 and 2 Samuel* (TOTC; Leicester; Downers Grove, IL: Inter-Varsity Press, 1972), p. 128, keeps open the possibility that David already had good contacts in Jerusalem. Goslinga, *Eerste boek Samuël*, p. 343, states that the head was immediately taken away (possibly to the tent Saul had allocated to him), and was brought to Jerusalem much later. This last solution seems to best match the whole body of data.

206. Wénin, 'David roi', p. 88; Goslinga, *Eerste boek Samuel*, pp. 343-44.

207. Stoebe, *Das erste Buch Samuelis*, p. 319: 'Das auffallende Zurücktreten seines Namens kann einen Grund mit darin haben, dass das Geschilderte über das konkret einmalige in das Paradigmatische emporgehoben werden soll.' McCarter, *I Samuel*, p. 298: 'highly idealized and symbolic form'.

208. Or at least: belonging to the Philistine army.

209. Rofé, 'Battle', p. 128). However, in the canonical version little is said about the exact contents of Goliath's words.

hubris.[210] And lastly, Goliath is compared to the animals lion and bear, with יד ('claw' as well as 'hand') as the most striking *tertium comparationis*.

There are not enough elements to prove conclusively that the author of this chapter was thinking beyond the historical data to an eschatological figure who could be described as the Antichrist.

Yet it is also clear that in later writings Goliath bears much more resemblance to the Antichrist.[211] This can only be explained by the evolution of the historical David into the messianic David. In our further studies of texts we will therefore certainly have to pay attention to the opponent of a messianic figure, even if at first he does not seem to have many links with the Antichrist: what is being said about the messiah will also reflect on his opponent.

c. *Zechariah 11.15-17*

God told the prophet to play the role of a shepherd. It is unclear in how far this should be taken literally, that is, whether the prophet really acted out this symbolic role. Especially vv. 15-17 seem to indicate a more 'normal' prophecy.[212] Here the prophet is commanded to play the role of a godless shepherd. The script for this second role-play is quite short, and in this aspect the first part of the passage (vv. 4-14) differs from the second part (vv. 15-17).

---

210. Cf. C. Begg, 'The David and Goliath Story According to Josephus', *Mus* 112 (1999), pp. 3-20 (19). If someone takes too many liberties in word and deed and if this leads to success, the person is guilty of hubris. The overconfident person believes that the results of his deceit will last, because he does not reckon with God. At some point, however, he has reached his limit and God's purpose is carried out: God's judgment humiliates the overconfident. For the Greek view, see J. de Romilly, *The Rise and Fall of States* (Jerome Lectures, 11; Ann Arbor: University of Michigan Press, 1977), pp. 43-44, 46. See also P. Humbert, 'Démesure et chute dans l'Ancien Testament', in maqqél shâqédh, *la branche d'amandier* (Festschrift W. Vischer; Montpellier: Causse, Graille, Castelnau, 1960), pp. 63-82 (63, 67).

211. For several elements of the definition, see Van Staalduine-Sulman, 'Song of the Lamb', pp. 269-70, 277, 279-80, 284-85, 287-88.

212. J. Ridderbos, *De kleine profeten*. III. *Haggai, Zacharia, Maleachi* (Korte Verklaring; Kampen: Kok, 2nd edn, 1952), pp. 143-44 ([two] vision[s] of two symbolic acts which have not been acted out in reality); A.S. van der Woude, *Zacharia* (Prediking van het Oude Testament; Nijkerk: Callenbach, 1984), p. 206 (only literary presentation); B. Tidiman, *Le livre de Zacharie* (Commentaire Evangélique de la Bible; Vaux-sur-Seine: Edifac, 1996), pp. 234-35 (symbolical acts).

Although the play is short, its message is clear. After reading these verses (vv. 15-17) the reader gets the impression that the preceding passage (vv. 4-14) refers to a good shepherd.

The future[213] wicked shepherd would not care for any lost sheep, or seek the young,[214] or heal the injured, or feed the healthy. He would even eat the meat of the choice sheep, tearing off their hoofs, the latter probably to make sure he got even the last scrap of meat.[215] He would work only for his own profit (vv. 15-16). His time was limited, however, for God already announced the judgment of this wicked shepherd: the conqueror was going to destroy his power.[216]

If vv. 4-14 are messianic, this could be another argument for seeing the Antichrist theme in vv. 15-17, although we have established that the Antichrist will establish himself as anti-God in the first place, not so much as an anti-Messiah. There is a lot of discussion about the character of the first part and we can conclude from their comments that the exegetes establish the nature of the first part partly by looking at the second part.

Van der Woude states that a first edition of vv. 4-14[217] certainly did not intend to discuss a good shepherd as such, but that in the last edition the addition of vv. 15-17 came with a good shepherd interpretation of the first part.[218]

---

213. T. Chary, *Aggée. Zacharie. Malachie* (SB; Paris: Gabalda, 1969), p. 193; W. Rudolph, *Haggai—Sacharja 1–8—Sacharja 9–14—Maleachi* (KAT; Gütersloh: Gerd Mohn, 1976), p. 210; J. Ridderbos, *Haggai, Zacharia, Maleachi*, p. 145; Van der Woude, *Zacharia*, p. 218 (cf. p. 212).

214. נְעַר instead of נַעַר, nifal ptc. of עדר (Van der Woude, *Zacharia*, p. 217); or 'straying' (נֵעָר) instead of נַעַר, niphal ptc. of נער, according to Zorell, *Lexicon, s.v.*). In both cases the powerful construction that C. Brouwer, *Wachter en herder: Een exegetische studie over de herder-figuur in het Oude Testament, inzonderheid in de pericopen Zacharia 11 en 13.7-9* (Wageningen: Veenman, 1949), pp. 188, 195, sees here is preserved.

215. Van der Woude, *Zacharia*, pp. 217-18.

216. A. van Hoonacker, *Les douze Petits Prophètes* (SB; Paris: Gabalda, 1908), p. 679. Many include 13.7-9 with this passage, but we will not study those verses. There are three reasons for this. First, the link between our passage and 13.7-9 is debatable (see, e.g., the structure of P. Lamarche, *Zacharia IX–XIV: Structure littéraire et messianisme* [Ebib; Paris: Gabalda, 1961], pp. 112-13). Secondly, this does not tell us much about the shepherd and, thirdly, it is unclear with which shepherd it actually matches (see Van der Woude, *Zacharia*, pp. 205-206).

217. Consisting of vv. 4-5, 7, 8b-14, with a text-critical intervention in v. 7 (Van der Woude, *Zacharia*, pp. 209-13).

218. Van der Woude, *Zacharia*, pp. 216, 218.

1. Introduction

Lamarche speaks of a 'Roi-Pasteur' and draws the conclusion that a historical figure, that is, Zerubbabel, was a model, but only in the sense that it was hoped he would be the messiah;[219] if that expectation would not come true, their hope would have to be shifted to the future.[220]

The use of v. 13 in Mt. 27.9-10 indicates a messianic interpretation in New Testament times. Rudolph and Laato assume a straightforward messianic interpretation.[221] It seems that two facets of the messiah—suffering and judgment—have been combined here.[222] The general context of persecution by the world pleads for an eschatological interpretation. In that case there is sufficient evidence to identify this wicked shepherd with the Antichrist. Before applying our own criteria, we should first check the literature.

Chary sees a development in the description of the bad shepherd in the last verses that is similar to Lamarche's development in the first part: the prophet foresaw that the wielding of power by a ruler would end in evil. What he said about this future ruler can however be applied to any wicked ruler, especially to the wicked eschatological shepherd, the 'anti-messie'.[223] Rudolph is cautious: he says it merely refers to a forerunner of the Antichrist.[224] Laato speaks of a 'model for the Antichrist'.[225] Van der Woude does not use the term itself in his exegetical part, he only uses it in his homiletical part.[226]

The other writers I consulted do not accept this interpretation, and most do not even mention it. Only Rigaux defends his rejection of this interpretation. He says that this passage cannot refer to the Antichrist, because

---

219. Against: Brouwer, *Wachter en herder*, p. 112.

220. In 9.9-10; 11.4-17; 12.10-13.1; 13.7-9. Lamarche, *Zacharia IX–XIV*, pp. 112-13, 118-23.

221. Rudolph, *Haggai—Sacharja 1-8—Sacharja 9-14—Maleachi*, p. 205; A. Laato, *Josiah and David Redivivus: The Historical Josiah and the Messianic Expectations of Exilic and Postexilic Times* (ConBOT, 33; Stockholm: Almqvist & Wiksell, 1992), p. 279.

222. See also Ridderbos, *Haggai, Zacharia, Maleachi*, pp. 147-49.

223. Chary, *Aggée. Zacharie. Malachie*, p. 193: 'Cette absence d'attaches concrètes facilitait l'application de ce portrait à tout mauvais chef et surtout au mauvais pasteur par excellence de l'avenir, l'anti-messie.'

224. Rudolph, *Haggai—Sacharja 1-8—Sacharja 9-14—Maleachi*, p. 211: 'Diese Gegenfigur ist dem AT sonst fremd und ist eine Art Vorläufer des Antichrists.'

225. Laato, *Josiah and David Redivivus*, p. 286.

226. Van der Woude, *Zacharia*, p. 218: 'In our text the figure of the anti-divine ruler of the end times is visible'; p. 221: '…that the Antichrist does not have everlasting life' (translated quotes).

'The bad shepherd succeeds to the good one'.[227] Perhaps Rigaux expects too much of this single prophecy if he expects to find in it the *full* eschatological development, since he would not want to deny that the Antichrist will come *after* a *specific* phase of the Good Shepherd.

Also Ridderbos mentions the interpretation that this passage may refer to the Antichrist, but he does not accept it. He thinks of a *future* fulfilment of the prophecy (from the perspective of the prophet), but not of an eschatological fulfilment.[228]

In view of the divided views of the authors it will certainly be worthwhile to apply our own criteria to this passage.

The comparison to a man, that is, a shepherd, seems to indicate that a man is being discussed here. This passage is definitely about the future, but it is clear that this future could be seen on an eschatological level. The link with Satan is not discussed at all, but there is mention of unrighteousness and murderousness. In the religious area it can be said that the wicked shepherd acts in a way that is squarely opposed to God's ways. The occurrence of a messianic interpretation in the history of the reading of the first part should be mentioned here as important, but it is not indicative of the functioning of an Antichrist theme. We do not find any reference to secondary elements of our definition, for example, Beast, false prophet or hubris.

The general conclusion is that the data are limited, that nothing pleads against identification, and even that the combination of 'unrighteous and murderous eschatological man' actually pleads *for* it.

d. *Conclusion*

I hope I have proven from these passages that the Antichrist theme was present in the Old Testament (even outside the book of Daniel), albeit in a very limited way and although the word Antichrist does not occur.[229] Of course I could have discussed many more passages, had I wished to mention all the elements that occur in the Antichrist theme. I have however limited this study to those passages in which some of the elements of our definition converge.

The religious aspects of the Antichrist theme appear to be discussed reasonably fully in the false prophet of Deut. 13.

---

227. 'Le mauvais pasteur *succède* au bon'. Rigaux, *Antéchrist*, p. 141 n. 4.
228. Ridderbos, *Haggai, Zacharia, Maleachi*, p. 163.
229. It is actually not necessary to always have a *Christ* opposite the *Antichrist*, so I have not used this as a requirement for these Old Testament passages.

1. Introduction

When establishing what happened later to the figure of Goliath in 1 Sam. 17, and looking again at the account itself, we must conclude that in Goliath a large part of the Antichrist theme is present in potential, as a man of force, as an 'anti-prophet' marked with hubris.

In Zech. 11.15-17 we find an unrighteous and murderous eschatological man. During the reading history of this text, this man has certainly been placed opposite a messianic figure, but even without that development we may say that in view of the limited length of the text a reasonably complete picture of the Antichrist can be found here.

This means that the core of the Antichrist theme according to our definition[230] not only occurs in the book of Daniel in the Old Testament, but elsewhere as well,[231] indeed from the earliest period onwards,[232] whether we assume this was the time of the historical Moses,[233] or several centuries later.[234] Our last text (Zech. 11) dates from roughly the same period as the book of Daniel.[235]

---

230. See above, section 2c. Some would suppose that I have adapted the interpretation of the studied texts to make them fit into my mould. I believe however that I have sufficiently placed the texts within their own context. I have also studied a number of texts that were not included in this selection because I do not find the Antichrist theme in them. It is therefore not true that I was determined to find the theme in all the texts.

231. Against: Lietaert Peerbolte, *Antecedents*, pp. 10, 87.

232. The Minimalists have not been included in this overview. See E. Yamauchi, 'The Current State of Old Testament Historiography', in A.R. Millard, J.K. Hoffmeier and D.W. Baker (eds.), *Faith, Tradition, and History: Old Testament Historiography in its Near Eastern Context* (Winona Lake, IN: Eisenbrauns, 1994), pp. 1-36 (21-36); I.W. Provan, 'Ideologies, Literary and Critical: Reflections on Recent Writing on the History of Israel', *JBL* 114 (1995), pp. 585-86; B. Halpern, 'Erasing History: The Minimalist Assault on Ancient Israel', in V.P. Long (ed.), *Israel's Past in Present Research: Essays on Ancient Israelite Historiography* (Sources for Biblical and Theological Studies, 7; Winona Lake, IN: Eisenbrauns, 1999), pp. 415-26 (original edition 1995).

233. R.K. Harrison, *Introduction to the Old Testament* (Grand Rapids: Eerdmans, 1969), pp. 176-77, 636, 648 about Moses and Deut. 13. For a different dating of Moses, see J.J. Bimson, *Redating the Exodus and Conquest* (JSOTSup, 5; Sheffield: Almond Press, 1981).

234. O. Eissfeldt, *Einleitung in das Alte Testament*, (Tübingen: J.C.B. Mohr, 3rd edn, 1964), pp. 251-53, 308-10. For different datings within the same school, see, e.g., Buis and Leclercq, *Deutéronome*, p. 16.

235. Both were edited either in the fifth century (Harrison, *Introduction*, pp. 952-56, 1127; for Zechariah more clearly with Tidiman, *Zacharie*, pp. 42-44), or in the

From this we may deduce that the law concerning the false prophet formed the base of the Antichrist theme. The Goliath materials were available quite early, but were not developed. In Zech. 11 the Antichrist is shown from a different perspective, namely that of the wicked shepherd. *Hubris* is a characteristic that is often mentioned with the characters described.

centuries that followed immediately (Eissfeldt, *Einleitung*, pp. 593, 705-706; slightly more grouped according to Van der Woude, *Zacharia*, pp. 157, 213).

Chapter 2

THE ANTICHRIST IN THE APOCRYPHA AND PSEUDEPIGRAPHA

1. *Introduction*

What we have found so far in our study of the history of research into this subject is that finding a definition for the Antichrist concept is a central issue. We have developed an objective definition and studied the texts surrounding the intertestamental writings, that is the New and Old Testaments. We now wish to penetrate into the heart of the matter: the Antichrist theme in the intertestamental writings. The Qumran documents will be discussed in the next chapter; in this chapter we will focus on the Apocrypha and pseudepigrapha, and our limit will be the year 50 CE, because in this year the first New Testament writings were 'published'.

In this chapter we will study all relevant passages in the Apocrypha and pseudepigrapha. In doing this, we are not going into exhaustive discussions of the texts, including the motivations of the authors—which were probably more psychological than logical—and any parallels of the texts, since our theme is that of the Antichrist and not that of the texts themselves.

We will work in chronological order, since this will show any possible historical development in the Antichrist theme, although it is unlikely that we will find such a development, in view of the limited size of the material. Our subject is only a small eschatological detail: it does not concern the salvation of the saints, nor the punishment of the wicked, but the short period in which wickedness prospers in the person of one individual. Furthermore, in comparison to the ethical and parenetic aspects the eschatological aspect is limited in the intertestamental writings, even if the enormous interest in the 'apocalyptic' would lead us to suspect otherwise.

2. Psalm 152

a. *Setting*

Psalms 151–55,[1] also called the Syriac Psalms, were originally written in Hebrew. They are a reflection of individual godliness. An early Hellenistic date seems to offer the best possibilities.[2] The oldest preserved manuscript of Ps. 152 is in Syriac.[3]

At first glance, this early Hellenistic psalm seems to be a common lament based on David's experiences as a shepherd,[4] but the reference to 1 Sam. 17 demands our attention,[5] even though similar references also occur in other 'Syriac' psalms.[6]

Up until v. 6 this psalm could be discussing the struggle between David and a literal wolf or bear. If this is the case, Ps. 152 is not metaphorical. On the other hand, v. 4 seems exaggerated if the struggle is a purely physical fight against a zoological bear. Therefore we will take a closer look at Ps. 152.4-6.

b. *Psalm 152.4-6*

We work from the following Syriac text.[7]

ܣܘܐ ܚܙܐ ܬܠܝܬܠܥ 4
ܘܐܦ ܠܐܡܣܘ ܚܕ ܚܠܐ
ܕܐܚܐ ܕܠܬܚܙܐ ܕܝܠܗܘܢ ܒܐܝܪܗܘܡ,
ܘܠܚܫܐ ܠܐܫܐ ܘܠܒܣܐ
ܕܠܐ ܘܐܦܕܗܘ, ܡܕܢ ܐܢܐ, ܘܐܝܢ ܠܚܫܒܐ ܘܒܐܪܒ ܘܣܝܘܐ 5

---

1. The first, fourth, fifth, second and third Syriac Psalms respectively.

2. J.H. Charlesworth and J.A. Sanders, 'More Psalms of David', *OTP*, II, pp. 609-24 (612, 615-16); D. Flusser, 'Psalms, Hymns and Prayers', in M.E. Stone (ed.), *Jewish Writings of the Second Temple Period* (CRINT, 2.2; Assen: Van Gorcum; Philadelphia: Fortress Press, 1984), pp. 551-77 (559); A.S. van der Woude, 'Die fünf syrischen Psalmen (einschliesslich Psalm 151)', in *Poetische Schriften* (JSHRZ, 4.1; Gütersloh: Gerd Mohn, 1974), pp. 29-47 (31-33). Van der Woude dates these psalms considerably earlier than Charlesworth and Flusser. Pss. 151, 154 and 155 occur in Hebrew in 11Q5, but they did not originate in the Qumran Community. (See also Van der Woude, 'Die fünf syrischen Psalmen', pp. 31, 35.)

3. See also Van der Woude, 'Die fünf syrischen Psalmen', pp. 31, 33-35.

4. M. Noth, 'Die fünf syrisch überlieferten apokryphen Psalmen', *ZAW* 48 (1930), pp. 1-23 (20-21).

5. See above, Chapter 1.

6. Ps. 151, title, vv. 1, 6-7; 153 title.

7. Based on the Leiden edition, with an important variant from Mingana's MS 31, as rendered by Noth, 'Die fünf... Psalmen', p. 7.

2. The Antichrist in the Apocrypha and Pseudepigrapha

ܘܗܐ ܕܐܢܝܚܐ ܒܚܠܒܬܐ ܒܚܝܒ̈ܝ ܡ, ܩܒܠܬܥܡܝܚܐ ܕܚܝܘܬܐ
ܒܥܓܠ ܐܠܗܐ ܫܕܪ ܡܝ ܕܝܢ ܦܪܘܩܐ ܕܝܠܝ 6
ܡܥܡܘܩܬܐ ܕܥܕܪܘ ܐܠܗܐ ܕܗܘܡ ܘܐܠܝܬܐ

4   ḥws mryʾ gbyk
      wpṣʾ lḥsyk mn ḥblʾ
      dntʾ mn btš bḥtk bklhwn ʿdnwhy
      wnšbḥ lšmʾ drbwtk
5   mʾ dprqtyhy mn ʾydy ʾryʾ mḥblnʾ wdʾbʾ srwḥʾ
      wmʾ dʾ ʿdyt šbyty mn pwmhyn dḥywtʾ
6   bʿgl ʾdwny šdr mn qdmyk mšwzbnʾ
      wdlny mn hwtʾ pʿyrtʾ
      dṣbyʾ dtḥbšny bʿwmqyh

4   Have mercy, Lord, on your elect one,
      and save your holy one from destruction,
      so that he may continue in your praises during all his times
      and may praise your magnificent name,
5   when you have saved him[8] from the claws of the destroying lion and the deadly bear
      and when you have torn my captivity from the mouths of beasts.[9]
6   Quickly, Lord, send from your presence one who is redeeming me
      and lift me from the gaping abyss
      which is seeking to enclose me in its depths.

We have already noted that v. 4 seems to be exaggerated if it is not metaphorical.[10] The term 'elect one' in v. 4aα has messianic connotations.[11] The mention of 'holy'[12] in v. 4aβ suggests that there is a contrast with the ungodly.[13]

---

8. A. Ungnad, *Syrische Grammatik* (Clavis linguarum Semiticarum, 7; Munich: Beck, 1913), §25bγ, says that the perfect tense could indicate an unfinished action (imperfect) here, but a perfect tense translation is more logical and in view of the general meaning of the perfect tense it is not impossible.

9. This construction is a bit awkward, but the meaning is clear: 'when you have rescued me from captivity in the mouths of beasts'.

10. Cf. Noth, 'Die fünf... Psalmen', p. 21.

11. See *1 En.* 45; 48.6; 49.2; 51.3; 53.6; 55.4; *T. Benj.* 11.4; *Tg. 2 Sam.* 23.8; *Tg. Isa.* 42.1; (v. app. crit.!); *Tg. Isa.* 43.10 (cf. MT).

12. This translation is definitely legitimate: J.P. Smith Margoliouth, *A Compendious Syriac Dictionary* (Oxford: Clarendon Press, 1903), *s.v.*, mentions it as the first meaning and also mentions the phrase *ḥsy dmn 'lm'*: 'the Holy One Who is from everlasting'.

13. This phrase is also found in Ps. 153.2b and in a shortened form in Ps. 153.5b.

In v. 5 the correct rendering of the beast is of utmost importance. The Leiden edition reads *mwt' mḥbln'* (death of destruction); so apart from the title there is no mention at all of a specific animal. Noth's edition—based on a manuscript from Mingana—reads *d'b'* (also in the title and even in v. 2). These consonants could be referring to the wolf or the bear.[14] The bear is thematically more interesting, because the link between the bear and Goliath also appears elsewhere.[15]

The mention of the eschatological abyss in v. 6 is another reason to suspect a metaphorical meaning, but it remains strange that it is David, and not the bear, who is associated with the abyss.[16] We conclude that it is unclear whether it is a factor within an individual or an all-embracing eschatology.

c. *The Antichrist in Psalm 152*
We see that there are some links between Ps. 152 and the Antichrist theme: the struggle with a beast and the reference to Goliath (via the bear), the messianic context, and the eschatological abyss.

Yet many things remain unclear: Is the bear an eschatological evil-doer *par excellence*? If so, it may be a brief description of the Antichrist. In that sense we cannot say that Ps. 152 is about the Antichrist, but in view of our elaborate description of 'Antichrist', we must conclude that several elements of our description appear together in this Psalm and that therefore Ps. 152 deserves our special attention.

3. *Sirach: Laus Patrum*

a. *Setting*
Ecclesiasticus, or the Wisdom of Jesus Son of Sirach, was written in Hebrew, in Jerusalem, by a traditional scribe. It can be dated quite precisely: between 190 and 180. In 132, or shortly afterwards, a translation was made by Jesus Sirach's grandson in Egypt. Hebrew fragments have been found since the end of the nineteenth century, representing now more than 60 per cent of the text.[17]

---

14. M. Philonenko, 'L'origine essénienne des cinq Psaumes syriaques de David', *Sem* 9 (1959), pp. 35-48 (37).

15. Van Staalduine-Sulman, 'Song of the Lamb', p. 287.

16. Noth, 'Die fünf... Psalmen', p. 21, assumes on the basis of this (and of v. 1b), that the psalm did not belong to David originally.

17. Harrison, *Introduction*, pp. 1231-33; M. Gilbert, 'Wisdom Literature', in M.E.

2. The Antichrist in the Apocrypha and Pseudepigrapha 47

At the end of his book Jesus Sirach sings the praises of the fathers, in chronological order, concluding with an emphasis on the importance of Enoch, Joseph and Adam.[18] David is discussed in ten verses[19] in the historically appropriate place in the list of fathers. David's struggle with Goliath is mentioned in Sir. 47.4-5. Let us take a closer look at these verses.

b. *Sir. 47.4-5*
The Hebrew text is extant and reads as follows.[20]

4   בנעוריו הכה גבור ויסר חרפת עולם:
    בהניפו ידו על קלע וישבר תפארת גלית:
5   כי קרא אל אל עליון ויתן בימנו עז:
    להדף את איש יודע מלחמות ולהרים את קרן עמו:

4   In his youth he slew a hero and did away with eternal dismay,
    by whirling his hand around[21] a slingstone, and he broke Goliath's boasting.

Stone (ed.), *Jewish Writings of the Second Temple Period* (CRINT, 2.2: Assen, Van Gorcum; Philadelphia: Fortress Press, 1984), pp. 283-324 (291); T.C. Vriezen and A.S. van der Woude, *Oudisraëlitische en vroegjoodse literatuur* (Ontwerpen, 1; Kampen: Kok, 10th edn, 2000), pp. 419-21; P.W. Skehan and A.A. Di Lella, *The Wisdom of Ben Sira* (AB; Garden City, NY: Doubleday, 1987), p. 10. See also R.T. Beckwith, 'The Pre-History and Relationships of the Pharisees, Sadducees and Essenes: A Tentative Reconstruction', *RevQ* 11 (1982), pp. 3-46, who sees the Pharisees as the most loyal to tradition (p. 7 and *passim*) and rejects that Sirach could have had Sadducee origins (p. 4 n. 1).

18. Sir. 44-49; and the end in Sir. 49.14-16. This passage does not contain any references to any revelations given to Enoch. Since he is viewed as a model (also in Sir. 44.16), the fact that many traditions have been attributed to him could be viewed as legitimate. It should be noted that most of *1 Enoch* is of later date than Sirach Also Joseph plays an important role in the pseudepigrapha (*T. 12 Patr.*: see H.W. Hollander, *Joseph as an Ethical Model* [SVTP, 6; Leiden; Leiden: E.J. Brill, 1981]).

19. Sir. 47.2-11.

20. This text is from F. Vattioni, *Ecclesiastico: Testo ebraico con apparato critico e versioni greca, latina e siriaca* (Naples: Istituto orientale, 1968), p. 255. The new edition of the manuscripts, without reconstructions, in P.C. Beentjes, *The Book of Ben Sira in Hebrew: A Text Edition of All Extant Hebrew Manuscripts and a Synopsis of All Parallel Hebrew Ben Sira Texts* (VTSup, 68; Leiden: E.J. Brill, 1997), p. 83, does not exclude this text as a possibility.

21. The construction is unusual, but in view of the Greek χεῖρα ἐν λίθῳ, it must be original. In the reverse construction (בהניפו קלע על ידו) על could be explained locally. A. van den Born, *Wijsheid van Jezus Sirach (Ecclesiasticus)* (Boeken van het Oude Testament; Roermond: Romen, 1968), p. 227, translates the Greek text as follows:

5   because he called to God Most High and He gave strength in his[22] right hand
    to remove a man skilled in warfare and to lift up the horn of his people.

There are several discrepancies between the Hebrew and Greek texts. For example, the construction differs. The Greek has a rhetorical question where the Hebrew simply has an informative statement.[23] Furthermore, the Septuagint reads at the end of v. 4a: ὀνειδισμὸν ἐκ λαοῦ (together with the Syriac: ḥsd' d'mh), where Vattioni gives חרפת עולם for the Hebrew text. Apparently there once was a reading חרפת העם, which was linked more closely to 1 Sam. 17.26aβ: והסיר חרפה מעל ישראל.[24] Finally, the Greek γαυρίαμα leads to the negative translation of תפארת, which can by itself also mean 'honour'.

The horn in v. 5bβ is a symbol of pride and destructive power.[25] Its lifting up indicates triumph and a restoration of the people's national pride. The combination of הרים קרן with נתן עז is also found in 1 Sam. 2.10. The end of v. 5, the exaltation of Israel, is in stark contrast with the end of v. 4, where Goliath's honour is broken.[26]

c. *The Antichrist in the Laus Patrum*
In Sir. 47.2 David is compared to the best part of the sacrifice, the fat.[27] Do we reason too much from a New Testament perspective, when we conclude on the basis of this element that there is a messianic context here? In the next verse we see David playing with lions as if with goat kids, and with bears as if with lambs. This reminds us of Isa. 11.6-8, and thus messianic overtones are apparent in this verse. I have already mentioned 1 Sam. 2.10, where משיחו is mentioned as a genitive of קרן, which can of course be interpreted as messianic. Another important element is the mention of Goliath.

May we conclude—from the messianic overtones and the mention of

---

'doordat hij met zijn hand de slingersteen ophief' (because he lifted the slingstone with his hand). We probably ought to think of the meaning of 'because of', or 'in order to': 'he whirled his hand to launch a slingstone'; cf. P. Joüon, *Grammaire de l'hébreu biblique* (Rome: IBP, corr. edn, 1965), §170h.

22. Namely 'David's'.

23. This is also mentioned by T.R. Lee, *Studies in the Form of Sirach 44–50* (SBLDS, 75; Atlanta: Scholars Press, 1986), p. 222.

24. Skehan and Di Lella, *Wisdom*, pp. 524-25.

25. Zorell, *Lexicon*, s.v. קרן; E. Dhorme, *L'emploi métaphorique des noms de parties du corps en hébreu et en akkadien* (Paris: Gabalda, 1923), pp. 35-36, 40.

26. Skehan and Di Lella, *Wisdom*, pp. 525-26.

27. See Lev. 3–4; cf. Skehan and Di Lella, *Wisdom*, p. 525.

2. The Antichrist in the Apocrypha and Pseudepigrapha 49

Goliath—that Jesus Sirach was thinking of the Antichrist theme in these verses? If David was portrayed as a model, this puts the figures around him in the same perspective. We may therefore suppose that the struggle between young David and his opponent from the Philistine army meant more to Jesus Sirach than a single historical event. However, he and many other intertestamental writers did not think of the Antichrist theme. Yet this passage remains of importance to the tradition of the Antichrist theme in the intertestamental period.

4. Sibylline Oracles, Book 3, Oldest Parts

a. *Setting*

We know of two Sibyls: the Cumean Sibyl, who went to the Underworld with Aeneas and later managed to sell three books for the price of nine to king Tarquinius,[28] and the Jewish Sibyl, whose books are extant. She claimed that she was related to Noah[29] and therefore claims a dating of around the fourth millennium.[30]

Most researchers assume that the most important parts of *Sib. Or.* 3 were written in Leontopolis, around 160–150. *Sib. Or.* 3.97-349 and 489-829 belong to this main part, except v. 776, which is a Christian interpolation.[31] This means that vv. 381-400 date from more or less the same period.[32]

---

28. Either Tarquinius Priscus (fl. 619–579) or Tarquinius Superbus (fl. 534–510).

29. His daughter-in-law, wife, or niece? See V. Nikiprowetzky, *La Troisième Sibylle* (Etudes Juives, 9; The Hague: Mouton, 1970), pp. 44-45. This is yet another case of pseudonimy; see p. 539: '...une tradition prophétique qui masque sa nouveauté sous une revendication d'hyperbolique antiquité.' F. Torm, 'Die Psychologie der Pseudonymität im Hinblick auf die Literatur des Urchristentums (1932)', in N. Brox (ed.), *Pseudepigraphie in der heidnischen und jüdisch–christlichen Antike* (Darmstadt: Wissenschaftliche Buchgesellschaft, 1977), pp. 111-48, delves deepest into this problem.

30. Starting from the figures in the LXX; see, e.g., Harrison, *Introduction*, p. 150.

31. J.J. Collins, 'Sibylline Oracles', *OTP*, I, pp. 317-472 (354-56); idem, 'The Development of the Sibylline Tradition', *ANRW*, II 20.1 (1987), pp. 421-59 (430-32). M. Philonenko, 'Pseudépigraphes de l'Ancien Testament', in A. Dupont-Sommer and M. Philonenko (eds.), *La Bible: Ecrits intertestamentaires* (Bibliothèque de la Pléiade; Paris: Gallimard, 1987), pp. lix-cxlvi (xciii), dates this book much later, i.e., in the first century CE (in Alexandria). Nikiprowetzky, *Troisième Sibylle*, p. 329, interprets v. 776 in the Jewish sense, which implies that all of vv. 489-829 is a unity.

32. In that case, a first edition of this passage was directed to Alexander the Great —and was therefore much older. Later additions then applied this passage to Antiochus IV Epiphanes. Some scholars apply the passage, even in its current form, to Alexander

b. Sib. Or. 3.388-92
We follow Geffcken's[33] text:

"Ἥξει καί ποτ' ἄπιστος[34] ἐς Ἀσίδος ὄλβιον οὖδας
ἀνὴρ πορφυρέην λώπην ἐπιειμένος ὤμοις
390 ἄγριος ἀλλοδίκης[35] φλογόεις· ἤγειρε γὰρ αὐτοῦ[36]
πρόσθε κεραυνὸς φῶτα.[37] κακὸν δ' Ἀσίη ζυγὸν ἕξει
πᾶσα, πολὺν δὲ χθὼν πίεται φόνον ὀμβρηθεῖσα.

Also at a certain time there will come, faithlessly,[38] to the happy soil of Asia,
a man, wrapped in a purple mantle around his shoulders,
390 savage, strange in justice, fiery. For a thunderbolt
once awakened his life-light.[39] Then all of Asia will bear an evil yoke,
and the earth, deluged, will drink much blood.

Much discussion has taken place about the issue of whether these verses are about Alexander the Great[40] or Antiochus IV Epiphanes.[41] Perhaps they apply to both men, or even give a general picture.[42]

---

the Great (or at least the first part). See L.L. Gunderson, 'The Portrait of Alexander the Great in the Sibylline Oracles', in *Ancient Macedonia*, II (Thessaloniki: Institute for Balkan Studies, 1977), pp. 53-66 (54, 57-58); J. Geffcken, *Komposition und Entstehungszeit der Oracula Sibyllina* (TU, 23.1; Leipzig: J.C. Hinrichs, 1902), p. 3; W. Bousset, 'Die Beziehungen der ältesten jüdischen Sibylle zur chaldäischen Sibylle und einige weitere Beobachtungen über den synkretistischen Charakter der spätjüdischen Literatur', *ZNW* 3 (1902), pp. 23-49 (35); S.K. Eddy, *The King Is Dead: Studies in the Near Eastern Resistance to Hellenism* (Lincoln: University of Nebraska Press, 1961), p. 12.

33. The edition of A. Rzach, Χρησμοί Σιβυλλιακοί—*Oracula Sibyllina* (Vienna and Prague: Tempsky; Leipzig: Freytag, 1891), is not necessarily of poorer quality, but it is customary to use the most recent good edition. Moreover, J. Geffcken, *Die Oracula Sibyllina* (GCS, 8; Leipzig: J.C. Hinrichs, 1902) is less enthusiastic in the area of finding rationalising conjectures. A similar judgment is found with Nikiprowetzky, *Troisième Sibylle*, pp. 284-85.

34. Cj. Rzach: ἄπυστος; also Geffcken's text is a cj. The MSS offer ἄπιστ' ἐξ and ἄπιστόν τ' ἐξ.

35. See Nikiprowetzky, *Troisième Sibylle*, pp. 345-46.

36. Cj. Rzach: ἤγειρε δὲ τοῦτον; Geffcken's text is also a cj. The MSS offer ἤγειρε γὰρ αὐτόν.

37. Cj. Rzach: κεραύνιος ἄνδρα.

38. Cj.: 'unexpectedly'.

39. Cj.: 'him, a man' (instead of 'his life-light'), so rather colourless.

40. Hatred for Alexander is also expressed elsewhere: see, e.g., D. Flusser, 'The Four Empires in the Fourth Sibyl and in the Book of Daniel', *IOS* 2 (1972), pp. 148-75 (172 n. 84).

41. For Antiochus IV, see Daniel (G.W. Lorein, 'Fathers and their Exegetical

2. The Antichrist in the Apocrypha and Pseudepigrapha 51

Although ἄπιστος and ἄπυστος have different meanings, both apply to Alexander the Great and Antiochus IV Epiphanes. Foreign rulers were never perceived as trustworthy, and definitely not Antiochus IV (see, e.g., the interpretation of Dan. 11.22b-23): both kings came unexpectedly, Antiochus had not even been granted the title of king (Dan. 11.21).[43]

Against the identification of the man in *Sib. Or.* 3.389 with Antiochus IV it must be remarked that strictly speaking he was not yet a king when he set foot in Asia, and therefore was not πορφυρέην λώπην ἐπιειμένος ὤμοις,[44] but this could be explained with a simple prolepsis. Furthermore,

---

Basis', pp. 6-12), but also the *Potter's Oracle* (POx 22.2332.30-31: καθέξει δὲ ἐκ Συρίας βασιλεὺς ὅς ἔσται μεισητὸς πᾶσειν ἀνθρώποις; text by Roberts: E. Lobel and C.H. Roberts, *The Oxyrhynchus Papyri*, XII [Greek–Roman Memoirs, 31; London: Egypt Exploration Society, 1954]), or according to the interpretation of J.C.H. Lebram, 'König Antiochus im Buch Daniel', *VT* 25 (1975), pp. 737-72 (763-65)—and more recently J.W. van Henten, 'Antiochus IV as a Typhonic Figure in Daniel 7', in A.S. van der Woude (ed.), *The Book of Daniel in the Light of New Findings* (BETL, 106; Leuven: Peeters, 1993), pp. 223-43 (239)—and L. Koenen, 'Die Prophezeiungen des "Töpfers"', *Zeitschrift für Papyrologie und Epigraphik* 2 (1968), pp. 178-209 (187) (*contra* Lobel and Roberts, *Oxyrhynchus Papyri*, XII, pp. 91-93, and J.J. Collins, *The Sibylline Oracles of Egyptian Judaism* [SBLDS, 13; Missoula, MT: Scholars Press, 1974], p. 29: it was meant as general and we therefore should not look for particular historic events; against that, in 1994, J.J. Collins, 'The Sibyl and the Potter: Political Propaganda in Ptolemaic Egypt', in L. Bormann, K. del Tredici and A. Standhartinger [eds.], *Religious Propaganda and Missionary Competition in the New Testament World* [Festschrift D. Georgi; NovTSup, 74; Leiden: E.J. Brill, 1994], pp. 57-69 [67], sees Antioch IV as a prototype of the king who was hated by all). Possibly also PWien ÖN 10000, at least according to the interpretation of H.-J. Thissen, '"Apocalypse Now!", Anmerkungen zum *Lamm des Bokchoris*', in W. Clarysse, A. Schoors and H. Willems (eds.), *Egyptian Religion in the Last Thousand Years* (Mem. J. Quaegebeur; Orientalia Lovaniensia Analecta, 84–85; Leuven: Peeters; Oosterse Studies, 1998), pp. 1043-53 (1051-53).

42. Perhaps Cambyses was partly a model for both: see Herodotus, 2.25-33; A.E. Cowley, *Aramaic Papyri of the Fifth Century B.C.* (Oxford: Clarendon Press, 1923), no. 30 ll. 13-14 (וכזי כנבוזי על למצרין...ואגורי אלהי מצרין כל מגרו) and when Cambyses came to Egypt…[his soldiers] destroyed all the temples of the gods of Egypt [historical reference in a petition from Elephantine]); Lebram, 'König Antiochus', pp. 767-68. M. Hadas-Lebel, 'L'évolution de l'image de Rome auprès des Juifs en deux siècles de relations judéo-romaines -164 à +70', *ANRW*, II 20.2 (1987), pp. 715-856 (759), sees Pompey here, based on a much later date. We see that Sibylline literature can be interpreted in many ways.

43. Cf. V. Nikiprowetzky, 'La sibylle juive et le "Troisième Livre" des "pseudo-Oracles Sibyllins" depuis Charles Alexandre', *ANRW*, II 20.1 (1987), pp. 460-542 (527).

44. Gunderson, 'Portrait', p. 57; Eddy, *The King Is Dead*, p. 12.

he probably thought of himself as a king from the time he received news in Athens of Seleucus IV's death.

Both Alexander the Great and Antiochus IV were ἄγριος, ἀλλοδίκης and φλογόεις. Gunderson says about κεραυνός that Callisthenes of Olynth, Alexander's official biographer, had put the thunderbolt on him. This points at Alexander's relationship with Zeus.[45] Besides, we must note also that Antiochus had a special relationship with Zeus, which even led to identification.[46]

Also the next sentence, κακὸν δ' Ἀσίη ζυγὸν ἕξει πᾶσα, applies to Alexander the Great as well as Antiochus IV,[47] even though Ἀσίη was indeed larger for the first than for the other.

c. Sib. Or. *3.608-15*

Ὁππόταν[48] Αἰγύπτου βασιλεὺς νέος ἕβδομος ἄρχῃ
τῆς ἰδίης γαίης ἀριθμούμενος ἐξ Ἑλλήνων
610 ἀρχῆς, ἧς[49] ἄρξουσι Μακηδόνες ἄσπετοι ἄνδρες·
ἔλθῃ[50] δ' ἐξ Ἀσίης βασιλεὺς μέγας, αἰετὸς αἴθων,[51]
ὃς πᾶσαν σκεπάσει γαῖαν πεζῶν τε καὶ ἱππέων,[52]

---

45. Gunderson, 'Portrait', pp. 57-58.
46. See note 98 below.
47. Gunderson, 'Portrait', p. 57, and Eddy, *The King Is Dead*, p. 12, deny this for Antiochus IV. W.W. Tarn, *The Greeks in Bactria and India* (Cambridge: Cambridge University Press, 2nd edn, 1951), p. 195, confirms the use of the term for the Seleucid Empire. Nikiprowetzky, 'Sibylle juive', p. 527, points out—*contra* Eddy—that it is pointless to play Alexander the Great off against Antiochus IV, since Antiochus IV is portrayed as a cliché here.
48. Rzach: ὁππότ' ἄν (the normal epic form).
49. The usual expression is ἀρχὴν ἄρχειν (*figura etymologica*); this must therefore be an attraction of the case the antecedent takes. Or is γαίης the antecedent? In that case, the object genitive is with ἄρξουσι.
50. Conj. aor. pro fut.: does not occur in Attic; could be called a Homerism (P. Chantraine, *Grammaire homérique. II. Syntaxe* [Collection de philologie classique, 4; Paris: Klincksieck, 1963], §309), but occurs again in the Hellenistic period and with the *Sib. Or.* even more often than with Homer (BDR, §363; A. Rzach, *Kritische Studien zu den Sibyllinischen Orakeln* [Denkschriften der kaiserlichen Akademie der Wissenschaften. Philosophisch-historische Classe, 38.4; Vienna: Tempsky, 1890], p.13).
51. Although αἰετὸς αἴθων does occur with Homer (Ο 690; with thanks to Rzach, Χφησμοὶ Σιβυλλιακοί, p. 268) and although the text can be viewed as definite on the basis of this, references by Geffcken, *Oracula Sibyllina, ad loc.*, to Lycophron's *Alexandra* are pointless, since the *combination* of these two words does not occur there.
52. Cj. Rzach: πεζοῖς τε καὶ ἵπποις (see also Rzach, *Kritische Studien*, p. 38).

2. The Antichrist in the Apocrypha and Pseudepigrapha 53

πάντα δὲ συγκόψει καὶ πάντα κακῶν ἀναπλήσει·
ῥίψει δ' Αἰγύπτου βασιλήιον· ἐκ δέ τε πάντα
615 κτήμαθ' ἑλών[53] ἐποχεῖται[54] ἐπ' εὐρέα νῶτα θαλάσσης.

Whenever a young king[55] rules over Egypt, the seventh
of[56] his own land, counted from the Hellenic
610 rule, which the Macedonians, awesome men, will exercise,[57]
a great king will come from Asia, a tawny[58] eagle,
who will cover the whole earth with infantry and cavalry
and he will destroy everything and fill everything with evil.
He will cast down that which is royal in Egypt. And after having
615 taken all possessions, he rides on the broad back of the sea.

Depending on whether Alexander the Great himself is included in the count, the seventh king is either Ptolemy VI Philometor[59] or Ptolemy VIII Euergetes II Physcon.[60] Historically the text can be understood more easily

---

Rzach refers to Homer, ξ 267, where the genitive does occur (πλῆτο δὲ πᾶν πεδίον πεζῶν τε καὶ ἵππων), and where this is justified. Is it possible that the Sibyl copied Homer too slavishly, perhaps partly influenced by ἀναπλήσει in v. 613? If so, this 'grammatical error' is the correct reading. After all, the aim of a critical text is to find the correct reading.

53. ἐκ...ἑλών: ptc. aor. of ἐξαιρεῖν, with *tmesis*.
54. One would expect a fut. here (usually ἐποχήσεται). According to Nikiprowetzky, *Troisième Sibylle*, p. 271, this is a deviated form of the fut. (he wrongly writes this as ἐποιχήσεται.); cf. 274 (2.a.: 'Le présent est fréquemment employé au lieu du futur'); Rzach, *Kritische Studien*, p. 13 ('Schon der Abwechslung wegen hätten die Sibyllisten das Präsens öfter für das Futurum verwendet').
55. Or 'new'.
56. Also possible: 'over his own land' (gen. with ἀρχῃ). In both cases, τῆς ἰδίης γαίης does not contain much new information.
57. Also possible: 'over which...will rule' (antecedent γαίης instead of ἀρχῆς). In both cases, v. 610b does not offer much new information.
58. The expression αἰετὸς αἴθων comes straight out of Homer (see n. 51), and so we need to choose for the meaning of αἴθων which Homer apparently intended. (See LSJ, *s.v.*)
59. Collins, *Sibylline Oracles of Egyptian Judaism*, p. 30, as original interpretation; Collins, 'Sibylline Oracles', *ad loc.* (as the only interpretation); Lanchester, 'Sibylline Oracles', pp. 368-406 (*ad loc.*); J.H. Friedlieb, *Die Sibyllinischen Weissagungen: Vollstaendig gesammelt, nach neuer Handschriften-Vergleichung, mit kritischem Commentare und metrischer deutscher Uebersetzung* (Leipzig: Weigel, 1852), p. xxxv; A. Momigliano, 'La portata storica dei vaticini sul settimo Re nel terzo libro degli Oracoli Sibillini', in *Forma Futuri* (Festschrift M. Pellegrino; Turin: Erasmo, 1975), pp. 1077-84 (1082).
60. V. Nikiprowetzky, 'Oracles sibyllins', in A. Dupont-Sommer and M. Philonenko

if the seventh is Ptolemy VI. His tender age at the time of the invasion is also mentioned by Livy.[61] If he is our man, the invasion was carried out in 169 by Antiochus IV Epiphanes (the βασιλεὺς μέγας), who returned, not with complete victory, but anyhow with much plunder.[62]

Collins stated (in 1974) that even here we should not look for a specific historical event, but that this is about a general feeling, which had recently become personified in Antiochus IV Epiphanes.[63]

The aforementioned verses are followed by an account of the conversion of Egypt (*Sib. Or.* 3.616-18). This does not mean that the βασιλεὺς μέγας has Messianic characteristics, but rather the reverse.[64]

d. Sib. Or. *3.652-56*

Καὶ τότε ἀπ' ἠελίοιο Θεὸς πέμψει βασιλῆα,
ὃς πᾶσαν γαῖαν παύσει πολέμοιο κακοῖο,
οὓς[65] μὲν ἄρα κτείνας, οἷς δ' ὅρκια πιστὰ τελέσσας.

(eds.), *La Bible: Ecrits intertestamentaires* (Bibliothèque de la Pléide; Paris: Gallimard, 1987), pp. 1035-1140 (*ad loc.*), who claims that later it could also have been applied to Cleopatra VII. (Cf. Nikiprowetzky, *Troisième Sibylle*, p. 215.) According to Collins, *Sibylline Oracles of Egyptian Judaism*, p. 30, as a re-interpretation. This king is also called Ptolemy VII. This confusion arose because of the extremely short reign of Ptolemy VII Neus Philopator (only in 145) and the exile of the Ptolemy referred to here, from 163 until 145, which cut his reign into two periods: 170–163 (with Ptolemy VI Philometor) and 145–116.

61. Livy 42.29.5, 7: 'Antiochus inminebat quidem Aegypti regno, et pueritiam regis et inertiam tutorum spernens... Ptolemaeus propter aetatem alieni etiam arbitrii erat...' E. Will, *Histoire politique du monde hellénistique. II. Des avènements d'Antiochos III et de Philippe V à la fin des Lagides* (Nancy: Presses Universitaires, 2nd edn, 1982), pp. 311-16, 318.

62. Momigliano, 'Portata storica', p. 1081. Will, *Histoire politique*, pp. 317-20.

63. Collins, *Sibylline Oracles of Egyptian Judaism*, p. 30. In 1994, Collins, 'The Sibyl and the Potter', pp. 67-68, is of the opinion that a reminiscence of Antiochus IV can be seen here, but that there is obviously no position *against* him in this passage. Although a shift of focus has taken place in this time period of 20 years, there is some unity in Collins's vision. Antiochus IV did play a role in the edition of this oracle, but the oracle should be interpreted as general in the first place.

64. Collins, *Sibylline Oracles of Egyptian Judaism*, p. 40. Contra A. Peretti, *La Sibilla babilonese nella propaganda ellenistica* (Biblioteca di cultura, 21; Florence: Nuova Italia, 1943), pp. 389-93, who does accept an adaptation of Antiochus IV, which leads to a peculiar mix of messianic figure ('Il re messianico'!, p. 391) and Antichrist figure.

65. Rzach: τοὺς μέν τοῖς δέ, which indeed is 'more normal' Greek. (This does not mean, however, that it is therefore the right reading!)

2. The Antichrist in the Apocrypha and Pseudepigrapha

655 Οὐδέ γε ταῖς ἰδίαις βουλαῖς τάδε πάντα ποιήσει,
ἀλλὰ Θεοῦ μεγάλοιο πιθήσας δόγμασιν ἐσθλοῖς.

And then God will send a king from the sun,
who will stop the entire earth from evil war,
killing some, imposing loyal oaths on others.
655 He will not do all these things on the basis of his private plans,
but trusting the noble ordinances of the great God.

God will send a king from heaven (where the sun is)[66] or from the east (where the sun rises).[67] Collins argues that the expression ἀπ' ἠελίοιο cannot just mean 'from the east' and that such a king—with no further details—is unknown. A king from the sun is known in Egyptian context, and indicates—according to Collins—an Egyptian (or, more precisely, Ptolemaic) king, presented as the messiah[68] in the *Sibylline Oracles*. If Collins's references to Egypt are correct, a conclusion implying a *divine* king seems to be more obvious.[69] If that conclusion is right, this passage describes the coming of the messiah, in images understood and appreciated in Ptolemaic circles, but where the *origin* of this messiah is clearly presented as divine.

However, the figure has human characteristics as well, as is rightly remarked by Nikiprowetzky,[70] but that should not surprise us in a description of the messiah. This messiah will play a role at the end of times, when the Kingdom of Peace is ushered in, an event often referred to in the pseudepi-

---

66. Lanchester, 'Sibylline Oracles', *ad loc.*

67. Lanchester, 'Sibylline Oracles', *ad loc.*; Nikiprowetzky, *Troisième Sibylle*, pp. 136, 323; Peretti, *Sibilla babilonese*, pp. 387-88; Momigliano, 'Portata storica', p. 1081; H.G. Kippenberg, '"Dann wird der Orient herrschen und der Okzident dienen". Zur Begründung eines gesamtvorderasiatischen Standpunktes im Kampf gegen Rom', in N.W. Bolz and W. Hübener (eds.), *Spiegel und Gleichnis* (Festschrift J. Taubes; Würzburg: Königshausen & Neumann, 1983), pp. 40-48 (43-44, 47), who sees evidence in this for the rather strange hypothesis that in Judea too the farmers who could no longer pay their taxes, and were therefore ex-farmers, participated in a Levant-wide movement of opposition.

68. Collins, *Sibylline Oracles of Egyptian Judaism*, pp. 40-44; Collins, 'The Sibyl and the Potter', p. 64; cf. Momigliano, 'Portata storica', pp. 1081-82.

69. The link Collins, *Sibylline Oracles of Egyptian Judaism*, pp. 42-43, lays between the king of the sun and the 'seventh king' (mentioned in v. 608, etc.) is not strong enough to lead to identification (see Momigliano, 'Portata storica', p. 1081).

70. Nikiprowetzky, *Troisième Sibylle*, p. 136.

grapha.[71] He does not act of his own accord, but only by order of God, who will exercise judgment and dominion.[72]

It is clear that the Antichrist does not occur here. However, certain elements of this passage could be of importance to our research, albeit by analogy.

e. *The Antichrist in the oldest parts of the* Sibylline Oracles

Let us start with a discussion of the last passage. God will send a messiah who will eliminate some through warfare and who will bind others to himself by loyalty. He will do this in the form of a human figure, and in total dependence on God. It has been stated that the way the Antichrist is portrayed is determined in part by the messiah figure. A link between the messiah and the Antichrist does not seem necessary, but here the data are clearly similar. From our reading of this description of the messiah, we can conclude about the Antichrist: 'An Antichrist sent by Satan[73] will eliminate some through warfare and bind others to himself by loyalty; he will do this in a human figure and in total dependence on Satan'.

Perhaps it is not fully responsible to include the elements obtained by inversion into our view. However, it is remarkable that so many elements of the Antichrist can be found in these oldest parts of *Sib. Or.* 3 if we carry the reasoning all the way through.

The Antichrist is a man (everywhere in these passages) of non-earthly origin (vv. 390b-91a, 652 [by analogy]), who acts under the influence of Satan (vv. 655-56 [by analogy]). He is faithless (v. 388) and tyrannical (v. 390a: savage and a stranger to justice). He eliminates some by force (vv. 392, 612-13, 653-54a [by analogy]), others he influences ideologically (v. 654b [by analogy]). From the third part we should not conclude that the Antichrist is the counterpart of the messiah, because that conclusion was included in the argument from the start. However, the link with Antiochus

---

71. Nikiprowetzky, *Troisième Sibylle*, p. 137. Apart from the passage studied here, see also *1 En.* 10.7; 10.17–11.2; 91.12-14 (where the expectation for the future [*Fernerwartung*] is remarkable), cf. K. Koch, 'Sabbatsstruktur der Geschichte. Die sogenannte Zehn-Wochen-Apokalypse (I Hen 93, 1-10; 91, 11-17) und das Ringen um die alttestamentliche Chronologie im späten Israelitentum', *ZAW* 95 (1983), pp. 403-40 (420-21); *Jub.* 23.26-29; *Tr. Shem* 11.18.

72. For a more active role of the Messiah, see Isa. 9.5-6; 11.1-10 (cf. T.C. Vriezen, *Hoofdlijnen der theologie van het Oude Testament* [Wageningen: Veenman, 3rd edn, 1966], pp. 485-86).

73. This should not be interpreted in a dualistic way: Satan is not an anti-God.

2. The Antichrist in the Apocrypha and Pseudepigrapha

IV Epiphanes is clear in the first two parts, and this Seleucid king was important in filling in the Antichrist figure. It is therefore surprising that we do not find him here.

Even if the authors who do not immediately distinguish Antiochus IV Epiphanes here are right, *Sib. Or.* 3 remains of utmost importance: the individualizing is unique, and if we should see a general figure in vv. 388-400 and 611-15, these verses are eschatological and all elements point towards the Antichrist.[74]

5. Judith

a. *Setting*

Although the book of Judith has roots dating from Persian times, the present version originates from around 150 or shortly afterwards. A Greek translation of the Hebrew original is extant. The author lived in Palestine and had a puritan streak; he could be called an early Pharisee.[75]

Does the Antichrist occur in this apocryphal book, that originates from shortly after 150? At first glance this seems improbable in a work claiming to be historical. However, we must take a closer look. The work contains many historical impossibilities, so that we can definitely not speak of a 'historical' work. But does that mean that the book is unhistorical or metahistorical? There are so many elements, that it is worth taking a closer look at some passages.[76]

---

74. Collins, *Sibylline Oracles of Egyptian Judaism*, p. 40 ('closer to the figure of an anti-Christ') and *idem*, 'Sibylline Oracles', *ad loc.*

75. Vriezen and Van der Woude, *Oudisraëlitische en vroegjoodse literatuur*, pp. 412-14; Harrison, *Introduction*, pp. 1214-17; G.W.E. Nickelsburg, 'Stories of Biblical and Early Post-Biblical Times', in Stone (ed.), *Jewish Writings of the Second Temple Period*, pp. 33-87 (51-52). Cf. Beckwith, 'Pre-History', p. 29. The book was originally written in Greek: H. Engel, ' "Der Herr ist ein Gott, der Kriege zerschlägt". Zur Frage der griechischen Originalsprache und der Struktur des Buches Judit', in K.-D. Schunck and M. Augustin (eds.), *Goldene Äpfel in silbernen Schalen: Collected Communications to the XIIIth Congress of the International Organization for the Study of the Old Testament* (BEATAJ, 20; Bern: Peter Lang, 1992), pp. 155-68 (156-59).

76. This research has made clear that I was not the first to think this way. I shall refer to the work of E. Haag more than once. For the exegetical history, see also N. Poulssen, *Judith* (Boeken van het Oude Testament; Roermond: Romen, 1969), p. 11.

b. *Judith 2.1-3*[77]

1 Καὶ ἐν τῷ ἔτει τῷ ὀκτωκαιδεκάτῳ δευτέρᾳ καὶ εἰκάδι τοῦ πρώτου μηνὸς ἐγένετο λόγος ἐν οἴκῳ Ναβουχοδονοσὸρ βασιλέως Ἀσσυρίων ἐκδικῆσαι πᾶσαν τὴν γῆν καθὼς ἐλάλησεν.
2 Καὶ συνεκάλεσεν πάντας τοὺς θεράποντας αὐτοῦ καὶ πάντας τοὺς μεγιστᾶνας αὐτοῦ καὶ ἔθετο μετ' αὐτῶν τὸ μυστήριον τῆς βουλῆς αὐτοῦ καὶ συνετέλεσεν[78] πᾶσαν τὴν κακίαν τῆς γῆς ἐκ τοῦ στόματος αὐτοῦ,
3 καὶ αὐτοὶ ἔκριναν ὀλεθρεῦσαι πᾶσαν σάρκα οἳ οὐκ ἠκολούθησαν τῷ λόγῳ τοῦ στόματος αὐτοῦ.

1 And in the eighteenth year, on the twenty second (day) of the first month, it was decided in the house of Nebuchadnezzar, king of the Assyrians, to punish the whole earth just as he had said.[79]
2 And he summoned all his ministers and all his nobles, informed them of his secret decree, and revealed all the wickedness he desired to bring upon the earth[80] on the grounds of what he had said.[81]
3 And[82] they decided to kill everyone[83] who did not obey[84] the word of his mouth.

Although there are many problems with the chronological and geographical setting of Judith, the date mentioned is of significance. The eighteenth year of the king's reign is the year Jerusalem was destroyed.[85] The first month[86] is the month in which the kings used to go out into battle.[87] The

77. According to the Septuaginta Gottingensis.
78. This is claimed to be the translation of the Heb. ויכלה (and he finished), which is a wrong reading for ויגלה (and he revealed): C.A. Moore, *Judith* (AB; Garden City, NY: Doubleday, 1985), p. 132.
79. The aorist can take the meaning of a pluperfect: J. Humbert, *Syntaxe grecque* (Tradition de l'humanisme, 8; Paris: Klincksieck, 3rd edn, 1960), §243; BDR, §345.
80. Trans. on the basis of cj.; text: 'decided to realize the complete destruction of the earth'.
81. Lit. 'from his mouth'.
82. E. Zenger, *Das Buch Judit* (JSHRZ, 1.6; Gütersloh: Gerd Mohn, 1981), *ad loc.*, translates 'also'; although the advisers remained completely in line with the king, the text says that they agreed to do something entirely different from what the king had decided. The king's decision was to punish the whole earth, the council now decided to punish only those who would not agree with this policy. This means that Zenger's translation is not justified.
83. Lit. 'all flesh' (which is also a Hebraism, from כל בשר).
84. Lit. 'follow'.
85. The historical Nebuchadnezzar reigned as a Babylonian king from 605 until 562; during the eighteenth year of his reign (see, e.g., Jer. 52.29) Jerusalem was destroyed.
86. This is, if the year starts with the month of Nisan, but that seems to be the intended meaning.

2. The Antichrist in the Apocrypha and Pseudepigrapha 59

twenty-second of the month Nisan is just after the holy period of the Passover celebrations. The date therefore indicates a post-salvation period.[88] It was under these circumstances that a most solemn word of the illustrious king arrived: ἐγένετο λόγος is the usual formula in which God speaks.[89] Also καθὼς ἐλάλησεν is an expression often used in connection with God.[90]

The king informed his advisers of what had been known to himself only until that moment.[91] he had decreed that the whole earth must be rendered useless.

Naturally the king's advisers accepted this, and they decreed that all those who thought otherwise must be eliminated.

c. *Judith 3.8*

8 Καὶ κατέσκαψεν πάντα τὰ ὅρια[92] αὐτῶν καὶ τὰ ἄλση αὐτῶν ἐξέκοψεν, καὶ[93] ἦν δεδομένον αὐτῷ ἐξολεθρεῦσαι πάντας τοὺς θεοὺς τῆς γῆς, ὅπως αὐτῷ μόνῳ τῷ Ναβουχοδονοσὸρ λατρεύσωσιν πάντα τὰ ἔθνη, καὶ πᾶσαι αἱ γλῶσσαι καὶ αἱ φυλαὶ αὐτῶν ἐπικαλέσωνται αὐτὸν εἰς θεόν.

8 And (Holophernes) destroyed all their borders[94] and cut down their sacred groves, and[95] he had been commissioned to eliminate all native gods, so that the nations would worship him, Nebuchadnezzar, alone and all their languages and tribes should worship him as a god.

---

87. De Vaux, *Les institutions de l'Ancien Testament*, II, pp. 63-64.
88. Poulssen, *Judith, ad loc.*
89. Especially in Ezek. (in the LXX). (Zenger, *Buch Judit, ad loc.*; E. Haag, *Studien zum Buche Judith: Seine theologische Bedeutung und literarische Eigenart* [Trierer Theologische Studien, 16; Trier: Paulinus, 1963], p. 16.)
90. Zenger, *Buch Judit, ad loc.*; Haag, *Studien*, p. 16.
91. Some see in μυστήριον a religious, eschatological meaning, which is not impossible in this context. (See Zenger, *Buch Judit, ad loc.*; Haag, *Studien*, pp. 16-17.) It is also possible to think of the confidentiality to which people are bound in regard to private conversations with their king or queen.
92. Cj.: ἱερά, on the basis of the contents, of the Syr. *hyklyhwn*, and of an assumed Hebr. במות. (Poulssen, *Judith*, p. 91; Moore, *Judith*, p. 142; Zenger, *Buch Judit, ad loc.*; A. Miller, *Das Buch Judit* [Die Heilige Schrift des Alten Testamentes; Bonn: Hanstein, 1940], *ad loc.*; Haag, *Studien*, p. 23 n. 58). M.S. Enslin and S. Zeitlin, *The Book of Judith* (Dropsie University Edition. Jewish Apocryphal Literature, 7; Leiden: E.J. Brill, 1972), keep the text, with reference to Deut. 19.14.
93. V.l. ὅτι.
94. Cj.: 'sanctuaries'.
95. V.l. 'because...'

The people in the Phoenician–Philistine coastal area[96] surrendered to Holophernes, Nebuchadnezzar's general, without much difficulty. But this surrender did not lead to the hoped for results. Holophernes created terrible destruction, especially in the area of religion. For example, the poles devoted to the goddess Ashera were destroyed.[97] It slowly emerged that his task was to direct all worship to Nebuchadnezzar, thereby excluding all other gods (μόνῳ). Such monolatry is impossible in the ancient Near East.[98] Was the elimination of all gods a task given by the Lord God, or by Nebuchadnezzar? Perhaps it is premature to see a reference to God's acts in this phase of the story, but this solemn expression could refer to an opinion about Nebuchadnezzar[99] that is in perfect agreement with the worship given to him, and comparable only to the worship the God of Israel demands for himself.[100]

d. *Judith 6.9*

9   Καὶ εἴπερ ἐλπίζεις τῇ καρδίᾳ σου ὅτι οὐ λημφθήσονται, μὴ συμπεσέτω σου τὸ πρόσωπον· ἐλάλησα, καὶ οὐδὲν διαπεσεῖται τῶν ῥημάτων μου.

9   And if you hope in your heart that they will not be taken, then do not look downcast; I have spoken and none of my words shall fail to come true.

96. Poulssen, *Judith*, p. 26.

97. ἄλση is the usual rendering of אשרות (Enslin and Zeitlin, *Book of Judith, ad loc.*; Moore, *Judith*, p. 142; Zenger, *Buch Judit, ad loc.*).

98. Moore, *Judith*, p. 143, is right in saying that Assyrian, Neo-Assyrian, Babylonian, Neo-Babylonian and Persian kings would never (or at least hardly ever) deify themselves during their own lives. (See, e.g., W. Freiherr von Soden, *Einführung in die Altorientalistik* [Orientalistische Einführungen in Gegenstand, Ergebnisse und Perspektiven der Einzelgebiete; Darmstadt: Wissenschaftliche Buchgesellschaft, 1985], pp. 53-64; H. Goedicke, *Die Stellung des Königs im Alten Reich* [Ägyptologische Abhandlungen, 2; Wiesbaden: Otto Harrassowitz, 1960], pp. 92-93; W. Barta, *Untersuchungen zur Göttlichkeit des regierenden Königs: Ritus und Sakralkönigtum in Altägypten nach Zeugnissen der Frühzeit und des Alten Reiches* [Münchner Ägyptologische Studien, 32; Munich: Deutscher Kunstverlag, 1975], pp. 132-37.) With Antiochus IV Epiphanes one could probably speak of a far-reaching identification with Zeus: see G.W. Lorein, 'Some Aspects of the Life and Death of Antiochus IV Epiphanes. A New Presentation of Old Viewpoints', *Ancient Society* 31 (2001), pp. 157-71 (162-65). In contrast to what Haag, *Studien*, pp. 23-24, writes, there are more clues for deification in Mesopotamia than in Egypt. However, he is right in saying that deification never took place with the exclusion of other gods.

99. Cf. Poulssen, *Judith, ad loc.*; Zenger, *Buch Judit*, p. 502 (*ad* 11.19). A different interpretation of δεδόμενον with Moore, *Judith*, pp. 142-43.

100. Haag, *Studien*, p. 24.

2. *The Antichrist in the Apocrypha and Pseudepigrapha*

In Holophernes' speech to Achior (the commander of the Ammonites who did know of the greatness of God[101]), the speaker hinted several times that Nebuchadnezzar was divine.[102]

Finally Holophernes said that Achior should not think that the cities of Israel would not be taken. He also reproached him by saying that the sad expression on his face contradicted his conviction (i.e. that Israel's God could save his people). He used an expression derived from the Hebrew (נפלו פני 'פ), a variant of which is used in 1 Sam. 17.32 (נפל לב 'פ). He concluded by saying that his words would certainly come true and that none of them would fail, which also seems to put him on a divine level.

e. *Judith 11.19*

19 Καὶ ἄξω σε διὰ μέσου τῆς Ἰουδαίας ἕως τοῦ ἐλθεῖν ἀπέναντι Ἰερουσαλήμ καὶ θήσω τὸν δίφρον σου ἐν μέσῳ αὐτῆς, καὶ ἄξεις αὐτοὺς ὡς πρόβατα, οἷς οὐκ ἔστιν ποιμήν, καὶ οὐ γρύξει κύων τῇ γλώσσῃ αὐτοῦ ἀπέναντί σου· ὅτι ταῦτα ἐλαλήθη μοι κατὰ πρόγνωσίν μου καὶ ἀπηγγέλη μοι, καὶ ἀπεστάλην ἀναγγεῖλαί σοι.

19 And I shall lead you straight through Judea, until you come to Jerusalem, and I shall establish your throne in its centre and you will drive them like sheep who have no shepherd,[103] and no dog will sound its tongue at you;[104] for these things have been told me according to my foreknowledge and they have been announced to me, and I was sent to announce it to you.

Judith ended her first conversation with Holophernes (or, rather, her first speech to him) by announcing her programme: she would show him the way, she would install his throne (and thereby his divine power)[105] in Jerusalem, and he would overpower them without meeting resistance.[106] She compared the people to sheep that cannot resist, especially without a

---

101. Jdt. 5.5, 13.
102. Cf. Haag, *Studien*, p. 35.
103. Possessive dative.
104. This is probably a Hebraism (cf. Poulssen, *Judith*, *ad loc.*; Moore, *Judith*, p. 211; but not necessarily, since it is not non-Greek): cf. לא יחרץ־כלב לשנו in Exod. 11.7. (NB: In spite of the frequent references to Josh. 10.21, the expression does not occur there in the MSS.) In view of the concrete circumstances we may have to think of a sheepdog. However, this specific translation does not follow from the expression itself, and a reference to Isa. 56.10 does not provide any more clarity (*contra* Miller, *Buch Judit*, *ad loc.*).
105. Haag, *Studien*, p. 49.
106. Moore, *Judith*, p. 211.

shepherd or a sheepdog.[107] Holophernes would then be able to take the place of a shepherd. In the Greek text, the verbs used for Judith's leadership and Holophernes' driving are the same: Holophernes would not be able to act until Judith had done something for him.[108]

There are a number of phrases which also occur in the Bible. To us, especially the link with Zech. 11.16 is important.[109]

Judith was well aware of her task. The passive forms ἐλαλήθη, ἀπηγγέλη and ἀπεστάλην should be interpreted as divine passives;[110] Judith did everything that was within her power.

f. *Judith 13.9*

9 Καὶ ἀπεκύλισεν τὸ σῶμα αὐτοῦ ἀπὸ τῆς στρωμνῆς καὶ ἀφεῖλεν τὸ κανώπιον ἀπὸ τῶν στύλων· καὶ μετ' ὀλίγον ἐξῆλθεν καὶ παρέδωκεν τῇ ἄβρᾳ[111] αὐτῆς τὴν κεφαλὴν Ὀλοφέρνου.

And she rolled his body off his bed and took the mosquito net from the posts, and soon afterwards she went out and gave Holophernes' head to her maid.

Holophernes had not only figuratively, but also literally, fallen at Judith's feet. It is unclear what she intended to do with the mosquito net,[112] but Miller points out that it was costly and therefore could easily help to confirm the head's identity.[113] Judith did not keep Holophernes' head for very long: she gave it to her maid. However, we are strongly reminded here of David who walked around with Goliath's head.

g. *Judith 16.6*

6 Οὐ γὰρ ὑπέπεσεν[114] ὁ δυνατὸς αὐτῶν ὑπὸ νεανίσκων,
οὐδὲ υἱοὶ τιτάνων ἐπάταξεν αὐτόν,

---

107. See the second part of note 104 above.
108. Cf. Poulssen, *Judith, ad loc*.
109. See Poulssen, *Judith, ad loc*. For Zech. 11.16 see Chapter 1.
110. Poulssen, *Judith, ad loc*.
111. Cf. Aram. חברה. This indicates a worker who is more equal in rank, but compare the development in the meaning of the Dutch word *medewerker* which has developed from the meaning of 'co-worker' to 'subordinate'.
112. Moore, *Judith*, p. 227.
113. Miller, *Buch Judit, ad loc*. For a description of the mosquito net, see Jdt. 10.21.
114. A and B offer ὑπέπεσεν, many other MSS offer ἔπεσεν. The problem of the given text is a grammatical one: ὑποπίπτειν usually takes a dative ('become the victim of', whereas ὑποπίπτειν ὑπό is equivalent to 'become the victim because of'). Against this speaks the *lectio difficilior* argument. This should not be used for absurd

2. *The Antichrist in the Apocrypha and Pseudepigrapha* 63

οὐδὲ ὑψηλοὶ γίγαντες ἐπέθεντο αὐτῷ,
ἀλλὰ Ἰουδὶθ θυγάτηρ Μεραρὶ
ἐν κάλλει προσώπου αὐτῆς παρέλυσεν αὐτόν.

6 Not by youths their hero has fallen,
nor did sons of titans beat him,
no mighty giants attacked him,
but Judith, Merari's daughter,
undid him with the beauty of her face.

After having accomplished her task, Judith, Merari's daughter,[115] sang a song of thanksgiving. The middle part of this song (vv. 5-10) changes from Judith in the first person to Judith in the third person. We do not necessarily have to conclude from this that the middle part was sung by a choir: she may have been singing about herself.[116]

The hero[117] Holophernes, who had put not only his master, but also himself at a divine level, was killed, and not even at the battlefield by the hands of young men, sons of giants, or giants, but by a woman who had no other weapon than her beauty.[118]

We must remark several things about the giants. First there is the lexical problem of the τιτᾶνες. This does not belong in this literature, but it was probably necessary because the Hebrew original used two different terms for 'giants'.[119] Secondly, there is the literary phenomenon of gradation:[120] giants are stronger than sons of giants, who themselves are stronger than mere mortals. Thirdly, there is the question about the historical appearance of giants in this period. Whichever historical period the writer has intended, giants did not exist then. This is an indication that the writer did not intend a historical period, but had metahistorical information in mind.[121]

---

variants, but that is not the case here: ὑποπίπτειν is not impossible as regards to the meaning: 'become the victim' does fit into this context. (However, I did not opt for this translation, because it may give the impression that the Greek text offers a more specific word.) Cf. Enslin and Zeitlin, *Book of Judith*, ad loc.

115. For a complete genealogy, see Jdt. 8.1.
116. Moore, *Judith*, pp. 248, 253; *pace* Poulssen, *Judith*, ad loc.
117. Same term in 1 Sam. 17.51, about Goliath (גבור).
118. Cf. Zenger, *Buch Judit*, ad loc.
119. According to Enslin and Zeitlin, *Book of Judith*, ad loc. Making a reconstruction of the specific Hebrew words that were used would in this instance be slightly far-fetched.
120. Miller, *Buch Judit*, ad loc.
121. Haag, *Studien*, p. 57.

h. *The Antichrist in Judith*

The whole story is metahistorical. The date in 2.1 points to a post-salvation period and therefore to an eschatological interpretation (cf. 16.6).[122] On several points, Nebuchadnezzar is presented in a way one would present God (2.1; 3.8). Holophernes, who served him, partly shared in these divine actions (6.9). Nebuchadnezzar wished to be worshipped as the only god, and therefore he and Holophernes opposed all religion (3.8). Holophernes' actions took place at a military (2.1-2; 3.8; 6.9) and a political-religious level (11.19, referring to the religious value of the throne and to Zech. 11.16). All his actions are saturated with hubris[123] (6.9). All these elements of the Antichrist are present in Judith. There are also references to the story of 1 Sam.17 (6.9; 13.9; 16.6),[124] so that Holophernes is compared to Goliath. The author of 1 Sam. 17 did not conceive of Goliath as an Antichrist, but this link must have been added later. Finally Holophernes played the role of a shepherd (11.19). We may assume that he would not be regarded a 'good' shepherd and that this is therefore a reference to the wicked shepherd of Zech. 11.15-17.[125]

One could say that the military actions of Holophernes rather point at the figure of the 'enemy from the North',[126] also in view of the mention of Esdrelon (3.9),[127] but the presence of the religious element is too strong for this. However, we must admit that Holophernes is not presented as a false prophet.

All in all, there are sufficient indications to justify a comparison of Holophernes' metahistorical military and religious actions in his service of Nebuchadnezzar, with the eschatological political and religious actions of the Antichrist under the influence of Satan. It seems that he has worked at this more deliberately than the authors of the Laus Patrum.

---

122. Naturally, it only points at an eschatological interpretation. The whole story is presented as a historical account, and it is only logical that this concludes with an account of Judith's further life and her death (16.21-25). (*Pace* Poulssen, *Judith*, p. 12, and really also *pace* Haag, *Studien*, p. 78, who wishes to emphasize the metahistorical more than the eschatological.)

123. Cf. Poulssen, *Judith*, p. 28; Haag, *Studien*, pp. 22-25, 35.

124. See also Zenger, *Buch Judit*, p. 440.

125. For 1 Sam. 17 and Zech. 11 see Chapter 1.

126. This is, in my opinion, a different theme from that of the Antichrist.

127. Cf. Haag, *Studien*, p. 22.

6. 2 Maccabees

a. Setting

The Second Book of Maccabees is mainly a summary, written by a Jew with Pharisaic tendencies, of a five-volume history by Jason of Cyrene. Apart from the two letters at the beginning of the work, originally written in Aramaic, the Greek text is not a translation.[128] The letters may be original. If they are, they date from 124 and 164 respectively.[129] The general opinion is that the summary dates from the same time as 1 Maccabees, that is, around the year 100. It is often stated that at a later time, an editor wrote an introduction, and that the final edition was rendered still later, in 77 at the earliest.[130] Bunge, however, regards 1.10b–2.18 as the core passage of 2 Maccabees, whereby 1.1-10a is a covering letter, chs. 3–15 have been added as an appendix, and the complete set was sent to Leontopolis in 124, to refute carefully the objections to the Temple in Jerusalem.[131]

Bunge's clever hypothesis creates an order that deviates from the usual numbering, 2 Maccabees (124)—1 Maccabees (100)—*3 Maccabees* (80 or 20).[132]

Like 1 Maccabees, 2 Maccabees discusses the period of Antiochus IV Epiphanes, but follows a different pattern. Actually, the person who wrote the summary did not always manage to show the interconnection of events.

---

128. Harrison, *Introduction*, pp. 1268, 1276.

129. Harrison, *Introduction*, p. 1269; Flusser, 'Psalms, Hymns and Prayers', p. 572. *Contra*: K.-D. Schunck, *Die Quellen des I. und II. Makkabäerbuches* (dissertation, Greifswald; Halle: Niemeyer, 1954), p. 127.

130. Vriezen and Van der Woude, *Oudisraëlitische en vroegjoodse literatuur*, p. 437; H.W. Attridge, 'Historiography', in Stone (ed.), *Jewish Writings of the Second Temple Period*, pp. 157-84 (177-78).

131. J.G. Bunge, 'Untersuchungen zum zweiten Makkabäerbuch: Quellenkritische, literarische, chronologische und historische Untersuchungen zum zweiten Makkabäerbuch als Quelle syrisch-palästinensischer Geschichte im 2. Jh. v. Chr.' (Unpublished dissertation; Bonn, 1971), pp. 195-201, 601-606, 615-17, 635-36.

132. An early date of *3 Maccabees* could be combined with a late date for 2 Maccabees. This would mean *3 Maccabees* does not build on 2 Maccabees but on the work of Jason of Cyrene.

b. *2 Maccabees 1.15-16*[133]

15 Καὶ προθέντων αὐτὰ τῶν ἱερέων τοῦ Ναναίου κἀκείνου προσελθόντος μετ' ὀλίγων εἰς τὸν περίβολον τοῦ τεμένους, συγκλείσαντες τὸ ἱερόν, ὡς εἰσῆλθεν Ἀντίοχος,

16 ἀνοίξαντες τὴν τοῦ φατνώματος κρυπτὴν θύραν βάλλοντες πέτρους συνεκεραύνωσαν τὸν ἡγεμόνα καὶ μέλη ποιήσαντες καὶ τὰς κεφαλὰς ἀφέλοντες τοῖς ἔξω παρέρριψαν.

15 After the priests of the Nanea temple had set out the [temple treasures] and after [Antiochus IV] had gone ahead, with a few people, to the enclosure of the holy area, they closed the sanctuary as soon as Antiochus had entered,

16 opened the secret door in the ceiling, threw stones and struck down the leader. They dismembered [them], cut off the heads and threw them to those who were outside.

These verses are from the second letter at the beginning of the work (1.10[134]–2.18). This letter is presented as Judas Maccabeus's written description of the death of Antiochus IV Epiphanes. However, it is highly unlikely that the letter is authentic. This description of Antiochus's death differs from others,[135] but that is in itself not a conclusive argument. There is an impressive list of other arguments that all point to a late edition. Nelis[136] is one of those who argue for a late edition. He also points out some eschatological elements: the expectation that all Jews will be brought back to the Land (1.27, 29; 2.7) and then the Tabernacle, the Ark and the Incense Altar will be found (2.7).[137]

Bunge has a different view on this matter.[138] According to him, certain verses belong to a historical core,[139] including vv. 15-16. Bunge claims that this core can be called historical in the sense that it dates from 164. It

---

133. According to the Septuaginta Gottingensis.

134. Or perhaps v. 10b, if the date is part of the first letter; see, e.g., Bunge, 'Untersuchungen', p. 35.

135. Lorein, 'Life and Death', p. 169 n. 65.

136. J.T. Nelis, *II Makkabeeën* (Boeken van het Oude Testament; Bussum: Romen, 1975), pp. 51-55, 57; cf. Bunge, 'Untersuchungen', pp. 36-37.

137. Nelis, *II Makkabeeën*, p. 56. Cf. D. Arenhoevel, *Die Theokratie nach dem 1. und 2. Makkabäerbuch* (Walberger Studien der Albertus Magnus-Akademie. Theologische Reihe, 3; Mainz: Grünewald, 1967), p. 181, who gives a good overview, but the texts he quotes are not convincing.

138. Actually, Bunge's whole dissertation focuses on the second letter. (Bunge, 'Untersuchungen', p. 33.) However, pp. 35-46, 53-55, are useful as an introduction.

139. 1.18b-2.15 could be interpolated. (Bunge, 'Untersuchungen', pp. 46-52, 56.) To Bunge, this leaves 1.10b-18a and 2.16-18.

2. The Antichrist in the Apocrypha and Pseudepigrapha 67

does not give the correct rendering of the facts, because they were not yet known at the time of writing.[140]

Whatever the truth may be, these verses relate how Antiochus IV Epiphanes and some of his nobles[141] went to a temple of the Mesopotamian goddess Nanea—also known as Artemis and as Aphrodite—on what was once Persian territory.[142] As an experienced temple raider he tried to obtain the treasuries of this temple too, by staging a ἱερὸς γάμος.[143] He arrived on the holy site[144] with a small company. As soon as Antiochus had entered the temple proper, it was closed off. Within the building there was a coffer ceiling, and one of the ceiling panels could be removed, very much like a trap door.[145] Temple officials were sitting in the space between ceiling and roof.[146] Apparently the priests had not entered with Antiochus). They threw heavy rocks down the trap door, like thunderbolts (συγκεραυνοῦν). Antiochus, the ἡγεμών,[147] died, and possibly his company with him. His body (and perhaps also the bodies of his company) was mauled horribly, and all their heads were thrown out.[148]

---

140. Bunge, 'Untersuchungen', pp. 42-43.
141. Φίλοι (v. 14).
142. J.A. Goldstein, *II Maccabees* (AB; Garden City, NY: Doubleday, 1983), p. 170.
143. Nelis, *II Makkabeeën*, p. 59; Goldstein, *II Maccabees*, p. 170; contra O. Mørkholm, *Studies in the Coinage of Antiochus IV of Syria* (Historisk-filosofiske Meddelelser Kongelige Danske Videnskabernes Selskab, 43.3; Copenhagen: Munksgaard, 1963), p. 73, who argues that the ἱεροὶ γάμοι were not a trick.
144. In Jewish texts τέμενος indicates pagan temples (Goldstein, *II Maccabees*, p. 170), but in combination with περίβολος and with ἱερόν following quite closely, the classical translation of 'holy site' is more probable. Bunge, 'Untersuchungen', p. 72 ('heiliger Bezirk'); Nelis, *II Makkabeeën, ad loc.*
145. See LSJ, *s.v.* φάτνωμα. Contra Nelis, *II Makkabeeën, ad loc.*: it does not say that the trap door was hidden, but that it was not clear that there was some kind of door; we cannot expect the writer of these verses to describe the situation in the same way as Herodotus has done (5.16).
146. Or were they simply sitting on the roof?
147. The word ἡγεμών is not a usual description of Antiochus IV (see Bunge, 'Untersuchungen', p. 72), but this is clearly about him. Cf. 2 Macc. 9.19, where the term στρατηγός is used for Antiochus, albeit in combination with βασιλεύς. Goldstein, *II Maccabees*, p. 170, thinks this is a typical word that is used to describe Antiochus as an arrogant tyrant, after Isa. 10.5-19.
148. The Vulgate reads, 'percusserunt ducem et qui cum eo erant'. Nelis, *II Makkabeeën, ad loc.*, assumes that Antiochus was the only one who went in and reads, slightly further in the sentence, the singular κεφαλήν. S. Tedesche and S. Zeitlin, *The Second Book of Maccabees* (Dropsie College Edition. Jewish Apocryphal Literature;

c. 2 Maccabees 4.25

25 Λαβὼν δὲ τὰς βασιλικὰς ἐντολὰς παρεγένετο τῆς μὲν ἀρχιερωσύνης οὐδὲν ἄξιον φέρων, θυμοὺς δὲ ὠμοῦ τυράννου καὶ θηρὸς βαρβάρου ὀργὰς ἔχων.

25 After receiving the royal orders, [Menelaus] arrived [in Jerusalem], possessing nothing that is worthy of the high priestly status, but having the mind of a cruel tyrant and the temperament of a barbaric[149] beast.

During his visit to Antiochus IV in 172, Menelaus took the priesthood away from Jason by promising more money for the concession.[150] He returned to Jerusalem with at least two royal decrees: Jason's removal and his own appointment.[151] The only basis for Menelaus's position as a high priest was his appointment by Antiochus IV, who, by Jewish standards, did not have the right to appoint.[152] The Jewish people's appreciation of him is expressed in this verse: Menelaus is called tyrannical, even beastly.

d. 2 Maccabees 5.11-17

11 Προσπεσόντων δὲ τῷ βασιλεῖ περὶ τῶν γεγονότων διέλαβεν ἀποστατεῖν τὴν Ἰουδαίαν· ὅθεν ἀναζεύξας ἐξ Αἰγύπτου τεθηριωμένος τῇ ψυχῇ ἔλαβε τὴν μὲν πόλιν δοριάλωτον

12 καὶ ἐκέλευσε τοῖς στρατιώταις κόπτειν ἀφειδῶς τοὺς ἐμπίπτοντας καὶ τοὺς εἰς τὰς οἰκίας ἀναβαίνοντας κατασφάζειν.

13 Ἐγίνοντο δὲ νέων καὶ πρεσβυτέρων ἀναιρέσεις, γυναικῶν καὶ τέκνων ἀφανισμός, παρθένων τε καὶ νηπίων σφαγαί.

14 Ὀκτὼ δὲ μυριάδες ἐν ταῖς πάσαις ἡμέραις τρισὶ κατεφθάρησαν, τέσσαρες μὲν ἐν χειρῶν νομαῖς, οὐχ ἧττον δὲ τῶν ἐσφαγμένων ἐπράθησαν.

New York: Harper, 1954), p. 105, mentions the small difference between singular and plural in the Aramaic st. emph. (אַשָּׁרְ—אִשְּׁרָא).

149. For this meaning of βάρβαρος in the first century, see F.-M. Abel, *Les livres des Maccabées* (Ebib; Paris: Gabalda, 1949), ad loc.; Nelis, *II Makkabeeën*, ad loc.

150. Menelaus had not been able to deliver on his promise (2 Macc. 4.27-28). For the circumstances, see Eddy, *The King Is Dead*, pp. 208-209. Did Antiochus IV also see an advantage in Menelaus having a pro-Seleucid attitude? See J.G. Bunge, 'Münzen als Mittel politischer Propaganda: Antiochos IV. Epiphanes von Syrien', *Studii Clasice* 16 (1974), pp. 43-52 (46).

151. Goldstein, *II Maccabees*, ad loc.

152. Menelaus probably did belong to the priestly family. (A.S. van der Woude, 'Geschiedenis en godsdienst van het Palestijnse Jodendom vanaf Alexander de Grote tot aan de komst van de Romeinen', in Van der Woude [ed.], *Bijbels Handboek*. IIB. *Tussen Oude en Nieuwe Testament* [Kampen: Kok, 1983], pp. 5-89 [38]; Nelis, *II Makkabeeën*, p. 128.)

2. The Antichrist in the Apocrypha and Pseudepigrapha

15 Οὐκ ἀρκεσθεὶς δὲ τούτοις κατετόλμησεν εἰς τὸ πάσης τῆς γῆς ἁγιώτατον ἱερὸν εἰσελθεῖν ὁδηγὸν ἔχων τὸν Μενέλαον τὸν καὶ τῶν νόμων καὶ τῆς πατρίδος προδότην γεγονότα

16 καὶ ταῖς μιεραῖς χερσὶ τὰ ἱερὰ σκεύη λαμβάνων καὶ τὰ ὑπ' ἄλλων βασιλέων ἀνασταθέντα πρὸς αὔξησιν καὶ δόξαν τοῦ τόπου καὶ τιμὴν ταῖς βεβήλοις χερσὶν συσσύρων.

17 Καὶ ἐμετεωρίζετο τὴν διάνοιαν ὁ Ἀντίοχος οὐ συνορῶν, ὅτι διὰ τὰς ἁμαρτίας τῶν τὴν πόλιν οἰκούντων ἀπώργισται βραχέως ὁ δεσπότης, διὸ γέγονε περὶ τὸν τόπον παρόρασις.

11 When (news) of what had happened reached the king, he assumed that Judea was in revolt. So, raging in his spirit like a beast, he left Egypt and took the city by storm

12 and commanded his soldiers to cut down relentlessly whoever fell into their hands and to slaughter those who fled to their houses.

13 There were massacres of young and old, disappearance of women and children, slaughter[153] of girls and babies.

14 Within the total of three days eighty thousand were destroyed, namely forty thousand in hand-to-hand fighting,[154] and no less than the slaughtered ones were sold (as slaves).

15 Not content with this, he also dared to enter the holiest Temple on earth, with Menelaus as his guide, who thus became the traitor to the laws and his country.

16 With his dirty hands he took the holy vessels and what had been placed there by other kings to adorn, glorify and honour the place, he dragged along with his profane hands.

17 And Antiochus remained insolent in his mind,[155] because he did not perceive that the Lord had been angry for a short time because of the sins of those living in the city, thus disregarding the city.[156]

After former high priest Jason heard the false report that Antiochus IV Epiphanes had died in Egypt during the second phase of the Sixth Syrian War in 168, he tried to regain the office of high priest. This led to serious riots in Jerusalem, and Antiochus concluded—wrongly—that the city had rebelled against his authority. This, together with the unpleasant experiences he had had in Egypt, led to the king's strong reaction.[157]

---

153. Lit. slaughters (plural).
154. Lit. 'the roaming of their hands'. According to LSJ, *s.v.*, the term ἐν χειρῶν νόμῳ (by the law of hands) is original.
155. Gr. acc.
156. See Bunge, 'Untersuchungen', pp. 600-601.
157. Lorein, 'Life and Death', pp. 158-59, 161.

According to the author, Jason's rebellion was the cause of all this misery.[158] Eighty thousand people were affected, half of whom died, and half of whom were reduced to slavery.[159]

The author subsequently relates how the evil Antiochus entered the Temple and took the gifts of honour.[160] However, the plunder of the temple did not take place during this period: here the chronology of 2 Maccabees is wrong.[161]

Antiochus became insolent as a result of his success, but his insolence was unjustified. The only reason for his success was that the Jews had sinned and God did not mind his city for a short while, in other words, that God did not intervene. It has been claimed that the only purpose of this summary of the work of Jason of Cyrene[162] was to prove that the Temple of Jerusalem really is the only true temple, and that even though doom had come over Jerusalem, this was only the result of its own sins.[163] The author does not say that Antiochus acted under orders of God: Antiochus was led by his own wickedness.[164]

e. *2 Maccabees 9.7-12*

7 Ὁ δ' οὐδαμῶς τῆς ἀγερωχίας ἔληγεν, ἔτι δὲ καὶ τῆς ὑπερηφανίας ἐπεπλήρωτο πῦρ πνέων τοῖς θυμοῖς ἐπὶ τοὺς Ἰουδαίους καὶ κελεύων ἐποξύνειν

---

158. Bunge, 'Untersuchungen', pp. 597-98.

159. Both the author's intention and the concrete numbers (see Nelis, *II Makkabeeën, ad loc.*) are debatable.

160. For the gifts of honour, see Nelis, *II Makkabeeën*, p. 89.

161. See E. Bickerman, *The God of the Maccabees: Studies on the Meaning and Origin of the Maccabean Revolt* (SJLA, 32; Leiden: E.J. Brill, 1979), p. 12. 4Q248 (ll. 6-8) also indicates that Antiochus IV himself was in Jerusalem after the *first* phase of the Sixth Syrian War (in 169): M. Broshi and E. Eshel, 'The Greek King is Antiochus IV (4QHistorical Text = 4Q248)', *JJS* 48 (1997), pp. 120-29 (128). Apparently an earlier temple raid was added to the rigorous actions taken during the *second* phase of the Sixth Syrian War. Even if the details outlined above are left out of consideration, this is more probable than a projection of a temple raid to an earlier phase, whereby the raid and its effects are presented summarily and unexpectedly. (*Contra* Nelis, *II Makkabeeën*, pp. 144-45.)

162. 2 Macc. 3–15, by Bunge, 'Untersuchungen', pp. 602-603, 635-36, only viewed as an 'appendix' to the letter of 1.10b–2.18. (This in its turn was preceded by a 'covering letter' in 1.1-10a.)

163. Bunge, 'Untersuchungen', pp. 603-604, 606; Bickerman, *God of the Maccabees*, p. 19.

164. Arenhoevel, *Theokratie*, p. 151.

2. The Antichrist in the Apocrypha and Pseudepigrapha 71

τὴν πορείαν. Συνέβη δὲ καὶ πεσεῖν αὐτὸν ἀπὸ τοῦ ἅρματος φερομένου ῥοίζῳ καὶ δυσχερεῖ πτώματι περιπεσόντα πάντα τὰ μέλη τοῦ σώματος ἀποστρεβλοῦσθαι.

8 Ὁ δ' ἄρτι δοκῶν τοῖς τῆς θαλάσσης κύμασιν ἐπιτάσσειν διὰ τὴν ὑπὲρ ἄνθρωπον ἀλαζονείαν καὶ πλάστιγγι τὰ τῶν ὀρέων οἰόμενος ὕψη στήσειν κατὰ γῆν γινόμενος ἐν φορείῳ παρεκομίζετο φανερὰν τοῦ Θεοῦ πᾶσι τὴν δύναμιν ἐνδεικνύμενος,

9 ὥστε καὶ ἐκ τῶν ὀφθαλμῶν[165] τοῦ δυσσεβοῦς σκώληκας ἀναζεῖν καὶ ζῶντος ἐν ὀδύναις καὶ ἀλγηδόσι τὰς σάρκας αὐτοῦ διαπίπτειν, ὑπὸ δὲ τῆς ὀσμῆς αὐτοῦ πᾶν τὸ στρατόπεδον βαρύνεσθαι τὴν σαπρίαν.

10 Καὶ τὸν μικρῷ πρότερον τῶν οὐρανίων ἄστρων ἅπτεσθαι δοκοῦντα παρακομίζειν οὐδεὶς ἐδύνατο διὰ τὸ τῆς ὀσμῆς ἀφόρητον βάρος.

11 Ἐνταῦθα οὖν ἤρξατο τὸ πολὺ τῆς ὑπερηφανίας λήγειν τεθραυσμένος καὶ εἰς ἐπίγνωσιν ἔρχεσθαι θείᾳ μάστιγι κατὰ στιγμὴν ἐπιτεινόμενος ταῖς ἀλγηδόσιν.

12 Καὶ μηδὲ τῆς ὀσμῆς αὐτοῦ δυνάμενος ἀνέχεσθαι ταῦτ' ἔφη· Δίκαιον ὑποτάσσεσθαι τῷ Θεῷ καὶ μὴ θνητὸν ὄντα ἰσόθεα[166] φρονεῖν.

7 [Antiochus IV Epiphanes] did in no way stop his insolence, he even multiplied his arrogance by breathing fire against the Jews in his mind, and by ordering to drive up speed. Furthermore, he fell out of his chariot, which was carrying him at great speed, and because of this disagreeable fall all his limbs were dislocated and ended up in a totally different position.

8 While he had only recently seemed to command the waves of the sea by his superhuman boasting and thought he weighed the height of the mountains in a balance,[167] he ended up on the ground and was taken away in a litter, manifesting God's power to all,

9 so that worms swarmed even from the eyes[168] of th(is) ungodly (man) and so that while he was still alive, parts of his flesh fell off in smart and pain, while through his odour the whole army camp could hardly bear the stench.

10 And nobody could carry away him who shortly before seemed to touch the stars in the sky, because of the unbearable stench.

---

165. Especially in the Vetus Latina; MSS: τοῦ σώματος (lectio facilior; cf. Nelis, *II Makkabeeën, ad loc.*; Abel, *Livres des Maccabées, ad loc.* Against this speaks H. Bévenot, *Die beiden Makkabäerbücher* (Die Heilige Schrift des Alten Testamentes; Bonn: Hanstein, 1931), *ad loc.* ('wohl nicht speziell "aus den Augen"'). Conflation in Codex Venetus: τῶν τοῦ σώματος ὀφθαλμῶν.

166. A (as well as the Septuaginta Gottingensis) has ὑπερήφανα, which is obviously a simplification (cf. Abel, *Livres des Maccabées, ad loc.*).

167. See LSJ, *s.v.* ἵστημι, A IV 1. A different translation is possible ('with a whip make the heights of the mountains stand'), but this is less probable in view of the literary context, see below.

168. MSS: 'the body'.

11 Crushed, he then let go of much[169] of his insolence and came to his senses because of the scourge of God, encouraged by his pains every moment.
12 And when he could no longer endure his own odour, he uttered these words: 'It is reasonable to submit to God and not, as a mortal, to strive after things divine'.[170]

Antiochus IV went on raiding temples, but one day things went wrong for him. Shortly after that he heard of Nicanor's defeat, and decided to vent his frustration on the Jews. Instead, he met with his end—God struck him with a terrible illness. Although in a sense one could say this is a *topos*, the clinical picture described here (in v. 9) does exist.[171] To the author the most important conclusion is of course that this illness was sent by God (v. 5).

Antiochus IV's reaction is next in our passage. From its description it is plain what impression he made on the Jews. This is remarkable, because in 2 Maccabees (and in most other writings) very little is said about Antiochus IV. The explosion of negativity in reaction to the description of his death strikes us as unexpected.

It is unclear from what kind of chariot Antiochus IV fell. The word ἅρμα indicates a wagon drawn by horses that was not meant to carry freight, but to reach a certain speed, either in battle, or for travel.[172] The data in the text do not allow us to be more precise, but for fast passenger transport, wagons with two wheels and no safety margins were used. Their suspension left a lot to be desired, and they could not reach very high speeds.[173] Thus it is understandable that people could fall off when trying to go too fast.[174]

There are clear indications in the text of how powerful Antiochus IV was thought to be, both by himself and those around him: he seemed to command the sea, he thought he could weigh the mountains, he seemed to touch the stars. Commanding the sea is a privilege usually ascribed to God alone.[175] The image of weighing mountains occurs in Isa. 40.12,

169. See LSJ, *s.v.* πολύς IIIa: 'for the most part'.
170. V.l.: 'insolent'.
171. For the final journey and death of Antiochus IV Epiphanes, see Lorein, 'Life and Death', pp. 166-71.
172. LSJ, *s.v.*
173. E. Badian, 'Carriages', *OCD*², pp. 207-208; E.M. Jope, 'Vehicles and Harness', in C. Singer *et al.* (eds.), *A History of Technology*. II. *The Mediterranean Civilizations and the Middle Ages* c. *700 B.C. to* c. *A.D. 1500* (Oxford: Clarendon Press, 1956), pp. 537-62 (541-45).
174. E.R. Bevan, *The House of Seleucus*, II (London: Edward Arnold, 1902), p. 161 n. 1—apparently 2 Macc. 9.7 is intended here—suggests a different explanation: Antiochus IV could have had an epileptic fit.
175. See Exod. 14.21; Isa. 10.26; 51.15; Jer. 31.25; Ps. 65.8; 89.10; Job 26.12; 41.22. Cf. 2 Macc. 5.21.

2. The Antichrist in the Apocrypha and Pseudepigrapha 73

which explains that nobody can be compared to God.[176] Touching the stars can be compared to Isa. 14.13-14, where the image is used in the context of making oneself equal to the Most High.[177]

Antiochus's recognition of the truth, which came very late, was not honoured. Naturally, one could question its sincerity.[178]

f. *2 Maccabees 15.30-33*

30 Καὶ προσέταξεν ὁ καθ' ἅπαν σώματι καὶ ψυχῇ πρωταγωνιστὴς ὑπὲρ τῶν πολιτῶν, ὁ τὴν τῆς ἡλικίας εὔνοιαν εἰς ὁμοεθνεῖς διαφυλάξας τὴν τοῦ Νικάνορος κεφαλὴν ἀποτεμόντας καὶ τὴν χεῖρα σὺν τῷ ὤμῳ φέρειν εἰς Ἱεροσόλυμα.

31 Παραγενόμενος δὲ ἐκεῖ καὶ συγκαλέσας τοὺς ὁμοεθνεῖς καὶ τοὺς ἱερεῖς πρὸ τοῦ θυσιαστηρίου στήσας μετεπέμψατο τοὺς ἐκ τῆς ἄκρας.

32 Καὶ ἐπιδειξάμενος τὴν τοῦ μιεροῦ Νικάνορος κεφαλὴν καὶ τὴν χεῖρα τοῦ δυσφήμου, ἣν ἐκτείνας ἐπὶ τὸν ἅγιον τοῦ Παντοκράτορος οἶκον ἐμεγαλαύχησε,

33 καὶ τὴν γλῶσσαν τοῦ δυσσεβοῦς Νικάνορος ἐκτεμὼν ἔφη κατὰ μέρος δώσειν τοῖς ὀρνέοις, τὰ δ' ἐπίχειρα τῆς ἀνοίας κατέναντι τοῦ ναοῦ κρεμάσαι.

---

176. The disadvantage of a rhetorical question is that some things remain unclear: did *no-one* ever do the things described here, or has only *God* done them? Either way, what is pointed out here is that no-one can be compared to God.

177. A comparison to Dan. 8.10 seems obvious too, but the stars in Daniel are used in the meaning of 'idols'. Cf. especially Deut. 4.19; M. Delcor, *Le livre de Daniel* (SB; Paris: Gabalda, 1971), p. 173, and M. Delcor, 'L'histoire selon le livre de Daniel, notamment au chapitre 11', in Van der Woude, *The Book of Daniel in the Light of New Findings* (BETL, 106; Leuven: Leuven University Press; Peeters), pp. 365-86 (368-70). This means that this parallel does not really match the combination of sea, mountains and stars in this passage (*pace* E.J. Young, *The Prophecy of Daniel* [Grand Rapids: Eerdmans, 1949], p.171). A reference to Antiochus IV's coins is more appropriate here: J.G. Bunge, 'Der "Gott der Festungen" und der "Liebling der Frauen". Zum Identifizierung der Götter in Dan 11.36-39', *JSJ* 4 (1973), pp. 169-82 (177 n. 1); cf. Mørkholm, *Studies in the Coinage*, p. 58.

178. Cf. C. Gutberlet, *Das zweite Buch der Machabäer* (Alttestamentliche Abhandlungen, 10.3-4; Münster: Aschendorff, 1927), p. 139. It is not true that repentance is impossible in Judaism (cf. Jonah, Dan. 4, Jdt. 14.10) but possible in Christianity (e.g. in Lk. 23.42-43). Lactantius, *De morte persecutorum* 33–35, makes the situation of emperor Galerius (Caesar 293–305; Augustus 305–11) run completely parallel to that of Antiochus IV, albeit with even more repulsive details: rotting, worms, smell (33.6-8), confession and the promise of the restoration of the Temple (!) (33.11), edict (34), no more grace (35.3).

30 And [Judas the Maccabee], who had ever been the leading figure for his fellow citizens both with his body and his spirit, and who had maintained the goodwill of his youth toward his compatriots who had cut off Nicanor's head, ordered them to carry his arm and shoulder[179] to Jerusalem as well.

31 When he had arrived there, and had called his compatriots together and stationed the priests in front of the altar, he sent for those in the Citadel.

32 And after he had shown the dirty Nicanor's head and that profane man's hand, which he had stretched out boastfully against the holy house of the Almighty,

33 and after he had cut out the wicked Nicanor's tongue, he said he would give it piecemeal to the birds, and would hang the rest opposite the Temple as a reward for his evil inclination.

This passage discusses the battle of 8 March 161, also described in 1 Macc. 7.39-47. The author praises Judas the Maccabee, but presents Nicanor[180] as the great evildoer. Because of his victory, Judas too felt he was strong against 'those in the Citadel', by which is meant the Seleucid military garrison camped on the Acra.[181] Not only Nicanor's head was cut off, but his tongue and his right hand as well, because he had spoken wickedly, and had acted wickedly, and had even placed himself opposite the God of Israel.[182]

g. *The Antichrist in 2 Maccabees*

Again I have devoted many pages to the interpretation of some passages in which I believe elements of the Antichrist can be distinguished. In my opinion it is impossible to draw further conclusions without putting the passages concerned into their historical contexts. But after all it is the Antichrist we are looking for. We already knew that Antiochus IV Epi-

---

179. The Greek word for hand, χείρ, can also include the arm; the Greek word for shoulder, ὦμος, can also include the upper arm (see LSJ, *s.vv.*). Also the Hebrew and Aramaic hand (יד) goes further up the arm than in English. See R. Péter-Contesse, 'Main, pied, paume? Les noms des extrémités des membres (יד, רגל, כף) en Hébreu et en Araméen biblique', *RB* 105 (1998), pp. 481-91 (484-86, 490-91).

180. For the Nicanors, see J.T. Nelis, *I Makkabeeën* (Boeken van het Oude Testament; Roermond: Romen, 1972), pp. 149-50.

181. According to Nelis, *II Makkabeeën, ad loc.*, Judas did not have the right to summon the Antiochians, and they probably did not really want to come. It does not say that they complied. However, it should be remarked that the heydays of the Acra were already over in 161. The citadel returned into Jewish hands in 141 (1 Macc. 13.51).

182. R. Doran, 'The Jewish Hellenistic Historians before Josephus', *ANRW*, II 20.1 (1987), pp. 246-97 (287), with reference to 2 Macc. 15.3-5; Bévenot, *Die beiden Makkabäerbücher, ad loc.*

2. *The Antichrist in the Apocrypha and Pseudepigrapha* 75

phanes plays a role in the interpretation of this theme, and we have come across all elements of the Antichrist definition in this book, although not all of them have been applied to Antiochus IV.

It is said of Antiochus IV that he boasted in superhuman terms and he claimed divine prerogatives (9.8, 10, 11). Nothing is said of his relationship to Satan, but his human nature is indisputable.[183] His resistance to religion in general is underlined: temple plunder was not appreciated even in ancient times. In both versions of Antiochus's death the plunder of a pagan temple is mentioned (1.15-16; 9.2). The temple raid in Jerusalem (5.15-16) is a highlight. However, religious misbehaviour is also attributed to Menelaus: he was an unworthy high priest (4.25) who had become the traitor to everything Jewish (5.15). Menelaus is called a beast and a tyrant (4.25). This is also said about Antiochus IV[184] (5.11-14). The word ὕβρις does not occur in the discussed passages in 2 Maccabees,[185] but the concept does occur in relation to Antiochus IV (5.17; 7.36; 9.7). Finally, we have learned about Nicanor that he acted wickedly and spoke wickedly (15.30-33); he even placed himself in opposition to God (15.4-5).

Although all the elements are present, they are not combined and not placed in an eschatological framework. There are some eschatological elements in the second letter at the beginning of the work, which means that a later editor[186] has thought along eschatological lines for a while, but generally no eschatological overtone seems apparent.

On the other hand, there are many references to certain biblical passages in which links with the Antichrist can been discerned: the cutting off of Antiochus IV's (1.16) and Nicanor's (15.30) heads, after 1 Sam.17, and a string of references to Isa. 14 in 2 Macc. 9: the angry pursuit (Isa. 14.6; 2 Macc. 9.4), the words ἀνιάτῳ πληγῇ (Isa. 14.6;[187] 2 Macc. 9.5), the fall (Isa. 14.12; 2 Macc. 9.7), the attack on the divine prerogatives (Isa. 14.13-14; 2 Macc. 9.8, 10), the revelation of God's power to bystanders (Isa. 14.16; 2 Macc. 9.8), the worms (Isa. 14.11; 2 Macc. 9.9).[188]

The fact that these are embedded in biblical tradition seems to indicate that the authors[189] had an eschatological mindset. If we assume that the

---

183. Arenhoevel, *Theokratie*, p. 154.
184. Albeit without using the word τύραννος.
185. It does occur in 8.17, describing the ἔθνη. Arenhoevel, *Theokratie*, p. 153, says that Antiochus's hubris is the actual reason for his insubordination to God.
186. Bunge too claims that these elements do not belong to the historical core.
187. Only in the LXX and with a different meaning.
188. Goldstein, *II Maccabees*, *ad locc.*
189. After all, 2 Macc. 1.16 was not written by the author of the summary.

Antichrist theme already existed, we may conclude on the basis of all available data that this was another theme they wished to keep alive and in doing so ascribed a role to the period discussed.

In spite of the differences in character between 1 and 2 Maccabees, we may safely compare the conclusions of these books.[190] Lastly there is one other important difference, which is actually a small detail: the parallel with Cambyses, an extra-biblical figure.[191]

---

190. Arenhoevel, *Theokratie*, pp. 152-53, believes that Antiochus IV's role as enemy of God's people in 2 Macc. is more important than in 1 Macc. Our research has not led to this conclusion.

191. Parallels can be pointed out between Antioch IV Epiphanes and Cambyses (fl. 530–520; for this king see E.M. Yamauchi, *Persia and the Bible* [Grand Rapids: Baker Book House, 1990], pp. 93-128), so that Cambyses can be included with the factors which have influenced the Antichrist theme. One example is the picture Herodotus painted: his difficult character (3.25: ʿΟ Καμβύσης ὀργὴν ποιησάμενος), his wickedness (3.16: ἐκέλευσέ μιν ὁ Καμβύσης κατακαῦσαι, ἐντελλόμενος οὐκ ὅσια [cf. Yamauchi, *Persia and the Bible*, pp. 109-10]; 3.25: ἐνετέλλετο τὸ χρηστήριον τοῦ Διὸς ἐμπρῆσαι; 3.29: ʿΩς δὲ ἤγαγον τὸν Ἆπιν οἱ ἱρέες, ὁ Καμβύσης…παίει τὸν μηρόν [cf. Yamauchi, *Persia and the Bible*, pp. 115-22]); the elimination of his rivals (3.30-31: πρῶτα μὲν τῶν κακῶν ἐξεργάσατο τὸν ἀδελφεὸν Σμέρδιν…δεύτερα δὲ ἐξεργάσατο τὴν ἀδελφεήν), his madness (3.25: ἐμμανής; 3.29: ὑπομαργότερος; 3.30: ἐμάνη; 3.33: ἐξεμάνη), the circumstances surrounding his death (3.64: ἐν Ἀγβατάνοισι; 3.66: Μετὰ δὲ ταῦτα ὡς ἐσφακέλισέ τε τὸ ὀστέον καὶ ὁ μηρὸς τάχιστα ἐσάπη [cf. Yamauchi, *Persia and the Bible*, pp. 125-26]). Lebram, 'König Antiochus', pp. 767, 769, builds radical conclusions on this.

H. Lewy, 'The Babylonian Background of the Kay Kâûs Legend', *ArOr* 17.2 (1949), pp. 28-109 (104-105, 109 [summary]), claims that this legend was first applied to Nabonidus (fl. 556–539; for this king see R.P. Dougherty, *Nabonidus and Belshazzar: A Study of the Closing Events of the Neo-Babylonian Empire* [Yale Oriental Series Researches, 15; New Haven: Yale University Press, 1929]), worked like that of Isa. 14 and Daniel, and was later applied to Cambyses, which explains the name of the legend. This thesis proves that it is possible to draw lines from the Antichrist to Cambyses and Nabonidus and to the Bible books we have studied, but the Nabonidus part of this thesis is debatable and a real link between Cambyses and the Antichrist theme has not been shown conclusively. The parallels with Antiochus IV Epiphanes are interesting, but unfortunately many rulers had at least a few evil traits. The parallels with another extra-biblical character, Alexander the Great, are much clearer: see above re. *Sib. Or.* 3.388-92, below re. 1 Macc. 1.41 and Lorein, 'Life and Death', p. 163 n. 38, and now also P.S. Alexander, 'From Poetry to Historiography: The Image of the Hasmoneans in Targum Canticles and the Question of the Targum's Provenance and Date', *JSP* 19 (1999), pp. 103-28 (112). Again, we cannot simply conclude that the Antichrist theme has been influenced by the figure of Alexander the Great.

2. The Antichrist in the Apocrypha and Pseudepigrapha 77

7. 1 Maccabees

a. *Setting*

The First Book of Maccabees is a Greek translation of a Hebrew original. The book was written around the year 100, by a pro-Maccabean Jew from Jerusalem, who was orthodox but not attached to a party.[192]

The book also discusses Antiochus IV Epiphanes. Since he is an interesting figure as a background for the Antichrist theme, we shall delve into some of the passages.

b. *1 Maccabees 1.24*[193]

24 Καὶ λαβὼν πάντα ἀπῆλθεν εἰς τὴν γῆν αὐτοῦ καὶ ἐποίησε φονοκτονίαν καὶ ἐλάλησεν ὑπερηφανίαν μεγάλην.

24 And he took everything and went away to his land. And he acted murderously and spoke with great arrogance.

In 169, on his way back from the invasion of Egypt mentioned in Dan. 11.25-28 and in *Sib. Or.* 3.608-15 (the *first phase* of the Sixth Syrian War), Antiochus IV Epiphanes visited Jerusalem and raided the Temple, or—in his own view—took care of the settlement of the debts the Jewish nation, in the person of Menelaus, owed him.[194] Antiochus returned to Antioch[195] with the golden religious objects, artefacts, and all the deposits[196] that were in the Temple, but not without striking a blow.[197]

---

192. Vriezen and Van der Woude, *Oudisraëlitische en vroegjoodse literatuur*, pp. 434-35; Attridge, 'Historiography', p. 171; Harrison, *Introduction*, pp. 1260-262. Rather 'pro-Maccabean' than 'pro-Hasmonean': see Harrison, *Introduction*, p. 1260, and now esp. E. Haag, 'Die Theokratie und der Antijahwe nach 1 Makkabäer 1-2', *TTZ* 109 (2000), pp. 24-37 (24-25, 36-37).

193. According to the Septuaginta Gottingensis.

194. N. Hyldahl, 'The Maccabean Rebellion and the Question of "Hellenization"', in P. Bilde *et al.* (eds.), *Religion and Religious Practice in the Seleucid Kingdom* (Studies in Hellenistic Civilization, 1; Aarhus: University Press, 1990), pp. 188-203 (191-92, 197), mentions amounts, but does not give his sources, and incriminates (p. 194) Menelaus. See Lorein, 'Life and Death', pp. 158-59, 161, and 'Fathers and their Exegetical Basis', p. 116.

195. Cf. Josephus, *Ant.* 12.247 (χρήματα πολλὰ συλήσας ὑπέστρεψεν εἰς ᾽Αντιόχειαν).

196. Nelis, *I Makkabeeën*, pp. 54-55.

197. For the view that this is a wrong translation from the Hebrew, see Abel, *Livres des Maccabeées*, pp. 12-13, who fervently defends text and meaning.

Schunck wants to scrap this passage. Since the order of events in the text is not always correct,[198] he believes it must be a mixture of data that belong here and data from 2 Maccabees describing the events of 168. Something is wrong indeed, but even if the author intended to give all this information, there would always be a problem: a swap of v. 24a and v. 24b would have sounded strange, because it would be less obvious to which word πάντα refers; on the other hand, the word 'took' cannot be disconnected from 'went', but obviously the 'going away' was the end.[199] Therefore the order must be taken as follows: first the Temple raid (vv. 21-24), then the return coupled with general acts and words of insolence[200] (v. 24), and then mourning (vv. 25-28).

c. *1 Maccabees 1.41-43*

41 Καὶ ἔγραψεν ὁ βασιλεὺς πάσῃ τῇ βασιλείᾳ αὐτοῦ εἶναι πάντας εἰς λαὸν ἕνα
42 καὶ ἐγκαταλιπεῖν ἕκαστον τὰ νόμιμα αὐτοῦ. Καὶ ἐπεδέξαντο πάντα τὰ ἔθνη κατὰ τὸν λόγον τοῦ βασιλέως.
43 Καὶ πολλοὶ ἀπὸ Ισραηλ εὐδόκησαν τῇ λατρείᾳ αὐτοῦ[201] καὶ ἔθυσαν τοῖς εἰδώλοις καὶ ἐβεβήλωσαν τὸ σάββατον.

41 Then the king wrote to his whole kingdom that[202] all should be one people,
42 and that each should give up his (own) customs.[203] And all nations accepted,[204] according to the word of the king.
43 Also many from Israel agreed to his idolatry and sacrificed to the idols and profaned the sabbath.

---

198. K.-D. Schunck, *1. Makkabäerbuch* (JSHRZ 1.4; Gütersloh: Mohn, 1980), *ad loc.*

199. This argument is weaker if we read εἰσηνέγκεν (v. app. crit. in S. Tedesche and S. Zeitlin, *The First Book of Maccabees* [Dropsie College Edition. Jewish Apocryphal Literature; New York: Harper, 1950], *ad loc.*).

200. It is certainly possible that Antiochus started the temple raid immediately and that further clashes only took place later. Antiochus's actions were mainly driven by financial motives at that time (*contra* C. Gutberlet, *Das erste Buch der Machabäer* [Alttestamentliche Abhandlungen, 8.3-4; Münster: Aschendorff, 1920], pp. 19-20).

201. Subjective genitive: see transl. and discussion

202. Nuance of aim: see Abel, *Livres des Maccabées, ad loc.*

203. Abel, *Livres des Maccabées, ad loc.*, makes a comparison with the classical *mos maiorum*. τὰ νόμιμα can also be translated 'laws'.

204. They did not necessarily do this happily. (Cf. Gutberlet, *Das erste Buch der Machabäer*, p. 24. *Contra* Abel, *Livres des Maccabées, ad loc.*)

2. The Antichrist in the Apocrypha and Pseudepigrapha 79

Later, in 167, Antiochus IV decided to melt all the nations of the Hellenistic empire into one (v. 41). This covered the whole of their daily lives (v. 42a), but the religious facet is emphasized (v. 43).[205]

d. *1 Maccabees 4.30*

30 Καὶ εἶδε τὴν παρεμβολὴν ἰσχυρὰν[206] καὶ προσηύξατο καὶ εἶπεν· Εὐλογητὸς εἶ, ὁ[207] σωτὴρ Ισραηλ ὁ συντρίψας τὸ ὅρμημα τοῦ δυνατοῦ ἐν χειρὶ τοῦ δούλου σου Δαυιδ καὶ παρέδωκας τὴν παρεμβολὴν τῶν ἀλλοφύλων εἰς χεῖρας Ιωνάθου υἱοῦ Σαουλ καὶ τοῦ αἴροντος τὰ σκεύη αὐτοῦ.

30 [Judas the Maccabee] saw how strong the army camp was and prayed and said: 'Blessed are You, saviour of Israel, Who thwarted the threat[208] of the hero by the hand of your servant David. You also delivered the army camp of the foreigners[209] into the hands of Jonathan, son of Saul, and of his armour-bearer'.

In his prayer, occasioned by the arrival of Lysias, who actually replaced Antiochus IV in the west, in Beth-Zur (on the border between Idumea and Judea)[210] in the spring of 164,[211] Judas the Maccabee referred to the fight

---

205. See also Lorein, 'Life and Death', pp. 162-65.
206. Predicative placing of the adjective. Cf. trans.
207. In Hellenistic Greek, the vocative is hardly ever used, and certainly not before adjuncts (BDR, §§146-47).
208. This translation combines both nuances of the meaning of ὅρμημα: physical violence and psychological turmoil.
209. I.e. the Philistines (cf. Nelis, *I Makkabeeën*, p. 104).
210. See map 13 in B. Bar-Kochva, *Judas Maccabaeus: The Jewish Struggle against the Seleucids* (Cambridge: Cambridge University Press, 1989), p. 285.
211. The accounts of 1 Macc. 3–4, with a calculation of the dates according the most obvious calendar—for this problem see Lorein, 'Life and Death', n. 16—seem to indicate that the following reconstruction is the most probable.
After the defeat of the Seleucid army near Beth-Horon (1 Macc. 3.24), Antiochus IV travelled to the east and left Lysias to be the regent of the west. One of Lysias's tasks was to solve the problem in Judea (1 Macc. 3.31-36). He did this in the year 165 (1 Macc. 3.37: 147 SE). Lysias did not rush his actions against the Maccabees. Eventually this led to the debacle of Emmaus, which took place in the summer of 165. Lysias reviewed the situation and in the spring of 164 (1 Macc. 4.28) advanced to Beth-Sura. Then came the concessions from the Seleucids (who wished to focus their main attention on the east), as described in the first letter in 2 Macc. 11 (vv. 16-21), which dates from the autumn of 164. During the aftermath of this all, the Temple was cleansed and re-consecrated, in December 164 (1 Macc. 4.52). Meanwhile, Antiochus IV had died (November or December 164: A.J. Sachs and D.J. Wiseman, 'A Babylonian King List of the Hellenistic Period', *Iraq* 16 [1954], pp. 202-212), but the Jews only heard the news in early 163. During the upheavals of that moment, the second and

between David and Goliath[212] and to Jonathan's heroic act described in 1 Sam. 14.[213]

e. *1 Maccabees 7.34-35, 47*

34 Καὶ ἐμυκτήρισεν αὐτοὺς καὶ κατεγέλασεν αὐτῶν καὶ ἐμίανεν αὐτοὺς καὶ ἐλάλησεν ὑπερηφάνως·
35 καὶ ὤμοσε μετὰ θυμοῦ λέγων· Ἐὰν μὴ παραδοθῇ Ἰούδας καὶ ἡ παρεμβολὴ αὐτοῦ εἰς χεῖράς μου τὸ νῦν, καὶ ἔσται ἐὰν ἐπιστρέψω ἐν εἰρήνῃ, ἐμπυριῶ τὸν οἶκον τοῦτον. Καὶ ἐξῆλθε μετὰ θυμοῦ μεγάλου.
47 Καὶ ἔλαβον τὰ σκῦλα καὶ τὴν προνομὴν καὶ τὴν κεφαλὴν Νικάνορος ἀφεῖλον καὶ τὴν δεξιὰν αὐτοῦ, ἣν ἐξέτεινεν ὑπερηφάνως, καὶ ἤνεγκαν καὶ ἐξέτειναν παρὰ τὴν Ιερουσαλημ.

34 And [Nicanor] mocked them and laughed at them and defiled them and spoke arrogantly;
35 and he swore in anger, 'If this time Judas and his army camp are not delivered

---

third letter of 2 Macc. 11 (vv. 22-33) followed, written in March 163 by the new king, Antiochus V Eupator, who was readily inclined to grant amnesty at the beginning of his reign (for this detail, see Doran, 'Jewish Hellenistic Historians', p. 283; D. Gera and W. Horowitz, 'Antiochus IV in Life and Death: Evidence from the Babylonian Astronomical Diaries', *JAOS* 117 [1997], pp. 240-52 [250]).

The Macedonian variant of the Seleucid calendar dates the third letter in 2 Macc. 11 (vv. 27-33) on 11/12 March 164. This makes the second letter in 2 Macc. 11 (vv. 22-26) the product of an editor (see Schunck, *Quellen*, pp. 103-105), unless it should be regarded as completely independent of the second letter (see Nelis, *II Makkabeeën*, pp. 227-28; Doran, 'Jewish Hellenistic Historians', p. 283). If this is the right date and if it is a response to Judas' victory, there is little time left for Lysias' reaction: either towards the end of 165 (1 Macc. 4.28 does speak of τῷ ἐρχομένῳ ἐνιαυτῷ, but according to Schunck, *1. Makkabäerbuch*, ad loc., this could refer to the year following that which is mentioned in 1 Macc. 2.70, and therefore not in the Emmaus year), or in 164 but very early in the warring season—too early in the season, perhaps —since Antiochus wrote his letter as early as the beginning of March. Furthermore, with Antiochus IV such a radical change was improbable.

However, a solution for this is possible. Lysias may have had the letter written by Prince Antiochus (who later became Antiochus V Eupator), to give it an official touch without involving the authority of King Antiochus IV; cf. Goldstein, *II Maccabees*, pp. 117, 418-20, who assigns the main role to Menelaus and limits Lysias' influence and authority. This explanation is only possible by saying that Lysias took emergency steps whereby he made the prince annul a measure that the king had taken.

212. See above, Chapter 1.
213. This was before the fight between David and Goliath.

into my hands, then if I return safely,[214] I shall burn up this house'. And he went out in great anger.

47 And they took the armour and the supplies,[215] and they cut off Nicanor's head and his right hand which he had stretched out arrogantly, and they carried (them) away and put (them) out near Jerusalem.

While the Seleucid king Demetrius I Soter (fl. 162–150) was in the east, one Nicanor[216] was left to combat the Maccabees. He did not fully succeed. At one point he headed for the Temple, and because he was not allowed in, priests and senators met him to show their loyalty to the king. This restriction displeased Nicanor;[217] he became angry and arrogantly threatened the priests and senators, and defiled them, probably by spitting on them.[218]

On 8 March 161[219] Nicanor met his fate. The body parts he had used in his threats were cut off and displayed as a sign of victory.

f. *The Antichrist in 1 Maccabees*

Although the author of 1 Maccabees was more sober than the compiler of 2 Maccabees, he too wished to give more than an analytic history. He knew the old truths and hoped that Gods salvation, that is, the Davidic kingdom, would continue to materialize throughout history, and specifically in the Hasmonean royal family.[220] His familiarity with the Scriptures was also notable in other passages we have looked at.

---

214. ἐν εἰρήνῃ as a Hebraism (בשלום).
215. Cf. Gutberlet, *Das erste Buch der Machabäer*, p. 126.
216. For the Nicanors, see Nelis, *I Makkabeeën*, pp. 149-50.
217. Abel, *Livres des Maccabées*, p. 140.
218. Cf. Lev. 15.18, Num. 12.14 and Goldstein, *I Maccabees*, p. 340.
219. Of course there is also a chronological problem here. Apparently it is 13 Adar (in view of 1 Macc. 7.43) 151 SE (in view of 1 Macc. 7.1). The question is whether it was 151 SE Mac. (which is 8 March 161), or 151 SE Bab. (which is 27 March 160). As always, one question is whether our timeframe allows sufficient time for all the events to have taken place. If we assume that Nicanor's defeat took place in 161, there is very little time left for all the events preceding it, but it is possible. If we assume that it took place in the spring of 160, Judas the Maccabee only lived for several weeks after this event, which is too short for the contacts that took place between him and the Romans, and for the peace in the land, which is described in 1 Macc. 7.50. The Macedonian variant seems to offer the best possibilities (cf. Goldstein, *I Maccabees*, pp. 341-43). Nelis, *I Makkabeeën*, pp. 153, 168, opts for the Babylonian variant and recognizes that Judea has been free for a very short time and that Bakchides advanced very quickly.
220. Arenhoevel, *Theokratie*, pp. 65-68, 179, 181.

Which elements of the Antichrist do we find in 1 Maccabees? The Antichrist is an eschatological man who acts wickedly and speaks wickedly. Also, it has become apparent in the course of our research that Antiochus IV Epiphanes plays a role in the interpretation of the concept.[221]

In 1 Maccabees we find a similarly negative approach to Antiochus IV: it says that he acted murderously and spoke insolently (1.24). Furthermore, there is a clear ethical-religious dimension: Antiochus wished to lead the Jews away from their ancestral customs, to a new religion (1.41-43).[222]

We must admit, however, that Antiochus is not the only evildoer: Nicanor is also described as such (7.34-35). This shows that the importance of Antiochus IV should not be overestimated, on the one hand, but that there was some room for a clichéd evildoer also.

Also Goliath is mentioned again (4.30). The struggle between David and Goliath is only referred to as a historical event, and there is no eschatological perspective, but this reference proves again that the story of Goliath had become thematic during the period discussed, and that it was therefore open to expansion.

One aspect of Goliath's fortunes is found separately in 7.47: Nicanor's head was cut off. Also in this verse, the author of 1 Maccabees must have thought of Goliath, since he had a thorough grasp of the Scriptures.

In conclusion, we have found obvious elements of our definition. The fact that Antiochus IV Epiphanes and Goliath are mentioned draws our attention to the discussed passages even more. Yet one important element of our definition of the Antichrist is absent: everything is viewed from a historical perspective, and since there is no explicit theological indication, there is no eschatological indication either. We do not find the Antichrist figure in 1 Maccabees, but we do notice some elements that clearly existed around the year 100 and could therefore be used by other authors as they formed their ideas about the Antichrist.

---

221. See Lorein, 'Fathers and their Exegetical Basis', pp. 115-18.
222. For Antiochus IV Epiphanes as 'Antijahwe' (this expression is preferred by Haag to 'Antichrist': see E. Haag, 'Jesaja, Assur und der Antijahwe. Literar- und traditionsgeschichtliche Beobachtungen zu Jes 10,5-15', *TTZ* 103 [1994], pp. 18-37 [18-19]) in 1 Macc. 1–2, see now also Haag, *'Theokratie und der Antijahwe'*, pp. 27-29, 32-35. Moreover, ἀνὴρ ἁμαρτωλός in 1 Macc. 2.62 is probably meant to mean Antiochus IV (see Nelis, *I Makkabeeën, ad loc.*), which means that Antiochus IV is branded here as a sinner *par excellence*.

8. 3 Maccabees

a. *Setting*

The Third Book of Maccabees is claimed to originate from before 77, in Alexandria,[223] or more precisely in common circles opposed to emancipation, with those who saw the acceptance of Greek culture and civil rights as treason against God and country.[224] If, as has been claimed, such a negative portrayal of a Ptolemaic king is only possible in Roman times, the book dates from around 22 or slightly later. The issue of the concrete meaning of the word λαογραφία plays an important role in the dating of this book.[225] Tcherikover's argument is not very convincing, because he is perhaps a bit too technical in his dealing with this term; similar events have taken place during the time of Ptolemy IV.[226] In general, we can remark that Ptolemy IV was not presented in a way that is unjustified, and this means that a date closer to his time is more appropriate.[227] Against that we should state that *3 Maccabees* should be dated after 2 Maccabees (or after the work of Jason of Cyrene);[228] this would lead us to a date during the first century.

The Third Book of Maccabees is not about the Maccabees, but discusses a similar subject, that is Ptolemy IV Philopator's treatment of the Jews in

---

223. H. Anderson, '3 Maccabees', *OTP*, II, pp. 509-29 (510, 512); Vriezen and Van der Woude, *Oudisraëlitische en vroegjoodse literatuur*, p. 439; M. Hadas, *The Third and Fourth Books of Maccabees* (Dropsie College Edition. Jewish Apocryphal Literature; New York: Ktav, 1953), p. 23; D.S. Williams, '*3 Maccabees*: A Defense of Diaspora Judaism?', *JSP* 13 (1995), pp. 17-29 (20, 22).

224. V.A. Tcherikover, 'The Third Book of Maccabees as a Historical Source of Augustus' time', in A. Fuks and I. Halpern (eds.), *Studies in History* (ScrHier, 7; Jerusalem: Magnes Press, 1961), pp. 1-26 (23-24).

225. Tcherikover, 'Third Book of Maccabees', pp. 13-18. See also A. Paul, 'Le Troisième livre des Macchabées', *ANRW*, II 20.1 (1987), pp. 298-336 (317-18), who attempts to prove that the word λαογραφία can only have had the meaning he attributes to it for *3 Maccabees* during the Roman period.

226. Anderson, '3 Maccabees', p. 511. (It seems he did not read Tcherikover's article.)

227. This is certainly true for *3 Macc.* 1.1–3.1; the remaining part (and the final edition) could date from the end of the first century (at the latest). Cf. Nickelsburg, 'Stories', pp. 80-83.

228. Tcherikover, 'Third Book of Maccabees', pp. 6, 19. For *3 Maccabees* as a reaction to 2 Maccabees, see Williams, '*3 Maccabees*', p. 23 (think of Bunge's thesis, see above, p. [51]).

Egypt.[229] The Third Book of Maccabees is not regarded as Deutero-canonical by the Catholic Church in the West (because it was not included in the Vulgate),[230] but it does appear in some Septuagint manuscripts, so we have the original Greek text at our disposal. This text is included in the Septuaginta Gottingensis.

b. 3 Maccabees *2.1-23*

Text *3 Macc.* 2.2-3

2 Κύριε κύριε, βασιλεῦ τῶν οὐρανῶν καὶ δέσποτα πάσης τῆς κτίσεως, ἅγιε ἐν ἁγίοις, μόναρχε, παντοκράτωρ, πρόσχες ἡμῖν καταπονουμένοις ὑπὸ ἀνοσίου καὶ βεβήλου, θράσει καὶ σθένει πεφρυαγμένου.
3 Σὺ γὰρ ὁ κτίσας τὰ πάντα καὶ τῶν ὅλων ἐπικρατῶν δυνάστης δίκαιος εἶ καὶ τοὺς ὕβρει καὶ ἀγερωχίᾳ τι πράσσοντας κρίνεις.

Translation *3 Macc.* 2.2, 3

2 'Lord Lord, King of the heavens and Master of all creation, Holy one among that which is holy,[231] Absolute Sovereign, Almighty, pay heed to us, (for) we are suppressed by an unholy and profane (king) who acts with brutality and violence.
3 For You have created everything and are the just ruler who governs everything, and who judges those who act in insolence or arrogance.'

Discussion *3 Macc.* 2.1-23[232]

Ptolemy IV Philopator wished to visit the Temple in Jerusalem[233] after his victory over Antiochus III at Raphia in 217 (Fourth Syrian War), out of

---

229. Fl. 221–204. For this king, see Will, *Histoire politique*, pp. 26-44, 105-108; 110-11.

230. Also 1 and 2 Maccabees were not included by Jerome himself, but only later in the Vulgate: H. Dörrie, *Die Stellung der vier Makkabäerbücher im Kanon der griechischen Bibel* (Nachrichten von der Gesellschaft der Wissenschaften zu Göttingen. Philologisch-historische Klasse. Fachgruppe V. Religionswissenschaft. Neue Folge 1.2; Göttingen: Vandenhoeck & Ruprecht, 1937), pp. 45-46, 53. The four were included in the ancient Greek manuscripts (א only has 1 and 4 Maccabees), the Greek Church only declared 1, 2 and 3 Maccabees to be canonical (pp. 46-47, 53-54). An important factor in this inclusion was that *4 Maccabees* was attributed to Flavius Josephus (pp. 47-48).

231. This translation is based on Isa. 57.15 (LXX and MT); another possible translation is: 'among the holy'.

232. The same division is found with Tcherikover, 'Third Book of Maccabees', p. 2.

233. M. Hengel, *Judentum und Hellenismus: Studien zu ihrer Begegnung unter besonderer Berücksichtigung Palästinas bis zur Mitte des 2. Jh. v. Chr.* (WUNT, 10; Tübingen: J.C.B. Mohr, 1969), pp. 11-13; Paul, 'Troisième livre des Macchabées', pp. 299-303.

2. The Antichrist in the Apocrypha and Pseudepigrapha 85

interest in architecture²³⁴ and to honour the local gods.²³⁵ He even tried to enter into the Holy of Holies, but that was of course unacceptable to the Jews. High priest Simon II²³⁶ led them in a plea to God, wholly in the style of other Jewish works written in Greek.²³⁷ He requested that the evil king Ptolemy IV be punished and affirmed the belief that God is the actual ruler of the world.²³⁸

In answer to this prayer, God removed all power from Ptolemy IV. He was swiftly taken away by his companions.

c. 3 Maccabees *2.24–3.1*

Text *3 Macc.* 2.25-29; 3.1

2.25 Διακομισθεὶς δὲ εἰς τὴν Αἴγυπτον καὶ τὰ τῆς κακίας ἐπαύξων διά τε τῶν προαποδεδειγμένων συμποτῶν καὶ ἑταίρων τοῦ παντὸς δικαίου κεχωρισμένων

26 οὐ μόνον ταῖς ἀναριθμήτοις ἀσελγείαις διηρκέσθη, ἀλλὰ καὶ ἐπὶ τοσοῦτον θράσους προῆλθεν, ὥστε δυσφημίας ἐν τοῖς τόποις συνίστασθαι καὶ πολλοὺς τῶν φίλων ἀτενίζοντας εἰς τὴν τοῦ βασιλέως πρόθεσιν καὶ αὐτοὺς ἕπεσθαι τῇ ἐκείνου θελήσει.

27 Προέθετο δημοσίᾳ κατὰ τοῦ ἔθνους διαδοῦναι ψόγον· ἐπὶ τοῦ κατὰ τὴν αὐλὴν πύργου στήλην ἀναστήσας ἐκόλαψε γραφὴν

28 μηδένα τῶν μὴ θυόντων εἰς τὰ ἱερὰ αὐτῶν εἰσιέναι, πάντας δὲ τοὺς Ἰουδαίους εἰς λαογραφίαν καὶ οἰκετικὴν διάθεσιν ἀχθῆναι, τοὺς δὲ ἀντιλέγοντας βίᾳ φερομένους τοῦ ζῆν μεταστῆσαι,

29 τούς τε ἀπογραφομένους χαράσσεσθαι²³⁹ καὶ διὰ πυρὸς εἰς τὸ σῶμα παρασήμῳ Διονύσου κισσοφύλλῳ, οὓς καὶ καταχωρίσαι εἰς τὴν προσυνεσταλμένην αὐθεντίαν.

3.1 Ἃ καὶ μεταλαμβάνων ὁ δυσσεβὴς ἐπὶ τοσοῦτον ἐξεχόλησεν, ὥστε οὐ μόνον τοῖς κατὰ Ἀλεξάνδρειαν διοργίζεσθαι, ἀλλὰ καὶ τοῖς ἐν τῇ χώρᾳ βαρυτέρως ἐναντιωθῆναι καὶ προστάξαι σπεύσαντας συναγαγεῖν πάντας ἐπὶ τὸ αὐτὸ καὶ χειρίστῳ μόρῳ τοῦ ζῆν μεταστῆσαι.

234. Hadas, *Third and Fourth Books of Maccabees*, p. 17.
235. Tcherikover, 'Third Book of Maccabees', p. 6 n. 15; Hengel, *Judentum und Hellenismus*, p. 13.
236. Fl. 220–190. Hadas, *Third and Fourth Books of Maccabees*, p. 38.
237. Hadas, *Third and Fourth Books of Maccabees*, p. 22; Tcherikover, 'Third Book of Maccabees', p. 18; Paul, 'Troisième livre des Macchabées', pp. 308-10. (On p. 309 n. 37, however, he is mistaken as regards to Hadas's and Tcherikover's intentions.)
238. Paul, 'Troisième livre des Macchabées', pp. 303, 306, 312; Hadas, *Third and Fourth Books of Maccabees*, ad loc.
239. χαράσσειν could be a Semitic loan word (חרשׁ, 'to cut into, to plough'); see Paul, 'Troisième livre des Macchabées', p. 314 n. 58; Hadas, *Third and Fourth Books of Maccabees*, ad loc. However, it occurs frequently in Greek and could also be of Indo-European origin (LSJ, *s.v.*).

Translation *3 Macc.* 2.25-29; 3.1

25 After [Ptolemy IV] had come to Egypt and had increased the acts of his wickedness even more through his aforementioned guests and knights who had been cut off from all that is just,

26 he was not only lavish in his countless debaucheries, but also came to so much brutality that he got a bad reputation[240] (even) in the districts, and that many of his Friends[241] intently watched the meaning of the king, following his will.

27 He suggested to publicly denounce the nation.[242] putting up a pillar on the tower near the palace he had a text carved out:

28 'That none of those who do not sacrifice should go to their temples, and that all Jews would be forced to a census and to a position as slaves, and that those who opposed would be taken by force and made to depart this life

29 and that those who were noted down would receive a brand-mark[243] on their bodies in the shape of Dionysus' ivy emblem, and that they would also be registered in their restricted statute of before.'

3.1 After the impious one had received word of these things, he was so enraged that he not only became angry with those of Alexandria, but also bitterly opposed those in the province, and that he gave order to assemble all the zealous in one spot, and made them depart from this life with the most terrible fate.

Discussion *3 Macc.* 2.24-3.1

After a transitional sentence (v. 24)[244] the book reports that Ptolemy IV was a wicked king,[245] only equalled by his assistants (who had *not*[246] been mentioned before) (vv. 25-26). He displayed notices at the palace in

---

240. Translation based on LSJ, *s.v.*, III. Hadas, *Third and Fourth Books of Maccabees*, *ad loc.*, translates δυσφημίας with 'slander', on the basis of its use in papyri, but does not say to which situation it refers.

241. I.e. in the Hellenistic courts.

242. The translation above is unclear—no reprimand was given to the people—but the translation suggested by Paul, 'Troisième livre des Macchabées', p. 313 ('se proposa d'imposer le port d'une marque publique sur la nation') seems to be based on the context only.

243. Lit. 'engraved by fire'.

244. Tcherikover, 'Third Book of Maccabees', p. 2 n. 2.

245. Also Polybius paints a negative image of the king: πανηγυρικώτερον διῆγε τὰ κατὰ τὴν ἀρχήν (5.34.3); ...διὰ τοὺς ἀπρεπεῖς ἔρωτας καὶ τὰς ἀλόγους καὶ συνεχεῖς μέθας (5.34.10); ...οὔτε προνοούμενος τοῦ μέλλοντος...εὐήθως καὶ ἀλόγως (5.35.6); ἑλκόμενος ὑπὸ τῆς συνήθους ἐν τῷ βίῳ ῥαθυμίας καὶ καχεξίας (5.87.3). Hadas, *Third and Fourth Books of Maccabees*, p. 16 n. 26, p. 17, *ad loc.*

246. Many attribute this problem to the sloppy composition, but there are also indications that a part is missing from the beginning of the book. (Hadas, *Third and Fourth Books of Maccabees*, *ad loc.*; Tcherikover, 'Third Book of Maccabees', p. 2 n. 5.)

2. The Antichrist in the Apocrypha and Pseudepigrapha   87

Alexandria[247] announcing measures against—mainly[248]—the Jews. They were no longer allowed to visit their own temple (v. 28a),[249] they lost their citizenship (vv. 28b, 29b), which was very important to them,[250] and were branded with a Dionysus symbol (v. 29a).[251] Whoever protested was put to death (v. 28c). There was an alternative: those who agreed to be initiated into the Dionysus cult, would enjoy full civil rights (v. 30[252]).

Prior to this the author mentioned that the king, a great Dionysus adept, had suggested uniting Jews and Greeks in the Dionysus cult—after all, the

---

247. Hadas, *Third and Fourth Books of Maccabees*, *ad loc.*; Paul, 'Troisième livre des Macchabées', p. 316. The Jewish quarter is near the palace: see map with J. Vergote and G. Bartelink, 'Alexandrië', in J. Nuchelmans *et al.* (eds.), *Woordenboek der Oudheid*, I (Bussum: Romen, 1976), cols. 115-21 (117-18).

248. Hadas, *Third and Fourth Books of Maccabees*, *ad loc.*; Paul, 'Troisième livre des Macchabées', p. 314. According to Tcherikover, 'Third Book of Maccabees', p. 4, these words did not refer to the Jews at all in their original context; this issue is different from the question of what the current text attempts to say.

249. Hadas, *Third and Fourth Books of Maccabees*, p. 18. Paul, 'Troisième livre des Macchabées', p. 313 n. 57, is opposed to this interpretation, but gives arguments for it on the next page (p. 314, concerning ἔθνος and εὐσέβεια).

250. Paul, 'Troisième livre des Macchabées', pp. 318-19; Hadas, *Third and Fourth Books of Maccabees*, pp. 17-18. People could only lose their citizenship if they had it in the first place, but it is unclear whether the Jews did actually have citizenship (Hadas, *Third and Fourth Books of Maccabees*, p. 45; cf. S. Applebaum, 'The Legal Status of the Jewish Communities in the Diaspora', in S. Safrai and M. Stern [eds.], *The Jewish People in the First Century* [CRINT, 1; Assen: Van Gorcum, 1974], pp. 420-62 [434-40]). The λαογραφία—which is of great importance to the dating—was not necessary to full citizens of Alexandria, who had been exempted from paying tax, even during the beginning of the Roman period. This is the period in which many claim the book originated: Tcherikover, 'Third Book of Maccabees', pp. 13-15. This was also the case during the time of the Ptolemies: Paul, 'Troisième livre des Macchabées', pp. 317-18; Anderson, '3 Maccabees', p. 511.

251. For the branding of members of religious communities, see Hadas, *Third and Fourth Books of Maccabees*, *ad loc.*; Paul, 'Troisième livre des Macchabées', p. 315. Slaves and soldiers were branded in later times: P. Prigent, *L'Apocalypse de Saint Jean* (CNT; Genève: Labor et Fides, 2nd edn, 1988), p. 213. According to Tcherikover, 'Third Book of Maccabees', p. 4, we should not view this as a punishment, but that can only be true in the 'original' context. After all, why would people be branded with a symbol that was so clearly a religious one, if they refused categorically to belong to this religion? The author of *3 Maccabees* must have seen this as a punishment.

252. Tcherikover, 'Third Book of Maccabees', p. 5, claims that the Jews could not make this decision personally, but that if King Ptolemy IV was an ardent follower of the Dionysus cult, he may have been able to obtain a group arrangement.

Jews worship Sabaoth and Sabazius was another name for Dionysus—and the Jews had refused.[253]

Most of the Jews wished to be faithful to their own religion, even though they did not like the idea of martyrdom (vv. 31-33). Ptolemy IV was furious and ordered that all Jews in Egypt should be put to death. Following these verses, there is another confused account, which we will ignore since we do not need it for our sketch of Ptolemy IV.

d. *The Antichrist in* 3 Maccabees

Now that we have seen that historically the story discussed above (i.e. *3 Macc.* 1–2) matches the time of Ptolemy IV Philopator perfectly (Raphia and its consequences, citizenship and tax, Dionysus cult),[254] it would not make sense for me to state that the whole story sprouted from fantasy in the year 21. I do not claim that there are no other problems in *3 Maccabees*; or that all issues surrounding the first chapters have now been resolved. All I am saying is that the historical situation forces us to date the events of the account towards the end of the third century, and not towards the end of the first century. The author probably believed that the account also had a message for his own days, but apparently he did not just dress the events of his own time in the clothes of the third century.[255]

We must conclude, therefore, that by the end of the third century a situation had emerged in which a number of elements presented themselves, all at the same time, making this situation comparable to that of the time of Antiochus IV Epiphanes. Some elements of our definition of the Antichrist are present, but again no line was drawn from a historical Ptolemy IV to an intensification of his figure in an eschatological perspective.

We conclude that some elements are definitely present. One political figure, the king, was active in the religious arena: he acted wickedly (2.2, 25),

---

253. H. Heinen, 'The Syrian–Egyptian Wars and the New Kingdoms of Asia Minor', *CAH* (1984), pp. 412-45 (435); Hadas, *Third and Fourth Books of Maccabees*, pp. 16-17, 44; Paul, 'Troisième livre des Macchabées', p. 316; Hengel, *Judentum und Hellenismus*, pp. 126, 480; H. Jeanmaire, *Dionysos: Histoire du culte de Bacchus. L'orgiasme dans l'antiquité et les temps modernes. Origines du théâtre en Grèce. Orphisme et mystique dionysiaque. Evolution du dionysisme après Alexandre* (Paris: Payot, 1951), pp. 450-51.

254. Cf. Hadas, *Third and Fourth Books of Maccabees*, pp. 16-18, at least for the first two chapters.

255. For this one aspect we can agree with J. Tromp, 'The Formation of the Third Book of Maccabees', *Henoch* 17 (1995), pp. 311-28 (326). We cannot agree with the rest of his construction (pp. 318-22, 324-25).

2. The Antichrist in the Apocrypha and Pseudepigrapha

debaucherously (2.26) and brutally (2.2, 26), killed subjects (2.28; 3.1), travelled to the Temple (after Raphia) and opposed religion (2.2, 28; 3.1). The word ὕβρις is used (2.3) and elsewhere the concept is used (2.26). Remarkable parallels with passages discussed above are the branding (2.29; Rev. 13.16)[256] and being 'cut off from what is right' (2.25; *Sib. Or.* 3.390).[257]

9. Psalms of Solomon

a. *Setting*

The 18 *Psalms of Solomon* (not to be confused with the Odes of Solomon, which are Christian) were written in Jerusalem, between 70 and 45.[258] The attribution to Solomon is late, and in that sense the book is not really a Pseudepigraph.[259]

These psalms originate from a small community,[260] most probably even from one single author.[261] The Pharisaic flavour of the psalms has been debated on the basis of the Qumran discoveries,[262] but lately some have

---

256. χαράσσεσθαι and χάραγμα δοῦναι respectively. As here, we also find in Rev. 13.13-15 that those who refused to change their religion would be killed.

257. τοῦ παντὸς δικαίου κεχωρισμένοι and ἀλλοδίκης respectively.

258. R.B. Wright, 'Psalms of Solomon', *OTP*, II, pp. 639-70 (640-41); Philonenko, 'Pseudépigraphes', pp. lxxxi-lxxxii; A.-M. Denis, *Introduction aux pseudépigraphes grecs d'Ancien Testament* (SVTP, 1; Leiden: E.J. Brill, 1970), pp. 62-64.

259. J. Viteau, *Les Psaumes de Salomon: Introduction, texte grec et traduction* (Documents pour l'étude de la Bible; Paris: Letouzey et Ané, 1911), pp. 97-98.

260. Wright, 'Psalms of Solomon', p. 136.

261. Denis, *Introduction*, pp. 63-64; G. Maier, *Mensch und freier Wille: Nach den jüdischen Religionsparteien zwischen Ben Sira und Paulus* (WUNT, 12; Tübingen: J.C.B. Mohr, 1971), p. 300; Vriezen and Van der Woude, *Oudisraëlitische en vroegjoodse literatuur*, p. 457.

262. Essene: Philonenko, 'Pseudépigraphes', pp. lxxxii-lxxxiii, lxxxv.
Apocalyptic: Wright, 'Psalms of Solomon', pp. 137-46. The apocalyptic group was at the far margin of the Chasidim: see G.W. Lorein, '4Q448: Een gebed tegen Jonathan de Makkabeeër', *NedTTs* 53 (1999), pp. 265-73 (270).
Non-specific Hasidic: J. O'Dell, 'The Religious Background of the Psalms of Solomon (Re-evaluated in the Light of the Qumran Texts)', *RevQ* 3 (1961–62), pp. 241-57 (242-48, 251-52, 255-57); M. de Jonge, *De toekomstverwachting in de Psalmen van Salomo* (Leiden: E.J. Brill, 1965), p. 9; A.S. van der Woude, 'Nabloeiers en uitlopers: apocriefen, pseudepigrafen en Dode-Zeerollen', in T.C. Vriezen, *De literatuur van Oud-Israël* (Wassenaar: Servire, 4th edn, 1973), pp. 307-80, 408-33 (343); J.H. Charlesworth, in Wright, 'Psalms of Solomon', p. 642.

again defended the original opinion that the *Psalms of Solomon* eloquently describe Pharisaic spirituality of the first century.[263]

They have been preserved in a Greek translation of the Hebrew original.[264] The Syriac translation is slightly further removed from the Hebrew.[265] The *Psalms of Solomon* do not feature in the canon of the Roman Catholic Church, but they do appear in relatively late Septuagint manuscripts (originally probably even in the Alexandrinus and the Sinaiticus).[266] We will mainly use Rahlfs's 'pocket edition',[267] but where the Greek text is unclear we will consult the Syriac[268] and if necessary use the latter to choose from the variants that the Greek offers.

We will follow Viteau's dates for the individual psalms and discuss the passages to be researched in this order (dates between brackets): *Pss. Sol.* 1 (64), *Pss. Sol.* 15.9 (63), *Pss. Sol.* 17 (61), *Pss. Sol.* 2 (47).[269]

b. Pss. Sol. *1*

Text *Pss. Sol.* 1.5-8
5   Ὑψώθησαν ἕως τῶν ἄστρων
    εἶπαν Οὐ μὴ[270] πέσωσιν.[271]

---

263. Denis, *Introduction*, p. 64; J. Schüpphaus, *Die Psalmen Salomos: Ein Zeugnis Jerusalemer Theologie und Frömmigkeit in der Mitte des vorchristlichen Jahrhunderts* (ALGHJ, 7; Leiden: E.J. Brill, 1977), pp. 131-37; Maier, *Mensch und freier Wille*, pp. 299-300. (As regards the supposedly 'down-to-earth' Pharisaic eschatology, it should be noted that the Pharisees, and therefore also the Rabbinic period, never sympathized with apocalyptic speculations. See R.T. Beckwith, 'Daniel 9 and the Date of Messiah's Coming in Essene, Hellenistic, Pharisaic, Zealot and Early Christian Computation', *RevQ* 10 [1979–81], pp. 521-42, and 'Pre-History', pp. 41-46.)

264. J.L. Trafton, *The Syriac Version of the Psalms of Solomon: A Critical Evaluation* (SBLSCS, 11; Atlanta: Scholars Press, 1985), p. 207.

265. Trafton, *Syriac Version*, p. 215.

266. Denis, *Introduction*, pp. 60-62; Wright, 'Psalms of Solomon', p. 639; A. Rahlfs, *Septuaginta. Id est Vetus Testamentum Graece iuxta LXX interpretes*. II. *Libri poetici et prophetici* (Stuttgart: Privilegierte Württembergische Bibelanstalt, [1935]), p. 471.

267. A. Rahlfs, *Septuaginta: Id est Vetus Testamentum Graece iuxta LXX interpretes*, I (Stuttgart: Privilegierte Württembergische Bibelanstalt, 1935), p. XXI.

268. Leiden edition.

269. Viteau, *Psaumes de Salomon*, pp. 38-40. NB: Viteau, G.B. Gray, 'The Psalms of Solomon', *APOT*, II, pp. 625-52, and Syr. use a different verse numbering. We will follow Rahlfs's numbering and convert where necessary.

270. Elliptic for οὐ δέος ἐστὶ μή, 'there is no fear that'.

271. Act. conj. 2nd aor. Cj. Gray, 'Psalms of Solomon', *ad loc.*: πέσωμεν.

2. The Antichrist in the Apocrypha and Pseudepigrapha 91

6   καὶ ἐξύβρισαν ἐν τοῖς ἀγαθοῖς αὐτῶν
    καὶ οὐκ ἔγνωκαν.[272]
    Αἱ ἁμαρτίαι αὐτῶν ἐν ἀποκρύφοις,
    καὶ ἐγὼ οὐκ ᾔδειν·
    αἱ ἀνομίαι αὐτῶν ὑπὲρ τὰ πρὸ αὐτῶν ἔθνη,
    ἐβεβήλωσαν τὰ ἅγια Κυρίου ἐν βεβηλώσει.

Translation *Pss. Sol.* 1.5-8
5   [My children] were exalted to the stars,
    they said there was no chance that they would fall.[273]
6   And they became arrogant in their riches,[274]
    they had no insight[275]
7   Their sins (were) hidden,
    and I, I did not know;
8   their lawless actions sur(passed) the nations before them,
    they intensively[276] profaned the Temple[277] of the Lord.

Discussion *Pss. Sol.* 1
The author refers to Jerusalem in the first person singular. The city was thriving and had sent out its sons over the whole earth (vv. 3-4). Then there was a state of war (vv. 1-2), probably during the war with Pompey. The verses we will discuss do not refer to the Romans, but to the nation's own children. Among them is a group which thinks it can interfere with the privileges of God Himself (v. 5a[278]), and that it cannot be conquered (v. 5b). They are arrogant (again the element of hubris!), their shoulders

---

272. This cj. is based on the Syr. *yd'w* with the suspicion of a Hebr. הבינו and with reference to Isa. 1.2-3, which is also about children. (Gray, 'Psalms of Solomon', *ad loc.*; Trafton, *Syriac Version*, pp. 26-27.) MSS: ἤνεγκαν.

273. Cj.: 'they said, "there is no chance we would fall"'.

274. Lit.: 'goods'.

275. MSS: 'they could not bear it' (so M. de Goeij, *De Pseudepigrafen: Psalmen van Salomo. IV. Ezra, Martyrium van Jesaja* [Kampen: Kok, *s.d.*], p. 18), or possibly: 'they did not bring sacrifice' (cf. Ps. 67.30 [LXX] and Ps. 75.12 [LXX] [οἴσουσιν δῶρα] or Ps. 68.30 [MT] and 76.12 [MT] [יובילוש׳], which could explain the Syrian *yd'w* [הבילו mistakenly read as הבינו]). Wright, 'Psalms of Solomon', *ad loc.* ('they did not acknowledge [God]'), does not really take MT reading of Ps. 29.1-2 and Ps. 96.7-8 (הבו) into consideration. The cj. offers the best solution and has the additional advantage that, like *Pss. Sol.* 1.8, it offers a reference to Isa. 1.

276. ἐν βεβηλώσει interpreted as a transl. of Hebr. inf. abs.

277. Syr. has *hyklh*. τὰ ἅγια can also have this meaning. (Gray, 'Psalms of Solomon', *ad loc.*; Trafton, *Syriac Version*, p. 28.)

278. For the image with the stars, see Isa. 14.13-14 and 2 Macc. 9.10 (see above, pp. 72-73).

cannot bear their riches (v. 6) and they are more sinful (albeit less obviously) than many before them (vv. 7-8). Generally this is a very negative picture.

However, this is a description of their own children, the Jews. The Hasmoneans had known tremendous economic growth, but they had also completely grown away from the ideals of their ancestors (vv. 5-6). They had sinned through their kings and high priests, which meant that the sin was less obvious than if it had been committed by an invading foreign enemy. They even profaned τὰ ἅγια, the Temple[279] (vv. 7, 8b). Because of this all they greatly surpassed their non-Jewish attackers in their wickedness (v. 8a). In the first instance one should think of the last great enemy before the economic upsurge, the Seleucids, against whom the Maccabees, the ancestors of these sinners, had fought. However, Gentiles did not take part in temple worship after they had sinned.[280]

As a punishment for it all, Pompey was now standing at their gates (v. 2).

c. Pss. Sol. *15.9*

9 Ὡς ὑπὸ πολεμίων ἐμπείρων καταλημφθήσονται,
τὸ γὰρ σημεῖον τῆς ἀπωλείας ἐπὶ τοῦ μετώπου αὐτῶν.

9 [The impious] will be caught as by experts in warfare.[281]
for the mark of destruction is on their forehead.

In this psalm, which is mostly about the believer's trust that God will make the sinners perish, one verse is of special interest to us. It says that those who act impiously will not escape, but will be dealt with immediately and thoroughly, as if by people with a lot of military experience. They are clearly recognizable by a mark on their foreheads, the mark of destruction. This contrasts the just, who bear God's mark for salvation (v. 6). This mark is not the cause of their eternal doom, it simply is the result of their lifestyle.[282] The mark on their foreheads reminds us of certain parallels: the mark of the beast on everybody's forehead (Rev. 13.16), Ptolemy IV's brand mark with ivy emblem on Jewish people's bodies (*3 Macc.* 2.29).

From this passage it is not clear who the author is describing here. The context of the *Psalms of Solomon* suggests that the impious are the Has-

---

279. Viteau, *Psaumes de Salomon, ad loc.*, specifies τὰ ἅγια and consequently does not take the Syr. (*hyklh*) into account. However, cf. his p. 53.
280. Viteau, *Psaumes de Salomon, ad loc.*
281. Or: 'experienced enemies'.
282. Viteau, *Psaumes de Salomon, ad loc.*

moneans (led by Aristobulus II) and the soldiers are the Romans (led by Pompey). However, the word ‛Ως[283] should make us cautious.

d. Pss. Sol. *17*

Text *Pss. Sol.* 17.5-6, 11-15, 20, 23, 32, 35
5   Καὶ ἐν ταῖς ἁμαρτίαις ἡμῶν ἐπανέστησαν ἡμῖν ἁμαρτωλοί·
    ἐπέθεντο ἡμῖν καὶ ἔξωσαν[284] ἡμᾶς,
    οἷς οὐκ ἐπηγγείλω,[285] μετὰ βίας ἀφείλαντο
    καὶ οὐκ ἐδόξασαν τὸ ὄνομά σου τὸ ἔντιμον ἐν δόξῃ.[286]
6   Ἔθεντο βασίλειον ἀντὶ ὕψους αὐτῶν,
    ἠρήμωσαν τὸν θρόνον Δαυιδ ἐν ὑπερηφανίᾳ ἀλλάγματος.
11 Ἠρήμωσεν ὁ ἄνομος τὴν γῆν ἡμῶν ἀπὸ ἐνοικούντων αὐτήν,
    ἠφάνισαν νέον καὶ πρεσβύτην καὶ τέκνα αὐτῶν ἅμα·
12 ἐν ὀργῇ κάλλους[287] αὐτοῦ ἐξαπέστειλεν αὐτὰ ἕως ἐπὶ δυσμῶν
    καὶ τοὺς ἄρχοντας τῆς γῆς εἰς ἐμπαιγμὸν καὶ οὐκ ἐφείσατο.
13 Ἐν ἀλλοτριότητι ὁ ἐχθρὸς ἐποίησεν ὑπερηφανίαν,
    καὶ ἡ καρδία αὐτοῦ ἀλλοτρία ἀπὸ τοῦ Θεοῦ ἡμῶν.
14 Καὶ πάντα, ὅσα ἐποίησεν ἐν Ιερουσαλημ,
    καθὼς καὶ τὰ ἔθνη ἐν ταῖς πόλεσι τοῖς θεοῖς[288] αὐτῶν.
15 Καὶ ἐπεκρατοῦσαν αὐτῶν οἱ υἱοὶ τῆς διαθήκης ἐν μέσῳ ἐθνῶν συμμίκτων,
    οὐκ ἦν ἐν αὐτοῖς ὁ ποιῶν ἐν[289] Ιερουσαλημ ἔλεος καὶ ἀλήθειαν.

283. Syr.: ’yk.
284. Grammar would dictate that the word here should be ἐξέωσαν, but perhaps the augment was lost under the influence of Homer's ὦσα.
285. Med. ind. aor. 2 sg. The Syr. retained the (supposed) Hebrew construction: *dl' pqdt lhwn* (להם...אשׁר) (Trafton, *Syriac Version*, p. 161.) For the allocation to v. 5bα, see translation.
286. The Syr. lets *btšbḥt'* link up with v. 7a (v. 5bβ in the Greek), and starts a new thought with *wsmw mlkwt'* in v. 7b (6a in the Greek). This means that ἐν δόξῃ should link up with v. 5bβ and is (together with ἐδόξασαν) the reflection of an inf. abs. in the Hebrew. This makes translation easier, but we do end up with a less regular verse arrangement.
287. This is undoubtedly the correct reading of the MSS, but it could be an incorrect interpretation of the Hebrew, i.e., יפי instead of the correct אף (see Gray, 'Psalms of Solomon', *ad loc.*; P. Prigent, 'Psaumes de Salomon', in A. Dupont-Sommer and M. Philonenko [eds.], *La Bible: Ecrits intertestamentaires* [Bibliothèque de la Pléiade; Paris: Gallimard, 1987], pp. 945-92 [*ad loc.*]; Viteau, *Psaumes de Salomon, ad loc.*; S. Holm-Nielsen, *Die Psalmen Salomos* [JSHRZ, 4.2; Gütersloh: Gerd Mohn, 1977], *ad loc.*).
288. MSS (and Syr.) (one MS: τοὺς θεούς); cj. τοῦ σθένους (see Gray, 'Psalms of Solomon', *ad loc.*).
289. For MSS, see Holm-Nielsen, *Psalmen Salomos, ad loc.*

Ἀπὸ ἄρχοντος αὐτῶν καὶ λαοῦ²⁹⁰ ἐλαχίστου ἐν πάσῃ ἁμαρτίᾳ,
ὁ βασιλεὺς ἐν παρανομίᾳ καὶ ὁ κρίτης ἐν ἀπαθείᾳ καὶ ὁ λαὸς ἐν ἁμαρτίᾳ.
23 ἐν σοφίᾳ, ἐν δικαιοσύνῃ²⁹¹ ἐξῶσαι²⁹² ἁμαρτωλοὺς ἀπὸ κληρονομίας,
ἐκτρῖψαι²⁹³ ὑπερηφανίαν ἁμαρτωλοῦ ὡς σκεύη κεραμέως,
32 Καὶ αὐτὸς βασιλεὺς δίκαιος διδακτὸς ὑπὸ Θεοῦ ἐπ' αὐτούς,
καὶ οὐκ ἔστιν ἀδικία ἐν ταῖς ἡμέραις αὐτοῦ ἐν μέσῳ αὐτῶν,
ὅτι πάντες ἅγιοι, καὶ βασιλεὺς αὐτῶν χριστὸς Κυρίου. ²⁹⁴
35 Πατάξει γὰρ γῆν τῷ λόγῳ τοῦ στόματος αὐτοῦ εἰς αἰῶνα,
εὐλογήσει λαὸν Κυρίου ἐν σοφίᾳ μετ' εὐφροσύνης.

Translation *Pss. Sol.* 17.5-6, 11-15, 20, 23, 32, 35
5   But²⁹⁵ because of²⁹⁶ our sins, sinners rose up against us,
    they attacked us and drove us out.
    Those to whom You did not make a promise,²⁹⁷ took away with force,
    and they did not intensively glorify your honourable name.
6   They have established²⁹⁸ the kingdom to compensate for their ambition,²⁹⁹
    they laid waste the throne of David with the arrogan(t idea they could) replace³⁰⁰ him.
11 The lawless one desolated our land from those who lived on it,

---

290. Incorrect trans. (reading ועם instead of ועד). Cf. Gray, 'Psalms of Solomon', *ad loc.*; Holm-Nielsen, *Psalmen Salomos, ad loc.*
291. MSS; cj. Rahlfs, δικαιοσύνης. Cf. Holm-Nielsen, *Psalmen Salomos, ad loc.*
292. NB: accentuated as an infinitive (cf. Syr. [v. 26] *lmwbdw*); ἐξῶσαι is act. opt. aor. 3 sg.
293. NB: accentuated as an infinitive (cf. Syr. [v. 26] *lmšḥq*); ἐκτρίψαι is act. opt. aor. 3 sg.
294. MSS: χριστὸς κύριος (Syr. *mšyḥ 'mry'*), interpreted as a Christian emendation (Rahlfs; De Jonge, *Toekomstverwachting*, p. 18 n. 41 [pp. 38-39]), or an incorrect trans. (Gray, 'Psalms of Solomon', *ad loc.*; Holm-Nielsen, *Psalmen Salomos, ad loc.*). On the other hand, see Wright, 'Psalms of Solomon', *ad loc.*, Prigent, 'Psaumes de Salomon', *ad loc.*, and Viteau, *Psaumes de Salomon*, p. 72 and *ad loc.*
295. καὶ interpreted as a transl. of the Hebr. ו adversative.
296. ἐν interpreted as a transl. of the Hebr. ב.
297. These words could also link up with v. 5aβ: see De Goeij, *Pseudepigrafen, ad loc.* Wright, 'Psalms of Solomon', *ad loc.*, and Viteau, *Psaumes de Salomon, ad loc.*, opt for the arrangement used here.
298. Viteau, *Psaumes de Salomon, ad loc.*
299. Viteau, *Psaumes de Salomon, ad loc.* Gray, 'Psalms of Solomon', *ad loc.*: 'instead of (what) their fame (should have made)'. Other translations of ἀντί are confronted with the problem of the Syr. *ḥlp*. The Hebr. must have been תחת. (Cf. Holm-Nielsen, *Psalmen Salomos, ad loc.*)
300. Viteau, *Psaumes de Salomon, ad loc.*

2. *The Antichrist in the Apocrypha and Pseudepigrapha*

they[301] made young and old and their children disappear together.
12   In the anger of his mind[302] he sent them away to the West,
also the rulers of the land, as a ridicule, and he did not spare them.
13   Because of his foreign status the enemy was proud,
and his heart was a stranger to our God.
14   And all he did in Jerusalem (was)
in accordance with (that which) the nations also (do) with their gods[303] in the cities.
15   But[304] the sons of the covenant had[305] surpassed them among the mingled nations,
no-one among them did mercy and truth in Jerusalem.
20   From their leader to the most common[306] (they lived) in every kind of sin,
the king in transgression and the judge in disobedience[307] and the people in sin.
23   In wisdom (and) in righteousness[308] may [the son of David] drive out[309] the sinners, away from the inheritance,
may he crush[310] the arrogance of the sinners like the potter's jars.
32   And he is a righteous king over them, taught by God,
and in his days there exists no unrighteousness among them,
because all are holy, and their king is an[311] Anointed One of the Lord.[312]
35   He will strike the earth with the word of his mouth until eternity,
he will bless the Lord's people in wisdom with joy.

Discussion *Pss. Sol.* 17
The main sinners in this Psalm are the Hasmoneans,[313] who were able to harm the people because the nation ('the righteous') had sinned (v. 5a).[314]

301. This is still about the lawless one and his followers (cf. Viteau, *Psaumes de Salomon*, *ad loc.*). Cf. Schüpphaus, *Psalmen Salomos*, p. 68 n. 313.
302. Transl. of reconstruction. MSS: 'anger of beauty' (Wright, 'Psalms of Solomon', *ad loc.*: 'blameless wrath'). Also A. Caquot, 'Les Hasmonéens, les Romains et Hérode: observations sur *Ps. Sal.* 17', in Caquot *et al.* (eds.), *Hellenica et Judaica* (Mem. V. Nikiprowetzky; Leuven: Peeters, 1986), pp. 213-18 (215), keeps the text ('en s'irritant contre Sa beauté'), but his identification with Jerusalem (p. 216) is improbable.
303. Cj.: 'of their might'.
304. καί interpreted as a transl. of the Hebr. ו adversative.
305. For the transl. of a Gr. imperf. as pluperfect, see Humbert, *Syntaxe grecque*, §239.
306. Transl. of reconstruction.
307. Syr. (v. 22b) *bmrgznwtʾ*: 'in anger'.
308. Cj.: 'in righteous wisdom'.
309. Lit. 'in order to drive away' (inf. subordinate to ὑπόζωσον...τοῦ in v. 22).
310. Lit. 'in order to crush' (inf. subordinate to ὑπόζωσον...τοῦ in v. 22).
311. If translating the supposed Hebr. יהוה משיח, it is possible to have 'the' here.
312. MSS: 'the anointed Lord', 'Christ, the Lord'. (Cf. Lk. 2.11.)
313. Wright, 'Psalms of Solomon', *ad loc.*
314. Righteous people do sin, but their basic attitude is different, and they accept

In contrast to the house of David, the Hasmonean house had not been given a promise (v. 5b).[315] It is clear that when the Hasmoneans were not satisfied with their exalted offices of high priest and prince,[316] they also usurped David's throne[317] and in this way harmed it, but otherwise many of the details in v. 6 remain unclear. In the following verses Pompey is portrayed as the foreigner who offers the national enemies compensation for their misdeeds (vv. 7-9). The way Pompey is presented here is quite positive.[318]

Pompey also plays a role in the verses following this, but there he is called the lawless one. Schüpphaus is right in seeing certain tensions here,[319] but it is possible that these had been evoked in the soul of a poet confronted with two evils simultaneously. Pompey had taken Aristobulus II and his children to Rome as exiles and had displayed them there in his third triumphal procession (vv. 11, 12).[320] It is peculiar that the poet was so upset about the horrible treatment the Hasmoneans received from the Romans (v. 12b); apparently the psalmist was satisfied with the punishment of the Hasmoneans, but did not appreciate the Romans very much either.[321] Do the following verses (vv. 13, 14) sound like an excuse?[322]

God's actions as discipline: Schüpphaus, *Psalmen Salomos*, pp. 121-23; Viteau, *Psaumes de Salomon*, pp. 53-54. The same idea is found in 2 Macc. 5: see above, p. 69.

315. See 2 Sam. 7.16 and C.J. Goslinga, *Het tweede boek Samuël* (Commentaar op het Oude Testament; Kampen: Kok, 1962). The promise was 'pending' from that moment onwards: Schüpphaus, *Psalmen Salomos*, p. 93.

316. Cf. Gray, 'Psalms of Solomon', *ad loc.*; Prigent, 'Psaumes de Salomon', *ad loc.*; Trafton, *Syriac Version*, p. 162.

317. Aristobulus I (fl. 104–103) was the first to proclaim himself king.

318. An earlier researcher even saw a description of the Messiah here: see Schüpphaus, *Psalmen Salomos*, p. 68 n. 305. Cf. J. Van Ooteghem, *Pompée le Grand, bâtisseur d'Empire* (Mémoires de l'Académie Royale de Belgique. Classe des lettres et des sciences morales et politiques, 49; Brussels: Palais des Académies, 1954), p. 648 and *passim*.

319. Schüpphaus, *Psalmen Salomos*, pp. 67-68. Comp. the discussion about another irregularity with v. 32, but on p. 73 he definitely presents the issue from too sombre a viewpoint.

320. Josephus, *Ant.* 14.79; Plutarch, *Vitae Pompeius* 39.3, 45.5. See also Van Ooteghem, *Pompée le Grand*, pp. 281-87, who also mentions links with Alexander the Great (pp. 283-84).

321. Viteau, *Psaumes de Salomon*, *ad loc.* The punishment of the wicked by a wicked enemy is a recurring theme; see De Jonge, *Toekomstverwachting*, p. 14. Cf. the attitude of the Qumran Community to the evil that overcame the Pharisees according to 4QpNah 3-4 i 6-8 (see below, Chapter 3).

2. The Antichrist in the Apocrypha and Pseudepigrapha 97

That would confirm our impression that the greatest evildoers with whom the poet was confronted were the Hasmoneans, but that there was a point at which he would return to their side. On the one hand, one could say that v. 14 is completely applicable to Pompey,[323] but on the other hand there is the Syriac version:[324] 'Jerusalem did everything like the nations did...'[325] This is confirmed in the next verse (v. 15). The reference is probable not to Pompey's times, but to earlier events, which took place in the time of Alexander Janneus.[326]

In response to this, pious people with whom the author sympathized at the least, had fled to the desert (v. 17). It is tempting to link this with the foundation of the Qumran community, but Qumran had been inhabited for a long time before Pompey's invasion, and even before Alexander Janneus's actions. We ought therefore to think of events at the time of Alexander Janneus and Aristobulus II.[327]

Of the wicked, the king and the judge are mentioned by their function (v. 20). This must be a reference to the Hasmonean regime, which means that the king is not necessarily Aristobulus II.[328] No-one offers an identification for the judge, and it is unclear to whom he had been disobedient: the Syriac talks about 'wrath'.

Faced with this hopeless situation, the poet fully trusted God to give a Son of David to be the king of Israel. The poet knew of this promise, and he also knew that somewhere there must be relatives of David, although at that moment there were certainly no 'pretenders to the throne'.[329] The king

---

322. They do in our translation, based on Prigent, 'Psaumes de Salomon', *ad loc.*; Gray, 'Psalms of Solomon', *ad loc.*; Viteau, *Psaumes de Salomon, ad loc.* See also Maier, *Mensch und freier Wille*, p. 274. For other possible translations of ἀλλοτρι-, see Schüpphaus, *Psalmen Salomos*, p. 69 n. 316.

323. Prigent, 'Psaumes de Salomon', *ad loc.*; Viteau, *Psaumes de Salomon, ad loc.*

324. *wklmdm gbrt ʾwršlm ʾyk dʾp ʿmmʾ gbrw bmdynthwn lʾlhyhwn*

325. The problem is linked to the problem of the translation of the preposition ⊃: it can indicate equality as well as inequality (albeit only if there is similarity) (Joüon, *Grammaire*, §133g).

326. Fl. 103–76. Schüpphaus, *Psalmen Salomos*, p. 69; Maier, *Mensch und freier Wille*, p. 274.

327. See Josephus, *Ant.* 13.379, 383; 14.21. Cf. Charlesworth, in Wright, 'Psalms of Solomon', p. 642.

328. However, Viteau, *Psaumes de Salomon, ad loc.*, says it is. Cf. Schüpphaus, *Psalmen Salomos*, p. 70 n. 325.

329. Viteau, *Psaumes de Salomon*, pp. 68-70.

would remove the Hasmonean sinners from the inheritance, that is Judea[330] (v. 23a), and crush the sinner's[331] arrogance (v. 23a).

While the expected king is mainly portrayed as Davidic in vv. 21-23, in vv. 32-43 he is mainly described as the Anointed One.[332] This does not indicate a break between vv. 31 and 32, but rather that the one expectation has two elements. Because the king is instructed by God and is God's Anointed One, and because all are holy, that is, converted,[333] there will be no more injustice among the nations[334]—in contrast to the Hasmonean period (v. 32)—and the whole world will finally be judged[335] in justice (there is a clear reference to Isa. 11.4[336]), and the believers (not just Jewish believers!) will be blessed (v. 35). Military operations will apparently no longer be necessary, and the king's power will rest in another domain.[337]

e. Pss. Sol. 2

Text: *Pss. Sol.* 2.1-3, 9b, 24-29

1 Ἐν τῷ ὑπερηφανεύεσθαι τὸν ἁμαρτωλὸν[338] ἐν κριῷ κατέβαλε τείχη ὀχυρά,
   καὶ οὐκ ἐκώλυσας.
2 Ἀνέβησαν ἐπὶ τὸ θυσιαστήριόν σου ἔθνη ἀλλότρια,
   κατεπατοῦσαν ἐν ὑποδήμασιν αὐτῶν ἐν ὑπερηφανίᾳ,
3 ἀνθ' ὧν οἱ υἱοὶ Ιερουσαλημ ἐμίαναν τὰ ἅγια Κυρίου,
   ἐβεβηλοῦσαν τὰ δῶρα τοῦ Θεοῦ ἐν ἀνομίαις.
9b ...οὐκ ἐποίησε πᾶς ἄνθρωπος ἐπ' αὐτῆς ὅσα ἐποίησαν.
24 Ὅτι οὐκ ἐν ζήλει ἐποίησαν, ἀλλ' ἐν ἐπιθυμίᾳ ψυχῆς,
   ἐκχέαι τὴν ὀργὴν αὐτῶν εἰς ἡμᾶς ἐν ἁρπάγματι.
25 Μὴ χρονίσῃς, ὁ Θεός, τοῦ ἀποδοῦναι αὐτοῖς εἰς κεφαλάς,

---

330. See Viteau, *Psaumes de Salomon, ad loc.* In view of the link with v. 22b, Schüpphaus, *Psalmen Salomos*, p. 70, suspects that this is about Gentile sinners.

331. This sg. after the pl. in the first half of this verse is remarkable. It probably refers to the same group, in this case to a Hasmonean. (This is also what Schüpphaus, *Psalmen Salomos*, p. 70, thinks, but he has a Gentile sinner in mind.)

332. Schüpphaus, *Psalmen Salomos*, p. 71. The attribution of title 'Anointed' to the future king is claimed to be an innovation of this psalm. (De Jonge, *Toekomstverwachting*, p. 18.)

333. Viteau, *Psaumes de Salomon*, p. 358 and *ad loc.*

334. This is what αὐτούς seems to indicate. A different view is presented by Holm-Nielsen, *Psalmen Salomos, ad loc.* (Israel).

335. Schüpphaus, *Psalmen Salomos*, p. 92.

336. This whole psalm could be compared to the whole of Isa. 11.1-5, 9–10.

337. De Jonge, *Toekomstverwachting*, p. 22.

338. Acc. subject with inf.

2. The Antichrist in the Apocrypha and Pseudepigrapha

τοῦ ῥίπτειν[339] τὴν ὑπερηφανίαν τοῦ δράκοντος ἐν ἀτιμίᾳ.
26 Καὶ οὐκ ἐχρόνισα ἕως ἔδειξέν μοι ὁ Θεὸς τὴν ὕβριν αὐτοῦ,
    ἐκκεκεντημένον ἐπὶ τῶν ὀρέων[340] Αἰγύπτου
    ὑπὲρ ἐλάχιστον[341] ἐξουδενωμένον ἐπὶ γῆς καὶ θαλάσσης·
27 τὸ σῶμα αὐτοῦ διαφερόμενον[342] ἐπὶ κυμάτων ἐν ὕβρει πολλῇ,
    καὶ οὐκ ἦν ὁ θάπτων.[343]
    Ὅτι ἐξουθένωσεν αὐτὸν ἐν ἀτιμίᾳ,
28 οὐκ ἐλογίσατο ὅτι ἄνθρωπός ἐστιν,
    καὶ τὸ ὕστερον οὐκ ἐλογίσατο.
29 Εἶπεν· Ἐγὼ κύριος γῆς καὶ θαλάσσης ἔσομαι.[344]
    καὶ οὐκ ἐπέγνω ὅτι ὁ Θεὸς μέγας,
    κραταιὸς ἐν ἰσχύι αὐτοῦ τῇ μεγάλῃ.

Translation *Pss. Sol.* 2.1-3, 9b, 24-29
1 In his arrogance the sinner broke down strong walls with[345] a battering ram and You did not prevent it.
2 Foreign nations went up your altar, they trampled (the Temple) with their shoes in arrogance,
3 in return for the fact that the sons of Jerusalem had defiled the Temple of the Lord, had profaned the offerings of God in lawlessness.
9b ...no man on [earth] has done what they did.
24 Because they did not act out of zeal, but in the greediness of (their own) spirit, so that they in (their) plunder poured out their anger against us.
25 Do not wait long, O God, to repay to them on their heads,

---

339. The reading τοῦ εἰπεῖν (MSS) is a serious textual problem. (However, see transl. by Wright, 'Psalms of Solomon', *ad loc.*, and the comments by Viteau, *Psaumes de Salomon*, *ad loc.*, for a translation.) The cj. τοῦ ῥίπτειν (according to Viteau, *Psaumes de Salomon*, *ad loc.*) is the best solution, confirmed by the Syrian *lmrmyw* (in order to cast down). The reading of the MSS can be explained by supposing the Hebr. לרמה, or even לרמא (from רמה: see Joüon, *Grammaire*, §79p; cf. Aram. למרמא [*LLAVT, s.v.*]), mistakenly read as לאמר, which would explain the Gr. τοῦ εἰπεῖν. Holm-Nielsen, *Psalmen Salomos*, p. 66, points out certain parallels between *Pss. Sol.* 2.26 and Isa. 14.19 LXX. Added to this we could say that the word ῥιφήσῃ occurs there, which is also an argument for the form of ῥίπτειν in this verse. For other cj., see Trafton, *Syriac Version*, pp. 42-44.

340. In the LXX this form only occurs for the pl. gen. of τὸ ὄρος (LSJ, *s.v.*); for cj. ὀρίων (from τὸ ὅριον, 'border'), see discussion.

341. Cj.; MSS: ἐλαχίστου.

342. V.l. διεφθαρμένον; see discussion.

343. For the verse division, see transl.

344. Rendering of the Hebr. imperf., which indicates a present? (See Schüpphaus, *Psalmen Salomos*, p. 29 n. 63.)

345. ἐν interpreted as a transl. of the Hebr. ב.

to cast down in disgust the arrogance of the dragon.³⁴⁶

26 And I did not wait too long until God showed me his insolence,
    (he was) pierced on the mountains of Egypt,
    less honoured than the smallest³⁴⁷ on the earth and in the sea.
27 His body dashing on³⁴⁸ the waves in much insolence,
    and there was no-one to bury him.
    Because he had despised Him³⁴⁹ with contempt,
28 he had not considered that he was a man,
    and he had not considered what comes after.
29 He said 'I shall be³⁵⁰ lord of land and sea',
    but³⁵¹ he did not recognize that God is great,
    powerful in his great strength.

Discussion *Pss. Sol.* 2

One (single) sinner,³⁵² Pompey,³⁵³ had battered the northern temple wall, which was also a city wall (v. 1a).³⁵⁴ The psalmist was surprised that God had allowed this³⁵⁵ (v. 1b). The Romans had even been on the altar,³⁵⁶ and

346. Transl. of a reconstruction. For other possibilities, see text.
347. Transl. of the cj.
348. V.l.: 'destroyed near'; see discussion.
349. This translation is based on the variant verse division of one MS and Syr. (Cf. Holm-Nielsen, *Psalmen Salomos*, ad loc.) Other possibilities—while retaining the connection of v. 27c with v. 27b—are: 'He...him' (the previous expressed subject is ὁ Θεός [v. 26]—see Viteau, *Psaumes de Salomon*, ad loc.; Prigent, 'Psaumes de Salomon', ad loc.; Gray, 'Psalms of Solomon', ad loc.; Wright, 'Psalms of Solomon', ad loc.); or 'one...him' (cf. B.K. Waltke and M. O'Connor, *An Introduction to Biblical Hebrew Syntax* [Winona Lake, IN: Eisenbrauns, 1990], §4.4.2).
350. Or possibly 'am'.
351. καί interpreted as a transl. of Hebr. ו adversative.
352. This is not someone who commits one or several sins, but someone who is alienated from God and misjudges his own righteousness. (Viteau, *Psaumes de Salomon*, p. 55; Schüpphaus, *Psalmen Salomos*, p. 97.)
353. Holm-Nielsen, *Psalmen Salomos*, ad loc.; Viteau, *Psaumes de Salomon*, ad loc.; Schüpphaus, *Psalmen Salomos*, p. 25; Gray, 'Psalms of Solomon', ad loc.; Prigent, 'Psaumes de Salomon', ad loc.; Wright, 'Psalms of Solomon', ad loc.
354. Josephus, *War* 1.145, 147, 149; Van Ooteghem, *Pompée le Grand*, pp. 232-33; Viteau, *Psaumes de Salomon*, ad loc.; cf. J.J. Bimson and J.P. Kane, *New Bible Atlas* (Leicester: Inter-Varsity Press, 1985), p. 104. Pompey did not need to make any effort for the other city walls: Josephus, *Ant.* 14.59.
355. Schüpphaus, *Psalmen Salomos*, p. 26.
356. The altar was elevated slightly above ground level. See H.G. Koekkoek, *De geheimen van de offers* (Alphen aan den Rijn: Licht des Levens, 1986), p. 97; cf. T.A. Busink, *Der Tempel von Jerusalem: Von Salomo bis Herodes. Eine archäologisch-*

2. *The Antichrist in the Apocrypha and Pseudepigrapha* 101

had been walking around with their shoes on.[357] The deeper cause lay in the lawless acts of the Hasmoneans and their supporters.[358] They had unjustly assumed the high-priestly office (vv. 2-3) and surpassed everybody in their sin (v. 9b[359]), and God had passed his righteous judgment upon them (vv. 4-9a, 10, 15-18).

Although the psalmist rejoiced[360] that lawlessness was punished,[361] he was not pleased that the punishment was carried out by Gentiles (vv. 19-23), who did not do this out of zeal for God's righteousness, but for financial gain[362] (v. 24). The psalmist had prayed that God would intervene, and in his prayer called Pompey 'the dragon' (v. 25). The psalmist lived long enough to witness the answer to his prayer: Pompey, who regarded himself to be great[363] and superhuman, and who did not think of the shortness of life,[364] was pierced with a sword in 48, near Mount Cassius[365] near Pelu-

---

historische Studie unter Berücksichtigung des westsemitischen Tempelbaus. II. *Von Ezechiel bis Middot* (Leiden: E.J. Brill, 1980), pp. 830-31. The Romans had even entered the Holy of Holies (Josephus, *Ant.* 14.72), but this is not mentioned, at least not specifically.

357. Instead of barefoot: Koekkoek, *Geheimen van de offers*, p. 113. Cf. A. Maes, 'Le costume phénicien des stèles d'Umm el-'Amed', in E. Lipiński (ed.), *Studia Phoenicia.* XI. *Phoenicia and the Bible* (Orientalia Lovaniensia Analecta, 44; Leuven: Oriëntalistiek; Peeters, 1991), pp. 209-30 (227, 229). Going barefoot in the Temple was customary, in obedience to Exod. 3.5 and Josh. 5.15.

358. Sadducees? (According to Holm-Nielsen, *Psalmen Salomos, ad loc.*)

359. Elaborated on in vv. 11-14. The concept occurs earlier in the text in v. 1.8a.

360. However, deep concern is expressed in v. 14: τὰ σπλάγχνα μου πονῶ ἐπὶ τούτοις (I suffer within because of these things). For this personal concern, see also *Pss. Sol.* 1.7b.

361. Schüpphaus, *Psalmen Salomos*, pp. 24-25, starts a second main part with v. 19 too. He claims that this verse should be traced back to a different historical situation from the first main part. However, that does not mean that the poet did not mean this psalm to be one unit.

362. Schüpphaus, *Psalmen Salomos*, p. 98. Pompey did not touch the objects in the Holy of Holies, as Gray, 'Psalms of Solomon', *ad loc.*, rightly remarks (Josephus, *Ant.* 14.72; Cicero, *Pro Flacco* 67 ['Cn. Pompeius captis Hierosolymis victor ex illo fano nihil attigit.']), but his actions cost Jerusalem cities as well as a lot of money (ten thousand talents) (Josephus, *Ant.* 14.74, 77-78).

363. Comp. his cognomen 'Magnus', an honorary title granted to him as early as around 80, by Sulla (think of Alexander the Great! see Plutarch, *Vitae Pompeius* 13.7-9, and Van Ooteghem, *Pompée le Grand*, pp. 65-66), with ὁ Θεὸς μέγας in v. 29b: Viteau, *Psaumes de Salomon, ad loc.*

364. As a result Pompey did not think he needed God's righteousness, thereby

sium, while he was on his way to Egypt to find shelter.[366] The decapitated[367] body was thrown out of the boat,[368] and eventually cremated on an improvised pyre[369] (vv. 26-29). We conclude that the story agrees so much with data known form other sources, that not one point should be interpreted as topical.[370]

f. *The Antichrist in the* Psalms of Solomon
After the many passages in which we dealt with only a few elements of our definition of the Antichrist, we are now confronted with a wealth of data. In view of our vision on the authorship, we take the liberty to formulate one single conclusion for all of the Psalms of Solomon.

The historical identification is certain, but the expectation in *Pss. Sol.* 17 contains a clearly eschatological perspective, which is however only apparent in the verses about the Anointed One (*Pss. Sol.* 17.30, 35).

It is peculiar that the singular is often used (*Pss. Sol.* 17.11-13 and 2.1 with reference to Pompey; 17.23 to Aristobulus II; 17.14 is unclear). It could be explained as a purely grammatical or even a poetic detail, but we deduce that the focus is not on a group of wicked people, but on a person who is wicked *par excellence*. We know we are dealing with *people*:

committing the greatest sin (Schüpphaus, *Psalmen Salomos*, p. 97; see Heb. 9.27 for an elaboration of this idea).

365. This detail is found in a review by Cassius Dio 42.5.5 (πρὸς...τῷ Κασσίῳ). In general, the judgment of J. Van Deuren, 'Het beeld van Pompeius bij Dio Cassius in vergelijking met de Pompeius-Vita van Plutarchus' (licentiate's thesis Leuven, 1977), p. 123, is correct: Plutarch is better than Cassius Dio, both with his information and his literary style.

366. Plutarch, *Vitae Pompeius* 76.4–79.5. Those who are surprised about the 'mountains' can take refuge in the cj. ὁρίων ('borders'; thus Prigent, 'Psaumes de Salomon', *ad loc.*; the Syr. has *ṭwr*', 'mountain' or 'mountain range'!); this is inherently true. But Plutarch, *Vitae Pompeius* 77, does not claim that this happened on the Nile (78.4 clearly speaks of the sea): *contra* Holm-Nielsen, *Psalmen Salomos, ad loc.*

367. See Plutarch, *Vitae Pompeius* 80.2. In view of the frequency with which this motif returns, it is surprising that the Psalmist did not mention it.

368. Plutarch, *Vitae Pompeius* 80.2. Apparently it did not dash on the waves, but was touched by the waves (cf. Strabo 16.2.26). Of course the possibility remains that the group of MSS which has διεφθαρμένον instead of διαφερόμενον has retained the original text. (Cf. Gray, 'Psalms of Solomon', *ad loc.*: διαφερόμενον is the correct text, but διεφθαρμένον is historically more correct.)

369. Plutarch, *Vitae Pompeius* 80.3.

370. *Contra* Bickerman, *God of the Maccabees*, pp. 16-17, and Holm-Nielsen, *Psalmen Salomos, ad loc.* Cf. Maier, *Mensch und freier Wille*, p. 269.

2. The Antichrist in the Apocrypha and Pseudepigrapha

Pompey and Aristobulus II, as representatives of the Hasmoneans. Even where the plural is used, it does not just refer to wicked people, but to people who had reached the ultimate in wickedness, that is, in their contempt for God and his righteousness they heaped sin upon sin[371] (*Pss. Sol.* 1.8; 17.15, 20; 2.9b referring to the Hasmoneans).

In the political arena they acted tyrannically (*Pss. Sol.* 17.5 on the Hasmonean; 17.11-12 and 2.24 on Pompey) and lawlessly (*Pss. Sol.* 15.9; 17.6, 20 on the Hasmonean; 17.11 on Pompey). In the religious arena they regarded themselves as divine (*Pss. Sol.* 1.5 on the Hasmonean; 2.28-29 on Pompey) and harmed the worship of the true God (*Pss. Sol.* 1.7-8; 17.5bβ; 2.3 on the Hasmonean; 2.2, 27c, 29 on Pompey; 17.14 is unclear). There is also mention of insolence (ὕβρις) (*Pss. Sol.* 1.5-6 on the Hasmonean; 2.26-27 on Pompey; in *Pss. Sol.* 17.13; 2.1, 25 Pompey is said to have ὑπερηφανία;[372] in 17.23 it is the Hasmonean).

Pompey is called 'dragon' (*Pss. Sol.* 2.25): an animal is used as an image of an evil man. It is often pointed out that the use of the word 'dragon' for a foreign king occurs several times in the Old Testament.[373] We wish to simply refer to the general principle of the animal as a substitute for another entity, as in Dan. 7, 8 and in the book of Revelation.[374]

There are also parallels with passages we have already discussed: *3 Macc.* 2.29 (the mark on the forehead in *Pss. Sol.* 15.9), 2 Macc. 9.10 (reaching out to the stars in *Pss. Sol.* 1.5).

---

371. See Schüpphaus, *Psalmen Salomos*, p. 97.

372. Cf. Hadas-Lebel, 'Evolution de l'image de Rome', pp. 773-74, on 'superbia' and 'avaritia' as Roman vices.

373. Holm-Nielsen, *Psalmen Salomos, ad loc.*; Wright, 'Psalms of Solomon', *ad loc.*; de Jonge, *Toekomstverwachting*, p. 13; Viteau, *Psaumes de Salomon*, p. 50. Against those who regard this verse as a proof that the Antichrist is only the humanification of a mythical monster (thus D.S. Russell, *The Method and Message of Jewish Apocalyptic: 200 BCE–AD 100* [OTL; London: SCM Press, 1964], pp. 276-77, with a general reference to Gunkel, *Schöpfung und Chaos*, and to Bousset, *Antichrist*, p. 93 [Strecker's reference is incorrect]), G. Strecker, *Die Johannesbriefe* (KEK; Göttingen: Vandenhoeck & Ruprecht, 1989), p. 342 n. 39, deduces from the strong link between Pompey and the Antichrist in this verse, that the Antichrist figure cannot simply be deduced from the mythical.

374. For Revelation see Lorein, 'Fathers and their Exegetical Basis', pp. 121-24. We should also think of Balaam (the first false prophet according to 4Q339 1-2!), about whom J. de Vaulx, *Les Nombres* (SB; Paris: Gabalda, 1972), p. 271, says 'Balaam… est plus bête que son ânesse.' This French pun could be translated as 'Balaam is more of an ass than his ass'.

Balaam, Goliath,[375] and Antiochus IV Epiphanes are not mentioned in this passage. We have found two new figures that fit in the Antichrist theme: Pompey and Aristobulus II.

I wish to make a distinction between the Antichrist theme and the theme of the enemy from the north (Gog).[376] In *Pss. Sol.* 17 it is quite clear who is being referred to: Pompey is the military enemy from the north.[377] Aris-

---

375. Pompey's decapitation is not even mentioned!

376. If we must assume that Ezekiel and Revelation (and possibly Num. 24.7; see immediately below) all stand in the same biblical tradition and that they were careful with the information available to them (especially the latest of the three, Revelation), then we must conclude that Gog does not fit into the Antichrist theme: there is a chronological as well as a functional difference between the actions of the Antichrist and those of Gog. Gog belongs to the (admittedly related) theme of the 'enemy from the north'. Cf. H. Berkhof, *Christus, de zin der geschiedenis* (Nijkerk: Callenbach, 1958), pp. 145-46; R.H. Mounce, *The Book of Revelation* (NICNT; Grand Rapids: Eerdmans, 1977), pp. 361-62.

In Num. 24.7b, the reading 'Gog' occurs in SamP, LXX, α', σ', θ', Vulgate. This could indicate an eschatological interpretation of this passage by the textual witnesses mentioned (de Vaulx, *Nombres*, p. 284). The reading of SamP is most intriguing. We generally find in SamP an old text type (B.K. Waltke, 'The Samaritan Pentateuch and the Text of the Old Testament', in J.B. Payne [ed.], *New Perspectives on the Old Testament* [Evangelical Theological Society Supplementary Volumes. Symposium Series, 3; Waco, TX: Word Books, 1970], pp. 212-39 [232-34]). In that case we would have to assume that the Samaritans borrowed the Gog theme from Ezek. 38–39. Although the Samaritans focused completely on the Pentateuch, this appeal to Ezekiel is not impossible: Ezek. 37.16, 19 indicates sympathy for the north (J. Bowman, *Samaritanische Probleme: Studien zum Verhältnis von Samaritanertum, Judentum und Urchristentum* [Stuttgart: W. Kohlhammer, 1967], p.39), here 'Samaritans' were living even in Ezekiel's time. (The 'split' between 'Jews' and 'Samaritans' must not be viewed as a sudden event, but rather as a slow development that first started at the split of the Kingdom and experienced a last crisis during the reign of John Hyrcanus I: J. van Bruggen, *Wie maakte de bijbel? Over afsluiting en gezag van het Oude en Nieuwe Testament* (Kampen: Kok, 1986), pp. 25-26; H.G. Kippenberg, *Garizim und Synagoge: Traditionsgeschichtliche Untersuchungen zur samaritanischen Religion der aramäischen Periode* (Religionsgeschichtliche Versuche und Vorarbeiten, 30; Berlin: W. de Gruyter, 1971), pp. 35-87. Ezekiel's sympathy for the Samaritans may have given him some power to influence them. It is also useful to note that the chapters studied here are of great importance to Samaritan theology (incl. eschatology): cf. Bowman, *Samaritanische Probleme*, p. 20. This pleads for the view that the reading 'Gog' is very ancient, albeit not original (cf. B. Maarsingh, *Ezechiël*, III [Prediking van het Oude Testament; Nijkerk: Callenbach, 1991], p. 102).

377. Also geographically did he come from that direction: Orontes—Lebanon—Damascus—Jordan—Jerusalem (see Van Ooteghem, *Pompée le Grand*, pp. 229-31).

2. The Antichrist in the Apocrypha and Pseudepigrapha 105

tobulus II, who belongs to the land and supersedes Pompey in his wickedness, is the Antichrist. In *Pss. Sol.* 2, matters are more complicated: Pompey definitely serves as a pattern for the Antichrist theme. At least it is now clear that to the psalmist, there is not much difference between a wicked Jew and a wicked Gentile.[378]

We have stated that where a combination of these elements occurs, we will have to think of the Antichrist theme. Here the combination does occur, and even more clearly than ever before in intertestamental literature. The only aspect that has apparently not been worked out is the eschatological aspect of the possible Antichrist. However, we may state that the psalmist was expecting the Anointed One and believed himself to be on an eschatological turning point in at least this aspect. The reason he eagerly awaited the Anointed One is that he believed that a specific man had reached the culmination of evil and that only eschatological intervention from God could bring salvation now.[379] The psalmist was not expecting the Antichrist in the future, because he placed himself in the (pre-)*eschaton*. For this reason, Aristobulus II and especially Pompey can be recognized in detail (in parallel with historical sources), while becoming 'typical'[380] at the same time.

In that sense, all the elements we need to freely claim that this text discusses the Antichrist are present.

g. *The Antichrist and The Anointed One in* Pss. Sol. *17*

It is definitely not my aim to research systematically the figure of the Anointed One in the intertestamental writings here, but the question does arise of how the Antichrist theme relates to the Christ theme.[381] The two figures are not systematically treated as opposites (only in a very basic

---

378. Cf. Schüpphaus, *Psalmen Salomos*, pp. 98, 120.
379. Cf. De Jonge, *Toekomstverwachting*, pp. 14, 17, 21. Russell, *Method and Message*, p. 270, points out that in this second part of *Pss. Sol.* 17 the prophetic approach (about this age, nationalistic, political) and the apocalyptic approach (about the future, universalistic, transcendent) merge. Cf. Viteau, *Psaumes de Salomon*, p. 63 ('le peuple juif et le monde entier'); *contra* H. Braun, 'Vom Erbarmen Gottes über den Gerechten. Zur Theologie der Psalmen Salomos', *ZNW* 43 (1950–51), pp. 1-54 (50). Schüpphaus, *Psalmen Salomos*, pp. 125-26, therefore speaks of a 'double Messiah image' here. This merge of nationalism and universalism may be typical in moderate Pharisaic eschatology.
380. Cf. Schüpphaus, *Psalmen Salomos*, p. 96.
381. Cf. above with 1 Sam. 17, and with *Sib. Or.* 3.652-56. For the Anointed One in *Pss. Sol.* 17 in general, see De Jonge, *Toekomstverwachting*, pp. 20-23.

way, for example, in v. 23, and also in vv. 22, 24, 27-28). However, we see numerous inverted elements of the Antichrist theme here, as shown in the verses selected from *Pss. Sol.* 17.23-43.

Simply his title of 'Anointed One' (*Pss. Sol.* 17.32) makes him a potential counterpart to the Antichrist.[382] The activities of the Anointed One will last for ever (*Pss. Sol.* 17.35).[383] The Anointed One will act under God's influence (*Pss. Sol.* 17.35).[384] The Anointed One will reign in mercy and justice (*Pss. Sol.* 17.23, 32).[385] The Anointed One will prophecy in truth (*Pss. Sol.* 17.35).[386] The Anointed One will eliminate the arrogance of the Antichrist (*Pss. Sol.* 17.23).[387] Actually only two elements are missing: keeping the Law[388] (although this is certainly part of 'reigning in justice'), and acting as a man where the imagery is that of animals (that imagery is simply not present in this psalm).

We may therefore conclude that in *Pss. Sol.* 17, the theme of the Anointed One almost completely mirrors the Antichrist theme.

10. Testaments of the Twelve Patriarchs

a. *Setting*
In the *Testaments of the Twelve Patriarchs*, the 12 sons of Jacob speak to their descendants from their deathbeds. A testament typically discusses the future, whereby the apocalyptic is incidental; the *Testaments of the Twelve Patriarchs* are however mainly paraenetical.[389]

---

382. We are using the term 'potential' because our research has shown that the Antichrist does not necessarily act as the immediate opponent of the Messiah, but possibly also as a false god.

383. Also in *Pss. Sol.* 17.30. The Antichrist is an eschatological figure. This point is of course a direct, not an inverse, analogy.

384. Also in *Pss. Sol.* 17.22, 34, 37. The Antichrist will act under the influence of Satan.

385. Also in *Pss. Sol.* 17.26, 29, 40-41. The Antichrist will be a tyrant.

386. Also in *Pss. Sol.* 17.43; cf. 17.25, 42. The Antichrist will be a false prophet.

387. Moreover, the Anointed One will not be insolent himself, see *Pss. Sol.* 17.34, 39-41. Insolence is a characteristic of the Antichrist.

388. De Jonge, *Toekomstverwachting*, p. 23, outlines the link between the expectation of *Pss. Sol.* 17 and the Torah.

389. A. Kolenkow and J.J. Collins, 'Testaments', in R.A. Kraft and G.W.E. Nickelsburg (eds.), *Early Judaism and its Modern Interpreters* (The Bible and its Modern Interpreters, 2; Atlanta: Scholars Press; Philadelphia: Fortress Press, 1986), pp. 259-85 (259); M. Hengel, 'Anonymität, Pseudepigraphie und "Literarische Fälschung" in der jüdisch-hellenistischen Literatur', in K. von Fritz (ed.), *Pseudepi-*

2. The Antichrist in the Apocrypha and Pseudepigrapha 107

We do not wish to delve deeper into the origins of any of these writings. Therefore we will (and must) base our research on the results of earlier research, in the understanding that we wish to assume as much as possible that the work has been a unit during the longest part of its existence.[390] Where we note a consensus for most other writings, or in the worst case a discussion without any substantial consequences for our research, dating the *Testaments of the Twelve Patriarchs*[391] is actually quite difficult. Do they originate from the second century BCE or the third century CE? If the writings simply contain interpolations, there is no objection against including the *Testaments* in our research, but if the edition of these writings actually took place after 50 CE, they are outside the domain of this research. Even if we could establish that they originate from before 50 CE, one problem remains. Since we have chosen to discuss the texts to be researched in chronological order, we must make a relatively precise choice.

grapha. I. *Pseudopythagorica—Lettres de Platon—Littérature pseudépigraphique juive* (Entretiens sur l'Antiquité Classique, 18; Geneva: Fondation Hardt, 1972), pp. 229-329 (261); B. Noack, 'Satanás und Sotería: Untersuchungen zur neutestamentlichen Dämonologie' (dissertation Aarhus; Copenhagen: Gads, 1948), p. 44 (cf. p. 48); Hollander, *Joseph as an Ethical Model*, Thesis II; H.W. Hollander and M. de Jonge, *The Testaments of the Twelve Patriarchs: A Commentary* (SVTP, 8; Leiden: E.J. Brill, 1985), p. 50; M. de Jonge, 'The Testaments of the Twelve Patriarchs: Central Problems and Essential Viewpoints', *ANRW*, II 20.1 (1987), pp. 359-420 (393). To J.H. Ulrichsen, *Die Grundschrift der Testamente der Zwölf Patriarchen: Eine Untersuchung zu Umfang, Inhalt und Eigenart der ursprünglichen Schrift* (Acta Universitatis Upsaliensis. Historia Religionum, 10; Stockholm: Almquist & Wiksell, 1991), pp. 71-206, 315-36, the non-paraenetical is also incidental, in the sense that it is not part of the basic document ('Grundschrift'). Cf. E. von Nordheim, *Die Lehre der Alten*. I. *Das Testament als Gliedgattung im Judentum der Hellenistisch-Römischen Zeit* (ALGHJ, 18; Leiden: E.J. Brill, 1980), p. 71, on the priority of ethical dualism over cosmic dualism.

390. As regards to this, I fully agree with Hollander and De Jonge, *Testaments of the Twelve Patriarchs*, p. 25. For a literary critical approach, see J. Becker, *Untersuchungen zur Entstehungsgeschichte der Testamente der Zwölf Patriarchen* (AGJU, 8; Leiden: E.J. Brill, 1970), who actually goes very far (Hengel, 'Anonymität, Pseudepigraphie und "Literarische Fälschung"', p. 264—cf. De Jonge, 'Testaments of the Twelve Patriarchs', p. 389), or Ulrichsen, *Grundschrift*. Also a form-critical approach is not my aim here, but I refer to Von Nordheim, *Lehre der Alten*. As with other writings, I will only date the work, give a concise exposition of the passages concerned and then draw conclusions concerning the subject of my research.

391. For an overview of the problem, see, e.g., G. Vermes, 'Methodology in the Study of Jewish Literature in the Graeco-Roman Period', *JJS* 36 (1985), pp. 145-58 (152-56); Ulrichsen, *Grundschrift*, pp. 21-23.

108   *The Antichrist Theme in the Intertestamental Period*

We opt for treating the *Testaments of the Twelve Patriarchs* as texts from the middle of the first century[392] BCE, possibly from one single author,[393] and not from Judea.[394] The arguments for this choice are the Jewish elements,[395] the similarities[396] and differences with Qumran,[397] the Hellenistic[398] elements, the allusions to internal tensions during the declining years of the Hasmonean kingdom,[399] and the eschatology that is not especially Christian.[400] Hultgård seeks to deduce from the difference in precision with the *Psalms of Solomon*, that the *Testaments of the Twelve Patriarchs* are slightly *older* than the *Psalms of Solomon*.[401] The *Testaments of the Twelve Patriarchs* do indeed give the impression that they are somewhat further removed from the catastrophe in 63, but that does not necessarily indicate

---

392. P. Sacchi, *L'apocalittica giudaica*, p. 136; Philonenko, 'Pseudépigraphes', pp. lxxx-lxxxi; R.H. Charles, 'The Testaments of the XII Patriarchs', *APOT*, II, pp. 282-367 (290); A. Hultgård, *L'eschatologie des Testaments des Douze Patriarches*. II. *Composition de l'ouvrage, textes et traductions* (Acta Universitatis Upsaliensis. Historia Religionum, 7; Stockholm: Almqvist & Wiksell, 1982), pp. 226-27 (who dates it slightly earlier, between 100 and 63). Also Ulrichsen, *Grundschrift*, pp. 343-44, supposes a first completion during this period.

393. Hultgård, *Eschatologie*, II, p. 164, but see also p. 214.

394. Hultgård, *Eschatologie*, II, pp. 223-25 (Galilee); H.C. Kee, 'Testaments of the Twelve Patriarchs', *OTP*, I, pp. 775-828 (778) (Syria), J.J. Collins, 'Testaments', in Stone (ed.), *Jewish Writings of the Second Temple Period*, pp. 325-55 (344) (Egypt); Vriezen and Van der Woude, *Oudisraëlitische en vroegjoodse literatuur*, p. 488 (Egypt); Becker, *Untersuchungen*, pp. 193-95, 235-36 (Hellenistic synagogues in Egypt).

395. F.-M. Braun, 'Les testaments des XII Patriarches et le problème de leur origine', *RB* 67 (1960), pp. 516-49 (528-30, 533).

396. Braun, 'Testaments des XII Patriarches', pp. 535, 537-38; K.G. Kuhn, 'Die beiden Messias Aarons und Israels', *NTS* I (1954-55), pp. 168-79 (172-73); Van der Woude, *Die messianischen Vorstellungen*, pp. 193, 213, 216; A.I. Baumgarten, *The Flourishing of Jewish Sects in the Maccabean Era: An Interpretation* (JSJSup [*olim* SPB], 55; Leiden: E.J. Brill, 1997), p. 105 n. 65.

397. Braun, 'Testaments des XII Patriarches', pp. 544-48; Becker, *Untersuchungen*, pp. 149-51; Kolenkow and Collins, 'Testaments', p. 269. Clear and generally accepted definitions of 'Essenes' and 'Qumran Community' would perhaps clarify the issue.

398. Becker, *Untersuchungen*, pp. 193-94, 373-74; Kee, 'Testaments of the Twelve Patriarchs', p. 778; Hollander, *Joseph as an Ethical Model*, thesis I.

399. Hultgård, *Eschatologie*, II, p. 226.

400. Braun, 'Testaments des XII Patriarches', pp. 541, 543-44.

401. A. Hultgård, *L'eschatologie des Testaments des Douze Patriarches*. I. *Interprétation des textes* (Acta Universitatis Upsaliensis. Historia Religionum, 6; Stockholm: Almqvist & Wiksell, 1977), p. 135.

2. The Antichrist in the Apocrypha and Pseudepigrapha 109

an earlier date. I realize that these arguments have all been debated, but we still cannot really escape from this general impression.

That does not mean, however, that no older basic manuscript have ever existed.[402] Neither does it mean that there have been no later Christian revisions.[403] We will assume that the revisions have been minor, the interpolations limited[404] and partly traceable, possibly via the Armenian version,[405] and that the possible reductions have not structurally changed the parts that remained the same.[406]

---

402. Collins, 'Testaments', pp. 333, 344; Hengel, 'Anonymität, Pseudepigraphie und "Literarische Falschung"', p. 264; Becker, *Untersuchungen*, pp. 373, 376 (Hellenistic-Jewish); Eissfeldt, *Einleitung*, pp. 861-62 (Hebrew); Van der Woude, *Die messianischen Vorstellungen*, pp. 192-93, 215 (Aramaic); Hultgård, *Eschatologie*, II, pp. 165, 181-82 (Aramaic); Ulrichsen, *Grundschrift*, p. 343 (Hebrew or Aramaic); Vermes, 'Methodology', pp. 155-56. Kee, 'Testaments of the Twelve Patriarchs', pp. 777-78, dates all Testaments in the second century (Christian interpolations excepted); Collins, 'Testaments', pp. 343-44, only accepts this date for parts of *T. Levi* and *T. Naph.*; R.T. Beckwith, 'The Significance of the Calendar for Interpreting Essene Chronology and Eschatology', *RevQ* 10 (1979–81), pp. 167-202 (174), at least for *T. Levi*. Parts or parallels of *T. Levi* and *T. Naph.* have been found in Qumran; A. Caquot, 'Ecrits qoumrâniens', in Dupont-Sommer and Philonenko (eds.), *La Bible: Ecrits intertestamentaires*, pp. xxx-xliv (xxxi).

403. Van der Woude, *Die messianischen Vorstellungen*, pp. 193-94; Hultgård, *Eschatologie*, II, pp. 228-30; J. Becker, *Die Testamente der zwölf Patriarchen* (JSHRZ, 3.1; Gütersloh: Gerd Mohn, 1981), p. 25; Ulrichsen, *Grundschrift*, pp. 315-19, 344. Also Braun, 'Testaments des XII Patriarches', p. 543, draws this conclusion, but actually his whole article pleads for a date in the first century. Collins, 'Testaments', pp. 342-43 (but see also Kolenkow and Collins, 'Testaments', p. 276: 'the Testaments can be used much more confidently in the study of second century Christianity than of pre-Christian Judaism'). Cf. de Jonge, 'Testaments of the Twelve Patriarchs', p. 414; this author generally stresses the Christian date of edition of *T. 12 Patr.*

404. See the 'minimal list' of Braun, 'Testaments des XII Patriarches', p. 520. According to M. Philonenko, *Les interpolations chrétiennes des Testaments des Douze Patriarches et les Manuscrits de Qoumrân* (Cahiers de la RHPR, 35; Paris: PUF, 1960), p. 59, there are none at all (apart from a few very clear ones). This is an exaggeration, but see the remarks of Hultgård, *Eschatologie*, II, pp. 237-38.

405. Hultgård, *Eschatologie*, II, p. 228; Becker, *Untersuchungen*, pp. 66-67; C. Burchard, 'Zur armenischen Überlieferung der Testamente der zwölf Patriarchen', in W. Eltester (ed.), *Studien zu den Testamenten der Zwölf Patriarchen* (BZNW, 36; Berlin: Alfred Töpelmann, 1969), pp. 1-29 (27). Cf. Van der Woude, *Die messianischen Vorstellungen*, p. 193. Unfortunately it is not possible in this study to give an independent evaluation of the Armenian text. We will therefore not refer to Armenian editions.

In this we go along with the view that has most recently been defended by Dupont-Sommer and Philonenko. Although Philonenko's arguments[407] are impressive, we will not yield to his pan-Essenism, because his arguments are also valuable without assuming an Essene origin. The assumed dating does in my view not indicate a definite Essene origin.

We may assume that the Greek version is the original text of the present edition. Where the passage to be researched has been published by Hultgård, we will use his edition,[408] otherwise we will use De Jonge's[409] *editio minima*.[410]

b. T. Levi *16.1-2; 18.12*

16.1 Καὶ νῦν ἔγνων ἐν βιβλίῳ Ἐνὼχ ὅτι ἑβδομήκοντα ἑβδομάδας πλανηθήσεσθε καὶ τὴν ἱερωσύνην βεβηλώσετε καὶ τὰς θυσίας μιανεῖτε.

2 Καὶ τὸν νόμον ἀφανίσετε καὶ λόγους προφητῶν ἐξουδενώσετε ἐν διαστροφῇ,[411] καὶ διώξετε ἄνδρας δικαίους καὶ εὐσεβεῖς μισήσετε, ἀληθινοὺς λόγους βδελύξεσθε.

18.12 Καὶ ὁ Βελιὰρ δεθήσεται ὑπ' αὐτοῦ
καὶ δώσει ἐξουσίαν τοῖς τέκνοις αὐτοῦ πατεῖν ἐπὶ τὰ πονηρὰ πνεύματα.

16.1 Well,[412] I have read in the book of Enoch that you will wander for seventy sevens and profane the priesthood and defile the sacrifices.

---

406. Hultgård, *Eschatologie*, II, p. 213; Van der Woude, *Die messianischen Vorstellungen*, p. 194.

407. Philonenko, *Interpolations chrétiennes*.

408. Hultgård, *Eschatologie*, II, pp. 239-72.

409. It should be taken into account that even in determining the *stemma codicum*, and with it the text, any conclusions will inevitably be based on one's view of the history of the development of a text (cf. De Jonge, 'Testaments of the Twelve Patriarchs', p. 363; M. de Jonge, *Testamenta XII Patriarcharum: Edited According to Cambridge University Library* MS *Ff 1.24 fol. 203a-261b* [PVTG, 1; Leiden: E.J. Brill, 2nd edn, 1970], p. xvii; Charles, 'Testaments of the XII Patriarchs', p. 286; Hultgård, *Eschatologie*, II, p. 22). Therefore the combination of text-critical notes and notes regarding content into one critical apparatus is certainly justifiable (*pace* M. de Jonge, 'Testament Issachar als "typisches" Testament. Einige Bemerkungen zu zwei neue Übersetzungen der Testamente der Zwölf Patriarchen', in M. de Jonge [ed.], *Studies on the Testaments of the Twelve Patriarchs* [SVTP, 3; Leiden: E.J. Brill, 1975], pp. 291-316 [292]). Admittedly the use of an eclectic text is subjective, but so is the diplomatic issue of one MS (*pace* De Jonge, 'Testament Issachar', pp. 293-94).

410. A diplomatic edition of MS *b* from the tenth century CE.

411. In the Arm. ἐν διαστροφῇ is absent, which, according to Becker, *Testamente der zwölf Patriarchen*, *ad loc.*, leads to a better symmetry.

412. καὶ νῦν interpreted as Semitism: Hultgård, *Eschatologie*, II, p. 181.

2. The Antichrist in the Apocrypha and Pseudepigrapha 111

2   And you will make the law disappear and you will despise and distort[413] the words of the prophets, and you will chase just men and hate the pious, you will abhor truthful words.

18.12 And Beliar will be bound by [the new priest] and he will grant his children authority to trample the evil spirits.

Just like the other Patriarchs in their testaments, Levi says that his descendants will do evil in eschatological times. This prophecy is based on a message Levi had read in a book of Enoch that is not now extant.[414] Levi's descendants will even do this for a long time, in their own field of expertise, religion. This not only applies to the cultic aspect; they will also twist the meaning of Law and Prophets,[415] and will even end up persecuting those who oppose them (16.1-2).

These verses could point to the period in which the Pharisees and Essenes did not appreciate the actions of the Hasmoneans and the Sadducees,[416] and do not necessarily refer to the priests' involvement in the death of Christ.[417]

In eschatological times the New Priest[418] will bind Beliar.[419] This New Priest is a messianic figure with priestly but also kingly features.[420] The

413. Lit.: 'in distortion'.
414. Cf. *T. Levi* 14.1; *T. Sim.* 5.4; *T. Jud.* 18.1; *T. Dan* 5.4, 6; *T. Naph.* 4.1; *T. Benj.* 9.1 and also *T. Iss.* 6.1; *T. Zeb.* 9.5; *T. Dan* 7.3; *T. Gad* 8.2; *T. Ash.* 7.2 (the last series without mention of Enoch). Cf. Hultgård, *Eschatologie*, I, pp. 82-84.
415. Hultgård, *Eschatologie*, I, p. 101. For this division into two, see Mt. 5.17 etc. (cf. F.W. Grosheide, *Het Heilig Evangelie volgens Mattheus* [Kommentaar op het Nieuwe Testament; Amsterdam: Van Bottenburg, 1922], pp. 54-55 [*pace* Hollander and De Jonge, *Testaments of the Twelve Patriarchs, ad loc.*]).
416. M. Philonenko, 'Testaments des Douze Patriarches', in Dupont-Sommer and Philonenko (eds.), *La Bible: Ecrits intertestamentaires*, pp. 811-944; Charles, 'Testaments of the XII Patriarchs', *ad loc.* Cf. *Pss. Sol.* 2.3.
417. This is what Kee, 'Testaments of the Twelve Patriarchs', p. 794, says about the following verse. Also the MSS (in the margin) say this about the following verse. (Hultgård, *Eschatologie*, II, p. 31 n. 2). For non-interpolation interpretations of *T. Levi* 16.3, see Philonenko, 'Testaments des Douze Patriarches', *ad loc.*; Charles, 'Testaments of the XII Patriarchs', *ad loc.*; Hultgård, *Eschatologie*, I, p. 102-106; Beckwith, 'Significance of the Calendar', p. 180 (cf. pp. 174-75).
418. According to Van der Woude, *Die messianischen Vorstellungen*, p. 211, it is God Himself who should be regarded as the subject, but that would mean a break between v. 9 and v. 10.
419. The binding element seems to be based mainly on *1 En.* 10.4. (cf. Hultgård, *Eschatologie*, I, pp. 285, 325).
420. Charles, 'Testaments of the XII Patriarchs', p. 314. (However, his identification of the Messiah is incorrect.) See vv. 3-4; cf. 8.4-7, 11-15.

children of the New Priest[421] will receive authority to overcome demons[422] (18.12).

This could be a reaction to the evils[423] mentioned in 16.1-2 and is not necessarily a Christian interpolation. Of course one could think of Heb. 5.5-6, but that passage actually builds on Old Testament data.[424]

c. T. Jud. *2.4; 25.3*

2.4 Καὶ λέοντα ἀπέκτεινα καὶ ἀφελόμην ἔριφον ἐκ τοῦ στόματος αὐτοῦ. Ἄρκον λαβὼν ἐκ τοῦ ποδός, ἀπεκύλησα[425] εἰς κρημνόν· καὶ πᾶν θηρίον, εἰ ἐπέστρεφε πρός με, διήσπουν[426] αὐτὸ ὡς κύνα.

25.3 Καὶ ἔσται[427] εἷς λαὸς Κυρίου καὶ γλῶσσα μία καὶ[428] οὐκ ἔσται ἔτι πνεῦμα πλάνης τοῦ Βελιάρ[429] ὅτι ἐμβληθήσεται ἐν τῷ πυρὶ εἰς τὸν αἰῶνα καὶ ἐπέκεινα.[430]

2.4 And I killed a lion and removed a kid from its mouth. I seized a bear by its paw and turned[431] it away to an abyss. And every beast, when it approached me, I tore apart like a dog.

25.3 And there will[432] be one people of the Lord and one language

---

421. Apparently, grammatically v. 12 is about the children of the New Priest (Philonenko, 'Testaments des Douze Patriarches', p. 873; *pace* Van der Woude, *Die messianischen Vorstellungen*, p. 211; also according to Charles, 'Testaments of the XII Patriarchs', *ad loc.*, it is about God's children, but Charles is influenced by his identification of the Messiah, which makes the grammatical interpretation even harder for him than for us). In vv. 8, 13, both possibilities are open.

422. Hultgård, *Eschatologie*, I, p. 285; idem, *Eschatologie*, II, pp. 159-60; Noack, *Satanás und Sotería*, p. 46. Cf. especially *T. Sim.* 6.6 and *T. Zeb.* 9.8. As with *Pss. Sol.* 17 we refer to Isa. 11, esp. v. 8. Cf. also Lk. 10.19.

423. Charles, 'Testaments of the XII Patriarchs', *ad loc.*

424. Cf. S. Bénétreau, *L'épître aux Hébreux*, I (Commentaire Evangélique de la Bible; Vaux-sur-Seine: Edifac, 1989), pp. 209-10. Think also of the thesis that Heb. was written for Essenes who had not yet come to faith: H. Kosmala, *Hebräer—Essener —Christen* (Leiden: E.J. Brill, 1959), p. x.

425. Apparently the Armenian reading was ἀπηκόντισα. Cj. ἀπεκύλισα (indeed, the inf. is ἀποκυλίειν, not ἀποκυλεῖν / ἂν; itacism).

426. Irregular imperf. of διασπᾶν.

427. V.l. ἔσεσθε.

428. Arm. 'to you'.

429. τοῦ Βελιάρ is lacking in Arm.

430. 25.3c Arm.: 'because the evil spirits will be thrown into judgment for the eternities'.

431. Arm. 'slung'.

432. V.l. 'you will'.

2. The Antichrist in the Apocrypha and Pseudepigrapha 113

and Beliar's spirit of error will be no more[433]
because he will be thrown into the fire for ever and always.[434]

In 2.4 Judah relates an adventure from his youth.[435] Like David he had killed lions and bears. The adventures in the previous and following verses strongly remind us of Hercules, but apparently this verse is grafted into 1 Sam. 17.34-36.[436] The story strongly resembles an event from Gad's youth.[437]

According to 25.3a, there will only be one nation in eschatological times, after the resurrection of the Patriarchs, with only one language,[438] as in the time before the confusion of tongues when the tower of Babel was built. According to the reading ἔσεσθε this promise is only for the descendants of Judah, which seems less meaningful. The Armenian translation does not mention Beliar in 25.3b, and therefore speaks also consistently about evil spirits in 25.3c.[439] In the Greek too it is possible that it is the spirit of error that will be thrown into the fire, and not Beliar himself.[440] The eternal fire also occurs in *T. Zeb.* 10.3, but elsewhere in the *Testaments of the Twelve Patriarchs* the words 'fire' and 'eternal' rarely occur together.

d. *T. Dan* 5.6, 10-11; 6.1-4

5.6 Ἀνέγνων γὰρ ἐν βίβλῳ Ἐνὼχ τοῦ δικαίου ὅτι ὁ ἄρχων ὑμῶν ἔσται[441] ὁ Σατανᾶς καὶ ὅτι πάντα τὰ πνεύματα τῆς πορνείας καὶ τῆς ὑπερηφανίας

---

433. Arm. 'for you there will be no more spirit of error'.
434. Lit. 'until eternity and onwards'. Cf. Hebr. לעלם ועד, where the two meanings of עד (prep. and subs. ['eternity']; cf. Zorell, *Lexicon, s.vv.*) must be compared to ἐπὶ ἐκεῖνα. Arm. 'because the evil spirit will be thrust into judgment for the eternities'.
435. Because Levi and Judah are the main two patriarchs, there is more room for biographical data in their testaments: Hultgård, *Eschatologie*, II, p. 201.
436. Philonenko, 'Testaments des Douze Patriarches', *ad loc.*
437. *T. Gad* 1.3.
438. Hultgård, *Eschatologie*, I, pp. 239-40. Nation and language go together, as in Dan. 3.4, 7; Rev. 5.9; 7.9: Hollander and De Jonge, *Testaments of the Twelve Patriarchs, ad loc.*
439. Hultgård, *Eschatologie*, I, p. 240 n. 5.
440. This is the translation of Hollander and De Jonge, *Testaments of the Twelve Patriarchs, ad loc.*, p. 229. However, only one demon being thrown into the fire does not seem to match the Final Judgment character of this text. Could the 'spirit of error' (sg.!) perhaps be one of his characteristics? Cf. Hultgård, *Eschatologie*, II, pp. 159-60 (on people), and Noack, *Satanás und Sotería*, p. 46. A characteristic can not be thrown into the fire, so even if a characteristic is referred to in 25.3b, v. 3c must refer to Beliar himself.
441. Arm.; MSS (and Hultgård's text) ἐστιν.

114 *The Antichrist Theme in the Intertestamental Period*

τῷ Λευὶ ὑπακούσονται τοῦ παρεδρεύειν τοῖς υἱοῖς Λευὶ τοῦ ποιεῖν αὐτοὺς ἐξαμαρτάνειν ἐνώπιον Κυρίου.

10 Καὶ ἀνατελεῖ ὑμῖν ἐκ τῆς φυλῆς Ἰουδὰ καὶ Λευὶ τὸ σωτήριον Κυρίου
    καὶ αὐτὸς ποιήσει πρὸς τὸν Βελιὰρ πόλεμον
    καὶ τὴν ἐκδίκησιν τοῦ νίκους δώσει ἐχθροῖς[442] αὐτοῦ[443]

11 καὶ τὴν αἰχμαλωσίαν λήψεται ἀπὸ τοῦ Βελιὰρ
    καὶ ψυχὰς ἁγίων καλέσει πρὸς ἑαυτόν[444]
    καὶ ἐπιστρέψει καρδίας ἀπειθεῖς πρὸς Κύριον
    καὶ δώσει τοῖς ἐπικαλουμένοις αὐτὸν εἰρήνην αἰώνιον.

6.1 Καὶ νῦν φοβήθητε τὸν Κύριον τέκνα μου καὶ προσέξετε ἑαυτοῖς[445] ἀπὸ τοῦ Σατανᾶ καὶ τῶν πνευμάτων αὐτοῦ.

2 Ἐγγίσατε τῷ Θεῷ καὶ τῷ ἀγγέλῳ τῷ παραιτουμένῳ ὑμᾶς ὅτι οὗτός ἐστι μεσίτης Θεοῦ καὶ ἀνθρώπων· καὶ ἐπὶ τῆς εἰρήνης Ἰσραὴλ καὶ κατέναντι τῆς βασιλείας τοῦ ἐχθροῦ στήσεται.

3 Διὰ τοῦτο σπουδάζει ὁ ἐχθρὸς ὑποσκελίζειν πάντας τοὺς ἐπικαλουμένους τὸν Κύριον.

4 Οἶδε γὰρ ὅτι ἐν ᾗ ἡμέρᾳ πιστεύσει Ἰσραὴλ συντελεσθήσεται ἡ βασιλεία τοῦ ἐχθροῦ.

5.6 For I read in the book of Enoch, the righteous one, that your ruler will be[446] Satan, and that all spirits of fornication and arrogance will obey Levi, to assist the sons of Levi and to cause them to commit sin in the presence of the Lord.

10 And from the tribes of Judah and Levi the salvation of the Lord will arise for you;[447] and he will wage war against Beliar
    and he will bring the wrath of (his) victory over his enemies

11 and he will take the captives from Beliar

442. MSS (and Hultgård): πατράσιν; cj. (possibly πολεμίοις, in view of the context) based on Charles, 'Testaments of the XII Patriarchs', *ad loc.*; Becker, *Testamente der zwölf Patriarchen*, *ad loc.* A wrong reading of Hebr. אויבינו as אבותינו is assumed.

443. Cj. based on the Arm. MSS mainly ἡμῶν, but also ὑμῶν; I believe that this cj. could be combined with the previous.

444. καλέσει (this form for fut. s. in LXX) πρὸς ἑαυτόν: addition based on the Arm. (Cf. Hultgård, *Eschatologie*, II, p. 36.)

445. In Hellenistic Greek this is usual instead of ὑμῖν αὐτοῖς (BDR §64.1).

446. Arm.; MSS: 'is'.

447. Van der Woude, *Die messianischen Vorstellungen*, p. 205, is the only one of the authors consulted who offers the other possible translation: 'And He will also make the salvation of the Lord arise for you from the tribes of Judah and Levi.' In this translation, God is also the subject in the sentences that follow (referent of αὐτός and thereafter implicitly). This is problematic in v. 11c, and actually even in v. 10a, because God would there be the subject and also be referred to in Κυρίου. However, Van der Woude's translation does not necessarily lead to the conclusion that v. 10b has an unexpected personification of salvation.

2. The Antichrist in the Apocrypha and Pseudepigrapha 115

and he will call the souls of holy ones unto him[448]
and he will turn disobedient hearts to the Lord
and grant eternal peace to whoever calls on Him.

6.1 Now,[449] my children, fear the Lord, and for yourselves guard against Satan and his spirits.
2 Draw near to God and to the angel who pleads for you, because he is mediator of God and man. And he will rise up for the peace of Israel and against the kingdom of the enemy.
3 Therefore the enemy hastens to cause all who call on the Lord to stumble.
4 For he knows that on the day that Israel will believe, the kingdom of the enemy will have come to an end.

As in the other *Testaments*, also in the *Testament of Dan* there is a point at which the patriarch foretells, on the basis of the book of Enoch, that his descendants will sin terribly.[450] Since this clearly refers to the future and the following verbs are in the future tense, we will follow the Armenian version and read ἔσται. The threat to the Danites is very severe: Satan himself will be their ruler. However, his actions are not directed towards the Danites in the first place, but to the Levites. Here again the sins of the priests are pointed out, probably at the time of writing of the *Testaments of the Twelve Patriarchs*. The Danites will tempt the Levites to do so, under the direct command of Satan.[451] Fornication and arrogance will form the main threats to the priestly rank (5.6).

The Danites themselves will join in the sinning, and will consequently be taken into exile, but they will repent (5. 7-9). Thus salvation will yet[452] come out of Judah and Levi, who apparently are regarded as one tribe. The order (Judah first) is unusual[453] as well. Salvation is personified from 5.10 onwards and in certain manuscripts (περὶ) (τοῦ) Χριστοῦ is noted in the

---

448. 'he will call...unto him': addition on the basis of the Arm.; MSS 'namely souls of saints'.
449. καὶ νῦν interpreted as a hebraism: Hultgård, *Eschatologie*, II, p. 181.
450. Cf. note [414].
451. Von Nordheim, *Lehre der Alten*, I, p. 70, mentions this passage as an example of the combination in *T. 12 Patr.* of cosmic dualism and ethical dualism. The fact that Satan plays a part does not take away personal responsibility: Noack, *Satanás und Sotería*, p. 47.
452. Much simpler in 5.4! There is a contrast here between the actual Levi (i.e. priesthood) and the ideal, eschatological Levi (new priesthood).
453. According to Philonenko, *Interpolations chrétiennes*, p. 10, this is a reflection of a later phase of messianology, in which one messiah is both son of Levi and son of Judah. Cf. Van der Woude, *Die messianischen Vorstellungen*, p. 197. Cf. Hollander and De Jonge, *Testaments of the Twelve Patriarchs*, pp. 60-61.

margin.⁴⁵⁴ The bearer of salvation will wage war against Beliar and by conquering him he will take revenge on his enemies.⁴⁵⁵

The Bearer of Salvation will then deliver from Beliar's power the people who had fallen⁴⁵⁶ during the eschatological struggle. Does this mean that the captives are the same as the saints? According to the Greek text they are. (If so, they are people who enjoy God's special care and protection.)⁴⁵⁷ According to the Armenian version they may not be, and here a different localization is possible: the captives in hell, the saints in heaven; once they have been called back, they can be re-deployed on the battlefield. Some (not necessarily Jews) will be converted through the Bearer of Salvation and there will be eternal peace for those who call upon the Lord.⁴⁵⁸ This is worked out in the following verses (12-13).

In concluding, Dan exhorts his descendants to choose for the Lord, for the victory is his. However, there will be fighting,⁴⁵⁹ since the enemy knows that his kingdom will fall when Israel believes. At least that is the condition in the reading we have chosen. Hultgård prefers the reading ἰσχύσει on the basis of the Armenian version, but another explanation for this is possible⁴⁶⁰ and the redundancy of ἰσχύσει is extensive. The Greek manuscripts offer πιστεύσει and ἐπιστρέψει. The latter is, however, used transitively in 5.11c. On the basis of this objection and Charles's explanation of the Armenian version, we opt for πιστεύσει, although there are some objections to the absolute use of this verb.⁴⁶¹ As regards to the contents of the text, it is significant that the author stressed that Israel must repent.⁴⁶² Strangely, the margin has not mentioned τοῦ Χριστοῦ up to this point (v. 3).⁴⁶³

To what extent is there a Christian influence in these verses? The captivity reminds us of Eph. 4.8, but this is a quote from the Old Testament

---

454. Hultgård, *Eschatologie*, II, p. 31 n. 2.

455. This is the most reasonable interpretation, but it is only possible by making several text-critical changes.

456. Hultgård, *Eschatologie*, I, p. 294.

457. Charles, 'Testaments of the XII Patriarchs', *ad loc.*; Hollander and De Jonge, *Testaments of the Twelve Patriarchs, ad loc.*

458. Hollander and De Jonge, *Testaments of the Twelve Patriarchs, ad loc.* (see the references); Hultgård, *Eschatologie*, I, p. 295; cf. 1QM 12.1, 4.

459. For ὑποσκελίζειν cf. Hebr. הכשיל, to be interpreted as *terminus technicus* in Qumran (Philonenko, *Interpolations chrétiennes*, p. 45).

460. Charles *apud* Hultgård, *Eschatologie*, II, p. 36.

461. Becker, *Testamente der zwölf Patriarchen, ad loc.*

462. Hollander and De Jonge, *Testaments of the Twelve Patriarchs, ad loc.*

463. Hultgård, *Eschatologie*, II, p. 31 n. 2.

2. The Antichrist in the Apocrypha and Pseudepigrapha 117

(Ps. 68.19). Where many have regarded 'souls of saints' as a Christian interpolation,[464] these words do occur in the less 'Christian' Armenian version. The commentary by Hollander and M. de Jonge indicates that the link 'souls of saints' also occurs in old-testamental and intertestamental literature.[465] The most 'Christian' verses are 5.11c-d and 6.2β.[466] The rest can easily be read from an intertestamental perspective. However, there are old-testamental and intertestamental parallels[467] for 5.11c-d too, and 6.2aβ as a Christian addition would be peculiar, because Christ is not portrayed as an angel in the New Testament.[468] Messianic expectations around the archangel Michael[469] do occur in the intertestamental period, when angels were also presented as mediators between God and man.[470]

e. T. Gad *4.7–5.1*

4.7 Τὸ γὰρ πνεῦμα τοῦ μίσους διὰ τῆς ὀλιγοψυχίας συνεργεῖ τῷ Σατανᾷ ἐν πᾶσιν εἰς θάνατον τῶν ἀνθρώπων τὸ δὲ πνεῦμα τῆς ἀγάπης ἐν μακροθυμίᾳ συνεργεῖ τῷ νόμῳ τοῦ Θεοῦ εἰς σωτηρίαν ἀνθρώπων.

5.1 Κακὸν τὸ μῖσος ὅτι ἐνδελεχεῖ συνεχῶς τῷ ψεύδει, λαλῶν κατὰ τῆς ἀληθείας, καὶ τὰ μικρὰ μεγάλα ποιεῖ, τὸ σκότος φῶς προσέχει, τὸ γλυκὺ πικρὸν λέγει, καὶ συκοφαντίαν ἐκδιδάσκει καὶ πόλεμον καὶ ὕβριν καὶ πᾶσαν πλεονεξίαν κακῶν, καὶ ἰοῦ διαβολικοῦ τὴν καρδίαν πληροῖ.

4.7 For the spirit of hatred works through narrowmindedness in everything, to-

---

464. Charles, 'Testaments of the XII Patriarchs', *ad loc.*; Becker, *Testamente der zwölf Patriarchen*, *ad loc.*
465. Hollander and De Jonge, *Testaments of the Twelve Patriarchs*, *ad loc.*
466. 5.11c-d: cf. Lk. 1.17; Jn 14.27; 2 Thess. 3.16. The similarity of the wording with Lk. 1.17 is striking, but that verse is about John the Baptist. For this, see Hultgård, *Eschatologie*, I, p. 377. However, it is remarkable that Luke twice quotes the passages we are discussing here, and almost literally. This points to a dependency that can only be explained in one direction: Luke must have read *T. 12 Patr.* (cf. C.A. Evans, 'Luke and the Rewritten Bible: Aspects of Lukan Hagiography', in J.H. Charlesworth [ed.], *The Pseudepigrapha and Early Biblical Interpretation* [JSPSup, 14; Sheffield: JSOT Press, 1993], pp. 170-201 [175-76]). For 6.2aβ, cf. 1 Tim. 2.5.
467. Hollander and De Jonge, *Testaments of the Twelve Patriarchs*, *ad loc.*
468. See Heb. 1.4-8, 13. However, see also Hollander and De Jonge, *Testaments of the Twelve Patriarchs*, *ad loc.*
469. He is not mentioned by name here. However, see Charles, 'Testaments of the XII Patriarchs', *ad loc.*; Philonenko, 'Testaments des Douze Patriarches', *ad loc.*; Hultgård, *Eschatologie*, I, p. 253.
470. Bénétreau, *Epître aux Hébreux*, I, pp. 93-95; Philonenko, *Interpolations chrétiennes*, pp. 44-45.

gether with Satan, for the death of humankind. But through forbearance the spirit of love collaborates with God's law for the salvation of humankind.

5.1 Hatred is evil, since it continually consorts with deceit, speaks against the truth, and makes the small big, presents the darkness as light, says the sweet is bitter, teaches blackmail and war, insolence and a host of evil things, and fills the heart with diabolical venom.

The theme of *T. Gad* is hatred, and these verses give a good theological description of the psychology of hatred.[471] A characteristic of hatred is ὀλιγοψυχία, which should be interpreted as the opposite of μακροθυμία. 'Narrow-mindedness' would be the most literal translation, meaning 'easily offended',[472] which fits in well as a contrast to 'forbearance'. The Testament mentions love[473] as a characteristic of God's law, whereby love and hatred, the theme of this Testament, form an antithetical pair.[474]

In the following verse it is difficult to give a correct translation of συκοφαντία. The 'Sycophants' formed a proverbial group in ancient Athens. They harmed their opponents by reporting them, sometimes even wrongly, in which case we can say they were using slander.[475] The Sycophants would sometimes demand money from their opponents, by threatening to bring in false charges. This is how the word συκοφαντία took on the meaning of 'blackmail'.[476]

f. T. Ash. *7.2-3*

2 Οἶδα γὰρ ὅτι ἁμαρτήσετε καὶ παραδοθήσεσθε εἰς χεῖρας ἐχθρῶν ὑμῶν ἐρημωθήσεται καὶ τὰ ἅγια ὑμῶν καταφθαρήσεται καὶ ὑμεῖς διασκορπισθήσεσθε εἰς τὰς τέσσαρας γωνίας τῆς γῆς, καὶ ἔσεσθε ἐν διασπορᾷ ἐξουδενωμένοι ὡς ὕδωρ ἄχρηστον.[477]

3 Ἕως οὗ ὁ ὕψιστος ἐπισκέψηται τὴν γῆν καὶ αὐτὸς ἐλθὼν ὡς ἄνθρωπος μετὰ ἀνθρώπων ἐσθίων καὶ πίνων καὶ ἐν ἡσυχίᾳ συντρίβων τὴν κεφαλὴν

---

471. Not a *Christian* description: Philonenko, 'Testaments des Douze Patriarches', *ad loc.* Cf. Sacchi, *Apocalittica giudaica*, p. 292. Cf. *T. Dan* 4.7–5.1, but the passage discussed here is clearer.

472. As in Hollander and De Jonge, *Testaments of the Twelve Patriarchs, ad loc.*

473. Hollander and De Jonge, *Testaments of the Twelve Patriarchs, ad loc.*

474. According to Von Nordheim, *Lehre der Alten*, I, p. 55 n. 128, such a pair is typical for paraenesis.

475. See Charles, 'Testaments of the XII Patriarchs', *ad loc.*; Kee, 'Testaments of the Twelve Patriarchs', *ad loc.* Cf. LSJ, *s.v.* συκοφάντης.

476. D. Schouten, 'Sycophant', in J. Nuchelmans *et al.* (eds.), *Woordenboek der Oudheid*, III (*s.l.*: Romen, 1986), col. 2885; cf. LSJ, *s.v.*

477. Hultgård's spelling must be a printing error.

2. The Antichrist in the Apocrypha and Pseudepigrapha 119

τοῦ δράκοντος ἐπὶ τοῦ ὕδατος· οὕτως σώσει τὸν Ἰσραὴλ καὶ πάντα τὰ ἔθνη Θεὸς εἰς ἄνδρα ὑποκρινόμενος.

2 For I know that you will sin and will be delivered into the hands of your enemies and that your land will be made desolate and that your temple will be destroyed and that you will be scattered to the four corners of the earth, and that in the dispersion you will be regarded as nothing, as useless water.

3 Until the Most High visits the earth and comes Himself, like a man eating and drinking with the people, and quietly crushes the dragon's head on the water. Thus He will save Israel and all nations, God Who answers man.

Also in the *Testament of Asher* the point arrives at which the patriarch foretells that his descendants will sin.[478] This testament adds a few historical details: sin will result in the defeat and dispersion of Asher's descendants (who could be interpreted as all Israelites), and the destruction of the Temple. In the dispersion they will share the fate of water that in spite of its enormous potential value (especially in a dry climate!) just drains off unused, without any use for man, animal or plant.[479]

Also for the tribe of Asher there will be a turning point. These verses have been interpreted as Christian[480] and may have been interpolated by Christians,[481] but the core of the text indicates that God Himself will defeat the dragon. He will do this without having to make any special effort.[482] The dragon has not been mentioned previously in this Testament, but these verses do remind us of *Pss. Sol.* 2.1-3, 25–27, where God Himself—and not a messianic figure—is described as eliminating the dragon, thus answering man's cries.[483]

---

478. See note [414].

479. We find the same comparison (ὡς ὕδωρ ἄχρηστον) in Wis. 16.29. The cj. of Charles, 'Testaments of the XII Patriarchs', *ad loc.*, is therefore not necessary.

480. (περὶ) (τοῦ) Χριστοῦ in the margin of, or as a gloss in v. 3: Hultgård, *Eschatologie*, II, p. 256 (*app. crit.*).

481. Kee, 'Testaments of the Twelve Patriarchs', *ad loc.*: vv. 3aβ and 3bβ. However, cf. Philonenko, *Interpolations chrétiennes*, p. 34; K. Koch, 'Die Entstehung der Heilandserwartung in Israel und ihre kanonische Rezeption', in H.M. Niemann *et al.* (eds.), *Nachdenken über Israel, Bibel und Theologie* (Festschrift K.-D. Schunck; BEATAJ, 37; Bern: Peter Lang, 1994), pp. 235-50 (243).

482. This is the explanation of ἐν ἡσυχίᾳ; compare the v.l. ἐν ἰσχύι; cf. Hultgård, *Eschatologie*, II, p. 156. A different explanation is given by Hollander and De Jonge, *Testaments of the Twelve Patriarchs, ad loc.*

483. Cf. CšD (MS Antonin B 798) ii 1: אל עונה לעבדו (God who answers His servant).

g. *The Antichrist in the* Testaments of the Twelve Patriarchs

1. *The Bear and the Antichrist?* The first text we will approach with our definition of the Antichrist is *T. Jud.* 2.4., about Judah fighting a bear. Is this a normal fight? Thinking of 1 Sam. 17 and of Ps. 152, and considering the combination with the elimination (by turning or slinging) of the bear into the abyss, we must find out whether there is more to this than is immediately apparent.

There seem to be fewer indications of a metaphoric interpretation than in Ps. 152, since Ps. 152 is about the (near) future and this is about Judah's past. Judah has messianic links (albeit fewer than Levi), but is not presented here as a warrior acting out of principle who perhaps was idealized later on. However, we can distinguish David behind Judah in several places: both are royal and sinful at the same time.[484] Also the context of the links with the travails of Hercules could indicate a thematic element in the fight with the bear.

In any case we now have the elements 'Judah–David–Blessed One',[485] 'Bear–Goliath–Antichrist' and 'abyss'. The abyss is even linked with the obvious participant, in contrast to Ps. 152.6.

2. *The dragon and the Antichrist? Testament of Asher* 7.2-3 discusses the pre-eschatological times in which the Temple will be destroyed, as well as the eschatological times in which the Most High will visit the earth and come himself, calmly crushing the dragon's head on the water,[486] thereby saving Israel and all nations.[487] As in *Pss. Sol.* 2.25, the dragon could refer to the Antichrist. Whether the dragon in *T. Ash.* 7.3 also refers to Pompey, is a harder question. I have already pointed out that the *Testaments of the Twelve Patriarchs* are farther removed from the events of 63 than the *Psalms of Solomon*. The data found here are less precise and limited to 'an eschatological opponent who will be conquered by God Himself after the destruction of the Temple'. In itself this is a bit meagre for a conclusion that this is about the Antichrist (we could also think of a king from the

---

484. Hultgård, *Eschatologie*, II, p. 201.
485. *T. Jud.* 2.1 (ἔδωκέ μοι Κύριος χάριν), comparable to the 'elect one' and the 'holy one' in Ps. 152.4a.
486. Is there a link with Rev. 13.1 here?
487. When following the view of Kee, 'Testaments of the Twelve Patriarchs', *ad loc.*, on the Christian interpolations, we end up with the above-mentioned elements in v. 3.

2. The Antichrist in the Apocrypha and Pseudepigrapha 121

north), but the combination with the data in *Pss. Sol.* 2 seems to justify the conclusion.[488]

3. *Hatred as a motive for the Antichrist.* Data of a completely different nature are found in *T. Gad* 4.7–5.1. Here we find a number of elements of the Antichrist's character together: hatred, deceit, aiming to kill people, the culmination of evil, a heart completely under the influence of Satan.[489] No matter how interesting this theme of hatred,[490] and how compelling the combination of hatred with other elements of our Antichrist definition, we must conclude that this is not a description of an eschatological individual, but a psychological description that is applicable to everybody.

4. *The Wicked Priests and the Antichrist.* The sons of Levi themselves will treat holy matters in an unholy way (*T. Levi* 16.1), will act lawlessly, hate good people (*T. Levi* 16.2) and be arrogant (*T. Dan* 5.6).[491] The old priesthood will thus become so evil[492] (in pre-eschatological times?) that in eschatological times a New Priest will be needed (*T. Levi* 18).

The sons of Dan will also play a role in this deterioration, but it is unclear what the relations between Danites and Levites will be like (*T. Dan* 5.6). What is clear, however, is that there is a special relationship between this act of the Danites and Satan. Many have deduced from this that the Antichrist will be a descendant of Dan.[493] We have seen here that the Antichrist is a man acting under the influence of Satan. Since the Antichrist is not really discussed, and since there will be more tribes that will be sinning

---

488. King of the North: cf. above n. 376. It is also possible to think of Satan, who is called 'the dragon' (see Rev. 20–22). With the date used here, *Pss. Sol.* 2 is the first text to compare this text with.

489. The relationship to the Law (cf. the Antichrist's lawlessness) is only discussed in its mirror-image, love.

490. Also for Antiochus IV Epiphanes it could be said that he was driven by hatred. Cf. J.T. Nelis, *Daniël* (Boeken van het Oude Testament; Maaseik: Romen, 1954), p. 21; H.L. Jansen, *Die Politik Antiochos' des IV* (Skrifter Norske Videnskaps-Akademi Oslo. II. Historisk-Filosofiske Klasse, 1942, 3; Oslo: Dybwad, 1943), p. 15.

491. The use of βδελυγ– in *T. Levi* 16.2 reminds us of τὸ βδέλυγμα τῆς ἐρημώσεως (Mt. 24.15; Dan. 11.31), but that is only a link of association.

492. Cf. Van der Woude, *Die messianischen Vorstellungen*, p. 227.

493. E.g. Charles, 'Testaments of the XII Patriarchs', *ad loc.* Cf. Bousset, *Antichrist*, pp. 112-15 (do take a critical look at each of the passages quoted there!); K. Berger, *Die griechische Daniel-Diegese: Eine altkirchliche Apokalypse* (SPB, 27; Leiden: E.J. Brill, 1976), p. 110.

towards the end of times,[494] it is difficult to find a specific link between Dan and the Antichrist in this passage. It is not impossible that this text was used to find such a link in later times.[495]

In general we must say that in these texts we are on eschatological ground, but that contrary to the situation described in the *Psalms of Solomon*, there is no culmination of evil in one particular person here.

5. *Beliar Is the Enemy but not the Antichrist*. In the past people have tried to see the Antichrist in Beliar. However, Beliar does not only act in eschatological times, but throughout the course of history.[496] This means that it is better to identify him with Satan,[497] which is usually done in the pseudepigraphic writings.[498]

494. Only Ruben and, naturally, Joseph are not mentioned.
495. Hultgård, *Eschatologie*, I, p. 90; Becker, *Testamente der zwölf Patriarchen, ad loc.*; Hollander and De Jonge, *Testaments of the Twelve Patriarchs*, p. 49. The concept occurs in Christian literature, but not in the New Testament!
496. Eschatologically: *T. Levi* 3.3 (is partly absent in the Arm.); 18.12; *T. Jud.* 25.3 (not in Arm.); *T. Iss.* 6.1 (not in shorter text of Arm.); *T. Zeb.* 9.8 (not in shorter text of α-MSS and Arm.); *T. Dan* 5.10, 11; *T. Benj.* 3.8 (not in shorter text of Arm.). Historically: *T. Reu.* 2.2 (not in α-MSS); 4.7, 11; 6.3 (not in Arm.); *T. Sim.* 5.3 (not in MS c); *T. Levi* 19.1 (not in MS k); *T. Iss.* 7.7; *T. Dan* 1.7; 4.7 (not in shorter text of MS *l*); 5.1 (not in shorter text of MS *a*); *T. Naph.* 2.6 (not in shorter text of MS *l*); *T. Ash.* 1.8; 3.2; *T. Jos.* 7.4; 20.2; *T. Benj.* 3.3, 4 (twice not in shorter text of 3.2-5 in Arm.); 6.1, 7; 7.1 (not in Arm.), 2. NB: There is no tradition where the term 'Beliar' is completely absent! (Based on A.-M. Denis and Y. Janssens, *Concordance grecque des pseudépigraphes d'Ancien Testament: Concordance. Corpus des Textes. Indices* [Louvain-la-Neuve: UCL, 1987], *s.v.*; Hultgård, *Eschatologie*, II, *app. crit.*; Charles, 'Testaments of the XII Patriarchs', *ad locc.*; M. de Jonge, *The Testaments of the Twelve Patriarchs: A Critical Edition of the Greek Text* [PVTG, 1.2; Leiden: E.J. Brill, 1978], v. app. crit.).
497. Hultgård, *Eschatologie*, I, p. 90; Sacchi, *Apocalittica giudaica*, pp. 213-14, 291-92; Van der Woude, *Die messianischen Vorstellungen*, p. 22; Noack, *Satanás und Sotería*, p. 44. Cf. Hollander and De Jonge, *Testaments of the Twelve Patriarchs*, p. 49, albeit that 'always as name for Satan or for the "Antichrist"' is insufficient for this study. Nikiprowetzky, *Troisième Sibylle*, pp. 138-40, is not precise enough when describing Beliar as 'une figure métaphysique dont la fonction double celle de Satan' (p. 138). Only Satan can be the driving force behind all enemies of God, the Messiah and the believers. Further on (pp. 138-39) he gives a good definition of the Antichrist ('un faux prophète et un tyran militaire…à la fin des temps'), only without sufficient precise references on pp. 139-40, but he wrongly makes a transition from 'driving force behind all enemies' to 'Antichrist' and therefore fails to prove that the *Testaments of the Twelve Patriarchs* is about the Antichrist. On p. 140 he describes Beliar as differing from and more metaphysical than the Antichrist, but without drawing these conclusions.

2. The Antichrist in the Apocrypha and Pseudepigrapha 123

Therefore, *T. Levi* 18.12 is about Satan, who will be bound at the end of times (as in Rev. 20.2). In *T. Jud.* 25.3[499] Satan is cast into the fire for ever (as in Rev. 20.10[500]), so that the people will no longer go astray. In *T. Dan* 5.10-11 Satan will lose in the final battle[501] and he will have to give up his captives.[502]

Although the Antichrist's aim is to make people stumble, it is best to view the Enemy in *T. Dan* 6.3-4 as synonymous with Satan,[503] as mentioned in *T. Dan* 6.1. In view of the Antichrist's subordination to Satan, it would be presumptuous to speak about the Antichrist's kingdom in such absolute terms.[504]

Even if this is a description of an eschatological evildoer who opposes a messianic figure, we cannot state that this must therefore necessarily be the Antichrist. Neither should the actions of the New Priest in *T. Levi* 18.12 and the Bearer of Salvation in *T. Dan* 5.10 persuade us to see the Antichrist here.

What we can say however, is that in the intertestamental writings, the absolute *contrast* between God and Beliar is stressed to a certain extent, whereas the Old Testament stresses the *subordination* of Satan,[505] and that

---

The transition of the Beliar figure occurs much later. (This confusion is partly based on Nikiprowetzky's date of *Sib. Or.* 3.63-74 in the era BCE, which conflicts with the date other researchers have given.) H.H. Rowley, *The Relevance of Apocalyptic: A Study of Jewish and Christian Apocalypses from Daniel to the Revelation* (London: Lutterworth, 3rd edn, 1963), p. 72, clearly works from a definition that differs from ours, and which makes an identification of Beliar with the Antichrist possible.

498. Van der Woude, *Die messianischen Vorstellungen*, p. 22.
499. In the Arm., 'Beliar' is absent!
500. Admittedly, the Antichrist will also end up there (see Rev. 19.20).
501. Sacchi, *Apocalittica giudaica*, p. 292, rightly remarks that the author of the *Testaments of the Twelve Patriarchs* pays more attention to the end of evil than to its origins.
502. The latter element can hardly be applied to the Antichrist.
503. Noack, *Satanás und Sotería*, p. 44; Philonenko, *Interpolations chrétiennes*, p. 45.
504. Also the 'Prince of Error' (which in itself is a good term with which to describe the Antichrist, who is a tyrant and a false prophet) from *T. Sim.* 2.7 and *T. Jud.* 19.4 cannot be identified with the Antichrist, but with Satan, also known as Beliar. This is not an eschatological situation; cf. Noack, *Satanás und Sotería*, p. 44; Philonenko, 'Testaments des Douze Patriarches', p. 827.
505. Cf. Noack, *Satanás und Sotería*, p. 47; E. Pagels, 'The Social History of Satan, the "Intimate Enemy": A Preliminary Sketch', *HTR* 84 (1991), pp. 105-28 (107). Cf. E. Noort, 'JHWH und das Böse. Bemerkungen zu einer Verhältnisbestimmung', *OTS* 23 (1984), pp. 120-36.

this may have created some space for an Antichrist as a false god (actually much more an ἀντίθεος than an ἀντίχριστος), but this hypothesis is not based on very strong arguments.[506]

h. *Conclusion*

Although love for God is the highest commandment and an important subject in the *Testaments of the Twelve Patriarchs*,[507] and although one would expect to find only few data on the Antichrist, love is the opposite of hatred, and the genre of the testaments demands some apocalyptic.[508] So in what sense do we find the Antichrist in this writing?

The Antichrist theme is present in the *Testaments of the Twelve Patriarchs*, but not where it has been sought the most, that is, in the Beliar figure.

In the description of hatred and in the evaluation of priesthood we only find some elements, and as regards priesthood this only becomes apparent through studying the *Psalms of Solomon*.

Actually we find the Antichrist most clearly in the bear and the dragon, although even this is only clear after having read Ps. 152 and *Pss. Sol.* 2.

Especially in comparison to the previous section, which is about the *Psalms of Solomon*, we have not reached any further conclusions. We note that it is remarkable that the much more apocalyptic[509] *Testaments of the Twelve Patriarchs* say less about the Antichrist than the more devotional *Psalms of Solomon*.

These conclusions lead to some remarks on the dating. The similarities with *Pss. Sol.* 2 seem to confirm the similarity in date of origin that we have accepted, but this could be because of circular reasoning. If Beliar should be identified with Satan and not with the Antichrist here, then the *Testaments of the Twelve Patriarchs* join in with the idiomatic usage of the Pseudepigrapha and not with that of later writings. To confirm this objection, we would need to research later idioms. If the Gospel of Luke is the only Gospel that follows the *idiom* of the *Testaments of the Twelve Patriarchs*, then that could lead to deductions about the date. This ought to be re-

---

506. Even the etymology of שׂטן makes it debatable (cf. H.J. Koorevaar, 'God of men [iemand], Satan of een tegenstander', in G.W. Lorein [ed.], *Naar een nieuwe bijbelvertaling?* [Leiden: Groen, 1994], pp. 88-100 [93]).

507. Becker, *Untersuchungen*, pp. 381-401 (albeit only for the basic document).

508. Hultgård even uses two volumes for the eschatology of the *Testaments of the Twelve Patriarchs*!

509. Even though the paraenetic is the main issue here. For this combination in a *Testament*, cf. below note [561].

2. *The Antichrist in the Apocrypha and Pseudepigrapha*

searched more exhaustively, of course with the exclusion of Christian interpolations. Finally, many issues in connection with the setting of the *Testaments of the Twelve Patriarchs* evolve around the question whether certain details match the *Old* or the *New* Testament. The question cannot be answered very easily, however, and this illustrates how strong the many links between the Old and the New Testament are.

11. Sibylline Oracles, *Book 3, Old Additions*

a. *Setting*

The entire third book of Sibylline Oracles could be called 'old', but several layers can be distinguished. The verses we will discuss in this chapter were added to the corpus around 31 BCE, and an obvious chronological order can be distinguished.

The verses 401-88 are much older[510] as a unit (but not as a part of the collection). *Sib. Or.* 3.350-80 was added to the corpus during the same period, but also originates from that time.[511]

The last passage we will discuss, *Sib. Or.* 3.75-77, is only marginally younger, but it is separated from the preceding verses by the important boundary of 31 BCE. The longest passage, vv. 1-92, apparently originated in Egypt,[512] from shortly after 31 BCE, with the exception of vv. 63-74.[513]

---

510. J.J. Collins, 'The Sibylline Oracles', in Stone (ed.), *Jewish Writings of the Second Temple Period*, pp. 357-81 (369).

511. Collins, 'Sibylline Oracles', p. 358; *idem*, 'The Sibylline Oracles', p. 368.

512. The main fragments, *Sib. Or.* frr. 1 and 3, link up with this beginning of the (current) third book. Actually *Sib. Or.* 1 and 2 were originally the first book, and part of the second book has been preserved in *Sib. Or.* 3.1-92 and in *Sib. Or.* frr. 1, 2 and 3: Collins, 'Sibylline Oracles', pp. 330, 359-60, 469.

513. Collins, 'Sibylline Oracles', pp. 359-60, 469; Collins, 'The Sibylline Oracles', pp. 370-71. This matches the suggestion of Nikiprowetzky, *Troisième Sibylle*, pp. IX, 216-17, of 42 BCE as a publication date for the third book. (He stresses the unity of the current third book [p. 70: 'une œuvre composée et en définitive pourvue d'une certaine unité'], and also includes the first verses [p.64].) L.J. Lietaert Peerbolte, *The Antecedents of Antichrist: A Traditio-Historical Study of the Earliest Christian Views on Eschatological Opponents* (JSJSup [*olim* SPB], 49; Leiden: E.J. Brill, 1996), p. 326, dates this passage after 70 CE, but the only way he can appeal to general opinion is by presupposing that the whole passage should be dated late because of the dating of vv. 63-74.

b. Sib. Or. 3.434-35

As before, we will use Geffcken's text as a starting point. Geffckens generally stays in line with Rzach, but it should be remarked that both deviate considerably from manuscriptal tradition.

    Χαλκηδὼν στεινοῖο πόρον πόντοιο λαχοῦσα,
435 καί σε μολών ποτε παῖς Αἰτώλιος ἐξεναρίξει.

    Chalcedon, to whose lot has fallen the way of the sea strait,
435 to you also an Aetolian youth will come at some time and chase you out of your suit of armour.

This oracle is part of a group of oracles against many foreign nations. Chalcedon was situated opposite Byzantium (and would now be part of Istanbul) at the Bosphorus, where the sea reaches its narrowest point and could easily be used as a road.

Aetolia is an area north of the Peloponnesus. Politically it was an important confederation, with Thermum as its capital. Strangely, Chalcedon was allied to this confederation,[514] but that does not help to explain what the oracle means.

c. Sib. Or. 3.470-73

470 Ἀλλ' ὅτ' ἀπ' Ἰταλίης λυμήτης[515] ἵξεται ἀνήρ,
    τῆμος, Λαοδίκεια, καταπρηνὴς ἐπιροῦσα,
    Καρῶν ἀγλαὸν ἄστυ Λύκου παρὰ θέσκελον ὕδωρ,
    σιγήσεις μεγάλαυχον ἀποιμώξασα τοκῆα.

470 But when a destructive man comes from Italy,
    then Laodicea, dashed down headlong,
    beautiful town of the Carians by the wonderful waters of Lycus,
    you will be silent, bemoaning a conceited parent.

Laodicea was a prosperous city in the southern end of the valley of the Lycus, a subsidiary of the river Meander in the Carian area.

---

514. J. Nuchelmans, 'Aetolische bond', in Nuchelmans et al. (eds.), Woordenboek der Oudheid, I (Bussum: Romen, 1976), cols. 68-69; Will, Histoire politique, p. 122 (about events of 202).

515. Nomen agentis of λυμαίνεσθαι; instead of an adj. a subs. is used here. Apparently the word only occurs in Sib. Or. (It is not included in LSJ.) PGL, s.v., refers for its meaning to λυμεών, which is used for Satan, evil spirits, Simon Magus, false teachers and heretics, or in short for beings who are linked to the Antichrist in patristic literature. The question remains whether we may project this back to the first century BCE. If the early Christian writers had thought of this passage, they would probably not have used the related word λυμεών, but the word λυμήτης itself.

2. *The Antichrist in the Apocrypha and Pseudepigrapha* 127

Commentators have claimed that the evildoer is either Sulla, who travelled to Greece in 87,[516] or Pompey, who travelled extensively in Asia between 67 and 63.[517] The parent is claimed to be Zeus, who was considered to be the guardian god of Laodicea. Laodicea was going to be turned upside down, either by an earthquake (although nothing is known about earthquakes for this period)[518] or as a result of the First Mithridatic War (88–85)[519] (although Laodicea did not play an important part in it and Sulla was never there),[520] or else because of Pompey's actions[521] (although Laodicea did not take part in that war either, at least as far as we know[522]). The third hypothesis has the advantage that it shows a link between the man from Italy and the fall of Laodicea.

The destruction would make clear that their trust in Zeus was unjustified and that he could not help them at all.

d. Sib. Or. *3.365-66*

365 Σμύρνης δ' ὀλλυμένης οὐδεὶς λόγος. Ἔκδικος ἔσται,
     ἀλλὰ κακαῖς βουλῆσι καὶ ἡγεμόνων κακότητι.

365 No word from Smyrna, which is perishing. There will be an avenger, but with evil intentions and the evil of (his) lords.

Smyrna is located in Lydia, on a bay in the Aegean Sea.

The Greek word ἔκδικος has two very different meanings. The idea 'enforce the law' occurs most often, especially in Jewish writings. The meaning 'outside the law'[523] is etymologically so obvious that the Sybil could well have intended it. However, the fact that the 'evil' of v. 366 (κακαῖς βουλῆσι, κακότητι) is seen as a contrast (ἀλλά) to that which was mentioned before indicates a positive meaning of ἔκδικος in v. 365.

The meaning of the oracle is unknown.

---

516. Lanchester, 'Sibylline Oracles', *ad loc.*; Peretti, *Sibilla babilonese*, pp. 324, 326; Collins, 'Sibylline Oracles', *ad loc.*
517. Nikiprowetzky, 'Oracles sibyllins', *ad loc.*
518. Lanchester, 'Sibylline Oracles', *ad loc.* and p. 395 (re. *Sib. Or.* 4.107).
519. Collins, 'Sibylline Oracles', *ad loc.*; Peretti, *Sibilla babilonese*, pp. 324-25; Momigliano, 'Portata storica', p. 1080.
520. See Will, *Histoire politique*, pp. 477-86.
521. Nikiprowetzky, 'Oracles sibyllins', *ad loc.*
522. Will, *Histoire politique*, pp. 499-517: Pompey travelled a lot in Asia, but mostly in the area east of Laodicea.
523. Both meanings LSJ, *s.v.*

e. Sib. Or. 3.75-77

75 Καὶ τότε δὴ κόσμος ὑπὸ ταῖς[524] παλάμῃσι γυναικός
    ἔσσεται[525] ἀρχόμενος καὶ πειθόμενος περὶ παντός.
    Ἔνθ᾽ ὁπόταν[526] κόσμου παντὸς χήρη βασιλεύσῃ...

75 And then indeed the world will be ruled by the hands[527] of a woman
    and (it will) obey her in everything.
    Then when a widow will rule the whole world...

Although these verses start with Καὶ τότε, we must remember that they do not immediately follow the previous verses (*Sib. Or.* 3.63-74) and perhaps do not logically follow from *Sib. Or.* 3.62. *Sib. Or.* 3.63-74, in which the Antichrist is often referred to,[528] has been added to the oracles at a later date, and this may be of importance for the interpretation (in past and present) of the verses we are studying here.

The only aspect of these verses that should be commented on is the identification of the woman (possibly linked to the widow of v. 77). Many have identified her with Cleopatra VII, ruler of Egypt and the whole Roman Empire, a widow several times over, and also linked to the goddess Isis, who was also a widow through the death of Osiris, and ruler of the earth.[529] Others opt for a less simple metaphor: the woman is not an image of a woman, but of a city, originally Babylon, now Rome.[530] A problem is, however, that Rome in all its wealth can hardly be called a 'widow',[531] unless such a term can be used proleptically.[532] Whatever the case may be, the woman portrays an evil figure.[533]

---

524. Following a note by C. Alexandre, *Χρησμοὶ Σιβυλλιακοί* (Paris: Didot, 2nd edn, 1869), Rzach suggests a different text: Καὶ τότε δὴ πᾶς κόσμος ὑπαὶ παλάμῃσι γυναικός. Apart from the more Homeric absence of the article, this conjecture also has the advantage that it is better verse. (Cf. Nikiprowetzky, *Troisième Sibylle*, p. 276.) However, this is not a guarantee that the conjecture is right.

525. This periphrastic conjugation occurs several times in the *Sib. Or.*: see Nikiprowetzky, *Troisième Sibylle*, p. 274.

526. Rzach: ὁπότ᾽ ἄν. (The normal epic form would be ὁππότ᾽ ἄν.)

527. Lit. 'palms'.

528. Cf. Nikiprowetzky, *Troisième Sibylle*, pp. 138-43, who, however, dates these verses differently; Alexandre, *Χρησμοὶ Σιβυλλιακοί*, ad loc.

529. Collins, *Sibylline Oracles of Egyptian Judaism*, pp. 67-71; Nikiprowetzky, *Troisième Sibylle*, pp. 144-45; a challenge to this hypothesis on pp. 145-47.

530. Nikiprowetzky, *Troisième Sibylle*, pp. 147-48.

531. Collins, *Sibylline Oracles of Egyptian Judaism*, pp. 67-68.

532. Nikiprowetzky, *Troisième Sibylle*, p. 147.

533. Nikiprowetzky, *Troisième Sibylle*, pp. 149-50, and *idem*, 'Oracles sibyllins',

f. *The Antichrist in the Old Additions to* Sib. Or. *3*
These passages hardly mention the Aetolic youth, the evildoer from Italy and the avenger from Smyrna. For this reason, a detailed comparison with the Antichrist is not useful. The only remarkable element in these passages is that the evildoer is individualized, while the intertestamental writings usually discuss evildoers as a group and rarely mention the individual evildoer. However, the three passages discussed in this chapter show that the concept of an individual evildoer did exist.

More can be said about the last passage (*Sib. Or.* 3.75-77), because even if it points to Cleopatra VII in the first place, there could be a secondary meaning[534] in which womankind in general, and the Jewish attitude towards Cleopatra VII in particular, played a role.[535] This does not prove without doubt that this passage refers to the Antichrist, but it is sufficient proof that there is room for seeing an individual, eschatological opponent to God here, who will destroy the earth;[536] in other words: the Antichrist.[537]

The additions to *Sib. Or.* 3 are a continuation of two lines; first the line of the original core of the book, which gave more room to the Antichrist than other literature of that period; secondly (at least if our interpretation of *Sib. Or.* 3.470-72 is correct), the line that starts in the *Psalms of Solomon* and gives a lot of weight to Pompey in the development of the Antichrist theme.

12. Treatise of Shem

a. *Setting*
The *Treatise of Shem* is an astrological writing preserved in Syriac, which originated in the twenties, probably in Alexandria.[538] The original was

---

gives as a consideration the view that the widow (not the woman!) could be a messianic figure or the new Jerusalem.

534. Without involving all kinds of sea monsters, as Bousset, *Antichrist*, p. 62, does.

535. For this, see Collins, *Sibylline Oracles of Egyptian Judaism*, pp. 69-70. In order to defend the eschatological character, he appeals to the link with Isis and the changed attitude ('disillusionment') of the Jews towards Cleopatra VII after 31 BCE. Cf. Collins, 'Development of the Sibylline Tradition', pp. 434-35, where he also lays a link with Isa. 47.8-9. Perhaps the feminine element could point to a symbolic (in this case: an eschatological) meaning.

536. See *Sib. Or.* 3.78-81.

537. Collins, *Sibylline Oracles of Egyptian Judaism*, p. 69; Rowley, *Relevance of Apocalyptic*, p. 77 (albeit with a different dating).

538. K. von Stuckrad, *Das Ringen um die Astrologie: Jüdische und christliche*

probably written in Aramaic, or perhaps in Hebrew.[539] It has been studied very little until recently; it was Charlesworth especially who promoted it.[540] His text edition is used below.

In this writing, Shem discusses the events taking place in the course of a year, especially in agriculture,[541] based on the sign of the zodiac in which the year started.

b. Treatise of Shem *11.14-18*

ܘܢܦܘܩ ܓܒܪܐ ܐܘܟܡܐ ܕܒܥܐ ܡܠܟܘܬܐ 14
ܘܒܝܬܐ ܕܡܠܟܘܬܐ ܢܐܒܕ. 15
ܘܡܠܟܐ ܒܥܐ ܕܢܫܡܥ ܡܢܘ ܐܡܪܝܢ ܒܢܝܢܫܐ 16
ܘܡܚܪܒ ܡܕܝܢܬܐ ܣܓܝܐܬܐ
ܘܠܝܬ ܐܢܫ ܕܡܫܟܚ ܕܢܟܠܝܘܗܝ 17
ܘܕܚܠܬܐ ܕܐܠܗܐ ܘܪܚܡܘܗܝ ܦܪܝܩܝܢ ܡܢܗ
ܘܒܫܘܠܡܗ ܕܫܢܬܐ ܕܗܘܐ ܫܢܝܐ ܘܡܠܟܐ ܒܒܢܝܢܫܐ 18
ܘܫܒܩܐ ܘܐܘܦܬܐ ܬܗܘܐ ܒܝܢܬ ܠܗܘܢ ܠܡܠܟܐ
ܕܐܝܬ ܒܟܠܗ ܐܪܥܐ

14 *wnpwq gbr' 'wkm' db'' mlkwt'*
15 *wbyt' dmlkwt' n'bd*[542]
16 *wmlk' b'' dnšm' mnw 'mryn bnynš' wmḥrb*[543] *mdynt' sgy't'*
17 *wlyt 'nš dmškḥ*[544] *dnklywhy wdḥlt' d'lh' wrḥmwhy pryqyn mnh*

Beiträge zum antiken Zeitverständnis (Religionsgeschichtliche Versuche und Vorarbeiten, 49; Berlin: W. de Gruyter, 2000), p. 391, dates slightly earlier. There are elements from Syro-Palestine as well as from Alexandria (first-class astronomics!). It seems more obvious that a Jew working in Egypt would include other elements than the other way around. Cf. Charlesworth, 'Treatise of Shem', *OTP*, I, pp. 473-86 (p. 475); *contra* von Stuckrad, *Ringen um die Astrologie*, pp. 366-67, who assumes an Egyptian origin elsewhere (p. 384).

539. Charlesworth, 'Treatise of Shem', pp. 473-74.

540. A. Mingana, 'Some Early Judaeo-Christian Documents in the John Rylands Library', *BJRL* 4 (1917–18), pp. 59-118, first published it. E.R. Goodenough, *Jewish Symbols in the Greco-Roman Period*. VIII. *Pagan Symbols in Apocalyptic Literature*, II (Bollingen Series, 37.8; New York: Pantheon, 1958), p. 198, only used a few sentences to discuss it. J.H. Charlesworth published an introduction to, and a discussion of it: 'Rylands Syriac MS 44 and a New Addition to the Pseudepigrapha. The Treatise of Shem', *BJRL* 60 (1978), pp. 376-403; *idem*, 'Treatise of Shem'; *idem*, 'Die "Schrift des Sem": Einführung, Text und Übersetzung', *ANRW*, II 20.2 (1987), pp. 951-87.

541. Mingana, 'Some Early Judaeo-Christian Documents', p. 77.

542. East Aram. form of imperf. 3 sg. m.

543. Completive with *b''*, just like *dnšm'*.

544. Aphel ptc.

2. The Antichrist in the Apocrypha and Pseudepigrapha 131

18   wbšwlmh dšnt᾿ dhw᾿ šyn᾿ wšlm᾿ bbnynš᾿
     whwb᾿ w᾿wywt᾿ thw᾿ bynt klhwn mlk᾿ d᾿yt bklh ᾿r⟨᾿⟩

14   There will come forth a black man who will seek the kingdom.
15   And the royal house will perish
16   And the king will seek to hear what the people are saying, and lay waste many cities[545]
17   And no-one will be able to stop him and reverence for God and love for Him will be absent[546] from him.
18   And at the end of the year there will be peace and prosperity with the people and there will be love and harmony among all kings who are on the entire earth.

In ch. 11 we find a description of the *last* year.[547] After the usual agricultural statements (vv. 2-9), the author speaks of warfare and fighting with the Romans (vv. 10-13), after which an individual will rise up to bring the Roman dynasty to an end (vv. 14-15). The new king will spy, conquer and rule without acknowledging God (vv. 16-17). Finally there will be a time of peace and prosperity, which Strobel claims is exactly the object of hope during the Augustine period[548] (v. 18).

Apparently it was appreciated that the Romans strove for safety, and people were afraid that this safety would be lost.[549]

Charlesworth says that it is pure 'coincidence' in which sign of the zodiac a year will start. He reaches this conclusion by starting from the assumption that the sign in question is the sign of the zodiac that is in view at the determined *hour* of the start of the year[550] through the earth's rotation around its axis. However, Charlesworth also points out that the first

---

545. 'Provinces' is also possible, but usually it is cities that are destroyed, not provinces.

546. *pryqyn* is ptc. pass., but this translation seems to be better than 'liberated'.

547. Apparently (12.1) a copyist accidentally skipped the chapter that originally was the eleventh, and included it at the end, so that it became the current twelfth chapter. The verses we will study here were therefore meant as a conclusion of the treatise. Cf. Charlesworth, '"Schrift des Sem"', pp. 952-53, 987 n. 150.

548. A. Strobel, 'Weltenjahr, grosse Konjunktion und Messiasstern. Ein themageschichtlicher Überblick', *ANRW*, II 20.2 (1987), pp. 988-1187 (1011).

549. Cf. Charlesworth, '"Schrift des Sem"', p. 955. Cf. Hadas-Lebel, 'Evolution de l'image de Rome', p. 765, on the attitude the Jews in Egypt had towards the Romans during the days of Caesar and Augustus.

550. Charlesworth, '"Schrift des Sem"', p. 967 n. 42. Cf. M.D. Herr, 'The Calendar', in S. Safrai and M. Stern (eds.), *Jewish People in the First Century*, pp. 834-64 (845-50, 853-57), for the determination of the start of the month and the year. It was then based on lunar months, but they tried to keep in pace with the solar year (spring equinox).

chapter describes a much less favourable situation than the last.⁵⁵¹ This is not completely true (the last chapter also knows sorrow and misery), but it does open up another, eschatological perspective.⁵⁵² The text could be referring instead to the sign of the zodiac that is in view during the equinox because of the earth's rotation around the *sun*. Because of the precession (rotation of the Milky Way), this sign of the zodiac moves every 2,160 years,⁵⁵³ in the *opposite* order to the normal (based on the projection of the sun in a certain constellation at a certain point in time in the subsequent months of the year). There are 12 signs of the zodiac and thus we arrive at a total of 25,920 years.

Or less? The author describes the signs of the zodiac in their *usual* order,⁵⁵⁴ so that chronologically speaking the first chapter should be followed by the last (presently the eleventh). The rest is 'padding', although references to certain situations may occur.⁵⁵⁵ The author starts by describing his own situation (age of Aries), and foresees that one more period will follow (age of Pisces), which will end in a Kingdom of Peace.⁵⁵⁶ The writer of this treatise was not alone in his views about a time of peace based on astronomical observances. Virgil too constantly focused on the Golden Age.⁵⁵⁷

The exact moment of transition from the age of Aries to the age of Pisces

---

551. Charlesworth, '"Schrift des Sem"', p. 953.

552. Cf. Strobel, 'Weltenjahr', p. 999. If this interpretation is correct, Goodenough, *Jewish Symbols*, p. 198, is wrong in saying that it is only the name Shem and the mention of the Passover which give the writing a Jewish flavour. Also Von Stuckrad, *Ringen um die Astrologie*, pp. 392-93, sees more Jewish elements.

553. Strobel, 'Weltenjahr', p. 1011.

554. Charlesworth, '"Schrift des Sem"', p. 952, turns the tables twice by saying that the *Tr. Shem* discusses the signs of the Zodiac 'in entgegensetzter Reihenfolge'.

555. A similar scheme is also found in other years: agriculture, warfare, opportunity to escape. Cf. Von Stuckrad, *Ringen um die Astrologie*, p. 370.

556. The argumentation of Von Stuckrad, *Ringen um die Astrologie*, pp. 369-70, seems impressive, but is based on the translation of the text in Charlesworth, '"Schrift des Sem"', p. 985, and not on the original in Syriac.

557. In the fourth Eclogue as an image of the future, in the first Georgic as the past, in the second Georgic as realized in agricultural life on the condition of a right application of *labor*, i.e. a labour ethics. Astronomy plays a role, clearly in the fourth Eclogue (cf. v. 6), but also in the second Georgic (cf. v. 474). For the broader movement in the time of Virgil, see Strobel, 'Weltenjahr', pp. 999, 1011, 1029-63, and for the area of Herod, see pp. 1063-82 (which should be put into perspective in places, especially near the word 'unschwer').

is still being debated,[558] but we may assume that at the time of editing this was seriously discussed and considered in circles that showed an interest in astrology.[559]

c. *The Antichrist in the* Treatise of Shem
What we have found about the Antichrist in the Treatise of Shem are the following ideas: At the end of the next astronomic age, which will come soon, a political figure will come who will eliminate the Romans. This new king will act tyrannically through his intelligence service and with military violence. He is invincible and anti-religious. Then the Kingdom of Peace will come.

We have found political as well as religious aspects of this eschatological figure. He is portrayed as an opponent, not really of God but of the Jewish nation (the target readership). His relationship to Satan and to the law are not discussed, and the number of elements is very limited in this short passage.

13. Assumption of Moses

a. *Setting*
Influenced by Charles, most authors refer to this writing as the 'Testament' of Moses.[560] There are formal similarities to other testaments,[561] but a quo-

---

558. This is a very technical question, which far outstretches the area of biblical studies. At that time the dimensions of the constellations had not been established, a disc through the equator could not be determined, and measurements were taken at different heights above the horizon. The differences in opinion did not make this impossible (cf. Von Stuckrad, *Ringen um die Astrologie*, pp. 371-73). Von Stuckrad himself (pp. 368-84) works from a 'lunare Tages-Deutung', but it is unclear what the implications of this are for our passage. After reading his pp. 371-73, my impression is that the 'horoskopos' hypothesis remains a possibility.

559. Charlesworth, '"Schrift des Sem"', pp. 956 n. 12, 964.

560. See the extensive description with E.-M. Laperrousaz, 'Le Testament de Moïse (généralement appelé "Assomption de Moïse"). Traduction avec introduction et notes', *Sem* 19 (1970), pp. i-xx, 1-140 (29-62).

561. Our modern categories of genres should not be used to determine what the original name was. *Ass. Mos.* has some characteristics of a testament—there are both rebuking and prophesying passages: see Von Nordheim, *Lehre der Alten*, I, p. 204; cf. Kolenkow and Collins, 'Testaments', p. 259. It also has some characteristics of an apocalypse: see J. Tromp, *Assumption of Moses: A Critical Edition with Commentary* (SVTP, 10; Leiden: E.J. Brill, 1993), pp. 113 n. 2, 123.

tation by Gelasius[562] indicates that the old name 'Assumption' of Moses would be more accurate. Naturally, this use of the word 'assumption' needs some explanation.[563]

Much discussion has taken place on the position of chs. 6 and 7: Are they in the right place?[564] Are they part of the original edition or have they been interpolated later? In this study I have tried to avoid this kind of discussion, in view of the large amount of sources that need to be consulted, but here the outcome of the discussion will also determine the *nature* of the chapter that demands our special attention.

Although the structural argument of Nickelsburg (who believes *Ass. Mos.* 6–7 is an interpolation)[565] seems to be very strong, Collins has found an answer[566] to it. Collins's original view on the situation is in my opinion the most convincing.[567] The vision of Collins *et al.* is as follows:

---

562. Fl. 475 CE (Denis, *Introduction*, p. 129 n. 2). See E. Brandenburger, 'Himmelfahrt Moses', in *Apokalypsen* (JSHRZ, 5.2; Gütersloh: Gerd Mohn, 1976), pp. 57-84 (61), and Laperrousaz, 'Testament de Moïse', pp. 29-30, 60-61.

563. Cf. Tromp, *Assumption of Moses*, p. 101. Cf. Laperrousaz, 'Testament de Moïse', p. 85.

564. R.H. Charles, 'The Assumption of Moses', *APOT*, II, pp. 407-424, would place chs. 8–9 between chs. 5 and 6. This is typical for Charles's rationalizing way of working. For a defence of the unity of chs. 7–10 in their current order, see D. Maggiorotti, 'La datazione del Testamento di Mose', *Henoch* 15 (1993), pp. 235-62 (253, 256, 260). For a defence of the unity of chs. 5–6, see Laperrousaz, 'Testament de Moïse', pp. 119-20.

565. See G.W.E. Nickelsburg, 'An Antiochan Date for the Testament of Moses', in Nickelsburg (ed.), *Studies on the Testament of Moses: Seminar Papers* (SBLSCS, 4; Cambridge: SBL, 1973), pp. 33-37 (33).

566. J.J. Collins, 'The Date and Provenance of the Testament of Moses', in Nickelsburg (ed.), *Studies on the Testament of Moses*, pp. 15-32 (18); worked out by Tromp, *Assumption of Moses*, p. 121.

567. Collins, 'Date and Provenance', pp. 17-29. Later, J.J. Collins, 'Some Remaining Traditio-Historical Problems in the Testament of Moses', in Nickelsburg (ed.), *Studies on the Testament of Moses*, pp. 38-43 (39-40, 43), gave in to the arguments of Nickelsburg, 'Antiochan Date', pp. 33-34, and in my view this was wrong. Collins, 'Some Remaining Traditio-Historical Problems', pp. 40-42, did remain sceptical, and rightly so, about the viewpoint of Nickelsburg, 'Antiochan Date', p. 36, about Taxo. The view that Collins takes (namely, that the whole writing dates from the first century CE), is also found with Laperrousaz, 'Testament de Moïse', pp. 15-16, 99, 122; Brandenburger, 'Himmelfahrt Moses', pp. 60, 62-63; Von Nordheim, *Lehre der Alten*, I, p. 195; Tromp, *Assumption of Moses*, pp. 120-23. The viewpoint that Nickelsburg takes (that *Ass. Mos.* 6–7 is an interpolation) is also found with J. Licht, 'Taxo or the Apocalyptic Doctrine of Vengeance', *JJS* 12 (1961), pp. 95-103 (101-103); J.A.

2. The Antichrist in the Apocrypha and Pseudepigrapha

The *Assumption of Moses* was written shortly after 6 CE, when Herod Archelaus had already been dethroned, but the memory of Herod the Great and of Varus's actions were still alive.[568] The book describes the last words Moses spoke to Joshua (*Ass. Mos.* 1). The events from Moses until the Herods (*Ass. Mos.* 2–6) are summarized in this book, which views its own period as pre-eschatological (*Ass. Mos.* 7). In *Ass. Mos.* 8 we find a picture of the eschatological period, part of which is described on the basis of the events that took place at the time of the Seleucid king Antiochus IV. The messianic actions of Taxo[569] lead to further development in the events (*Ass. Mos.* 9–10). Finally there are sayings of Joshua[570] (*Ass. Mos.* 11) and Moses (*Ass. Mos.* 12). The ending is absent.

Goldstein, 'The Testament of Moses: its Content, its Origin, and its Attestation in Josephus', in Nickelsburg (ed.), *Studies on the Testament of Moses*, pp. 44-52 (46-47) (in spite of his views on p. 45, according to which this interpolation is too large to be credible), and Maggiorotti, 'Datazione', pp. 253-56, 260-61 (only *Ass. Mos.* 6 is an interpolation, as well as a part of 10.8, following A. Yarbro Collins, 'Composition and Redaction of the Testament of Moses 10', *HTR* 69 [1976], pp. 179-86 [185]; however, see the comparison to *1 En.* 91-104, *2 Bar.* and *4 Ezra* on her p. 258). NB: Nickelsburg, 'Antiochan Date', p. 35, dates the interpolation in the Herodian epoch too. With the interpretation of the interpolation, Nickelsburg, 'Antiochan Date', pp. 35, 38, actually moves back to a position of agreement with Collins.

568. Collins, 'Date and Provenance', p. 17; Brandenburger, 'Himmelfahrt Moses', p. 60; Tromp, *Assumption of Moses*, pp. 116-17, 203-204. As far as Tromp is concerned, it is my opinion that Varus's actions (in 4 BCE!; shortly after that Varus left Syria; see W. John, 'Quinctilius 27. P. Quinctilius Varus', PW, XXIV, cols. 907-84 [917]) could be the historical truth behind the phase the author regards as pre-eschatological, in which only a 'pars' and 'aliqui' will suffer, compared to the eschatological phase. On the basis of his interpretation of *Ass. Mos.* 7, C. Lattey, 'The Messianic Expectation in "the Assumption of Moses"', *CBQ* 4 (1942), pp. 9-21 (13), dates it slightly later, since the Sadducees could only be hated after their influence had grown, which was after 6 CE.

569. Here and elsewhere we will use a broad definition of 'messianic': a person who, depending on God, makes a structural contribution to humankind's salvation. Naturally, Taxo is not an 'Anointed One' in the strict sense of the word (he is neither king, nor priest, nor prophet), but that is not necessary: A.S. van der Woude, ' "Hij zal Zoon des Allerhoogsten genoemd worden…" ', in J.A. Hofman and D. Jorissen (eds.), *Hoogten en diepten* (Festschrift A.A. Spijkerboer; Kampen: Kok, 1993), pp. 137-44 (141). He does, however, contribute to the salvation of Israel: Lattey, 'Messianic Expectation', pp. 16-19. For an overview of the hypotheses, see Tromp, *Assumption of Moses*, pp. 124-28.

570. Such an interruption is unusual in the genre of the testament: Von Nordheim, *Lehre der Alten*, I, p. 202.

136   *The Antichrist Theme in the Intertestamental Period*

Although some of the data in 3.1 and 6.1 remind us of passages we have already discussed, these verses are only portrayed as future from Moses' viewpoint and not as eschatological from the author's viewpoint. Only *Ass. Mos.* 8 can be studied as a depiction of eschatology.

The *Testament of Moses* was written by someone from the wider Pharisaical movement (perhaps from its rigorous internal opposition[571]), who was not influential,[572] and who championed non-violence.[573] It may have been written in Hebrew,[574] but the Latin text which is extant[575] is a translation out of Greek.[576]

b. Ass. Mos. *8*

1   Et cita adveniet[577] in eos ultio et ira quae talis non fuit in illis a saeculo usque ad illum[578] tempus in quo suscitabit[579] illis regem regum terrae et potestatem a

571. Brandenburger, 'Himmelfahrt Moses', p. 65. Cf. Beckwith, 'Daniel 9 and the Date of Messiah's Coming', p. 529; Collins, 'Date and Provenance', pp. 30-32; M.-J. Lagrange *apud* Laperrousaz, 'Testament de Moïse', pp. 90-91; Maggiorotti, 'Datazione', p. 257 (no universalism at all). In my view, *Ass. Mos.* 7.3-4 could refer to the Sadducees. The criticism by Tromp, *Assumption of Moses*, p. 209 n. 3, on the interpretation of 'impii' by Geiger and Charles is unjustified. A pun might be a personal evaluation, but must also have a historical background, and specific accusations are always directed to a specific person or group, even in our time. *Ass. Mos.* 7.6-10 could then be about the mainstream Pharisees. In view of the absence of v. 5 this is certainly possible (*contra* Charles, 'Assumption of Moses', *ad loc.*). Although our interpretation of *Ass. Mos.* 7.6-10 differs from Charles's, our conclusion about its authorship runs parallel to his ('Assumption of Moses', p. 407).

572. Tromp, *Assumption of Moses*, p. 119.

573. Collins, 'Date and Provenance', p. 30; Collins, 'Some Remaining Traditio-Historical Problems', p. 39; cf. Licht, 'Taxo', p. 97; Laperrousaz, 'Testament de Moïse', p. 87.

574. According to Charles, 'Assumption of Moses', p. 410; Laperrousaz, 'Testament de Moïse', pp. 17-25 (Hebrew or Aramaic). Tromp, *Assumption of Moses*, pp. 81, 118, believes this is not proven and opts for a Greek original.

575. We will use the text of Tromp, *Assumption of Moses*, pp. 16, 18, but wish to stay closer to the MS on several points (provided a different interpretation is given) or get closer to the originally intended text (to improve ease of reading). The only MS that is extant is in such a bad condition (E.A. Lowe *apud* Laperrousaz, 'Testament de Moïse', p. 12), that it is not really a problem that Tromp used other editions and has not seen this MS himself (Tromp, *Assumption of Moses*, p. 1 n. 4).

576. Tromp, *Assumption of Moses*, p. 78; Laperrousaz, 'Testament de Moïse', p. 16.

577. Laperrousaz, 'Testament de Moïse', p. 74, prefers to read 'Et altera veniet'.

578. Classical: 'illud'.

579. MS 'suscitavit'. Since the intervocal 'b' was spirantized in popular Latin, a con-

2. The Antichrist in the Apocrypha and Pseudepigrapha 137

    potentia magna, qui confitentes circumcisionem in cruce suspendet.[580]
2 Nam negantes[581] torquebit, et tradet[582] duci vinctos in custodiam,
3 et uxores eorum diis donabuntur[583] gentibus. Et filii eorum pueri secabuntur a medicis pueri[584] inducere acrobistiam illis.
4 Nam illi in eis punientur in tormentis et igne et ferro, et cogentur palam bajulare idola eorum inquinata quomodo sunt pariter contingentibus[585] ea.
5 Et a torquentibus illos pariter cogentur intrare in abditum locum eorum, et cogentur stimulis blasfemare verbum contumeliose. Novissime post haec et leges quod habebunt[586] supra altarium suum.

1 And quickly[587] will come upon them revenge and wrath such as has not been with them from of old until that time when He stirs up for them the king of kings of the earth and might through great power, he who will hang upon a cross those who confess circumcision.
2 Yes,[588] those who deny[589] (it), he will torture, and will hand them over to be led into prison in chains,

---

fusion with 'suscitabit' seems obvious: V. Väänänen, *Introduction au latin vulgaire* (Bibliothèque française et romane. A. Manuels et études linguistiques, 6; Paris: Klincksieck, 3rd edn, 1981), §107; Tromp, *Assumption of Moses*, pp. 34, 55 (§§21, 94).

    580. MS 'suspendit'. Since in popular Latin, the pronunciation of the short 'i' moved towards 'e' (Väänänen, *Introduction au latin vulgaire*, §43), confusion with 'suspendet' seems obvious: Tromp, *Assumption of Moses*, pp. 29-30 (§2); cf. Väänänen, *Introduction au latin vulgaire*, §55.

    581. MS 'necantes'. Apparently 'negantes' was a writing error by the copyist, either because the intervocal 'c' became voiced in popular Latin (thereby becoming a 'g': Väänänen, *Introduction au latin vulgaire*, p. 104), or because the 'C' and 'G' are of similar shape (Tromp, *Assumption of Moses*, p. 34 [§22]). Charles, 'Assumption of Moses', *ad loc.*, has 'celantes' as a cj.

    582. MS: 'tradidit ; Tromp: 'tradit'. Tromp does not go as far as the original cj. of Hilgenfeld ('tradet'; *v. app. crit.* with Tromp), apparently because he tries to explain the error ('tradidit') via the form of 'tradit'. Cf. n. 580 above.

    583. Cj. Tromp: 'disdonabuntur'. NB: there is no consistent division of words in the MS: Charles, 'Assumption of Moses', p. 409, illustrated by Laperrousaz, 'Testament de Moïse', p. 101.

    584. Tromp discards this word.

    585. MS: 'continentibus'.

    586. MS 'haberent'. In view of the similar shape of 'R' and 'B', a confusion with 'habebunt' seems obvious: Tromp, *Assumption of Moses*, p. 14 (*app. crit.* with *Ass. Mos.* 6.7).

    587. Laperrousaz: 'another' or 'a new'. Tromp, *Assumption of Moses*, p. 216, prefers not to translate with 'quickly' but with 'suddenly'. However, the writer is trying to indicate that the readers will not have to wait for the end times much longer. Also lexically 'quickly' is more obvious.

    588. Tromp, *Assumption of Moses*, p. 69 (§145) (*pace* Tromp, *Assumption of Moses*, p. 146); already in classical Latin: see P.G.W. Glare (ed.), *Oxford Latin Dictionary*

3   and their spouses will be given to the gods among the nations. And their sons will be operated upon as children by paediatricians, to give them their foreskins.[590]
4   Yes, they will be punished by[591] them with torture and fire and the sword, and they will be forced to openly carry their gods around,[592] who are unclean, as are those who touch them.[593]
5   They will also be forced by their torturers to go into their hidden place, and they will be forced with goads to offensively insult the Word.[594] Finally, after this, the Laws as well, by[595] what they will have upon their altars.

After the pre-eschatological period described in *Ass. Mos.* 7, the most sorrowful time will come. It will even be more serious than during the time of Varus, described in 6.8-9[596] (v. 1a). God Himself will cause a great evil-doer to rise up. This 'king of the kings[597] of the earth' cannot really point to Antiochus IV. It could refer to the Roman emperor,[598] but rather as a

(Oxford: Clarendon Press, 1982), *s.v.*, 1 and 4; cf. Väänänen, *Introduction au latin vulgaire*, p. 370.

589. MS: 'kill'; Tromp: 'deny'; Charles: 'hide'.

590. Different, but also keeping the second 'pueri', Brandenburger, 'Himmelfahrt Moses', *ad loc.* ('Knabenvorhaut').

591. See Tromp, *Assumption of Moses*, p. 46 (§70).

592. For the choice of words, see Tromp, *Assumption of Moses*, p. 38 (§36).

593. MS: 'guard'? See Laperrousaz, 'Testament de Moïse', *ad loc.* The construction remains difficult, even after the explanation of Tromp, *Assumption of Moses*, p. 75 (§171), as appears from his 'must'. Because of the construction with 'quomodo' the situation is not quite comparable to A. Ernout and F. Thomas, *Syntaxe latine* (Nouvelle collection à l'usage des classes, 38; Paris: Klincksieck, 2nd edn [5th edn], 1972), §82. The alternative, 'as they are for those who touch/guard them', is not at all satisfactory.

594. Possibly: 'the Name (of God)'.

595. Tromp, *Assumption of Moses*, p. 76 (§174). The antecedent can be dropped, even where it would not take the same case as the relative pronoun: Väänänen, *Introduction au latin vulgaire*, §371.

596. Laperrousaz, 'Testament de Moïse', *ad loc.* For the formula 'quae talis non fuit…' see Berger, *Die griechische Daniel-Diegese*, pp. 70-74. Although 'altera' could refer to a final, eschatological punishment (Collins, 'Date and Provenance', p. 20), the mention of 'in eos' pleads for the restoration of 'cita adveniet'. Cf. J. Priest, 'Testament of Moses', *OTP*, I, pp. 919-34 (*ad loc.*).

597. The title 'king of kings' was already in use with the Assyrian king Tukulti-Ninurta (end of the thirteenth century): R. Borger, *Einleitung in die assyrischen Königsinschriften*. I. *Das zweite Jahrtausend v. Chr.* (HO, 1.5.1.1; Leiden: E.J. Brill, 2nd edn, 1964), p. 74.

598. Laperrousaz, 'Testament de Moïse', *ad loc.*

2. The Antichrist in the Apocrypha and Pseudepigrapha 139

'superlative' king, after the kings in 3.1, 6.1 and 6.8.[599] The evildoer will not crucify *some* believers, as Varus did ('aliqui' in 6.9),[600] but *all* believers who confess circumcision, that is, Jewish religion. Tromp defends the translation 'renounce'[601] for 'negare' in this context, and claims that this second group will be tortured[602] but not killed. This leads to a very rationalistic interpretation indeed, and the following verses do not give the impression that this passage only refers to people who deny their Jewish beliefs and their relatives. A less technical translation of 'negantes' (or of Charles's conjecture 'celantes'), 'those who deny, who hide', seems to be a better choice (vv. 1b-2). The spouses (v. 3a) and children (v. 3b-5) are defiled in many ways. 'Illi' (v. 4a) sounds strange, but grammatically it seems to refer to the 'filii'; this would mean that all of vv. 3b-5 is about the children, which is not impossible in view of the content of the passage.

Crucifixion took place under the Hasmonean king Alexander Janneus,[603] but probably not under the Seleucid king Antiochus IV; Flavius Josephus's testimony concerning this[604] has been debated.[605] No historical parallels are noted for v. 2. If the 'squandering' of the women indicates prostitution,[606] this threat could be based on practices attested in the time of Antiochus IV.[607] If the text could be slightly amended, however, we would

---

599. Cf. Tromp, *Assumption of Moses*, pp. 60 (§113), 162, 217 (*ad* 3.1; 6.8).

600. There were two thousand of them (Josephus, *Ant.* 17.295), but according to the writer, the Jewish people would suffer much more in eschatological times.

601. Tromp, *Assumption of Moses*, p. 217.

602. Tromp, *Assumption of Moses*, p. 218.

603. Josephus, *Ant.* 13.380; the reference to 4QpNa (4Q169) 1.7-8 by Laperrousaz, 'Testament de Moïse', *ad loc.*, is inaccurate, since Alexander Janneus is not mentioned there by name (cf. F.F. Bruce, *Second Thoughts on the Dead Sea Scrolls* [Grand Rapids: Eerdmans, 2nd edn, 1961], p. 79). That passage has even been applied to Antiochus IV: H.H. Rowley, 'The Kittim and the Dead Sea Scrolls', *PEQ* 88 (1956), pp. 92-109 (107-109). In any case, Jews who were faithful to the law were opposed to the actions of the later Hasmonean kings; see *Pss. Sol.*

604. Josephus, *Ant.* 12.256.

605. Laperrousaz, 'Testament de Moïse', *ad loc.* This doubt has its drawbacks, since Josephus is generally a trustworthy source.

606. Tromp, *Assumption of Moses*, p. 218 n. 4, finds this difficult, because the author of the *Assumption of Moses* would avoid using such a euphemism. It could be remarked that perhaps the word is not really that euphemistic. There is, however, a lexical problem. Would 'deus' be used in the *Assumption of Moses* in the meaning of 'idol'?

607. See 2 Macc. 6.4. Thus Laperrousaz, 'Testament de Moïse', *ad loc.*, with addition of 'in' (in the text or in thought) with 'gentibus'. 'Diis' is a normal form of 'deus' and does not need amendment into 'deis'.

be dealing with the verb 'disdonare', which would mean that the women were sold as slaves to foreign lands after being captured in the war.[608] For this we refer to an order issued by Antiochus IV after his second return from Egypt.[609] Antiochus IV did indeed forbid circumcision,[610] but never ordered corrective surgery.[611] This means that we are dealing with the expectation of a persecution that will be even worse than during the reign of Antiochus IV.[612] The combination of 'sword and fire' also occurs in Dan. 11.33 (בחרב ובלהבה). The problem with the idols is reminiscent of something attributed to Antiochus IV in 2 Macc. 6.7b, but that is a difficult passage.[613] It is unclear whether the Jews will be forced to enter[614] the Holy of Holies, or the *cella* of the pagan temples, the part where the image of the idol stood.[615] Actually both possibilities have no historical parallels,[616] but there is a slight grammatical and lexical preference for the second possibility.[617] 'Verbum' may be a metaphrase of God here (as a translation of שם[618]). Another possibility is that it refers to the word spoken by God, but

---

608. Tromp, *Assumption of Moses*, pp. 218-19; cf. Laperrousaz, 'Testament de Moïse', *ad loc.*

609. Tromp, *Assumption of Moses*, p. 219. See 1 Macc. 1.32 and 2 Macc. 5.24 (in 168; see Lorein, 'Life and Death', p. 161).

610. See 1 Macc. 1.48 and Josephus, *War* 1.34.

611. This surgery was carried out, however: see 1 Macc. 1.15; Nelis, *I Makkabeeën*, *ad loc.*; Tromp, *Assumption of Moses*, p. 219. (Both scholars give medical details.) R.G. Hall, 'Epispasm and the Dating of Ancient Jewish Writings', *JSP* 2 (1988), pp. 71-86 (71-72, 74-76, 82), points out that corrective surgery did take place from the times of Jason until rabbinical days, but mainly during the first century CE. In view of the importance of circumcision to the Covenant, this part of the persecution could be described as a compulsory break with the Covenant. *Jubilees* 15.33 has been referred to in this context (e.g. Hengel, *Judentum und Hellenismus*, p. 528), but this text is not very clear.

612. Hall, 'Epispasm', p. 73.

613. Cf. *3 Macc.* 2.29.

614. Laperrousaz, 'Testament de Moïse', *ad loc.*

615. Tromp, *Assumption of Moses*, pp. 220-21.

616. The passages to which Laperrousaz refers are not very specific.

617. Grammatical: the use of 'eorum': cf. n. 622. Lexical: the use of 'cella': Tromp, *Assumption of Moses*, p. 221.

618. No hypostasis! The examples are actually quite late: V. Hamp, *Der Begriff 'Wort' in den aramäischen Bibelübersetzungen: Ein exegetischer Beitrag zur Hypostasen-Frage und zur Geschichte der Logos-Spekulationen* (Munich: Neuer Filser-Verlag, 1938), pp. 138-39; Laperrousaz, 'Testament de Moïse', *ad loc.*; cf. Collins, 'Date and Provenance', p. 20; K. Beyer, *Die aramäischen Texte vom Toten Meer samt den Inschriften aus Palästina, dem Testament Levis aus Kairoer Genisa, der Fasten-*

in that would case it would be strange that there is no adjunct[619] in the sentence. There is no known parallel of people being forced to slander the Word. What is above the altar could be a reference to the βδέλυγμα τῆς ἐρημώσεως, if the altar in question is the original Temple altar;[620] if it is altars anywhere in the country, this may be a reference to the pork on pagan altars.[621] The second explanation would imply that more people will personally be forced to do something against the Laws; in an eschatological perspective this explanation therefore deserves our preference.[622]

c. *The Antichrist in the* Assumption of Moses
In *Ass. Mos.* 8 we find many elements of our Antichrist definition. Before we started our detailed discussion of this chapter, we have shown that an eschatological picture is definitely given here.[623] There is mention of an *individual* evildoer in the eschatological period, which makes this passage remarkable. Tromp's comparisons to all kinds of *multiple* or *collective* enemies[624] fall short on this important point.

The king of the kings of the earth is clearly portrayed as a tyrant. He has enormous power: this is already clear from his title ('regem regum terrae') and also from the remark that follows ('potestatem a potentia magna'). His terrible tyrannical actions, worse than ever before, will focus on Jewish religious life. He will crucify and torture Jewish people, whether they openly confess, or try to deny their identity; he will not only medically remove their sons from Judaism, but also force them to slander the Word and the Law (which is an active form of lawlessness). But this is not all; in

---

rolle und den alten talmudischen Zitaten (Göttingen: Vandenhoeck & Ruprecht, 1984), *s.v.*

619. Tromp, *Assumption of Moses*, p. 221.
620. See Lorein, 'Life and Death', p. 166.
621. Tromp, *Assumption of Moses*, pp. 221-22. Cf. 1 Macc. 1.47.
622. It is also advisable to either see the Temple twice in v. 5a and v. 5b, or not to see it in either of these verses. According to the classical syntax of eius/suus this seems the best explanation: cf. Tromp, *Assumption of Moses*, p. 43 (§57) (*pace* his p. 44 [§57]). We could wonder whether the author of the *Assumption of Moses* thought of a repetition of τὸ βδέλυγμα τῆς ἐρημώσεως in eschatological times. (This is the case in Mt. 24.15/Mk 13.14.)
623. For the eschatology of the *Assumption of Moses*, see, e.g., Laperrousaz, 'Testament de Moïse', pp. 85-86, who rightly remarks that there is no mention of a Kingdom of Peace in this writing (p. 85).
624. Tromp, *Assumption of Moses*, p. 214.

his hatred[625] he will also lead his victims into idolatry; he will sacrifice the women to idols and force the children to take part in idolatry.

The relationship of the king of the kings of the earth to Satan is not discussed directly. The text says that God will rise him up (v. 1), but that does not take away his function (and any possible dependence on Satan).[626] Noack remarks that, against all expectation, it is not the Antichrist's downfall that is discussed in *Ass. Mos.* 10.1, but Satan's, which creates a relationship between the two figures.[627] Of course such a substitution does not reveal any extra information concerning the nature of their relationship.

This figure looks very much like the Seleucid king Antiochus IV, not only because of the historical parallels, but also because of the description we can now give of him on the basis of our Antichrist definition: he will be active in the religious area, but mainly by politico-military means, and not so much through temptation. How this king will see himself (in the area of religion) is not mentioned. This is not the first time that Antiochus IV is used to fill in a typical figure in the Pseudepigrapha,[628] but here in the Testament of Moses it is clearer than ever.

14. *2 Enoch*

a. *Setting*

Any study of *2 Enoch* will be complicated by a number of factors: the language, the variations in verse numbering, the existence of two different versions of different lengths. The short version does not contain any Christian elements and is probably the oldest.[629] A later Christian expansion

---

625. Tromp, *Assumption of Moses*, p. 215.
626. For the theology proper of the *Assumption of Moses*, see Laperrousaz, 'Testament de Moïse', pp. 80-81. Cf. Tromp, *Assumption of Moses*, p. 216, and Maggiorotti, 'Datazione', p. 256 (on Antiochus IV!).
627. Noack, *Satanás und Sotería*, p. 31.
628. See *Sib. Or.* 3.388-92 and 3.608-15.
629. For the priority of the short version see A. Vaillant, *Le livre des secrets d'Hénoch: Texte slave et traduction française* (Textes publiés par l'Institut d'Etudes slaves, 4; Paris: Institut d'Etudes slaves, 1952), p. iv; U. Fischer, *Eschatologie und Jenseitserwartung im hellenistischen Diasporajudentum* (BZNW, 44; Berlin: W. de Gruyter, 1978), pp. 37-38; E. Turdeanu, *Apocryphes slaves et roumains de l'Ancien Testament* (SVTP, 5; Leiden: E.J. Brill, 1981), pp. 37-38 [sic]; Philonenko, 'Livre des secrets d'Hénoch', in Dupont-Sommer and Philonenko, *Ecrits intertestamentaires*, pp. 1165-1223 (1168); Denis, *Introduction*, p. 28; Sacchi, *Apocalittica*, pp. 302-303.

2. The Antichrist in the Apocrypha and Pseudepigrapha 143

probably resulted in the long version.[630] We will study the short version here.

There is no full consensus about the date of the first two main parts of *2 Enoch*, but we can say that its short version was written by a Jewish person, during the first century CE and before 70 CE, and apparently in Egypt.[631] We may therefore assume that this text is still within the domain of our study.

It is harder to date the third main part, mainly because—through Charles's influence—it has been studied less.[632] However, there are sufficient indications to assume that this third main part is an integral part of the short, Jewish version of *2 Enoch*,[633] and therefore also belongs to our study domain. Böttrich attempts to classify *2 Enoch* even more specifically within the general apocalyptic[634] genre: he claims that the third main part is mainly legend, and that *2 En.* 70.3-10 is the account of a vision.[635]

---

630. Vaillant, *Livre des secrets d'Hénoch*, p. v; Fischer, *Eschatologie und Jenseitserwartung*, p. 39.

631. J.J. Collins, 'The Genre Apocalypse in Hellenistic Judaism', in D. Hellholm (ed.), *Apocalypticism in the Mediterranean World and the Near East* (Tübingen: J.C.B. Mohr, 1983), pp. 531-48 (533-34); C. Böttrich, *Weltweisheit, Menschheitsethik, Urkult: Studien zum slavischen Henochbuch* (WUNT, 2.50; Tübingen: J.C.B. Mohr, 1992), pp. 197-99, 201-202; Fischer, *Eschatologie und Jenseitserwartung*, pp. 39-41; M. Philonenko, 'La cosmogonie du "livre des secrets d'Hénoch"', in P. Derchain (ed.), *Religions en Egypte Hellénistique et Romaine* (Paris: PUF, 1969), pp. 109-16 (109-10); Vaillant, *Livre des secrets d'Hénoch*, p. iv; M.E. Stone, 'Apocalyptic Literature', in Stone (ed.), *Jewish Writings of the Second Temple Period*, pp. 383-441 (306-307); Vriezen and Van der Woude, *Oudisraëlitische en vroegjoodse literatuur*, p. 470; B.A. Pearson, 'Jewish Sources in Gnostic Literature', in Stone (ed.), *Jewish Writings of the Second Temple Period*, pp. 443-81 (455). Not necessarily Egypt: Sacchi, *Apocalittica*, pp. 304, 308; F.I. Andersen, '2 (Slavonic Apocalypse of) Enoch', *OTP*, I, pp. 91-221 (96-97) (God-fearing men?). For later adaptations to the short version, see Böttrich, *Weltweisheit, Menschheitsethik, Urkult*, pp. 128-29.

632. In R.H. Charles and W.R. Morfill, *The Book of the Secrets of Enoch* (Oxford: Clarendon Press, 1896), it has been included as an appendix; in *APOT* it is not included at all. This part is also from N. Bonwetsch, *Das slavische Henochbuch* (Abhandlungen der Königlichen Gesellschaft der Wissenschaften zu Göttingen. Philologisch-historische Klasse, 1.3; Berlin: Weidmann, 1896). Fischer, *Eschatologie und Jenseitserwartung*, p. 40, views the Melchisedek story as secondary.

633. Böttrich, *Weltweisheit, Menschheitsethik, Urkult*, pp. 125, 147-49, 196-201; A. Caquot, 'La pérennité du sacerdoce', in *Paganisme, judaïsme, christianisme: Influences et affrontements dans le monde antique* (Festschrift M. Simon; Paris: de Boccard, 1978), pp. 109-16 (109); Sacchi, *Apocalittica*, p. 307.

634. See Collins, 'Genre Apocalypse', p. 532, but also Sacchi, *Apocalittica*, p. 318

A number of elements can be pointed out in *2 Enoch* that are also present in the New Testament,[636] but that does not mean that these elements have been copied from it, since the New Testament made use of Old Testament data.[637] Furthermore, there are also elements that a Christian author could hardly have used.[638] In the tenth century the book may have been translated by monks in Bulgaria from Greek into Old Church Slavonic.[639] The Hebraisms do not necessarily indicate that the work must originally have been written in Hebrew.[640]

The function Böttrich attributes to *2 Enoch*[641] can be compared to that of the *Sibylline Oracles*. In a sense they are apologetical towards the outside world (making outsiders more appreciative of Judaism), but they were mainly intended for internal use and reflection (making Jews indifferent to paganism).[642]

(third main part far removed), and Andersen, '2 Enoch', p. 91 (midrash with apocalyptic material).

635. Böttrich, *Weltweisheit, Menschheitsethik, Urkult*, p. 210.

636. A. Rubinstein, 'Observations on the Slavonic Book of Enoch', *JJS* 13 (1961), pp. 1-21 (14), uses this as a basis for his supposition of a Christian origin.

637. Fischer, *Eschatologie und Jenseitserwartung*, p. 39; Böttrich, *Weltweisheit, Menschheitsethik, Urkult*, p. 125; Sacchi, *Apocalittica*, p. 306.

638. Collins, 'Genre Apocalypse', p. 533; Andersen, '2 Enoch', pp. 96-97; Caquot, 'Pérennité du sacerdoce', pp. 111, 113. Based on the importance the author attributed to the priestly service, Caquot, 'Pérennité du sacerdoce', pp. 113, 115, supposes an Essene origin; cf. Philonenko, 'Cosmogonie', p. 116. S. Pines, 'Eschatology and the Concept of Time in the Slavonic Book of Enoch', in R.J.Z. Werblowsky and C.J. Bleeker (eds.), *Types of Redemption* (Studies in the History of Religions [NumenSup], 18; Leiden: E.J. Brill, 1970), pp.72-87 (75), doubts this, and it hardly seems to match the generally accepted hypothesis that the writing originates from the Egyptian diaspora. (Philonenko, 'Cosmogonie', p. 116, deduces from *2 Enoch* that several very different movements must have converged in Egypt.)

639. Böttrich, *Weltweisheit, Menschheitsethik, Urkult*, pp. 103, 105; Vaillant, *Livre des secrets d'Hénoch*, pp. i, viii, xii-xiii; Van der Woude, 'Nabloeiers en uitlopers', p. 470; Philonenko, 'Livre des secrets d'Hénoch', p. c.

640. Pines, 'Eschatology and the Concept of Time', p. 73; Andersen, '2 Enoch', p. 94; Stone, 'Apocalyptic Literature', p. 406, keep that possibility open.

641. Böttrich, *Weltweisheit, Menschheitsethik, Urkult*, pp. 208, 211-14.

642. Cf. Hengel, 'Anonymität, Pseudepigraphie und "Literarische Fälschung"', pp. 306-307.

2. The Antichrist in the Apocrypha and Pseudepigrapha 145

b. 2 Enoch 70.5-7 (69.7-9)[643]

5 (7) *Jako vo dni ego*[644] *budet*[645] *nestroenie*[646] *veliko po zemli, zane vzavidě*[647] *člověkŭ iskrenemu svoemu, i ljudie na ljudi* ₃*sogrězjat sja i jazykŭ na jazykŭ vozmuti rati, napolnit sja vsja* ₄*zemlja krovi i nestroenia zla;*

6 (8) *k tomu že ostavjat tvorca svoego* ₅*i poklonjat sja utverženiemŭ na nebesi i choženiemŭ po zemli i* ₆*volnam moŕiskymŭ, i vŭzveličit sja protivnik i poraduet sja o dělech* ₇*ichŭ v raždelenie moe.*

7 (9) *Vsja zemlja prěměniti ustroenie svoe i* ₈*vesi plodŭ i vsja trava premenjati vremena svoja; počajuti bo* ₉*vremeni pogybelnago. I vsi jazyci izměnjat sja na zemli i vŭ sŭžale* ₁₀*nie moe.*

5 (7) For in [Nir's] days there will be a great chaos on earth, because man has begun[648] to envy[649] his neighbour, and people will attack people and nation will wage war against nation, the whole earth will be filled with blood and evil chaos;

6 (8) Moreover, they will abandon their Creator, and worship mountings in the sky and movements on the earth and sea waves, and an[650] adversary will glorify himself and rejoice in their acts, to my distress.

7 (9) The whole earth will change its order, and all fruit, all herbs will change their seasons, for they will await the time of destruction. And all nations will change on earth, to my distress.

---

643. In order to link up with Charles's tradition as much as possible, and to be able to refer to the long version as well, we will use the chapter and verse numberings of *OTP*; the references in brackets are according to *Ecrits intertestamentaires*. The lines of the edition of Vaillant, *Livre des secrets d'Hénoch*, p. 70 (= p. [35]), are also given in the transcription and the translation. According to the chapter division he uses (originally from the edition by Sokolov: see Philonenko, 'Livre des secrets d'Hénoch', p. 1168), this is ch. XXII.

Thanks to Dr H. Seldeslachts I have obtained some insight in the source text of this passage.

644. This non-reflexive possessive pronoun refers to Nir, who is mentioned in the previous verse.

645. All verb forms in this text except *vzavidě* are perfective presents with the value of a future.

646. *Ne-* (negative) + *stroenie* (verbal subst. with *stroiti*, 'arranging'); cf. *ustroenie* in v. 7 (v. 9).

647. Aor. of *vzaviděti*, 'envy' (perfective of *zaviděti*). MS *vzanavidě*. (Possibly instead of *vznenavidě*, aor. of *vznenaviděti*, 'hate' (perfective of *nenaviděti*), but in that case we would expect an acc. instead of a dative.)

648. The only verb of this text that is in past tense.

649. MS 'hate' (if the reading is *vznenavidě*).

650. Or 'the': Old Church Slavonic does not have the articles.

This passage describes how, before the time of Nir, who was the apocryphal brother of Noah, God announced a period of sorrow, both in the social and the military domain, to Methuselah. People will even start to worship stars, animals and fish,[651] that is, all kinds of idols.[652] Because of this, an Opponent will triumph. The word *protivnik* is a term that is used for Satan in some instances,[653] but the word could of course indicate another figure. Even nature will suffer. Also the people will change, but it is unclear what that means. What is clear, however, is that everything seems to point to destruction.

c. *The Antichrist in* 2 *Enoch*
These verses seem to refer to the Flood, not to an eschatological period. However, Böttrich states that *2 Enoch* does not have a chronological linear eschatology, and that the writing assumes the concurrence of an upper world and a lower world (earth). The eschatological event takes place in the interface of the earthly and the upper world,[654] whereby the Flood plays a specific role.[655]

Although Böttrich is right in saying that *2 Enoch* does not strive for the Eschaton as much as other apocalypses,[656] the story definitely contains chronology. It shows how the earthly priesthood has come to an end through the ascension of Melchizedek, the eternal priest, and judgment by the Flood as a finishing point is referred to throughout the book, as Böttrich admits himself.[657] With 70.5 (69.7) we can also refer to Jesus' sermon on the end

---

651. Philonenko, 'Livre des secrets d'Hénoch', *ad loc.* Vaillant, *Livre des secrets d'Hénoch*, *ad loc.*, with reference to Exod. 20.4.
652. Böttrich, *Weltweisheit, Menschheitsethik, Urkult*, p. 186.
653. Andersen, '2 Enoch', *ad loc.*; Philonenko, 'Livre des secrets d'Hénoch', *ad loc.*
654. Böttrich, *Weltweisheit, Menschheitsethik, Urkult*, pp. 167-69; cf. Fischer, *Eschatologie und Jenseitserwartung*, pp. 53-62. Is there an Iranian influence here? See Philonenko, 'Cosmogonie', pp. 112-16, but also Sacchi, *Apocalittica*, p. 315. Andersen, '2 Enoch', pp. 91, 96-97, points out that *2 Enoch* does not have a systematic world view.
655. Böttrich, *Weltweisheit, Menschheitsethik, Urkult*, p. 181.
656. Böttrich, *Weltweisheit, Menschheitsethik, Urkult*, p. 167; cf. Sacchi, *Apocalittica*, p. 311.
657. Böttrich, *Weltweisheit, Menschheitsethik, Urkult*, p. 125; cf. Fischer, *Eschatologie und Jenseitserwartung*, pp. 42-53; Collins, 'Genre Apocalypse', p. 537; Sacchi, *Apocalittica*, p. 300.

2. The Antichrist in the Apocrypha and Pseudepigrapha

times (Mk 13.8; Mt. 24.7).[658] The change of seasons refers to the end of the age.[659]

On the basis of this, I believe we can view this text in an eschatological perspective, and to analyze it in view of our definition of the Antichrist.

In this text, terrible things are happening in the area of military and religion, all within an eschatological framework, and all of mankind is involved. Animals are being worshipped, and there are no indications that these animals represent anything else. During all this an (individual) Opponent is present. It is unclear how great his influence is and where it is exercised.

Actually, we have arrived at the same situation we arrived at when studying the oldest parts: there are elements, there is room for the Antichrist, but there is no systematic picture of the Antichrist to speak of. In studying the oldest writings we would have called this a remarkable result; in this period the result must be called very meagre indeed.

---

658. The link is also clear in the long version of 70.10.
659. Andersen, '2 Enoch', *ad loc.*

Chapter 3

THE ANTICHRIST IN THE QUMRAN WRITINGS

1. *Introduction*

In this chapter we will continue the research of the previous chapter by focusing on the documents found in Qumran. To a certain degree, the Qumran documents form a separate category that has generated its own secondary literature (even in enormous quantities).

As before, we will be building on the work of others. We will assume that in general the person who has studied a specific writing in depth will know the writing better than we do. In my discussion of the texts I shall not strive for completeness, but only focus on our theme. For example, higher textual criticism and literary-critical research will not be taken into account unless we have reason to believe that they are of importance to the meaning the text in question had at the height of its importance.

As before, we will be looking for any chronological development. Fortunately the texts that are of most interest to our theme and that will be discussed in this chapter can be dated with some degree of certainty. There are a few instances where only palaeographic dating is possible, but even in those instances the time in which a document was copied will give a clear indication of the period in which the Qumran Community was interested in it. We will therefore start our overview with the oldest documents written at Qumran. Texts that were kept there but did not originate there will as much as possible be discussed in relation to texts that did originate there or at least to their functioning within the Qumran Community.

The Qumran Community was a communal cult,[1] and although its writ-

---

1. For the cult in general, see F. Boerwinkel, *Kerk en secte* (The Hague: Boekencentrum, 1953), pp. 17, 20-25; L.A. Coser, *Greedy Institutions: Patterns of Undivided Commitment* (New York: Free Press; London: Collier Macmillan, 1974), pp. 14, 16, 106-107; R. Enroth, *Youth, Brainwashing, and the Extremist Cults* (Grand Rapids:

ings are marginal in the same way in which the Apocalyptic Apocrypha are marginal writings, they belong to the documents from that period that are by far the most relevant to us, both in terms of the understanding of the Old Testament in those days and of the understanding of the New Testament in our time.[2]

Zondervan; Exeter: Paternoster Press, 1977), pp. 121, 155, 159-64, 166-68; W.R. Martin, *The Kingdom of the Cults* (Minneapolis: Bethany Fellowship, 3rd edn, 1977), pp. 18-24, 26, 32-33; G. Vanacker, *De Religieuze Sekten: Religie, waanzin of bedrog?* (Kapellen: DNB-Pelckmans, 1986), pp. 33-34, 42, 44, 85, 89. For the Qumran Community as a cult, see J. Carmignac, 'Les esséniens et la Communauté de Qumrân', in A. George and P. Grelot (eds.), *Introduction à la Bible*. III 1. *Au seuil de l'ère chrétienne* (Paris: Desclée, 1976), pp. 142-61 (143); J. Duhaime, 'Relative Deprivation in New Religious Movements and the Qumran Community', *RevQ* 16 (1993), pp. 265-76 (266-67, 272, 274); W.S. LaSor, 'Interpretation and Infallibility: Lessons from the Dead Sea Scrolls', in C.A. Evans and W.F. Stinespring (eds.), *Early Jewish and Christian Exegesis* (Mem. W.H. Brownlee; Scholars Press Homage Series; Atlanta: Scholars Press, 1987), pp. 123-37 (130-32, 134); M. Weinfeld, *The Organizational Pattern and the Penal Code of the Qumran Sect: A Comparison with Guilds and Religious Associations of the Hellenistic–Roman Period* (NTOA, 2; Fribourg: Editions Universitaires; Göttingen: Vandenhoeck & Ruprecht, 1986), pp. 24, 29-30, 35.

For the general historical framework in which I see the Qumran writings, see F. García Martínez and A.S. van der Woude, 'A "Groningen" Hypothesis of Qumran Origins and Early History', *RevQ* 14 (1990), pp. 521-41 (536-41); Beckwith, 'Pre-History, pp. 6, 16; Lorein, '4Q448, pp. 270-73.

2. The views of the Qumran Community were well-known in Jerusalem: cf. H. Gabrion, 'L'interprétation de l'Ecriture à Qumrān', *ANRW*, II 19.1 (1979), pp. 779-848 (830-37). There are no explicit responses to their views in the New Testament, only implicit: an interesting example by D. Flusser, 'The Parable of the Unjust Steward: Jesus' Criticism of the Essenes', in J.H. Charlesworth (ed.), *Jesus and the Dead Sea Scrolls* (Garden City, NY: Doubleday, 1992), pp. 176-98; see also A.S. van der Woude, 'Fakten contra Phantasien: die Bedeutung der Rollen vom Toten Meer für die Bibelwissenschaft und die Kunde des Frühjudentums', in F. García Martínez and E. Noort (eds.), *Perspectives in the Study of the Old Testament and Early Judaism* (Festschrift A.S. van der Woude; VTSup, 73; Leiden: E.J. Brill, 1998), pp. 249-71 (268-70), H. Kvalbein, 'The Wonders of the End-Time. Metaphoric language in 4Q521 and the interpretation of Matthew 11.5 par.', *JSP* 18 (1998), pp. 87-110 (110), and M. Broshi, 'Hatred—An Essene Religious Principle and Its Christian Consequences', in B. Kollmann, W. Reinbold and A. Steudel (eds.), *Antikes Judentum und Frühes Christentum* (Festschrift H. Stegemann; BZNW, 97; Berlin: W. de Gruyter, 1999), pp. 245-52 (I assume only the first part of Broshi's reasoning is correct: Jesus reacted *against* the Essene teaching).

2. Pseudo-Ezekiel

a. Setting

Pseudo-Ezekiel is a writing compiled by Ms. Dimant from the following manuscripts: 4Q385 (4QpsEzek[a]), 4Q386 (4QpsEzek[b]), 4Q387 (4QpsEzek[c]), 4Q388 (4QpsEzek[d]) and 4Q391 (4QpsEzek[e] pap).[3] On palaeographic grounds it should be dated in the second half of the second century.[4] Whether it originates from the Qumran Community is unclear.[5]

b. *4QpsEzek (4Q386) ii 3-6*[6]

(3) ויאמ[ר] יהוה בן בליעל יחשב לענות את עמי (4) [ול]א אניחלו[8] ומשרו[7]
לאיהיה: (5) ואת (6) הרשע אהרג במף:

(ii 3) And the LORD said, 'A son of Belial will consider to suppress my people, (4) but I will not let him have (it) and his dominion will not last.' (5) And (6) I shall kill the evil one in Moph.

In this text, God answers Ezekiel's question whether Israel will be restored (i 1-2) by saying that someone who is dependent on Belial will first attempt to suppress God's people. We may deduce from this that the 'son

---

3. D. Dimant, 'New Light from Qumran on the Jewish Pseudepigrapha—4Q390', in J. Trebolle Barrera and L. Vegas Montaner (eds.), *The Madrid Qumran Congress* (STDJ, 11; Leiden: E.J. Brill; Madrid: Complutense, 1992), pp. 405-48 (409).

4. M. Smith, '4Q391. 4QpapPseudo-Ezekiel[e]', in M. Broshi *et al.*, *Qumran Cave 4. XIV. Parabiblical Texts, Part 2* (DJD, 19; Oxford: Clarendon Press, 1995), pp. 153-93 (154).

5. J. Strugnell and D. Dimant, '*4Q* Second Ezekiel', *RevQ* 13 (1988), pp. 45-58 (46-47); Dimant, 'New Light', p. 409.

6. We will work from the text and numbering by F. García Martínez and E.J.C. Tigchelaar, *The Dead Sea Scrolls Study Edition*. II. *4Q274–11Q31* (Leiden: E.J. Brill, 1998), *ad loc.*, with a small amendment according to PAM 42.598, as rendered by R.H. Eisenman and J.M. Robinson, *Facsimile Edition of the Dead Sea Scrolls* (Washington: Biblical Archaeology Society, 1991), Plate 921.

7. St. cstr. sg. m. + suff. 3 sg. m. of a masculine pendant of משרה. This word does not occur in the Old Testament, nor in the lists of E. Qimron, *The Hebrew of the Dead Sea Scrolls* (HSS, 29; Atlanta: Scholars, 1986), §§500.1-3.

8. García Martínez and Tigchelaar, *Study Edition*, II, *ad loc.*, read a form of the verb נוח, a space and then prep. + suffix. The space is not visible, but it is possible that the copier made a wrong estimation of the distance (because of the way ל was written). The way it is written here has the disadvantage of assuming a wrong placing of the י (hiphil imperf. 1 sg. + suff. 3 sg. m. of נחל).

of Belial' is not himself one of God's people.⁹ The combination of בליעל and the verb חשב is reminiscent of Nah. 1.11, especially in the version of the Targum, where עם occurs as well¹⁰ (as a buffer for the name of God). That biblical passage refers to Mesopotamia, as does 4Q386 1 iii. The combination of בן and the verb ענה could be a reference to Ps. 89.23 and here too the Targum brings us closer, because instead of עולה it uses a word which also occurs in 4Q386 1 ii 6, רשיעא.¹¹ Of course one may wonder what the value is of parallels that have fewer than a handful of words in common, but it is important that Ps. 89 refers to the opponent of the Anointed One.¹² Apparently there will be a short period of suppression, but this will not be permanent. Eventually God will have the victory (ii 3-4). That does not mean, however, that this will result in a perfect situation (ii 4-5).

In spite of it all, God will kill the Wicked One (הרשע) in Moph. This name also occurs in Hos. 9.6, where it refers to Memphis, which for many centuries remained the capital of Lower Egypt. Elsewhere, for example, in Ezek. 30.13, 16, this city is called Noph. These different names can all be explained from the Egyptian name Mennefer.¹³ The two passages mentioned here are also the two that can shed the most light on this passage. Ezekiel 30.1-19 is an oracle in which judgment is announced on Egypt, and this could also be the background against which these lines from *Pseudo-Ezekiel* must be placed. Ezekiel 30.13 mentions Noph and also the death of the ruler¹⁴ (which marks the end of the dynasty).¹⁵ In Hos. 9.1-6, the prophet

---

9. D. Dimant, '*4Q386 ii-iii. A Prophecy on Hellenistic Kingdoms?*', *RevQ* 18 (1998), pp. 511-29 (523). It is possible (in contrast to what is said by Dimant, '*4Q386*', p. 515) to interpret בליעל as a name here, since the name occurs not only in the Qumran Community, but also in apocryphal literature.

10. Dimant, '*4Q386*', p. 514. (The meaning in MT is the same as in *Tg*.)

11. Text according to L. Díez Merino, *Targum de Salmos: Edición Príncipe del MS. Villa Amil n. 5 de Alfonso de Zamora* (Bibliotheca Hispana Biblica, 6; Poliglota Complutense. Tradición sefardí de la Biblia Aramea 4, 1; Madrid: Instituto 'Francisco Suárez', 1982). This parallel was also added by Dimant, '*4Q386*', p. 514.

12. J. Ridderbos, *De Psalmen*. II. *Psalm 42–106* (Commentaar op het Oude Testament; Kampen: Kok, 1958), p. 385.

13. E. Drioton and J. Vandier, *L'Egypte: Des origines à la conquête d'Alexandre* (Paris: PUF, 7th edn, 1989), p. 386.

14. These elements have very few words in common: נף instead of מך; שיא instead of a derivate of שר. Only לא יהיה occurs in both texts.

15. G.C. Aalders, *Ezechiël*. II. *Hfdst. 25–48* (Commentaar op het Oude Testament; Kampen: Kok, 1957), *ad loc*.

announces judgment on those in Israel (i.e. the Northern Kingdom) who will flee to Egypt,[16] which is not what is described in *Pseudo-Ezekiel*, but Hos. 9.2 uses the word תירוש, which is also used in *Pseudo-Ezekiel* (4Q386 ii 5). This means that the background to *Pseudo-Ezekiel* can be found in Ezek. 30.[17]

Then God will show mercy on his children (ii 6). After this passage the text continues.

c. *The Antichrist in* Pseudo-Ezekiel
What we have found in this writing is an individual who is evil (הרשע), who acts tyrannically (משרו, ענות) and has close connections with Satan (בליעל). In view of the strong link with Ezek. 30 we can think of an eschatological context here, and the preceding passage seems to confirm this.[18] However, it is possible that the second-century author experienced his own time as pre-eschatological and portrayed the foreign ruler of his own days as a 'son of Belial' in a *vaticinium ex eventu*. Again the most obvious candidate is Antiochus IV Epiphanes.[19]

The word רשע may be a reference to the Wicked Priest, but of course the Qumran Community did not necessarily use this adjective for him only. There is also a link between Memphis and Antiochus IV: he was crowned

---

16. C. van Leeuwen, *Hosea* (Prediking van het Oude Testament; Nijkerk: Callenbach, 1968), pp. 185, 187. For the importance of Memphis in this period, see Drioton and Vandier, *Egypte*, pp. 531, 542, 544.

17. D. Dimant, 'Apocrypha and Pseudepigrapha at Qumran', *DSD* 1 (1994), pp. 151-59 (157).

18. 4Q385 2 = 4Q486 1 i and 4Q485 3 (cf. Mt. 24.22); E. Puech, *La croyance des Esséniens en la vie future: immortalité, résurrection, vie éternelle? Histoire d'une croyance dans le judaïsme ancien. I. Les données qumraniennes et classiques* (Ebib, NS 22; Paris: Gabalda, 1993), p. 611; Dimant, '*4Q386*', pp. 522, 527-28 (she regards this passage as a *vaticinium ex eventu*).

19. Dimant, '*4Q386*', pp. 522-24; cf. Lorein, 'Life and Death', pp. 161-66. In my view we cannot refer to 4Q246 (which is what Dimant does, albeit with reservations); cf., e.g., F. García Martínez, *Qumran and Apocalyptic: Studies on the Aramaic Texts from Qumran* (STDJ, 9; Leiden: E.J. Brill, 1992), pp. 162-79; J.J. Collins, 'The *Son of God* Text from Qumran', in M.C. de Boer (ed.), *From Jesus to John: Essays on Jesus and New Testament Christology in Honour of Marinus de Jonge* (JSNTSup, 84; Sheffield: Sheffield Academic Press, 1993), pp. 65-82; Van der Woude, '"Hij zal Zoon des Allerhoogsten genoemd worden..."', pp. 137-44. We cannot blame Flusser for being the basis of a completely different interpretation (Flusser, 'Hubris', pp. 31-37), since he did not have access to the complete text.

3. *The Antichrist in the Qumran Writings* 153

Pharaoh here during the first phase of the Sixth Syrian War.[20] This does not open any perspectives for the date: religious persecution did not start until after 170, when it had already become apparent that Antiochus IV was not killed in Memphis.[21] The setting in Egypt and the fact that the text continues plead against an explanation based on the Antichrist theme.

A discussion of all historical and future individuals and groups that opposed Israel should be avoided here. The text is too fragmented for us to base any statements about the Antichrist theme on it, but it does show that the author's thinking allowed for a human individual who had close connections with Satan and formed the apex of evil.

3. Wiles of the Wicked Woman

a. *Setting*

Manuscript 4Q184 originates from around the turn of the era.[22] The date of origin depends on its interpretation, and this writing has been the subject of many different interpretations. The text of the first fragment is probably a complete unit.[23]

Generally this writing is now regarded as having quite an early origin: at least from before the Qumran Community was formed, perhaps even the third or even the fourth century.[24] However, this early date is only correct

---

20. Porphyry *apud* Jerome, *De Antichristo in Danielem* (11.21) [IV] 62-65: 'Antiochus...ascendit Memphim, et ibi ex more Aegypti regnum accipiens...omnem Aegyptum subiugauit' (text according to F. Glorie, *S. Hieronymi presbyteri commentariorum in Danielem libri III <IV>* [CChr Series Latina, 75A; Turnholti: Brepols, 1964]).

21. Dimant, '*4Q386*', pp. 525-28, thinks of another figure and regards the period of 170–140 as the historical background of this text.

22. F. García Martínez and A.S. van der Woude, *De Rollen van de Dode Zee ingeleid en in het Nederlands vertaald*. I. *Wetsliteratuur en Orderegels, Poëtische teksten* (Kampen: Kok, Tielt: Lannoo, 1994), p. 399; A. Dupont-Sommer, 'Pièges de la femme', in Dupont-Sommer and Philonenko (eds.), *La Bible: Ecrits intertestamentaires*, pp. 441-51 (443).

23. J. Strugnell, 'Notes en marge du volume V des "Discoveries in the Judaean Desert of Jordan"', *RevQ* 7 (1970), pp. 163-276 (263); R.D. Moore, 'Personification of the Seduction of Evil: "The Wiles of the Wicked Woman"', *RevQ* 10 (1981), pp. 505-19 (508-509); *pace* Dupont-Sommer, 'Pièges de la femme', p. 443 (part of a larger paraenetic work).

24. A.S. van der Woude, 'Wisdom at Qumran', in J. Day *et al.* (eds.), *Wisdom in ancient Israel* (Festschrift J.A. Emerton; Cambridge: Cambridge University Press, 1995), pp. 244-56 (254-55).

if the *Wiles of the Wicked Woman* is wisdom literature and if no wisdom literature was written in the Qumran Community. Generally, one or two exceptions will be tolerated,[25] but Ms. Dimant has allocated an origin in Qumran to quite a number of works of wisdom literature.[26] Whether this work actually classifies as wisdom literature depends on the interpretation, as we have seen.

Carmignac is not terribly happy with the literary level of this writing,[27] but even this work has its champions.[28] Scholars now think they can point out literary qualities, a strong structure and many double meanings,[29] even though not all the elements that are noted may have been intended by the author.

With regard to the genre, many elements are repeated, but we will need to look at the whole text, since all of it is about the Woman.

b. *4QWWW (4Q184) frag. 1*[30]

(1) [...]א[...ו]ב הבל תוציא ה[...]
תועות תשחר תמיד [ות]שנן[32] דברי[31] [...]:
[...] (2) וקלס תחל[י]ק ולהלי[ץ[34] יחד בש[וא תו]עיל[33]
לבה יכין פחיז[35] וכליותיה מק[...]:

25. Van der Woude, 'Wisdom at Qumran', p. 255 n. 23.
26. D. Dimant, 'The Qumran Manuscripts. Contents and Significance', in D. Dimant and L.H. Schiffman (eds.), *Time to Prepare the Way in the Wilderness* (STDJ, 16; Leiden: E.J. Brill, 1995), pp. 23-58 (33 n. 25).
27. J. Carmignac, 'Poème allégorique sur la secte rivale', *RevQ* 5 (1965), pp. 361-74 (362-63).
28. Cf. B.P. Kittel, *The Hymns of Qumran: Translation and Commentary* (SBLDS, 50; Chico, CA: Scholars Press, 1981), for the Hymns.
29. Moore, 'Personification', pp. 508-10, 513-16; A.M. Gazov-Ginzberg, 'Double Meaning in a Qumran Work (The Wiles of the Wicked Woman)', *RevQ* 6 (1967), pp. 279-85 (280-84); H. Burgmann, '"The Wicked Woman": Der Makkabäer Simon?', *RevQ* 8 (1974), pp. 323-59 (346-48, 351, 358).
30. According to J.M. Allegro, *Qumrân Cave 4. I. 4Q158–4Q168* (DJD, 5; Oxford: Clarendon Press, 1968), *ad loc.*, with regard to Strugnell, 'Notes', pp. 263-68.
31. דברי seems to be certain, but what follows is not: Strugnell, 'Notes', p. 264; Carmignac, 'Poème allégorique', *ad loc.*
32. Reconstruction and reading by Carmignac, 'Poème allégorique', *ad loc.*
33. Reconstruction and reading by Carmignac, 'Poème allégorique', *ad loc.* This verse line is longer than the other, possibly because it is the end of a stanza.
34. Without the cj. תועיל by Carmignac it is impossible to explain what this inf. is subject to.
35. Allegro: פחוז (inf. abs. pro adv.?).

3. The Antichrist in the Qumran Writings

[עיניה] (3) בעול נגעלו[^36] ידיה תמכו שוח:
רגליה להרשיע ירדו וללכת באשמות [...]:

(4) מוסדי חושך ורוב פשעים בכנפיה:
[...]ה תועפות[^37] לילה ומלבשיה[...]:
(5) מכסיה[^40] אפלות נשף ועדיה[^39] נגועי[^38] שחת:
ערשיה יצועיה[^41] [...] יצועי שחת (6) מעמקי בור:
מלונותיה משכבי חושך ובאושני ליל[ה א]שלותיה[^42]:
ממוסדי אפלות (7) האהל שבת ותשכון באהלי דומה:
בתוך מוקדי עולם ואין נחלתה בתוך בכול (8) מאירי נוגה:

והיאה ראשית כול דרכי עול הוי הוה לכול נוחליה ושדדה לכ[ו]ל[
(9) תומכי בה:
כיא דרכיה דרכי מות ואורחותיה שבילי חטאת:
מעגלותיה משגות (10) עול ונתיבות[י]ה אשמות פשע:
שעריה שערי מות בפתח ביתה תצעד שאו[ל][^43]:
(11) כ[ו]ל[...] ישובון וכול נוחליה ירדו שחת:

וה[י]א במסתרים תארוב (12) [...] כול [...]:
ברחובות עיר תתעלף ובשערי קריות תתיצב:
ואין להרג[יעה] (13) מה[ן]זנו[ת תמ]יד [...]:
עיניה הנה והנה ישכיל[ו][^44] ועפעפיה בפחז תרים
לראו[ת ל]אי[ש][^46] (14) צדיק ותשיגהו[^45] ואיש [ע]צום ותכשילהו

---

36. Niphal perf. 3 pl. of געל, 'to defile' (Aramaism; see Carmignac, 'Poème allégorique', *ad loc.*, but he opts for a different translation).

37. Carmignac, 'Poème allégorique', *ad loc.*, opts for a link with תעפה (known from Job 11.17), 'dark mist'. The word תועפות was definitely known before: see Num. 23.22; 24.8; Job 22.25; Ps. 95.4 (Zorell, *Lexicon, s.v.*; *pace* Carmignac, 'Poème allégorique', *ad loc.*).

38. Deviation from the classical form (Qimron, *Hebrew*, §330.1d).

39. St. cstr. pl. (Qimron, *Hebrew*, §200.17c) m. + suff. 3 sg. fem. of עדי, 'adornment'.

40. St. cstr. sg. or pl. m. + suff. 3 sg. fem. of מכסה, 'cover, coat'. Since the predicate is pl. pl. is preferable with מכסיה.

41. This word has been dropped in the MS: Strugnell, 'Notes', p. 265.

42. This form apparently comes from אשל, 'tent, garden': Strugnell, 'Notes', p. 265.

43. Reconstruction according to Carmignac, 'Poème allégorique', *ad loc.*

44. Hiphil imperf. 3 pl. m. after subject pl. fem.: see Qimron, *Hebrew*, §310.128.

45. Conj. + imperf. 3 sg. fem. + suff. 3 sg. m. of נשג, 'to pursue, to reach' (hiphil). Whilst an interpretation of indir. juss. (Carmignac, 'Poème allégorique', *ad loc.*) is attractive thematically, it is difficult to explain both morphologically and syntactically: Joüon, *Grammaire*, §116; Qimron, *Hebrew*, §310.129.

46. Also the א and י are hardly distinguishable.

ישרים להטות דרך ולבחירי צדק (15) מנצור[47] מצוה
סמוכי י[צ]ר להביל בפחז והולכי ישר להשנות חו[ו]ק[48]
להפשיע (16) ענוים מאל ולהטות פעמיהם מדרכי צדק
להביא זד[ו]ן ב[לב]במה בל[49] ידרובו (17) במעגלי יושר
להשגות אנוש בדרכי שוחה ולפתות בהלקות [כול] בני איש:

(1) …her…she produces vanity, and in…
She constantly strives for confusion, and she sharpens the words of…
…and (2) she polishes absurdity,[50] and she is useful for leading the community into worthlessness.
Her heart organizes ambushes, and her kidneys…
Her eyes (3) are defiled with iniquity, (and[51]) her hands hold on tight to the Abyss.[52]
Her feet go down to act evilly and to go in wicked[53]…

…(4) foundations of darkness, and a multitude of transgressions is in her coat skirts.[54]
Her…are nightly heights and her clothes…
(5) Her coats are dusky darknesses, and her jewels are blows from the Abyss.[55]

Her bedsteads are beds of the Abyss,[56]… (6) depths (as) of a pit.
Her nightly quarters are dark sleeping-places, and her tents (stand) on nightly foundations.
She camps on dark foundations (7) in silence,[57] and she lives in tents of quietness;[58]
in the midst of eternal seats of fire, but she has no inheritance in the midst of all (8) who shine brightly.[59]

---

47. Prep. (see Joüon, *Grammaire*, §133e, for the construction!) + qal inf. cstr. of נצר 'to comply with'.

48. דרך by Carmignac, 'Poème allégorique', *ad loc.*, is impossible: Strugnell, 'Notes', p. 265.

49. Apparently this word takes the place of a conjunction.

50. Or: 'she makes smooth': cf. 4QWWW 17b!

51. Carmignac, 'Poème allégorique', *ad loc.*, points out that the ו could easily have been dropped from between a ו (from נגעלו) and a י (from ידיה).

52. Or: quicksand.

53. Literally: wrongdoings.

54. See Carmignac, 'Poème allégorique', *ad loc.*

55. Or: doom.

56. Or: doom.

57. שבת interpreted as adv. acc.

58. In Ps. 94.17 דומה is used to indicate eternal silence, i.e., the silence of death: Ridderbos, *Psalmen*, II, *ad loc.*

59. The Hebrew does not flow, and Carmignac suspects a copying error.

3. *The Antichrist in the Qumran Writings* 157

Indeed, she is the beginning of all evil ways;[60] woe, destruction for all who inherit her, and devastation for all (9) who hold on to her.[61]
For her ways are ways of death, and her paths are roads of sin.
Her tracks are evil paths of error,[62] (10) and her paths are wicked transgressions.[63]
Her gates are gates of death; at the opening of her house the realm of death approaches.
(11) All...return,[64] and all who inherit her go down to the Abyss.[65]

Indeed, she lays in ambush in hiding places...(12) all...
On the squares of the city she stands all dressed up,[66] and in the gates of the cities she has taken place,
and there is nothing to stop her (13) from her ongoing prostitution.
Her eyes flirt here and there, and she raises her eyelids with lust,
to look at a (14) righteous man and she pursues him, and (at) an important man and she makes him stumble;
and (to) upright (people) to mislead concerning the way, and to the righteous elect (15) to lead them away from observing the law;
(to) the steadfast of direction to confuse (them) into debauchery, and (to) those who walk upright to change the decree;
to (16) make the humble rebel against God, and to lead their steps away from the ways of righteousness;
to arouse insolence in their heart, so they will no (longer) walk (17) in the tracks of righteousness;

---

60. According to Moore, 'Personification', pp. 508-509, this half-verse is the core of the poem. The word דרכי provides a link with what follows, so we may wish to speak of 'a verse and a half' here rather than a 'half-verse'. Carmignac, 'Poème allégorique', *ad loc.*, assumes that the first half of the verse was dropped and that this was the second half. Because he prefers to assume that all stanzas have three verses, he must use a similar hypothesis elsewhere as well (at the change from v. 12 to v. 13; see his p. 370 n. 36). A verse division on the basis of content seems to be a safer device, and here we follow Moore, 'Personification', pp. 508-509, but without following his view on 8b as the core and without creating a division between 13b and 13c, because of the strong syntactic link.

61. The verse structure is different, and Carmignac, 'Poème allégorique', *ad loc.*, suspects a copying error.

62. Derived from the verb שגה (to wander); cf. Qimron, *Hebrew*, §500.3, *s.v.* מִשְׁגָּה (blunder).

63. Lit.: 'transgressions of violation'.

64. It is quite possible that there was a negation in the lacuna; in that case the translation of this clause should read 'no-one returns': Strugnell, 'Notes', p. 265; Moore, 'Personification', p. 516; but see also Carmignac, 'Poème allégorique', *ad loc.*

65. Or: 'doom'.

66. Lit.: 'she wraps herself'.

to make man wander into ways of the Abyss,[67] and to deceive all children of man with easy[68] things.

It is clear that this, like the *Hymns*, is a poetic text. The language is much more complicated than that of the other writings.

We see that alliteration was used in 1b.[69]

According to Moore, the words נחל and חלק, which are similar in sound, are of great importance to the structure, with נחל just before (7b) and just after (8b) the middle and חלק just after the beginning (2a) and just before the end (17b). The message is clear: by way of the smooth and easy, people end up in the hands of the woman.[70] This 'easy' way is also mentioned elsewhere in the Qumran Writings.[71]

The relationship between the terms שוח (3a, 3b), שחת (5a, 5b, 11a) and שוחה (17b) is unclear. The author's intention was probably to give at least the impression of repetition. This is why the translation uses the word 'Abyss' for all three, although each term carries its own range of meanings.[72]

The infinitives at the end seem at first to depend on the woman's flirtatious eyes (13b) and then to carry on independently. Within them there is another structure: they move from the single איש via the plural סמוכי, הולכי and ענוים, to the all-encompassing אנוש and כול בני איש.[73]

After discussing the structure of the poem itself, we also wish to take a closer look at some parallels, starting with those in Qumran writings.

In 2a we find a number of terms that are reminiscent of the competing group: חלק, ליץ and יחד.[74] line 17b also has the verb פתה, which is linked

67. Or: quicksand.
68. Or: smooth. Cf. 4QWWW 2a.
69. Carmignac, 'Poème allégorique', *ad loc.*
70. Moore, 'Personification', pp. 509-10. This structural message is not only applicable in Moore's own interpretation.
71. See the discussion of CD 1.18, 4Q171 i 19 and 4Q169 3-4 i 7.
72. Moore, 'Personification', p. 513. Note the parallelism with בור in 5b–6a. See Zorell, *Lexicon*, *s.vv.*, who also distinguishes two homonyms שחת. Cf. the remark by Strugnell, 'Notes', p. 268 (but see the apology of Allegro by P.R. Davies, '*Notes en marge*: Reflections on the Publication of DJDJ 5', in H.-J. Fabry, A. Lange and H. Lichtenberger, *Qumranstudien* [Schriften des Institutum Judaicum Delitzschianum, 4; Göttingen: Vandenhoeck & Ruprecht, 1996], pp. 103-109).
73. Moore, 'Personification', p. 519.
74. Carmignac, 'Poème allégorique', *ad loc.*; Moore, 'Personification', pp. 511-12. Cf., e.g., CD 1.18 and 4Q169 3-4 i 2, 7; CD 1.14, where the related לצון (arrogance) is used; CD 20.14, respectively.

with the competing group in the *Hymns*, and חלק again.⁷⁵ Carmignac also refers to שוא and מרמה (which is not very specific), but these two words do not occur in the unreconstructed text.⁷⁶

The woman has an inheritance in the midst of eternal seats of fire, but the light that would normally be produced in fire is excluded from them (7b-8a). We have also noted judgment by fire in 1QpHab 10.13. The combination of fire and darkness is unusual but not unique.⁷⁷

Significant biblical parallels are found in Prov. 8.22, where it is said that the Lord has obtained Wisdom as ראשית דרכו,⁷⁸ which means that 8b can be applied to Folly by inversion, and within the entirety of Prov. 7, where the polished (החליקה) in v. 5, dusk (נשף) and darkness (אפלה) in v. 9, squares (רחבות) in v. 12, intense searching (שחר) in v. 15, the ambush (פח) in v. 23, and ways (דרכיה) and paths (נתיבותיה) in v. 25 can be linked to an adulterous woman. The first meaning of the *Wiles of the Wicked Woman* can therefore be firmly placed against a biblical background.⁷⁹

c. *The Antichrist in the* Wiles of the Wicked Woman
We definitely have to look at the question whether the Woman answers to our own Antichrist definition. It is not impossible for this theme to be represented by a female figure. There are many similarities: the Woman is linked with the world of darkness, she acts against God's law and attempts

---

75. Carmignac, 'Poème allégorique', *ad loc*.
76. See the reconstruction of 2a and 16b by Carmignac, 'Poème allégorique', *ad loc*.; I chose against the use of מרמה. For שוא, cf. 1QpHab 10.10-11.
77. Moore, 'Personification', p. 514. Cf. *1 En.* 103.8 (ἐν σκότει...καὶ ἐν φλογὶ καιομένῃ); 1QS 2.8 (אפלת אש עולמים); 4.13 (אש מחשכים); Virgil, *Aeneid* 4.384 ('atris ignibus'). A. Kuyper, 'Locus de Consummatione Saeculi', in *Dictaten Dogmatiek*, V (Kampen: Kok, 2nd edn, 1910), p. 306, remarks that the biblical data on Gehenna are 'apparently contradictory', but interprets it as a non-raging fire that keeps glowing. A remarkable parallel is found with M. Vanderostyne, 'Hulpverleners sterven aan de lopende band', *De Standaard* (26 April 1996), p. 27, a description of the catastrophe at Chernobyl on 26 May 1986 CE: 'Het was een ongewone brand, je zag meer een gloed dan echte vlammen' (It was an unusual fire, one saw more of a glow than real flames).
78. Formally, Job 40.19 is closer than Prov. 8.22, but it is difficult to see a parallel with the hippopotamus. Think of the central place that Moore, 'Personification', pp. 508-509, wishes to give to half-verse 8b.
79. Moore, 'Personification', pp. 511-17. NB: Prov. 7 is about an adulterous woman even without metaphoric meaning, although the entire piece is embedded in a context of wisdom literature and wisdom is described as speaking in the surrounding chapters. Of course there are other parallels too, but they do not add much more to a better understanding of this text.

to lead people into doing the same, she opposes those who believe in God, in short she is an apex of evil. We could also refer to Sir. 25.15, where an evil woman is called even worse than a lion and a dragon, which means that an image of beasts can again play a role.[80] However, the activities of the woman described here do not seem to be eschatological but rather quite general, and they are directed toward individual persons rather than cast in the role of a religious and political world ruler. This means we cannot simply identify her with the Antichrist.

All that remains is the reconstruction set out by Burgmann in several articles, and linked in with Carmignac's thesis that the Woman refers to the rival group. This thesis has very strong arguments,[81] but some objections are its universal perspective and the slightly fatalistic character.[82] Whether the thesis is right or wrong, this group in its entirety cannot be the same as the Antichrist.

Burgmann builds on Carmignac's thesis (but without dealing with the objections first). He deduces from 8b-9a and 11a that the Woman had followers and she is therefore a reference to the founder of the rival group. He deduces from 1a, 1b and 1c-2a that this group was mainly known for its verbal violence.[83] This figure also occurs in other texts, as Man of Lies, Man of Arrogance and Saw.[84] He must have lived at the same time as the Teacher of Righteousness. This is actually a first phase in Burgmann's theory, which can certainly be defended.

His second phase cannot, however.[85] Burgmann claims that this refers to Hasmonean high priest Simon. Simon complied with all requirements: he was a demagogue and founded the group that eventually became the politico-religious group of the Pharisees,[86] to create division in the ranks of the Hasidim.

---

80. Sirach was written in the beginning of the second century, but the image may of course be older.

81. Carmignac, 'Poème allégorique', *passim*. J.M. Allegro, 'The Wiles of the Wicked Woman: A Sapiential Work from Qumran's Fourth Cave', *PEQ* 96 (1964), pp. 53-55 (53), thinks that 'perhaps' it refers to Rome. We must note here that Rome did not play a very important role in Qumranic thinking.

82. Van der Woude, 'Wisdom at Qumran', p. 247; Moore, 'Personification', pp. 506, 516, 519.

83. Burgmann, '"Wicked Woman"', pp. 326-34.

84. Burgmann, '"Wicked Woman"', pp. 335-37. Man of Lies: CD 20.15; 4QpPs i 18; 1QpHab 2.2; 10.9. Man of Arrogance: CD 1.14. Saw: CD 4.19; see also, as a summary, section 4g in this chapter.

85. Also Burgman, '"Wicked Woman"', p. 346, distinguishes these two phases.

86. Burgmann, '"Wicked Woman"', pp. 337-45, 359. The link between Simon and

3. *The Antichrist in the Qumran Writings* 161

What Burgmann does not mention in his article on the *Wiles of the Wicked Woman*, but does in his article on the Antichrist, is actually a third phase: Hasmonean high priest Simon (as Man of Lies, as father of two sons in the *Testimonia*, as mother of the serpent in the *Hymns* and as the Woman in this text) was a model for the Antichrist. While the thesis could be accepted for the *Testimonia*, it is impossible for the other texts, because we do not accept the preceding identification.[87]

What remains is the possibility that the woman refers to Saw. A female figure referring to a collective group seems more natural than a female figure portraying a male individual. However, since the leader is part of the group, it would be difficult to prove that it could be a reference to the opposing group but not to its leader.

Saw has been of importance to the development of the Antichrist theme,[88] but we cannot really distinguish the Antichrist in this text. Does that mean that this text is slightly older than the *Damascus Document*, and that the link between Saw and the Antichrist simply had not yet been laid?

If this writing has to be interpreted in the context of the Qumran Community—and aside from the interpretation as a whole and the use of certain specific words there are other words that seem to indicate this[89]—then this writing must be dated between 150 and 107.[90]

If we do not accept the aforementioned allegorical interpretations, then this writing is wisdom literature.

The document cannot be referring to women in general,[91] because the woman is clearly portrayed as a prostitute.[92] The members of the Qumran

---

the founding of the Pharisees is merely hypothetical! Burgmann, '"Wicked Woman"', p. 350, admits that the Testimonia (4Q175) are the most important texts for this identification.

87. H. Burgmann, 'Makkabäer Simon?', p. 161.

88. See this chapter, 4g. Cf. Burgmann, '"Wicked Woman"', p. 359: the people of the Qumran Community thought they were living in the pre-eschaton.

89. Carmignac, 'Poème allégorique', p. 363; Dupont-Sommer, 'Pièges de la femme', p. 450; Moore, 'Personification', pp. 510-11 (terms that are directly linked with the Qumran Community), 512, 514, 517-19. (Moore repeatedly appeals to reconstructions and interpretations that we have not accepted. He also struggles with the French language in which Strugnell's article was written: pp. 510 n. 14, 512 n. 20, 518.)

90. Burgmann, '"Wicked Woman"', p. 324 n. 3, dates it after the Nahum pesher, i.e., after 70.

91. According to Dupont-Sommer, 'Pièges de la femme', *passim*; cf. M. Philonenko, 'Essénisme et misogynie', *CRAIBL* (1982), pp. 339-53 (343-45).

92. Carmignac, 'Poème allégorique', p. 373.

Community were no misogynists,[93] and even outside the Qumran Community no circles would have been so misogynist as to portray all women as prostitutes. So is this a warning against prostitutes? I do not think so, because such a warning was probably not terribly relevant for any intended audience.[94]

There must be more to this, and the text itself seems to indicate that. The only solution that remains is that we are dealing here with the woman folly. The woman wisdom is mentioned in the Qumran Writings—and does not stand for the Qumran Community—so woman folly is a plausible option.[95] The argument of the woman folly becomes even stronger if the date of origin of this writing, together with most wisdom literature, is dated well before 150.[96]

This woman is influenced by evil spirits,[97] but that does not mean that the *Wiles of the Wicked Woman* is reminiscent of a specific demon or a sorceress.[98] There is not enough room for an identification of the woman folly with the Antichrist from a christological interpretation, since Christ and the Antichrist do not oppose each other that way.

We see that there are two clearly different main groups in the interpretations of the *Wiles of the Wicked Woman*. But do we really need to choose? Allegro believes that the writing clearly refers to a prostitute but is also about something else, perhaps Rome,[99] but he does not elaborate on this. Dupont-Sommer opts for a misogynist interpretation,[100] but his interpreta-

---

93. See R.T. Beckwith, 'The Qumran Calendar and the Sacrifices of the Essenes', *RevQ* 7 (1971), pp. 587-91 (591). Against Philonenko, 'Essénisme et misogynie', pp. 343-45; Dupont-Sommer, 'Pièges de la femme', p. 443.

94. Carmignac, 'Poème allégorique', p. 373; J.M. Baumgarten, 'On the Nature of the Seductress in *4Q184*', *RevQ* 15 (Mémorial Jean Starcky; 1991), pp. 133-43 (137).

95. Strugnell, 'Notes', pp. 266-67; Van der Woude, 'Wisdom at Qumran', p. 247; cf. A. Pezhumkattil, 'Husband–Wife Relationship in the Wisdom Literature', *Bible Bhashyam* 20 (1994), pp. 69-87 (69). Also think of Κακία and Ἀρετή in Xenophon, *Memorabilia* 2.1.21-33. Κακία has opened its eyes very wide (22; cf. 4Q184 1 13), wears revealing clothes (22; cf. 4Q184 1 4), has an overly luxurious bed (cf. 30; cf. 4Q184 1 5), tempts into doing what comes easily (23; cf. 4Q184 1 17) and into debauchery (cf. 30; cf. 4Q184 1 12, 15). Woman vice and woman folly are not identical, but the occurrence of these two women is an additional argument for this interpretation.

96. Van der Woude, 'Wisdom at Qumran', p. 255.

97. Baumgarten, 'On the Nature of the Seductress', pp. 133, 138-42.

98. Against Baumgarten, 'On the Nature of the Seductress', pp. 139-43.

99. Allegro, '"Wiles of the Wicked Woman"', p. 53.

100. Dupont-Sommer, 'Pièges de la femme', *passim*; cf. Philonenko, 'Essénisme et misogynie', pp. 343-45.

tion could also allow for the rival sect.[101] According to Carmignac, the author opted for this metaphor because to people who know the biblical texts no warning against the rival group could be stronger than a comparison to a prostitute.[102] Gazov-Ginzberg reads the entire text at both the level of a demonic and evil woman and that of a rival group.[103]

In my view, the text may refer to the woman folly, who has started a new life within the Qumran Community because this device would help to portray the leader of the rival group as the apex of misleading folly.[104] If this is true, it is an ancient writing that was copied because of a new interpretation, whereby the universal character of 4QWWW 17 was accepted as an extra. If this is the case, this text could have been the source of such typical terms as חלקות, שוא and לצון, and perhaps even יחר. The text then originated in the third century as a piece of wisdom literature and was copied before 107 (so it could have some influence on the Damascus Document).[105] It was copied again around the turn of the era, which resulted in our manuscript 4Q184.

4. Damascus Document

a. *Setting*

The *Damascus Document* (CD) was probably written around 107,[106] within the Qumran Community.[107] It mentions a Man of Arrogance and a Man of

---

101. Cf. Dupont-Sommer, 'Pièges de la femme', p. 451.

102. Carmignac, 'Poème allégorique', p. 374. Carmignac himself refers to Hos. 1–3 and Ezek. 16 and 23 here, but we could also think of Prov. 7 and Eccl. 7.26.

103. Gazov-Ginzberg, 'Double Meaning', p. 280 and *passim*.

104. Cf. Pezhumkattil, 'Husband–Wife Relationship', p. 83.

105. This would be, after the argument of the development of Saw, another argument for a date before 107, either for the writing itself or for its new interpretation. I must stress that this is a hypothesis. The issue is more complicated than described here, and with the availiable lexical aids and the current uncertainty regarding the date, a definite conclusion is impossible. Let me make a few last remarks: יחר excepted, the words that have been mentioned also occur in Hymns attributed to the Teacher of Righteousness, i.e., in texts from before 107 (D. Dimant, 'Qumran Sectarian Literature', in Stone [ed.], *Jewish Writings of the Second Temple Period*, pp. 483-550 [523 n. 199]); יחר also occurs in 4Q525 2 ii (as does מרמה!), which can be compared to the Wiles of the Wicked Woman (but if so, from when does 4Q525 date? See Van der Woude, 'Wisdom at Qumran', p. 255, and Dimant, 'Qumran Manuscripts', p. 44 n. 51!), and in 4Q372 1 10, but apparently not as a subst.

106. It was known from the Cairo Geniza, but 4Q266-73, 5Q12 and 6Q15 show that it originates from the Qumran Community.

Lies, and these descriptions are reminiscent of ὕβρις and the ἄνθρωπος τῆς ἀνομίας, which are linked to the false prophet as referred to in our definition of the Antichrist. We will now put this first impression concerning these figures to the test by studying the Qumranic data more closely. We will also discuss this figure and its link with the Antichrist on the basis of a passage in which Belial is mentioned.

b. *CD 1.11-18*[108]

(1.11) ויקֶם להם מורה צדק להדריכם בדרך לבו: ויודע (12) לדורות
אחרונים את אשר עשה בדור אחרון[109] בעדת בוגדים (13) הם סרי דרך:
היא העת אשר היה כתוב עליה כפרה סוֹרֵרָה[110] (14) כן סרר ישראל
בעמוד איש הלצון אשר הטיף לישראל (15) מימי כזב ויתעם בתוהו
לא דרך להשח גבהות[112] עולם ולסור (16) מנתיבות צדק ולסיע[111]
גבול אשר גבלו ראשנים בנחלתם למען (17) הדבק בהם את אלות
בריתו להסגירם לחרב נקמת נקם (18) ברית בעבור אשר דרשו בחלקות:

(1.11) And (God) raised for them a Teacher of Righteousness to guide them in the way of his heart. And He made known (12) to later generations what He was about to do for a latter generation with the congregation of the traitors, (13) of those who have departed from the way. This is the time of which it is written: 'Like a stubborn heifer, (14) thus Israel was stubborn', when the Man of Arrogance arose who trickled[113] over Israel (15) water of lies and caused them to wander in a pathless wilderness, lowering the

---

107. The year 107 does not indicate a precise date, but refers to the relationship between CD and 1QS and 1QSa. Cf. A.J.T. Jull, D.J. Donahue, M. Broshi and E. Tov, 'Radiocarbon Dating of Scrolls and Linen Fragments from the Judean Desert', *Radiocarbon* 37 (1995), pp. 11-19 (14) (4Q267).

108. This text will follow E. Qimron, 'The Text of CDC', in M. Broshi (ed.), *The Damascus Document Reconsidered* (Jerusalem: Israel Exploration Society; Israel Museum, 1992); the vocalisation of the MS has been preserved, the interpunction has been added on the basis of my translation.

109. No article!

110. This seems to be the intention of the MS. In fact the vocalization is supralinear, and is with the י.

111. Conj. + prep. + hiphil inf. cstr. of נסע. Deut. 19.14 has תסיג (from סוג); this means that again this is not a literal quotation!

112. גְּבֹהוֹת (although this is actually an adj.: 'higher things'), or גַּבְהוּת ('arrogance'); thus E. Lohse, *Die Texte aus Qumran. Hebräisch und Deutsch* [Darmstadt: Wissenschaftliche Buchgesellschaft, 2nd edn, 1971], *ad loc.*, but this would make the link to Hab. 3.6 less clear, since that has גְּבָעוֹת [hills]; however, the roots גבע, גבה [and גבח, גבן and גבל] are related: Zorell, *Lexicon, s.v.* גבע).

113. Or: 'whined'.

3. *The Antichrist in the Qumran Writings* 165

everlasting heights and straying (16) from paths of righteousness and removing the boundary markers which forefathers had planted in their inheritance, that (17) He might bring upon them the curses of his covenant by delivering them to the sword that avenges the covenant, (18) because they sought for that which is easy.

This passage is from the first part of the document, as are all the other passages of the *Damascus Document* we will be discussing.[114]

Four hundred and ten years after the beginning of the Babylonian Exile,[115] 20 years after the group which eventually formed the Qumran Community reluctantly started their search, the Teacher of Righteousness[116] arose (1.11).[117]

At first the Teacher of Righteousness viewed his own time as preeschatological: this was very nearly the very last period in history.[118] Furthermore, it was revealed[119] to him what would happen[120] during that very last period.[121] God was going to bring vengeance upon the 'others'

---

114. The first part consisting of CD 1–8, 19–20 (whereby 19 = 7-8). Cf. García Martínez and Van der Woude, *Rollen van de Dode Zee*, I, pp. 220-23.

115. Cf. M.A. Knibb, *The Qumran Community* (Cambridge Commentary on Writings of the Jewish and Christian World 200 BCE to CE 200, 2; Cambridge: Cambridge University Press, 1987), pp. 19-20, Burgmann, *Weitere lösbare Qumranprobleme*, pp. 92 n. 9, 147-48, and with a more detailed reconstruction, A. Steudel, 'אחרית הימים in the Texts from Qumran', *RevQ* 16 (1993), pp. 225-46 (236-38, 246).

116. 'Righteous Teacher' or 'True Teacher' might be better translations (cf. Van der Woude, *Die messianischen Vorstellungen*, p. 171), but the term 'Teacher of Righteousness' is so established that it would seem wrong to deviate from it.

117. Callaway, *History of the Qumran Community*, p. 101, believes that the *cause* was that God had noticed their repentance, and that the *aim* was that the Teacher of Righteousness would lead and teach the community.

118. C. Rabin, *The Zadokite Documents* (Oxford: Clarendon Press, 2nd edn, 1958), *ad loc.*

119. The subject of יודע is often debated: it could be the Teacher of Righteousness, who is mentioned just before this in the text: cf. P.R. Davies, *Damascus Covenant: An Interpretation of the 'Damascus Document'* (JSOTSup, 25; Sheffield: JSOT Press, 1983), p. 64, but he views מורה צדק as added (see J.G. Campbell 'Scripture in the Damascus Document 1.1-2.1', *JJS* 44 [1993], pp. 83-99 [98], about this). After all, the revelation is experienced as coming from God (thus also Knibb, *Qumran Community*, p. 22).

120. עשה as qal ptc.: cf. Davies, *Damascus Covenant*, p. 68. עשה could also be explained as qal perf. (עָשָׂה): see Davies, *Damascus Covenant*, pp. 67-69 (only with substantial amendments to the text).

121. L. Ginzberg, *An Unknown Jewish Sect* (New York: Jewish Theological Seminary of America, 1976), pp. 5-6, prefers to read בדור חרון instead of בדור אחרון.

(i.e. former members of their own group in the first place, since they receive most attention in the text[122]), those who had strayed from the true (i.e. Essene)[123] teaching under the guidance of the Man of Arrogance. They were now compared to a cow refusing to have its ploughing yoke put on[124] (1.11-14).

The Man of Arrogance described in this document will spread false teachings.[125] He will be like a constantly dripping leak in his preaching—unlike the Teacher of Righteousness, who will spread a mild rain of teaching[126]—because he will not know the true interpretation of the Law.[127] It is thought that what is said in Job 12.24b, Ps. 107.40b, Hab. 3.6 and Deut. 19.14 applies to him. Whereas God deprives prominent people of their reason to show his omnipotence (Job 12.24), or puts them several economic steps back (Ps. 107.40),[128] the Man of Arrogance will lead his group astray, through a spiritual desert. Whereas the age-old hills collapse when God comes (Hab. 3.6aδ), the Man of Arrogance will despise all 'things exalted', which is probably the Law.[129] Whereas arrogant Israelites were not allowed

---

Davies, *Damascus Covenant*, pp. 67-69, deletes איש הלצון and then deduces that דור אחרון and דורות אהרונים do not refer to the same period; but we are not interested in this (hypothetical) phase in the lifetime of the text.

122. However, see Callaway, *History*, p. 119. ישראל could also refer to all of Israel.

123. See Knibb, *Qumran Community*, p. 23, who claims the others are ex-Essenes, which, from the viewpoint of the Qumran Community, was definitely right. For הדרך, compare to ἡ ὁδός in the New Testament (Acts 9.2).

124. C. van Gelderen, *Het boek Hosea* (ed. W.H. Gispen; Commentaar op het Oude Testament; Kampen: Kok, 1953), p. 125, re. Hos. 4.16, with reference to the Peshitta. Apparently, the word 'cow' could have negative connotations in Hebrew, as in English.

125. מימי כזב refers to Jewish internal, not to pagan false teachings. This means that any identification with a pagan ruler, e.g. Antiochus IV Epiphanes, is out of the question: Ginzberg, *Unknown Jewish Sect*, p. 6; Rabin, *Zadokite Documents, ad loc.*; Knibb, *Qumran Community*, pp. 23-24; H.W. Huppenbauer, *Der Mensch zwischen zwei Welten: Der Dualismus der Texte von Qumrân (Höhle I) und der Damaskusfragmente. Ein Beitrag zur Vorgeschichte des Evangeliums* (ATANT, 34; Zürich: Zwingli Verlag, 1959), pp. 58-59. This sentence does not refer to political or military activities either: Callaway, *History*, p. 118.

126. W.H. Brownlee, 'The Wicked Priest, the Man of Lies, and the Righteous Teacher—the Problem of Identity', *JQR* 73 (1982), pp. 1-37 (10). הטיף from נטף (to drip, to moan—to prophesy, to preach [polysemy]); מורה from ירה (to rain—to teach [homonymy]).

127. Knibb, *Qumran Community*, p. 24.

128. For both texts the context should be taken into consideration.

129. Knibb, *Qumran Community*, p. 24. We could also think of a conflation with Isa.

3. *The Antichrist in the Qumran Writings* 167

to move boundary stones to appropriate to themselves the inheritance of their weaker neighbour as determined in the laws about the distribution of the land (Deut. 19.14),[130] the Man of Arrogance will mark the boundaries between the permissible and the forbidden at quite a different point than the ancient Law does (1.14-16).

The examples of Bible quotations in the previous paragraph seem to suggest that these are 'interpreting quotations', and that they were meant as quotations that do not violate the texts. The same exegetical method is used in the Midrash, but here we must note that the interpretation differs from the original meaning on a specific and sensitive point: that which is ascribed to God in the biblical text (Job 12.24; Ps. 107.40b) is here credited to an enemy. This begs the question whether the assumption that we are dealing with the same type of exegesis as in the Midrash is justified. We also need to determine whether we are closer to the truth if we assume that this is an interpretation that is far-fetched and simply uses biblical terminology. We might well be dealing with a linguistic-sociological phenomenon, a style of preaching in which as many biblical expressions as possible are used to make the message sound 'biblical'.[131]

God is described as responding to the behaviour of the Man of Arrogance by invoking curses and by bringing an avenging sword upon his group.[132] The use of the sword is here left to God and there is no mention of an armed conflict between the Teacher of Righteousness and the Man of Arrogance,[133] only a strong difference of opinion. The followers of the Man of Arrogance were too relaxed in their religious practices (1.17-18). The search for חלקות is also mentioned elsewhere.[134] It is usually assumed

---

2.17. (See Rabin, *Zadokite Documents, ad loc.*), but that would not make the interpretation of these lines any easier.

130. See Craigie, *Deuteronomy*, pp. 268 (re. Deut. 19.14), 322-33 (re. 27.17).

131. Cf. S. Holm-Nielsen, *Hodayot, Psalms from Qumran* (ATDan, 2; Aarhus: Universitetsforlaget, 1960), p. 60. However, this way of using Scripture also occurs in the Midrash of later Judaism. Compare the change of subject with the treatment of anthropomorphisms and the 'use of biblical terms hypothesis' with אסמכתא: see R. Kasher, 'The Interpretation of Scripture in Rabbinic Literature', in M.J. Mulder and H. Sysling (eds.), *Mikra* (CRINT, 2.1; Assen: Van Gorcum; Philadelphia: Fortress Press, 1988), pp. 547-94 (560-63).

132. If the Man of Arrogance is the subject of הדבק, this link is portrayed even more directly.

133. Callaway, *History*, p. 121.

134. The term also occurs in Isa. 30.10. This chapter has left a deep impression on this passage: see Campbell, 'Scripture in the Damascus Document', pp. 90-91, 98-99.

that this refers to Pharisees, and that may also be true for this text.[135] The description of the competing group is continued in the following lines.

c. *CD 4.12-20*

(4.12) ובכל השנים האלה יהיה (13) בליעל משולח בישראל כאשר דבראל
ביד ישעיה הנביא בן (14) אמוץ לאמר פחד ופחת ופח עליך יושב הארץ׃
פשרו (15) שלושת מצודות בליעל אשר אמר עליהם לוי בן יעקב (16) אשר
הוא תפש בהם בישראל ויתנם לפניהם[136] לשלושת מיני (17) הצדק הראשונה
היא הזנות השנית ההון[138] השלישית (18) טמא[137] המקדש׃ העולה מזה יתפש
בזה והניצל מזה יתפש(19) בזה׃ בוני החיץ אשר הלכו אחרי צו׃ הצו הוא
מטיף (20) אשר אמר הטף יטיפון׃

(4.12) And during all those years (13) Belial shall be sent away in Israel, as God has spoken by the prophet Isaiah the son of (14) Amos: 'Terror, pit, snare upon you, inhabitant of the earth'.[139] The interpretation of this: (15) the three nets of Belial about which Levi the son of Jacob spoke, (16) in which he caught Israel, and he placed them before them as three kinds of (17) righteousness: the first is fornication, the second is riches, the third (18) profanation of the temple. Whoever escapes the first will be caught in the other, and whoever is saved from the first will be caught (19) in the other. The builders of the wall, they follow after Saw. Saw is the preaching one (20) of whom He has said: 'They shall surely[140] preach'.

Our passage explains how a period of grace discussed in the preceding lines[141] will be followed by the period that precedes the end of times. Apparently the author thought that he was living in that period.[142]

---

135. Knibb, *Qumran Community*, p. 24. See also n. 1 above, second part.
136. Cj. by Lohse, *Texte aus Qumran, ad loc.*; MS: פניהם.
137. Piel inf. cstr. or else subst. st. cstr. (טמא, the unclean of the sanctuary).
138. Cj. by Lohse, *Texte aus Qumran, ad loc.*; MS: ההין.
139. Or: 'the land'.
140. This 'surely' is expressed both by the inf. abs. and by the *nun paragogicum*: see Waltke and O'Connor, *Biblical Hebrew Syntax*, §31.7.1b. In Mic. 2.6 the intention is probably a contrast rather than certainty. (The conclusion by J. Hoftijzer, *The Function and Use of the Imperfect Forms with Nun Paragogicum in Classical Hebrew* [SSN, 21; Assen: Van Gorcum, 1985], p. 70, about this verse means that this is an imperfect, in *contrast* [*pace* Hoftijzer, *Function and Use*, p. 67: 'no feature of contrastivity whatever'] with the jussive just before this form [אל תטפו]).
141. CD 4.9-10. Cf. Callaway, *History*, p. 120.
142. A. Dupont-Sommer, 'Ecrit de Damas', in Dupont-Sommer and Philonenko

3. *The Antichrist in the Qumran Writings* 169

The passage explains how, with God's permission,[143] Belial will play a role in Israel[144] (4.12-13). In order to explain this, the writer refers to Isa. 24.17 (4.14), provides a pesher of it (4.15-19) and a commentary on that (beginning in 4.20).[145]

The pesher speaks about Belial's threefold activity during this eschatological period. It is unclear whether a direct relationship exists between Isaiah's three terms and Belial's three snares. Also the reference to Levi is unclear.[146] What is clear, however, is that Belial—and not Levi—will harm Israel and that he will present as righteousness the things the Qumran Community experienced as unrighteousness.[147] We have here what seem to be three obvious and 'traditional' sins; only in the commentary the specific Qumranic aspect shines through (4.15-18). Sin, in any form, is unavoidable: those who manage to escape from one sin (with reference to the pit in Isa. 24.17) will be caught in another (with reference to the snare in Isaiah) (4.18-19).[148]

Meanwhile the builders of the wall are blamed for following Saw. The builders are probably the competing group.[149] Although the word צו occurs in the Old Testament as an appellative, in this instance it is probably the name of a person.[150] In the Old Testament our first reference is to Hos. 5.11,[151] where the same construction (הלך אחרי צו) is used, and Isa. 28.10,

(eds.), *La Bible: Ecrits intertestamentaires*, pp. 133-83 (*ad loc.*); Knibb, *Qumran Community*, p. 40; cf. Davies, *Damascus Covenant*, p. 108.

143. Pass. divinum; cf. Huppenbauer, *Mensch zwischen zwei Welten*, p. 60.

144. Israel is more inclusive here than the competing group. (Davies, *Damascus Covenant*, p. 111.)

145. It is unclear where the commentary on the three snares, which is incomplete, changes into a new tirade. On the basis of this carelessness, Knibb, *Qumran Community*, pp. 40-41, prefers to assume that 4.15-19 was already in existence as a literary unit.

146. Davies, *Damascus Covenant*, p. 110.

147. Ginzberg, *Unknown Jewish Sect*, pp. 17-18, gives an entirely different explanation, which is however unsatisfactory in all aspects: 'they [why pl.?] turned away from' (this translation of נתן פניהם ל' cannot be based on Gen. 30.40) 'the three chief virtues' (the introduction of any Greek thought here is not justifiable).

148. The image is from Isa. 24.18, but the words are not.

149. This is more limited than ישראל in 4.13; cf. Davies, *Damascus Covenant*, p. 111 (but see the whole of his pp. 111-13!).

150. Van Gelderen, *Hosea*, p. 189, point out that after הלך אחרי one would expect a person. Is the change from appellative to given name based on the Damascus Document?

151. Close to a passage which is of great importance to the Damascus Document (cf.

13 would only be our second reference.[152] As an appellative, צו seems to refer to a depreciating variant of the root צוה.[153] Probably Isa. 28[154] imitates language used to address children, but Isaiah had sufficient linguistic competence to have had a specific meaning in mind for צו as well. With regard to this opponent, the same word is used as in CD 1.16: הטיף (trickle, moan, preach). This leads the author to make use of God's words in Mic. 2.6, but it is unclear whether the meaning of this difficult verse contributes in any way to the meaning of CD 4.20. Apparently Saw will tell the people what they like to hear (4.19-20).[155]

d. *CD 19.22-26 (= 8.10-13)*

(19.22) התנינים[156] (23) מלכי העמים ויינם הוא דרכיהם וראש פתנים הוא
ראש (24) מלכי יון הבא עליהם לנקם נקמה: ובכל אלה לא הבינו בוני
(25) החיץ וטחי תפל: כי הולך רוח ושקל סופות ומטיף אדם (26) לכזב
אשר חרה אף אל בכל עדתו:

> (19.22) The dragons (23) are the kings of the peoples, and their wine means their ways and the venom of serpents means the head of (24) the kings of Greece, which came to them to wreak vengeance.[157] And they did not understand it all, those who (25) build the wall[158] and cover it with plaster. Surely, he follows the wind and weighs turbulence, and bespeaks man (26) to lies, so that God's anger is kindled against his whole assembly.

These lines are part of the first paragraph of CD 19.15–20.34.[159]

Campbell, 'Scripture in the Damascus Document', p. 99; Davies, *Damascus Covenant*, p. 112).

152. This too is an important passage for the Damascus Document. Cf. Isa. 28.14, where אנשי לצון occurs, albeit in plural.

153. Van Gelderen, *Hosea*, p. 189; E.J. Young, *The Book of Isaiah*. II. *Chapters 19 to 39* (Grand Rapids: Eerdmans, 1969), pp. 275-76.

154. A. Schoors, *Jesaja* (Boeken van het Oude Testament; Roermond: Romen, 1972), p. 166.

155. Ginzberg, *Unknown Jewish Sect*, p. 18.

156. Cj.: +הם.

157. Hebr.: internal acc. (*figura etymologica*).

158. Hebr.: poss. a pun (paronymy) of הבינו and בוני.

159. Van der Woude, *Die messianischen Vorstellungen*, pp. 36-37, divides as follows:

a—19.15-32: builders of the wall;
b—19.32-20.1: unfaithful ones;
c—20.13: unworthy people within the Community;
d—20.13-22: the coming judgment;

3. *The Antichrist in the Qumran Writings* 171

The metaphor from the Song of Moses[160] which refers to the enemies of God's people (Deut. 32.33) is here made topical, including all its details. The identification of the 'kings of the nations' is subject to the interpretation of the text that follows, but at this point we can already say that they are either the Seleucids or the Romans. We can easily deduce from the text that the wine refers to their ways, that is, their deeds.[161] The venom of vipers refers to the head of the kings of the Greeks, because of the homonym of ראש with the meaning of 'venom' and ראש with the meaning of 'head'. This refers to Gentiles, a completely different category from the other opponents of the Qumran Community.[162] Greece, יון, can of course refer to Ionia, but also to all of the Hellenized world, which would open up even more possibilities. We could think of Antiochus IV Epiphanes as the leader of the Seleucids.[163] Dupont-Sommer, however, thinks of Pompey as the leader of the Romans. He was not a king, but did rule (i.e. was 'head of') several kings, including the Hasmonean rulers, who had arrogantly assumed the title of 'king' and had adopted Hellenistic customs.[164] Although this explanation is appealing,[165] it brings Dupont-Sommer into conflict with the accepted date of the *Damascus Document*, which is 107[166] (19.22-24).

The military leader is said to be coming to wreak vengeance on the nation of Israel, which has sinned by not walking in the way of the

e—20.22-24: unfaithful ones;
f—20.25-26a: unworthy people within the Community;
g—20.26b-27a: unrighteous ones in Judah;
h—20.26b-34: redemption for the godly.

He contrasts *a*, *b* and *c* with *g*, *e* and *f*. This could be expanded by stating that *d* and *h* are parallels.

160. Used several times in CD: Campbell, 'Scripture in the Damascus Document', p. 99).

161. J. Ridderbos, *Het boek Deuteronomium*. II. *Hoofdstuk 16.18–34.12* (Korte Verklaring; Kampen: Kok, 1951), p. 116.

162. Huppenbauer, *Mensch zwischen zwei Welten*, p. 58 n. 220.

163. B. Reicke, 'Die Taʿāmire-Schriften und die Damaskus-Fragmente', *ST* 2 (1948), pp. 45-70 (54).

164. A. Dupont-Sommer, ' "Le Chef des rois de Yâwân" dans l'*Ecrit de Damas*', *Sem* 5 (1955), pp. 41-57 (42-46).

165. It would make this passage perfectly comparable to *Pss. Sol.* 1.6; 17.11-15; 2.1-3, 25 (see Chapter 2) with this difference that the author of the *Pss. Sol.* mourned over the events, whereas the author of the CD *rejoiced*, which could be explained on the basis of the spiritual differences between the Pharisees and the Qumran Community.

166. Dupont-Sommer, 'Ecrit de Damas', p. 137, dates it between 63 and 48.

Qumran Community. May we deduce from this that the Community itself had not been harmed by the enemy's military actions?[167] Apparently the competing group[168] had created a new framework of ideas. It was only a flimsy wall, but because they had plastered it with their smooth talk, it looked like a sturdy structure (the image is borrowed from Ezek. 13.10)[169] (19.24-25).

The subject of the next sentence is probably their leader. The shift of the focus to him is unannounced because the author assumed that the readers would be able to follow his line of thought. The grammatical construction of the sentence is slightly unusual, but part of it is borrowed from Mic. 2.11, which also uses a complicated structure.[170] This leader will give empty promises ('hot air') and tempt his audience into deceit (19.25-26). God did not withhold his judgment on this: his anger against the competing group was kindled (19.26).

e. *CD 20.13-15*

(20.13) ומיום (14) האסף יורה היחיד[171] עד תם כל אנשי המלחמה אשר
שבו (15) עם איש הכזב כשנים ארבעים:

(20.13) And from the day of (14) the decease[172] of the Teacher of the Community until the completing of all the men of war who have returned (15) with the Man of Lies is about[173] forty years.[174]

---

167. Dupont-Sommer, ' "Le Chef des rois de Yâwân" ', pp. 48-49, supposes that the pious Jews had fled to Damascus just before 63.

168. Whereas 19.22-24 is mainly military, 19.24-25 mainly discusses the attitude towards the Qumran Community. Apparently a group of Jews had moved across to the Qumran Community.

169. Aalders, *Ezechiël*, II, p. 226. Ezek. 13 is used several times in the Damascus Writing: Campbell, 'Scripture in the Damascus Document', p. 99.

170. Our translation is based on J. Ridderbos, *De kleine Profeten. II. Van Obadja to Zefanja* (Korte Verklaring; Kampen: Kok, 2nd edn, 1949), p. 68, with reference (p. 71 n. 2) to Prov. 2.7. (This does not mean that there are no other explanations for Mic. 2.11; see, e.g., A.S. van der Woude, *Micha* [Prediking van het Oude Testament; Nijkerk: Callenbach, 1976], pp. 90-92.)

171. Either the article with יורה is absent, or היחיד should be corrected into היחד (thus Qimron, 'Text of CDC', *ad loc.*; Lohse, *Texte aus Qumran*; Van der Woude, *Die messianischen Vorstellungen*, p. 37, prefers to read הַיָחוּד with the same meaning as היחד). Since the term יורה היחיד does not occur elsewhere, the second option is the preferred one.

172. This is a usual meaning of the niphal of אסף; lit. 'be gathered in'.

173. See Joüon, *Grammaire*, §133g.

3. *The Antichrist in the Qumran Writings* 173

These rules are part of a fourth section of CD 19.15–20.34.[175] It explains how it is expected that after the Teacher of Righteousness[176] will decease[177] at an old age and full of years, another 40 years will pass until all the people will have died who had returned from the Qumran Community to the Land under the influence of the Man of Lies, thereby rebelling against the Law.[178] This phrase is based on Deut. 2.14, and the idea of 40 years may also have found its origin here, even if other factors were involved.[179] The Man of Lies must have influenced some people who were members of the Qumran Community for some time, or who sympathized.[180] Apparently this incident took place shortly before the death of the Teacher of Righteousness.[181] It is unclear whether there was a military encounter (אנשי המלחמה!).

Davies assumes that all references to an individual leader or an individual opponent are secondary.[182] His claim that this passage is not original, therefore does not come as a surprise.

f. *4QpPs (4Q171) i 18–ii 1*[183]

(i 18) [פשר]ו על איש הכזב אשר התעה רבים באמרי (19) שקר כיא בחרו
בקלות ולוא שמ[עו] למליץ דעת למען (ii 1) יובדו בחרב וברעב ובדבר:

(i 18) Its interpretation: about the Man of Lies who has led many astray by (19) deceitful words, for they have chosen light things and they did not listen to the interpreter of knowledge, so that (ii 1) they shall perish by the sword, by famine and by the plague.

---

174. The Hebr. usually uses sg. here. See Waltke and O'Connor, *Introduction to Biblical Hebrew Syntax*, §15.2.3.
175. See above n. 159.
176. Generally the identity of the מורה צדק and the יורה היחד is assumed.
177. Burgmann, *Weitere lösbare Qumranprobleme*, pp. 57-59.
178. Cf. Deut. 1.26.
179. Knibb, *Qumran Community*, pp. 73-74; Steudel, 'אחרית הימים', p. 238; Davies, *Damascus Covenant*, pp. 187-88. For the context, see Deut. 1.26.
180. Van der Woude, *Die messianischen Vorstellungen*, pp. 35-36. It is my understanding that the Man of Lies was never a member of the Qumran Community.
181. Van der Woude, *Die messianischen Vorstellungen*, p. 36.
182. Davies, *Damascus Covenant*, p. 187; cf. Callaway, *History*, p. 121.
183. The text follows Allegro, with a correction by Strugnell, 'Notes', p. 216. We are using the old verse numbering.

174   *The Antichrist Theme in the Intertestamental Period*

The reason for the inclusion of this Psalm pesher in this chapter is that it mentions the Man of Lies[184] with reference to Ps. 37.7. The date of origin of this pesher is 75.[185]

The author of the pesher believes that the words of Ps. 37.7 apply to the Man of Lies, who will appear to be successful because of his large following, but who will speak deceitfully (i 18-19). Part of the responsibility lies with his followers, since they have chosen for the superficial things (קלות),[186] instead of listening to the voice—this might be a word play on קלות[187]—of him who has a real understanding of the Law (i 19). Therefore their fate is determined: they will perish by a number of causes which are often mentioned in one breath (ii 1).[188]

g. *The Antichrist in the* Damascus Document

1. *Relative Identifications.* The *Document* mentions a Teacher of Righteousness and a Teacher of the Community. These are undoubtedly two names for the same figure, who is not directly linked to our subject. The *Document* also mentions Belial. His figure is never linked with another description.

There is a Man of Arrogance called Saw, a leader of those who build the wall (or in short the 'wall leader'). There is also a Man of Lies, and here the identification is more complicated. The similarities between these figures is overwhelming. The verb נטף is used for the Man of Arrogance (1.14), Saw (4.19-20) and the wall leader (19.25). The word כזב is used for the Man of Arrogance (1.15), the wall leader (19.26) and the Man of

---

184. Further on in the text (4.13-16) there is another possible reference to the Man of Lies. The reasoning of the quotation (Ps. 37.35-36) is the same; the text of the exposition is too lacunary for us to be able to base conclusions on it. Cf. M. Wood, 'Pesher Habakkuk and the Targum of Jonathan ben Uzziel', *JSP* 19 (1999), pp. 129-46 (144 n. 41).

185. A. Steudel, *Der Midrasch zur Eschatologie aus der Qumrangemeinde (4Qmidr-Eschat*$^{a.b}$*): Materielle Rekonstruktion, Textbestand, Gattung und traditionsgeschichtliche Einordnung des durch 4Q171 ('Florilegium') und 4Q177 ('Catena A') repräsentierten Werkes aus den Qumranfunden* (STDJ, 13; Leiden: E.J. Brill, 1994), p. 208 n. 2.

186. Cf. D. Pardee, 'A Restudy of the Commentary on Psalm 37 from Qumran Cave 4 (Discoveries in the Judaean Desert of Jordan, vol. V n° 171)', *RevQ* 8 (1973), pp. 163-94 (172).

187. According to Brownlee, 'Wicked Priest', p. 25.

188. Jer. 14.12; Ezek. 5.13. It is therefore unlikely that these three causes of death should be applied to three actual events that took place when Jerusalem was conquered by the Romans in 63, as Dupont-Sommer, 'Ecrit de Damas', *ad loc.*, prefers to do (which also is made problematic by his dating).

Lies (20.15; 4QpPs i 18). The verb תעה is used for the Man of Arrogance (1.15) and the Man of Lies (4QpPs i 18). The חלקות of which the Man of Arrogance is accused (1.18) is contrasted with the קלות of the Man of Lies (4QpPs i 19). Both Saw (4.19) and the wall leader are linked with the building of the wall (19.24-26). All these names can therefore be linked to one figure, who will henceforth be referred to as Saw, even though this was probably not his real name.

The text mentions the head of the kings of Greece, who is probably not mentioned by another name or description elsewhere. There is also a Wicked Priest (but not in the *Damascus Document* or the *Psalms Pesher*). Some have wanted to reduce all descriptions of local opponents of the Community to one and the same person,[189] but their viewpoint seems to be far-fetched.

2. *Definite Identifications*. The passage we have just discussed could be interpreted as claiming that Belial is a man who will appear in a limited, eschatological period and lead people astray. This would mean that he answers to our description of the Antichrist. However, Belial generally refers to Satan in the Qumran documents.[190] Although we do not wish to dismiss the possibility that in some passages this name may refer to another figure, we must note that in this passage the identification of Belial with Satan makes sense and is therefore the preferred option. In our definition the Antichrist is a *man who is dependent on* Satan, which means that we do not need to study Belial any further.

There is insufficient material (within the limits of the accepted date of edition) to enable us to identify Saw with any figure known from sources outside the Qumran Community.[191]

Dupont-Sommer's identification of the head of the kings of Greece with Pompey is well founded in itself, but fails on the date of the *Damascus Document*.

---

189. E.g. Dupont-Sommer, '"Chef des rois de Yâwân"', p. 41 n. 2; Brownlee, 'Wicked Priest', p. 22 (who viewed Saw as one of the wicked priests).

190. B. Noack, *Satanás und Sotería*, p. 33; W. Foerster and K. Schäferdiek, 'σατανᾶς', *TWNT*, VII, pp. 152-53; Huppenbauer, 'Belial in den Qumrantexten', pp. 87-88; Van der Woude, *Die messianischen Vorstellungen*, p. 20 n. 7 (p. 22); Knibb, *Qumran Community*, p. 40; Dimant, 'Qumran Sectarian Literature', p. 534.

191. Callaway, *History*, pp. 118, 121; cf. Brownlee, *Midrash Pesher of Habakkuk*, p. 95 (with more than a dozen possibilities).

176 *The Antichrist Theme in the Intertestamental Period*

Also the identification with Antiochus IV Epiphanes is difficult, because a conflict between the Qumran Community and people without insight is hardly possible during this period, and because it is difficult to find an explanation for the 'building of a wall' in that period.

Although the building of a wall primarily refers to a framework of ideas, we must check history for someone who attempted to build walls, first of all in Jerusalem. Here we find Jonathan, who had the city walls around Jerusalem rebuilt in 153, and re-fortified them in 143 as well as building a wall between the Acra[192] and the city.[193] There was no opposition during the first occasion, but there was during the second: Tryphon pursued Jonathan and killed him.

To what degree can Tryphon be called 'head of the kings of Greece' who took 'revenge'? Tryphon was a general of Alexander Balas,[194] who after his death helped his young son Antiochus (VI)[195] to the throne as a ruler opposite king Demetrius II[196] and later opposite himself.[197] Initially the relationship between Jonathan and Tryphon was excellent, but when it appeared that Jonathan fought their mutual enemies with so much vigour that the situation became dangerous even to Tryphon, the latter treacherously imprisoned Jonathan and eventually killed him.[198] This means that Tryphon did not rule as a king during Jonathan's reign, but that he was a general, first of king Alexander Balas and later of King Antiochus VI. Now the word ראש can also indicate a military leader.[199] Although Tryphon was not an important figure from our perspective, the perspective of the Qumran Community may well have been different.[200] The word 'revenge' is quite a general term, but we know that Tryphon acted in response to Jonathan's

---

192. Lorein, 'Life and Death', pp. 159, 162.

193. Van der Woude, 'Geschiedenis en godsdienst', pp. 49, 51). For 153 see 1 Macc. 10.10-11. For 143 see 1 Macc. 12.25-37; Josephus, *Ant.* 13.181-83.

194. Fl. 150–145; an acclaimed son of Antiochus IV Epiphanes, who managed to fulfil his claims. See also Will, *Histoire politique*, II, pp. 373-78.

195. 148, fl. 145–142, d. 138. See also Will, *Histoire politique*, II, pp. 405-406.

196. 161, fl. 145–139 and 129–125, d. 125; see also Will, *Histoire politique*, II, pp. 277-78, 404-409, 432-33, 435-36.

197. In 142. Because of Antiochus VI's tender age, Tryphon was a regent in his place at first; d. 138. See also Will, *Histoire politique*, II, pp. 404-407, 410-12.

198. Van der Woude, 'Geschiedenis en godsdienst', pp. 51-52.

199. See Zorell, *Lexicon, s.v.* 4a.

200. Baumgarten, *Flourishing of Jewish Sects*, pp. 89-90, also mentions Tryphon as a possible identification but he suspects irony here.

actions, and that the author of the *Damascus Writing* borrowed the term נקם from Deut. 32.35aα.

3. *The Present as the End Times?* The most interesting figure seems to be Saw. Although we do not know who he was, it is clear that he was a historical person, not an eschatological figure. This leads us to the question whether perhaps the author viewed his own period as eschatological, and this would make Saw an eschatological figure after all.

CD 1.12 mentions דורות אחרונים. In that period, God let the Teacher of Righteousness know that in דור אחרון the revenge of the sword (1.17) was to come over Saw and his followers because of their transgressions. The thinking of the Qumran Community has never been very systematic;[201] otherwise they would have realized that according to CD 20.13-15 after the death of the Teacher of Righteousness 40 years would pass until all apostates would have died, the total of 490 years would have been reached and the Promised Land could be taken,[202] after which the *final battle* would come.[203] Although Saw may have survived the Teacher of Righteousness, he would not live to see this final battle, which means that his time can not be considered as the 'end times' in the strict sense, but apparently they can in a broader sense.[204]

The author dated the events described in CD 4.12-20 in his own days, and simultaneously presented them as taking place in a period that follows the period of grace and is therefore an eschatological period in my view.

CD 19.22-26 and the *Psalms Pesher* do not contain clues about the question we are trying to answer.

Although there is no need to discuss the Teacher of Righteousness, I should like to point out that although he was not considered to be a messianic figure, he was considered as akin to such a figure.[205]

We may therefore conclude that the Qumran Community viewed its own time, and therefore also Saw's time, as *a*—but not *the*—pre-eschatological period.[206]

---

201. Religious groups like the Qumran Community do not have a systematic, rational world view. If a researcher assumes that they do, he or she will inevitably end up with a wrong construction of the writings and history of such a group.
202. Cf. Craigie, *Book of Deuteronomy*, pp. 111-12 (re. Deut. 2.13-14).
203. This battle would possibly go on for another 40 years.
204. Cf. Steudel, 'אחרית הימים', p. 241.
205. Cf. Van der Woude, *Die messianischen Vorstellungen*, pp. 73, 171.
206. Cf. Steudel, 'אחרית הימים', p. 231; but also E. Puech, 'Messianism, Resurrec-

h. *Conclusion*

We have found in the *Damascus Document*, more specifically in the Man of Lies linked to the *Psalms Pesher*, a number of factors of our Antichrist definition, namely, in the figures of Saw and Tryphon. We have excluded Belial from an identification with the Antichrist by identifying him with Satan (and we wish to keep a clear distinction between Satan and the Antichrist).

The abrupt change in 4.19 suggests a close link between Saw and Belial, but a direct influence is not mentioned anywhere.

Rabin sees a direct link between the איש הכזב and the New Testament ἄνθρωπος τῆς ἀνομίας;[207] but it should be remarked that ἀνομία is not a straightforward translation of כזב and that Rabin's conviction is largely based on the Syriac and the Arabic. Of course it cannot be denied that 'lies' are a form of lawlessness and deceit. Also the straying from justice and the taking away of the boundary marker in 1.15-16, as well as the wind and turbulence in 19.25 and the words of deceit in 4QpPs i 18-19 confirm his view. The *Damascus Document* does not mention any use of violence by Saw: his role is much more that of the false prophet. He is an opponent in this period, which is viewed as pre-eschatological. He was the opposite number of the Teacher of Righteousness, who seems to have fulfilled a pre-messianic role.[208] He is the apex of hubris, because he is called the Man of Arrogance (איש הלצון, CD 1.14).

In 19.22-23 Tryphon (the 'head of the kings of Greece') is linked—but not identified—with dragons and serpents, that is, with animals. Tryphon was an opponent in this period, which is considered to be pre-eschatological; not, however, of the Qumran Community but of Israel as a whole.[209] He played the role of the violent tyrant: he took revenge (19.24). Although

---

tion, and Eschatology at Qumran and in the New Testament', in E. Ulrich and J. Vanderkam (eds.), *The Community of the Renewed Covenant* (Christianity and Judaism in Antiquity Series, 10; Notre Dame: University Press, 1994), pp. 235-56 (250, 253-54). This would mean that the term 'pre-eschatological' is the most appropriate one.

207. Rabin, *Zadokite Documents*, p. 40. A reference to 1 Jn 2.22 (cf. 2 Jn 7) would have been an even stronger indication of a link between the איש הכזב and the Antichrist. Burgmann, *Antichrist—Antimessias*, pp. 163-64, wrongly sees a link between 1 Jn 2.22 and the איש הלצון in CD 1.11-20.

208. The Antichrist is not necessarily an opposite of a Messianic figure, but where there are messianic figures in the text there will be parallels too.

209. Tryphon's actions could have served as a lesson for the competing group, which did not view them as such, but that does not mean there was an alliance between Tryphon and the Qumran Community.

3. *The Antichrist in the Qumran Writings* 179

we have dismissed the identification of the head of the kings of Greece with Antiochus IV Epiphanes, we must remember that Tryphon was one of his successors.

We conclude that all elements of our definition are present, albeit divided over two figures: the pseudo-prophetic Saw who is discussed most elaborately, and the tyrannical Tryphon, of whom is said a lot less.[210]

We deduce from the data in the *Damascus Document* that the Qumran Community could easily have developed teaching on the Antichrist which was very similar to the Christian view,[211] with the exception that they regarded their own days as pre-eschatological and expected the appearance of such a figure in their own days. Perhaps this desire to take the end times forward is an important differential between the canonical and the intertestamental writings.

5. *Testimonia*

a. *Setting*

The passage in the *Testimonia* that we will study (4Q175 21-30) also appears in the *Psalms of Joshua* (4Q379 22 ii), which is not so much a book of psalms as a description of events related to Joshua.[212] Palaeographically the *Psalms of Joshua* are younger than the *Testimonia*, but it is generally assumed that their last edition took place earlier. In other words, the compiler of the *Testimonia* must have found these lines in the *Psalms of Joshua*, which he apparently regarded as authoritative. If this is true, the *Testimonia* were written in the Qumran Community in the same period as CD and 1QS,[213] that is around 95. This would mean that the

---

210. Because of its location at the Dead Sea the Qumran Community was hardly troubled by him.

211. For this, see Lorein, 'Fathers and their Exegetical Basis', pp. 12-57.

212. C. Newsom, 'The "Psalms of Joshua" from Qumran Cave 4', *JJS* 39 (1988), pp. 56-73 (58).

213. Puech, 'Messianism, Resurrection', p. 242; H. Eshel, 'The Historical Background of the Pesher Interpreting Joshua's Curse on the Rebuilder of Jericho', *RevQ* 15 (1991), pp. 409-20 (409); C. Newsom, '4Q378 and 4Q379: An Apocryphon of Joshua', in Fabry, Lange and Lichtenberger, *Qumranstudien*, pp. 35-85 (76); F. García Martínez and A.S. van der Woude, *De Rollen van de Dode Zee ingeleid en in het Nederlands vertaald.* II. *Liturgische teksten, Eschatologische teksten, Exegetische literatuur, Parabijbelse literatuur en overige geschriften* (Kampen: Kok, 1995), p. 159; E. Schürer, G. Vermes and M. Black, *The History of the Jewish People in the Age of Jesus Christ (175 B.C.–A.D. 135)* (Edinburgh: T. & T. Clark, 2nd edn, 1973-87), III, pp. 446-47.

Psalms of Joshua date from the time before the Teacher of Righteousness, probably even before the formation of the Essene group,[214] that before 170. The opposite chronological order—the fourth part of the *Testimonia* was added to the *Psalms of Joshua* because it thematically fits in with them —has also been defended.[215]

In short, we are dealing with a series of 'Testimonia'[216] (proof texts) on a specific subject, namely the messiah. The two texts overlap to such an extent that in our reconstructed text I have felt free to make use of both sources.

b. *4QTest (4Q175) 21-30 (= 4Q379 22 ii 7-15)*[217]

(21) בעת אשר כלה ישוע להלל ולהודות בתהלותיהי[219] (22) ויאמר ארור היש[218]
אשר יבנה את העיר הזות[220] בבכורו (23) ייסדנה ובצעירו יציב דלתיה: ואנה
איש ארור אחד[221] בליעל (24) עומד להיות פ[ח י]קוש לעמו ומחתה לכול שכניו:
ועמד (25) [...]מ[...] לה[]יות שניהמה[222] כלי חמס ושבו ובנו את (26) [העיר

---

214. Cf. Newsom, '"Psalms of Joshua"', pp. 59-60; Burgmann, *Weitere lösbare Qumranprobleme*, p. 123; García Martínez and Van der Woude, *Rollen van de Dode Zee*, II, p. 420; cf. Eshel, 'Historical Background', p. 411: 4Q379 is not an autograph. Cf. n. 1 above, second part.

215. Eshel, 'Historical Background', p. 419. About the variant hypothesis on his p. 412, see T.H. Lim, 'The "Psalms of Joshua" (4Q379 fr. 22 col. 2): A Reconsideration of its Text', *JJS* 44 (1993), pp. 309-12 (309 n. 8). The reconstructed text by Eshel (his pp. 409-10) is indeed weak, but the other arguments have made it into an interesting hypothesis. On his p. 412 n. 10 Lim is willing to keep the original dating of the *Psalms of Joshua* for the main part. For more criticism see also Newsom, '4Q378 and 4Q379', p. 76, and J. Zimmermann, *Messianische Texte aus Qumran: Königliche, priesterliche und prophetische Messiasvorstellungen in den Schriftfunden von Qumran* (WUNT, 2.104; Tübingen: J.C.B. Mohr, 1998), p. 432.

216. For the term 'Testimonia', see J. Fitzmyer, '"4QTestimonia" and the New Testament', *TS* 18 (1957), pp. 513-37.

217. According to Allegro, *Qumrân Cave 4.*, I, *ad loc.*, with regard to Strugnell, 'Notes', pp. 225-29, and according to Newsom, '4Q378 and 4Q379', p. 72, with regard to Lim, '"Psalms of Joshua"', pp. 310-12.

218. Phonetic orthography instead of האיש (cf. הזות, ואנה): Newsom, '4Q378 and 4Q379', p. 74.

219. Aramaism. בתהלותיהו (thus Allegro) is a wrong reading: Qimron, *Hebrew*, §§322.142, 144.

220. 4Q379 simply has הזאת.

221. Strugnell, 'Notes', p. 228, used to suspect, on the basis of 4Q379, that this originally read איש, but now see Lim, '"Psalms of Joshua"', p. 312.

222. See Qimron, *Hebrew*, §322.18.

3. The Antichrist in the Qumran Writings

הזות ויצ[י]יבו לה חומה ומגדלים לעשות לעוז רשע (27) [בארץ223 ורעה
גדולה] בישראל ושערוריה באפרים וביהודה (28) [..וע]שו תנופה בארץ224
ונצה225 גדולה בבני (29) [יעקוב ושפכו ד]ם כמים על חל בת ציון ובחוק
ירושלם: (30)

(21) When Joshua had finished praising and giving thanks in his hymns of praise, (22) he said: 'Cursed be the man who will build this city; with his firstborn (23) he will lay its foundations, and with his youngest he will set its gate.' And behold, an accursed person, one from Belial, (24) will arise to be a fowler's snare to his people and a stumbling block to all his neighbours. And arise shall (25)…both being instruments of violence and they will (26) rebuild this city and they will erect a wall and towers for it to make (it) into a stronghold of ungodliness (27) in the land and a great evil in Israel and a horror in Ephraim and in Judah (28)… And they will cause alienation[226] from God in the land, and great blasphemy among the sons of (29) Jacob and they will shed blood like water on the ramparts of the daughter of Zion and within the boundaries of (30) Jerusalem.

Whereas Bible verses are quoted without any explanation in the first three parts of the *Testimonia*,[227] we here see a quotation from Joshua 6.26 embedded in the description of a situation only known to us from a document found in Qumran, and the quotation is even explained.

The context of the *Psalms of Joshua* might suggest that the destruction of Jericho had given occasion to Joshua's hymns of praise (21).[228]

In Josh. 6.26, Joshua pronounced a curse on the person who would rebuild Jericho, the city that had just been destroyed. This person would only be able to rebuild Jericho at the expense of two of his children. With this curse, Joshua hoped to ensure that Jericho's ruins would remain throughout the centuries, as a reminder of God's revenge on the Canaanites' sinful lives.[229] Anyone daring to rebuild the city would be regarded as

---

223. This word is omitted in Allegro's text.

224. This description of והחניפו את־הארץ is typical for the Qumran writings: Y. Thorion, 'Die Syntax der Präposition B in der Qumranliteratur', *RevQ* 12 (1985), pp. 17-63 (53-54).

225. 4Q379 has ונאצה here. This part of this MS was corrupted in an attempt to rectify a mistake in the homeoteleuton: see Newsom, '4Q378 and 4Q379', p. 73.

226. Or 'apostasy'.

227. Deut. 5.28-29; 18.18-19; Num. 24.15-17; Deut. 33.8-11.

228. Thus Newsom, '4Q378 and 4Q379', p. 72.

229. C. van Gelderen, *De Boeken der Koningen*. II. *1 Koningen 12–22 en 2 Koningen 1–4* (Korte Verklaring; Kampen: Kok, 1936), p. 145.

an evil aggressor.[230] It is believed that this curse was realized in Hiel, who was supported by the evil King Ahab (1 Kgs 16.33-34).[231]

We see an important difference from the original text here: this text does not mention Jericho and may not even be referring to it. The Qumran Community usually focused its attention on Jerusalem, and not necessarily in a positive sense.[232] The *Psalms of Joshua* do not mention Jericho either, but it is far from clear whether the author was actually thinking of Jerusalem. These words may not have carried the same meaning for its author as for the author of the *Testimonia*.[233] Incidentally the word 'Jericho' is also absent in the Septuagint (22-23).[234]

The Qumran Community expected another realization: the curse was meant for someone who belonged to Belial and was a plague[235] for his own people and neighbouring nations.[236] The question is whether it is presented here as a prophecy regarding a future event ('an accursed person, one from Belial, will arise...') or as a wish regarding a current event[237] ('an accursed man, may he be one of Belial, arising...') (23-24).

In both manuscripts a crucial portion following this, which could have made clear why there is a change from singular to plural (dual), is sadly missing. From what we do have it appears that the preposition ב was no longer understood to mean 'to the cost of', but 'with the help of'.[238] The figures referred to are weapons of violence (Gen. 49.5) and will make Jerusalem into a centre of corruption (Hos. 6.10)[239] and apostasy, which has

230. J.H. Kroeze, *Het Boek Jozua* (Commentaar op het Oude Testament; Kampen: Kok, 1968), *ad loc.*

231. H.A. Brongers, *I Koningen* (Prediking van het Oude Testament; Nijkerk: Callenbach, 1967), *ad loc.*

232. Van der Woude, *Die messianischen Vorstellungen*, pp. 121-22; A. Dupont-Sommer, 'Testimonia', in Dupont-Sommer and Philonenko (eds.), *La Bible: Ecrits intertestamentaires*, pp. 413-20 (*ad loc.*).

233. Newsom, '4Q378 and 4Q379', p. 74. Zimmermann, *Messianische Texte*, p. 433.

234. In the LXX the name of Jericho has been omitted, and also יקום and לפני יהוה, probably to give the verse a more general character: Kroeze, *Jozua, ad loc.* The tetragram may have been dropped in 4Q379 in an independent way.

235. The word פח also occurs in CD 4.14.

236. It is remarkable that sympathy for non-Jews is shown here.

237. The second suggestion is more probable in the original reading of 4Q379; cf. Newsom, '"Psalms of Joshua"', pp. 68, 77.

238. Newsom, '4Q378 and 4Q379', p. 77.

239. Cf. Van Leeuwen, *Hosea, ad loc.* On the basis of the use of שערוריה and the

3. *The Antichrist in the Qumran Writings* 183

consequences for Israel (the whole country?) but especially for Ephraim (Pharisees?) and Judah (the Qumran Community?)[240] (24-30).

Does this refer to a future—perhaps even an eschatological—event, or do these descriptions refer to people who were already part of history at that time (and were therefore perhaps pre-eschatological)?[241] This cannot be deduced from the Hebrew with absolute certainty.[242] Moreover, several researchers have proposed a historical identification. We need to make a distinction between those researchers who take the *three* people mentioned in Joshua's curse as a starting point, and those who start from the *two* people mentioned in the explanation 'both instruments of violence'. The first group has the clear advantage of the parallelism between curse and explanation. Such a parallelism was perhaps not really necessary for the Qumran Community, but it was for the author of the *Psalms of Joshua*.[243] The second group has the slight advantage that less is expected of the small lacuna at the beginning of 4Q175 25. It is possible, however, to fill in this lacuna with a text referring to three people.[244]

Milik claims that this refers to Mattathias (the elder) and his sons Jonathan and Simon, the builders of Jerusalem.[245] Vermes claims that it refers to the two sons, Jonathan and Simon. The advantage of this interpretation is that they were actual builders, both in a technical and a political sense. Jonathan and Simon are not linked in their deaths, however.

According to Cross, followed by Burgmann, the passage refers to the

---

combination of Ephraim, Israel and Judah we are forced to conclude that the author has used Hos. 6.10-11a but we cannot say with certainty that he wished to use the full contents of this verse.

240. Eshel, 'Historical Background', p. 416.

241. For an interpretation that places the four parts of 4Q175 in the time of writing of the Testimonia, see J. Lübbe, 'A Reinterpretation of 4Q Testimonia', *RevQ* 12 (1986), pp. 187-97. Whether his hypothesis is better than the 'testimonia hypothesis' is debatable.

242. Perf. cons. or conj. + perf.?

243. His interpretation may have been different, but he definitely used the same text.

244. Vermes, *Dead Sea Scrolls in English*, p. 296, seems to suppose a conjecture אחיו ומשלו להיות, but F.M. Cross Jr, *Ancient Library*, p. 149 (ובניו עמו להיות) apparently shows that the lacuna may also have contained a text that would support an interpretation with three persons. (However, this is not the place for a palaeographic study.) Both conjectures are more suitable than the *mera conjectura* by Lim, ' "Psalms of Joshua" ', pp. 311-12: וימשל בשקר להיות.

245. 1 Macc. 10.10-11; 12.36-37 (which according to Nelis, *I Makkabeeën*, p. 182, refers to Jonathan's extensive building works); 13.10, 52; 14.37.

Hasmonean high priest Simon, who terrorized neighbouring nations,[246] and who had the Dok fortress built in the Jericho area by his son-in-law. Because he was an Arab,[247] this man did not know the Scriptures very well and was killed there in 135, by Simon and his two sons Judas and Mattathias the Younger, while Antiochus VII Sidetes caused a bloodbath in Jerusalem[248] shortly afterwards. This interpretation provides a link between the building of the city and the deaths of both sons,[249] but not between the building works and the deaths of the three Maccabees in Jericho with the bloodshed in Jerusalem.

According to Starcky, followed by Eshel, it refers to John Hyrcanus I, who also terrorized the neighbouring nations[250] and who reportedly undertook important building projects in Jericho.[251] He was supposed to have had messianic tendencies.[252] His sons Aristobulus I and Antigonus, who acted violently towards Samaria,[253] both died in 103.[254] The bloodshed apparently took place later, during the days of Alexander Janneus.[255] This interpretation has the advantage of being close to the date of edition of the Testimonia[256] and is therefore our preferred interpretation.

---

246. With reference to 1 Macc. 13.49-51 (the occupation of the Acra); 14.7 (the occupation of Gezer and Beth-Sura); 15.28-29 (Acra, Gezer, Joppe).

247. According to Abel, *Livres des Maccabées*, *ad loc.*, he was from Idumea.

248. Cross, *Ancient Library*, p. 149; Burgmann, *Weitere lösbare Qumranprobleme*, p. 123; Burgmann, 'Antichrist—Antimessias', pp. 155-57; see 1 Macc. 16.15-16, and also Josephus, *Ant.* 13.228, 236-41.

249. According to Eshel, 'Historical Background', p. 413 n. 15, the youngest son, Mattathias the younger, was too young. It is unclear on what information Eshel has based this conclusion. 1 Maccabees 16.2-3 shows he was younger than his brothers, but his father's age suggests he cannot have been a small toddler. It would also mean that his title of 'instrument of violence' was a cliché.

250. With reference to Josephus, *Ant.* 13.254-58 (Syria, Moab, Samaria, Edom).

251. Eshel, 'Historical Background', p. 415. Against: Newsom, '4Q378 and 4Q379', p. 78.

252. See Josephus, *Ant.* 13.299. This idea has been strongly refuted: Zimmermann, *Messianische Texte*, p. 433.

253. Josephus, *Ant.* 13.276. The Qumran Community did not seem to have much sympathy for Samaria either.

254. Josephus, *Ant.* 13.307-309, 314-18.

255. Eshel, 'Historical Background', p. 417. However, see J. Sievers *apud* Newsom, '4Q378 and 4Q379', p. 78. Newsom eventually opts for a combination of John Hyrcanus I, Aristobulus I and Alexander Janneus, but with reservations.

256. This is not circular reasoning: the other hypotheses assume the same date of edition.

3. *The Antichrist in the Qumran Writings* 185

According to Allegro (and Dupont-Sommer) it refers to Alexander Janneus and his sons John Hyrcanus II and Aristobulus II, and to the destruction of Jerusalem in 63. This interpretation was made impossible by the palaeographic dating of the *Testimonia*.[257]

Van der Woude does not look for well-known Hasmoneans. He works with two people: 'one from Belial' and someone who has been 'lost' because of the lacuna. Together they form the 'two': the Wicked Priest and the Man of Lies.[258] When looking at the *Habakkuk Pesher*, we will deal with the question whether the Wicked Priest can be identified with a particular Hasmonean. Apart from this point, Van der Woude's interpretation coincides with the other interpretations. However, we must dismiss any identification of a Hasmonean with the Man of Lies.[259]

c. *The Antichrist in the* Testimonia

When comparing the two or three figures described in the *Testimonia* with our Antichrist definition, we see that we are dealing with a man (23) acting under the influence of Satan (23) who is violent (24-25, 29) and wicked (26-28). Because the fourth part of the *Testimonia* follows three messianic portions, we see that we are dealing with an opponent of the messiah, and that we clearly have to think of the Antichrist theme. What remains is the question about the eschatological content of this passage.

Most researchers have mainly focused on a historical identification. If the 'father with two sons hypothesis' is correct, Eshel's variant seems to be the most convincing. In spite of the historical reconstruction we should not forget that the Qumran Community may have experienced this event as a pre-eschatological phenomenon. According to Burgmann, the Qumran Community saw itself as elect and therefore presented its enemies as God's enemies.[260]

Others have pointed out that the messianic parts of the *Testimonia* are clearly eschatological, not pre-eschatological, and deduce from this that the figure (or figures) in the fourth part is still to be expected, that is eschato-

---

257. An overview of the hypotheses can be found with Schürer, Vermes and Black, *History of the Jewish People*, III, p. 447 n. 5, and with Eshel, 'Historical Background', pp. 413-14.

258. Van der Woude, *Die messianischen Vorstellungen*, p. 121.

259. Against: Burgmann, *Weitere lösbare Qumranprobleme*, p. 125; Brownlee, 'Wicked Priest', p. 12.

260. Burgmann, 'Antichrist—Antimessias', p. 153; cf. Burgmann, *Vorgeschichte und Frühgeschichte*, p. 486.

186   *The Antichrist Theme in the Intertestamental Period*

logical.[261] Similar multiple descriptions of the Antichrist appear elsewhere: we have seen this when studying Rev. 13.[262] A triple Antichrist also nicely corresponds with the three messianic parts in the *Testimonia*.[263]

Van der Woude takes the middle ground: in the pages in question he does not talk about historical identifications, but emphasizes the function of the multiple figure in the fourth part, that is the 'Doppelgestalt' (double figure) of the Antichrist.[264]

In short, we can say that in spite of the uncertainties in this passage[265] we should keep in mind that a remarkably clear description of the Antichrist is given here. Even if the author had a specific historical situation in mind, it apparently still led to the forming of ideas about the Antichrist in view of the messianic context of the *Testimonia*. However, after all the previous chapters it should be clear that this is not the single oldest text on the Antichrist.[266]

6. Hymns

a. *Setting*

On palaeographic grounds we must date the *Hymns* before 75.[267] Since a number of *Hymns* can be ascribed to the Teacher of Righteousness, the compilation could even be much older.[268] Whether the hymn we will study

---

261. García Martínez, *Qumran and Apocalyptic*, pp. 174-75; Callaway, *History of the Qumran Community*, p. 183; Lietaert Peerbolte, *Antecedents of Antichrist*, p. 285.

262. See Chapter 1, 2b, as a conclusion with the discussion of Rev. 13. Of course other writings have also given multiple descriptions of the Antichrist, but never this close together. In those cases the authors gave different images rather than different facets of the same image. Perhaps the descriptions of the Psalms of Solomon resembles this occurrence of multiple descriptions the most: cf. Chapter 2, section 9f.

263. Schürer, Vermes and Black, *History of the Jewish People*, III, p. 447.

264. Van der Woude, *Die messianischen Vorstellungen*, pp. 121-22; cf. Dimant, 'Qumran Sectarian Literature', p. 518; H. Stegemann, 'Some remarks to *1QSa*, to *1QSb*, and to Qumran Messianism', *RevQ* 17 (1996), pp. 479-505 (504).

265. Two or three persons, Jerusalem or Jericho, historical identification, pre-eschatological or eschatological.

266. Against: Burgmann, 'Antichrist—Antimessias', pp. 154-55; Burgmann, *Vorgeschichte und Frühgeschichte*, p. 487. This is however 'eine der ältesten Quellen': Van der Woude, *Die messianischen Vorstellungen*, p. 122.

267. García Martínez and Van der Woude, *Rollen van de Dode Zee*, I, p. 300.

268. Dimant, 'Qumran Sectarian Literature', p. 523; A. Dupont-Sommer, 'Hymnes' in Dupont-Sommer and Philonenko (eds.), *La Bible: Ecrits intertestamentaires*,

3. *The Antichrist in the Qumran Writings* 187

was also written by the Teacher of Righteousness, fully depends on the interpretation of the first part; the interpretation of the second part is irrelevant to this issue.[269]

The *Hymns* were published at a time when scholars were not yet convinced of the need of a consistent consecutive numbering system. For a while it was assumed that manuscript 1Q35 was actually a part of manuscript 1QH,[270] but this appeared not to be the case.[271]

The hard work of Stegemann and Puech[272] resulted in an important rearrangement of the *Hymns*. We will use the new column numbering, with the old numbering in brackets.

b. *1QH 11 (olim 3).12-18*[273]

(11.12) והרית[274] אפעה לחבל נמרץ ומשברי שחת לכול מעשי פלצות:
וירועו[276] (13) אוש[275]י קיר באוניה על פני מים ויהמו שחקים בקול המון:
ויושבי עפר (14) כיורדי ימים נבעתים מהמון מים:
וחכמיהם למו[277] כמלחים במצולות כי תתבלע (15) כול חכמתם בהמות
ימים ברתוח תהומות על נבוכי[278] מים:
[ויתרג]שו[279] לרום גלים (16) ומשברי מים בהמון קולם:

pp. 227-99 (230) (he dates the Teacher of Righteousness much later); cf. M. Mansoor, *The Thanksgiving Hymns* (STDJ, 3; Leiden: E.J. Brill, 1961), pp. 45-49.

269. G. Jeremias, *Der Lehrer der Gerechtigkeit* (SUNT, 2; Göttingen: Vandenhoeck & Ruprecht, 1963), pp. 171-73, 176-77, ascribes the Hymn to the Teacher of Righteousness.

270. D. Barthélemy and J.T. Milik, *Qumran Cave I* (DJD, 1; Oxford: Clarendon Press, 1955), p. 136.

271. A.S. van der Woude, 'Fünfzehn Jahre Qumranforschung (1974–1988)', *TRu* 57 (1992), pp. 1-57, 225-53 (17).

272. For this, see García Martínez and van der Woude, *Rollen van de Dode Zee*, I, p. 296, and E. Puech, 'Quelques aspects de la restauration du Rouleau des Hymnes (1QH)', *JJS* 39 (1988), pp. 38-55 (43 [n. 20!], 48, 51).

273. According to E.L. Sukenik, *The Dead Sea Scrolls of the Hebrew University* (Jerusalem: Magnes Press, 1955).

274. The י in the root was preserved, and the feminine ending came later.

275. Cf. Aram. אשׁ, 'foundation'.

276. Niphal imperf. cons. of רעע.

277. Sukenik: וחכמיה כולמו. See Holm-Nielsen, *Hodayot*, p. 51 n. 229 (pp. 58-59), for an explanation of the text that is generally accepted today.

278. Biblical Hebr. has נִבְכֵי as st. cstr. pl. (Job 38.16).

279. Van der Woude, *Die messianischen Vorstellungen*, p. 145 n. 30 (p. 150), suggests והתרגשו. However, there are no perfects in this passage. Lohse, *Texte aus Qumran*, *ad loc.*, suggests יתגרשו, but no sentence in 1QH begins with an imperf. that stands

ובהתרגשם יפתחו שא[ו]ל [ואבדון וכו]ל²⁸⁰ חצי שחת (17) עם מצעדם:
לתהום ישמיעו קולם ויפתחו שערי [שאול לכול²⁸¹] מעשי אפעה:
(18) ויסגרו דלתי שחת בעד הרית עול ובריחי עולם בעד כול רוחי אפעה:

(11.12) She who is pregnant with a serpent (will have) painful birth pangs, and the agony[282] of the grave (will lead) to all symptoms of fear. And (13) the foundations of the wall shall rock like a ship upon the face of the waters, and clouds roar with the sound of a multitude. And the inhabitants of dust (14) as well as those who travel the seas[283] (shall be) overrun by the mass of water.

And their wise men (shall be) to them like sailors in the deep, for swallowed will be (15) all their wisdom, by the roaring of the seas, and with the boiling of the oceans above the water sources. The waves shall be poured out until (they) rise (again) (16), and the breakers in the multitudes of their voice. And at their roaring Hades and Abaddon[284] shall open, and all arrows of the Abyss (17) (follow) in their footprints. They make their noise heard to the Ocean and the gates of Hades are opened to all acts of the serpent. (18) But the gates of the Abyss shall be closed behind those who are pregnant with calamity and eternal bolts behind all spirits of serpents.

After a discussion of a pregnancy in the first part of this hymn, another pregnancy is discussed in the second part.

This is a very difficult passage[285] which uses poetic language. Apart from the birth pains, the imagery used is mainly linked to shipping. In those

---

'on its own': L. Vegas Montaner, 'Some Features of the Hebrew Verbal Syntax in the Qumran Hodayot', in J. Trebolle Barrera and L. Vegas Montaner, *The Madrid Qumran Congress* (STDJ, 11; Leiden: E.J. Brill; Madrid: Complutense, 1992), pp. 273-86 (277). In general see Holm-Nielsen, *Hodayot*, p. 51 n. 33 (p. 59).

280. Van der Woude, *Die messianischen Vorstellungen*, 145 n. 31 (p. 150).

281. According to M. Delcor, *Les Hymnes de Qumrân (Hodayot): Texte hébreu—introduction—traduction—commentaire* (Paris: Letouzey et Ané, 1962), *ad loc.*; Lohse, *Texte aus Qumran, ad loc.* Van der Woude, *Die messianischen Vorstellungen*, p. 145 n. 32 (p. 150) suggests filling in the lacuna with מות ויובדו; see below: '…and the gates of Death will be opened and all deeds of the serpent will perish.'

282. The original word can mean both 'cervix' and 'sea billows'.

283. Lit.: 'those who go down the seas'; cf. Ps. 107.23.

284. For the translation see J.H. Kroeze, *Job* (Commentaar op het Oude Testament; Kampen: Kok, 1961), p. 288 (re. 26.6, where the same combination occurs, but note that אבדון is a reconstruction).

285. Dupont-Sommer, 'Hymnes', *ad loc.*: 'des plus difficiles à interpréter dans tout le recueil'; Burrows *apud* Mansoor, *Thanksgiving Hymns*, p. 91 n. 4: 'an exceptionally obscure passage'; A. Caquot, 'Le messianisme qumrânien', in M. Delcor (ed.), *Qumrân: Sa piété, sa théologie et son milieu* (BETL, 46; Gembloux: Duculot: Leuven: University Press, 1978), pp. 231-47 (244): 'trop équivoque pour que nous l'invoquions'.

3. *The Antichrist in the Qumran Writings* 189

days shipping was not as well advanced as it is today, and it carried many risks.[286] The two registers of imagery are linked through double meanings[287] that can generally not be reflected in the translation. Another literary tool is the *inclusio*,[288] which points to the second part of this hymn: the serpent.

The nature of the pregnancy is slightly problematic. The word אֶפְעֶה means 'serpent' but Biblical Hebrew also uses אֶפַע, although this is probably a writing error for אֶפֶס.[289] On the basis of this word, a number of researchers assume the meaning of vanity or idleness.[290] Not only the etymology, but also the improbability of an abstract word here, seem to indicate otherwise.[291] The pregnant woman will experience חבל: the root indicates birth pangs, but there is a homonymous[292] root with the meaning of 'destruction'. The word מַשְׁבֵּרִי could be derived from מַשְׁבֵּר, 'cervix', but also from מִשְׁבָּרִים, 'sea billows'[293] (11.12).

The suffering of the foundations apparently refers to an earthquake that will damage even the city walls[294] (11.12-13). The swallowing of wisdom (כול חכמתם תתבלע) also occurs in Ps. 107.27. It could be a reference to seasickness, but more probably to a storm that is so strong that the sailors' knowledge is insufficient to save them[295] (11.14-15). When the ocean is

---

286. Cf. J.P.M. van der Ploeg, *Psalmen. II. Psalm 76 t/m 150* (Boeken van het Oude Testament; Roermond: Romen, 1975), p. 228 (re. Ps. 107.23).

287. This style was used very often in the *Hymns*: Kittel, *Hymns*, p. 162.

288. Kittel, *Hymns*, p. 162.

289. Zorell, *Lexicon*, s.v.; Delcor, *Hymnes*, p. 114 n. 1; Holm-Nielsen, *Hodayot*, p. 51 n. 25 (p. 58), also mentions the root פעה, to 'groan'.

290. Lohse, *Texte aus Qumran, ad loc.*; Vermes, *Dead Sea Scrolls, ad loc.* Holm-Nielsen, *Hodayot*, p. 51 (see also n. 25 of that page [on p. 58]) speaks about 'wickedness'.

291. Knibb, *Qumran Community*, p. 177. This text would fit very nicely between Isa. 14.29 (to mention but one) and Mt. 3.7 (etc.), but that is not sufficient proof.

292. In view of the Arabic *ḥbl* and *ḫbl* I do not believe they are two different developments of meaning from the same root. See also Holm-Nielsen, *Hodayot*, p. 51 n. 12 (p. 53).

293. The two Hebrew words are interrelated. See also Holm-Nielsen, *Hodayot*, p. 51 n. 12 (p. 54).

294. Knibb, *Qumran Community*, p. 177. For the city, see the first part of the Hymn (11.7): J. Carmignac, 'Les Hymnes', in *idem* (ed.), *Les Textes de Qumrân traduits et annotés. I. La Règle de la Communauté—La Règle de la Guerre—Les Hymnes* (Paris: Letouzey et Ané, 1961), pp. 127-282 (*ad loc.*). Burgmann could be expected to think of the city walls being rebuilt by Simon, but this is not the case.

295. Van der Ploeg, *Psalmen*, II, pp. 228-29. Ps. 107.23 has been mentioned before. Ps. 107.18 could have influenced 1QH 11.17, especially if a different reconstruction is used: Holm-Nielsen, *Hodayot*, p. 51 n. 37 (p.59), 61.

boiling at a point near its floor,[296] then it is not only the surface that moves, but the whole water mass (11.15). The image at the end of 11.15 should probably be taken literally: the water mass will come down with such force that it bounces up again. This will unexpectedly be followed[297] by sudden calamity[298] that will sweep over the whole earth (11.16-17).

We have seen that the arrival of the serpent will be accompanied with all kinds of calamity, in which all registers of Hades will be opened. finally the doors of the Abyss will close. This probably means that all the wicked will be safely locked away (at the end of times). This thought is kept very short and follows the preceding lines[299] abruptly, without any introduction (11.18).

c. *The Antichrist in the* Hymns
In a first image, an author (i.e. the Teacher of Righteousness?) apparently compares himself to a woman in labour (with the emphasis on the pain and suffering). It seems that a later author linked this first image to the image of the birth of a policy maker (with messianic connotations).[300] Where the

---

296. נבכי in Job 38.16 is usually translated 'water sources'. L. Koehler and W. Baumgartner, *Lexicon in Veteris Testamenti libros* (Leiden: E.J. Brill, 2nd edn, 1958), *s.v.*, translates with 'sandy ground'.

297. It is unclear from the text *whom* the water will be following, but it is probably the Qumran Community, whose difficulties are mentioned throughout the poem: cf. Delcor, *Hymnes*, pp. 117-18.

298. See Van der Ploeg, *Psalmen*, II, p. 121 (re. Ps. 91.5); Holm-Nielsen, *Hodayot*, p. 51 n. 35 (p. 59).

299. According to Mansoor, *Thanksgiving Hymns*, p. 35; cf. Carmignac, 'Hymnes', p. 196 n. 49 (p. 197). Knibb, *Qumran Community*, p. 177, refers to Ps. 6.10 for a similar ending, but that verse is less abrupt. O. Betz, 'Past Events and Last Events in the Qumran Interpretation of History', in *Proceedings of the Sixth World Congress of Jewish Studies* (Jerusalem: World Union of Jewish Studies, 1977), pp. 27-34 (30), refers to 1QM 17.4-5; the thought is indeed comparable, but it fits better into the context in that verse. (His other references are not convincing.) The abruptness is less acute if we accept the restoration offered by Van der Woude, *Die messianischen Vorstellungen*, p. 145 n. 32 (p. 150): this would mean that the serpent's activities end in 11.17b (cf. Carmignac, 'Hymnes', *ad loc.*). NB: Hades could indeed be the domain of the serpent (cf. *2 En.* 42.1). For the abrupt character, cf. 2 Thess. 2.8b (by Christ's intervention); Rev. 19.20; Dan. 7.11; 8.25bβ; 11.45b; 1 Sam. 17.48-49 (by David's intervention); *Pss. Sol.* 2.26; *T. Ash.* 7.3 (by intervention of the Almighty); *Tr. Shem* 11.18.

300. Assuming some messianic expectation, Isa. 9.5 could have been read from a Messianic perspective at a very early date: cf. Vriezen, *Hoofdlijnen der theologie*, p. 485; E. Noort, 'Toekomstverwachting in het Oude Testament—enkele aspecten', in

3. The Antichrist in the Qumran Writings   191

first author probably thought of a pre-eschatological indication of his own time,[301] after the interpolation it becomes eschatological (11.9b-10a).[302] Following our usual views, the combination too must have had a special meaning within the Qumran Community, which is, however, unclear to us as yet.[303]

The second part could have been the work of the second author, linking in with his messianic interpolation without losing sight of the feeling of painful suffering. The second mother is of course not the Teacher of Righteousness, but she is not his opponent either. The second author had an eschatological interpretation in mind, and a search for historical identification is therefore useless.[304] The mother is the opposite number of the messiah's mother in the interpolation, and in that sense she has no significance on her own. In this interpretation only the serpent needs to be examined in the light of our Antichrist definition.

The serpent refers to a man who will be born in the end times, and who will therefore not be active before then. He will be called a 'serpent' because he is evil. He is the opposite number of the messiah.[305] He will cause

---

H. Baarlink, W.S. Duvekot and A. Geense (eds.), *Vervulling en voleinding* (Kampen: Kok, 1984), pp. 13-29 (29); Delcor, *Hymnes*, pp. 120-22 (note his 'y introduit un élément nouveau', which is in line with my 'two stages hypothesis'). *Pace* van der Woude, *Die messianischen Vorstellungen*, pp. 153-55. This view does not exclude the expectation of an earlier fulfilment of Isa. 9.5.

301. Cf. Holm-Nielsen, *Hodayot*, p. 63; Mansoor, *Thanksgiving Hymns*, pp. 90-91. This view does not mean that the first author attempted to make historical identification easy. This fact renders the passage useless for a *historical*, but not for an *ideological* reconstruction. (Cf. Callaway, *History*, pp. 192-93, 196-97.)

302. Cf. García Martínez, *Qumran and Apocalyptic*, p. 175.

303. Cf. Caquot, 'Messianisme qumrânien', p. 244 ('confusion de la pensée'). Neither the interpretation that it turns out to be the Teacher of Righteousness who gives birth to the Messiah—although he is sufficiently aware of the unusual grace bestowed upon him, giving him a special status—or to the Qumran Community, nor the interpretation that the Qumran Community gave birth to the Teacher of Righteousness seems very attractive. (See also Carmignac, 'Hymnes', p. 195; Holm-Nielsen, *Hodayot*, p. 62; Mansoor, *Thanksgiving Hymns*, p. 91; Delcor, *Hymnes*, p. 122.) If this reconstruction is correct, this throws into doubt the hypothesis that the Teacher of Righteousness is the author of the first passage: no-one would dare to add to his texts.

304. Burgmann, 'Antichrist—Antimessias', pp. 161, 168, who identifies the woman with high priest Simon and the Antichrist, is therefore wrong. Cf. Carmignac, 'Hymnes', p. 196 n. 37.

305. According to the interpretation presented above, i.e., interpolation in the first part.

fear, like the fear people have during an earthquake or a storm. All the usual rules of wisdom are pushed to the side by his actions. Assistance in many forms will be given from Satan's realm.[306]

All these points match our definition. The announcement of his end is very short, but can be harmonized with what we have seen about this elsewhere.[307] However, we need to point out that not much is said about the Antichrist theme in general. It is unclear how the mother should be interpreted, but apparently the passage was not meant to be clear about this.

This is the second writing—after the *Testimonia*—in which the Antichrist is not presented as pre-eschatological (i.e. in the days of the Qumran Community), but as eschatological.[308] Did the Qumran Community translate the pre-eschatological Antichrist into an eschatological one, or is the eschatological Antichrist of this text a continuation from older sources? In order to be able to give a verdict, we must look at all the texts in chronological order.

We could compare this to the Teacher of Righteousness, who also appears in two forms: historical (pre-eschatological) and eschatological.[309]

7. Nahum Pesher[310]

a. *Setting*

We will now focus on a pesher of the book of Nahum. Palaeographically, 4Q169 can be dated to between 40 and 20, and it does not seem to be an

---

306. For this interpretation, cf. Knibb, *Qumran Community*, p. 176.

307. Cf. 2 Macc. 9.7-12, *Pss. Sol.* 2.26; *Tr. Shem* 11.18; CD 1.11-18; 1QpHab 10.9-13 and also Rev. 17.17 and Dan. 7.26; 8.25; 11.45.

308. For a pre-eschatological Antichrist, see the Damascus Document.

309. Van der Woude, *Die messianischen Vorstellungen*, pp. 171, 174-75.

310. The pesher is a kind of topicalizing exegesis. In the past, scholars accentuated the *impression* left on us by the pesher: the interpretation deviates quite a lot from the original meaning. See for this approach, e.g., F.F. Bruce, *Biblical Exegesis in the Qumran Texts* (Exegetica, 3.1; The Hague: Van Keulen, 1959), pp. 7-17; A. Dupont-Sommer, *Les écrits esséniens découverts près de la mer morte* (Paris: Payot, 2nd edn, 1960) (p. 267: 'le texte n'est qu'un prétexte: on l'arrache au contexte, on le transpose...on le torture, de façon à lui faire dire ce dont on a soi-même l'esprit tout rempli'); in the same way in 'Le "Commentaire d'Habacuc" découvert près de la Mer Morte. Traduction et Notes', *RHR* 137.2 (1950), pp. 129-71 (p. 151: 'toutes les sentences bibliques sont...violemment transposées sur un plan historique et sur un plan théologique nouveaux'); E. Osswald, 'Zur Hermeneutik des Habakuk-Kommentars', *ZAW* 68 (1956), pp. 243-56 (p. 244: 'Jedes Stück des Textes wird ohne Beachtung des ursprünglichen Zusammenhanges für sich betrachtet'). In the present, scholars accentu-

autograph. Naturally the date of origin of the writing depends on its interpretation, but it is generally dated to around 70, the period preceding Pompey's capture of Jerusalem.[311]

Fragments 3 and 4 have been combined; they contain four columns of which the first is the best preserved.

b. *4QpNa (4Q169) 3-4 i 2-8*[312]

(i 2) [פשרו על דמי]טרוס מלך יון אשר בקש לבוא ירושלים בעצת דורשי החלקות (3) [ולוא נתן אל ירושלים] ביד[313] מלכי יון מאנתיכוס עד עמוד מושלי כתיים ואחר תרמס: (5) [פשרו על דמיטרוס אשר עשה מלחמה[314] על כפיר החרון אשר יכה[316] בגדוליו ואנשי עצתו (6) [וינוסו מלפניו[315]]:...
פשרו על כפיר החרון (7) [... נק]מות בדורשי החלקות אשר יתלה[317] אנשים חיים (8) [... אשר לא יעשה[318]] בישראל מלפנים:

(i 2) Its interpretation: about Demetrius, the king of Greece, who sought to come to Jerusalem, on the advice of those who sought smooth things. (3) And God did not deliver Jerusalem into the hand of the kings of Greece, from [the time of] Antiochus until the rulers of the Kittites arose, but then it will be trampled.
(5) Its interpretation: about Demetrius, who waged war against the Furious Lion which he defeated, together with his officials and advisors (6) and they fled from him.

ate the *intention* the writers seem to have had: representing the true meaning of each element of Scripture. See for this approach Gabrion, 'Interprétation de l'Ecriture', pp. 828-30 (p. 830: 'la connaissance des "choses cachées" et des "mystères" des prophéties …était avant tout le fruit d'une étude assidue'); M. Fishbane, 'Use, Authority and Interpretation of Mikra at Qumran', in M. Mulder and H. Sysling (eds.), *Mikra* (CRINT, 2; Assen: Van Gorcum; Philadelphia: Fortress Press, 1988), pp. 339-77 (340, 351, 361-62, 372, 374-75) (p. 351: 'the base text…determines the structure and developments of the new text'; p. 373: 'in order to understand the true intent of the ancient oracles').

311. Van der Woude, 'Fünfzehn Jahre' (1992), p. 233; García Martínez and Van der Woude, *Rollen van de Dode Zee*, II, pp. 216-17.

312. According to Allegro, *Qumrân Cave 4*, I, *ad loc.*, with regard to Strugnell, 'Notes', pp. 204-10, and M.P. Horgan, *Pesharim: Qumran Interpretations of Biblical Books* (CBQMS, 8; Washington: Catholic Biblical Association, 1979), p. 47.

313. The filling in of the lacuna is from Horgan. Allegro was unable to read the ב in ביד.

314. The addition is from Horgan.

315. The addition is from Horgan.

316. The imperf. could indicate repetition: Joüon, *Grammaire*, §113e.

317. In view of the imperf. the hanging was apparently not seen as a single event.

318. This addition is from the draft edition by J.M. Allegro, 'Further Light on the History of the Qumran Sect', *JBL* 75 (1956), pp. 89-95 (91).

Its interpretation: about the Furious Lion (7)…revenge against those who seek the smooth, who hangs people alive (8)…which had never been done before in Israel.

In this passage the writer offers several ideas regarding Nah. 2.12-13, but the biblical text seems to be of little importance in the pesher. Apparently the word that has caused the association is אריה, although כפיר is used in the explanation. One could therefore assume that the lion always refers to the same figure, or at least always to someone in the same category, but this is far from certain.

All commentaries assume that the four remaining letters טרוס indicate Demetrius, as this is the only Hellenistic royal name ending in these letters. This leads to the question to which the text is referring Demetrius to.[319] According to 1 Macc. 7, Demetrius I Soter[320] sent his commanding officer to Jerusalem in 161, in order to eliminate the people, after he was accused by the high priest, Alcimus. If this is true, דורשי החלקות refers to Alcimus and his party, whom the Essenes regarded as people who took the Law too lightly.[321] However, I must point out that the early dates mostly used during the first phase of research have since been abandoned. Nowadays an identification of דורשי החלקות with the Pharisees is generally assumed; the Qumran Community accused them of taking the Law too lightly. The Kittites seem to refer to a dynasty that was not that of the Seleucid king Antiochus IV Epiphanes,[322] which means they must be identified with the Romans and we are dealing with a period of immediate

---

319. And most importantly: why does this text give names, which was against common practice in Qumran? A.E. Palumbo Jr, 'A New Interpretation of the Nahum Commentary', *Folia Orientalia* 29 (1992–93), pp. 153-62 (155-56), suspects that this can best be explained by assuming that the Antiochus and Demetrius referred to lived a long time ago, and must therefore be Antiochus IV and Demetrius I. His further reconstruction offers no solution, however.

320. °189, fl. 162–150; for information on this man, see Will, *Histoire politique*, II, pp. 365-76.

321. Rowley, 'Kittim', pp. 107-108; cf. M. Burrows, *More Light on the Dead Sea Scrolls: New Scrolls and New Interpretations. With Translations of Important Recent Discoveries* (London: Secker & Warburg, 1958), p. 202. This judgment was specific to the Essenes (cf. García Martínez and Van der Woude, '"Groningen" Hypothesis', p. 540), either after 162, at a time when the Chasidim tolerated the so-called moderate Hellenistic Alcimus—unlike the Maccabees, which meant that the Essenes and Maccabees agreed on this point—or at a time when Alcimus had alienated the Chasidim from himself. See Will, *Histoire politique*, II, p. 369.

322. *Pace* Rowley, 'Kittim', p. 97.

3. The Antichrist in the Qumran Writings 195

Roman threat.[323] A search within these markers leads straight to Demetrius II Eucerus,[324] who allegedly attempted to go to Jerusalem in 88, on the instigation of the Pharisees. He never reached Jerusalem,[325] and so the city was free from foreign rule from the days of Antiochus IV until the arrival of the Kittites. Do we therefore need to think of the year 63, when Jerusalem was captured by Pompey?[326] I do not think so, because the text seems to indicate that תרמס is future, even though there is an immediate threat.[327] According to the old interpretations, מושלי כתיים refers to the numerous Seleucid pretenders to the throne during the end of the second century,[328] but it was still unclear what this end term indicated (i 2-3).

When Demetrius III set out to fight Jerusalem, Alexander Janneus was king of Jerusalem. It seems that 'a young lion' refers to him,[329] but this only becomes clear in the next paragraph in the pesher. The revelation in that paragraph is, however, not surprising in view of the interpretation of the quoted Bible text. This interpretation is not explicit in the text, but the Bible text says that the lion will kill for his lionesses, which might be a reference to crucifixions (whereby the crucified person died of suffocation) ordered by Alexander Janneus and watched by his harem.[330] The text of this para-

---

323. A. Dupont-Sommer, 'Commentaires bibliques', in Dupont-Sommer and Philonenko (eds.), *La Bible: Ecrits intertestamentaires*, pp. 333-80 (*ad loc.*); Knibb, *Qumran Community*, p. 212; Horgan, *Pesharim*, p. 174. (The reasoning of the latter is slightly too elaborate; this is not about finding freedom after a time of bondage, but about losing freedom.)

324. Fl. 95–97. About him, see Will, *Histoire politique*, II, pp. 449-50. Horgan, *Pesharim*, p. 173; Knibb, *Qumran Community*, p. 211. Demetrius II Nicator is hardly ever defended, but the data in the pesher are so imprecise that it is possible: cf. Bruce, *Biblical Exegesis*, p. 19.

325. Dupont-Sommer, 'Commentaires bibliques', *ad loc.* Josephus, *Ant.* 13.376. Allegro, 'Further Light', p. 92, deduces from this text that Demetrius aimed to settle in Jerusalem. He only got as far as Shechem, where he won a battle but never managed to capitalize on his victory: Josephus, *Ant.* 13.377-79.

326. Thus Knibb, *Qumran Community*, p. 212.

327. J. Carmignac, 'Interprétations de Prophètes et de Psaumes', in *idem* (ed.), *Les Textes de Qumrân traduits et annotés*. II. *Règle de la Congrégation—Recueil des Bénédictions—Interprétations de Prophètes et de Psaumes—Document de Damas—Apocryphe de la Genèse—Fragments des grottes 1 et 4* (Paris: Letouzey et Ané, 1963), pp. 43-128 (*ad loc.*).

328. Rowley, 'Kittim', p. 97.

329. The young lion was able to look after itself, and was therefore not a young cub: Zorell, *Lexicon, s.v.*

330. D.J. Halperin, 'Crucifixion, the Nahum Pesher, and the Rabbinic Penalty of

graph contains many lacunas. On the basis of other sources, more than on the basis of this text, we can say that Alexander Janneus counted on the Sadducee party, that Demetrius III defeated him near Shechem, and that they then fled[331] (i 5-6).

Alexander Janneus took revenge on the Pharisees—they had been advisers to Demetrius III—by crucifying eight hundred of them. Never before had crucifixion taken place on this scale,[332] at least not on the orders of a Jewish king. Flavius Josephus claims that Antiochus IV Epiphanes crucified the fathers who, being loyal to the Jewish laws, had circumcised their sons.[333] In view of the feelings in the Qumran Community towards the Pharisees, we must ask whether this action by Alexander Janneus, which implied that the victims were placed under God's curse (see Deut. 21.23) was viewed as a step too far, or whether *Schadenfreude* is implied.[334] In iii 4-5, and perhaps even in ii 9 in an indirect way, we detect some sympathy for the Pharisees in this pesher,[335] which means that the indignation described is real.

In the interpretation that was usual in an initial stage of the research (with early dates), Antiochus IV Epiphanes was the Angry Lion, both in these lines and the previous (i 6-8).

c. *The Antichrist in the* Nahum Pesher

Now that we have obtained more clarity about this text with its lacunas, is it possible to determine whether it refers to an Antichrist?

The Angry Lion is a man (Alexander Janneus) who is referred to by the name of an animal, which is an indication of his wickedness. According to the suggested interpretation he sinned horribly: his victims were 'only'

Strangulation', *JJS* 32 (1981), pp. 32-46 (34); for the link between crucifixion and suffocation, see his pp. 34-43.

331. Horgan, *Pesharim*, p. 175. See Josephus, *Ant.* 13.377-79.

332. According to Carmignac, 'Interprétations', *ad loc.*; Bruce, *Biblical Exegesis*, p. 22. For the question whether perhaps the regular, justified punishments with crucifixion were referred to, see Horgan, *Pesharim*, pp. 177-78. Dupont-Sommer, 'Commentaires bibliques', *ad loc.*, is right in remarking: 'Le passage est capital.'

333. This has been debated: see above, in the discussion of *Ass. Mos.* 8, Chapter 2, section 13b.

334. Cf. Knibb, *Qumran Community*, pp. 212-13.

335. It is possible that several persecuted Pharisees had fled to Qumran: cf. R. Marcus, *Flavius Josephus*. VII. *Jewish Antiquities, Books XII–XIV* (LCL, 365; Cambridge, MA: Harvard University Press; London: Heinemann, 1933), p. 419 (re. *Ant.* 13.383). See above, in the discussion of *Pss. Sol.* 17, Chapter 2, section 9d.

Pharisees, but the author of the pesher does think that he went too far in his tyrannical actions. Although he is a historical figure, we note the expression לאחרית הימים in ii 2. Apparently this refers to a situation that is experienced as being pre-eschatological. Nothing is said about a relationship with Satan. Few details are found in this text anyhow, especially when leaving all reconstructions out of consideration.

Antiochus IV, who had been important for the understanding of the term 'Antichrist', is mentioned in this text, but only plays a very minor role. At most we can say that the fact that Antiochus IV was still remembered at the time of writing shows how important he was to Jewish thinking, but this is a statement no-one would deny anyway.[336]

This text has revealed very little and can only be used in combination with other texts: a Hasmonean king and high priest may have been regarded as a pre-eschatological Antichrist.[337]

8. Habakkuk Pesher

a. *Setting*

The third pesher we will study is the most elaborate, the first published and the most studied pesher.

It is a pesher on Hab. 1–2; ch. 3 was not included because its genre is different.

The manuscript dates from around 40,[338] and is apparently not an autograph.[339] The text was probably finished just before 60.[340] The period under discussion is that the second half of the second century and the beginning of the first.[341]

---

336. Mertens, *Das Buch Daniel*, p. 78, opts for a close connection between those who suffered under Antiochus IV and the Qumran Community.

337. Cf. for the pre-eschatological element and for the Hasmonean high priest above the discussion of the *Damascus Document*, of 4QTest 21-30, and—below—of the *Habbakuk Pesher*.

338. Van der Woude, 'Fünfzehn Jahre' (1992), p. 233; Jull *et al.*, 'Radiocarbon Dating', p. 14.

339. On the basis of 2.5: see Horgan, *Pesharim, ad loc.*

340. Van der Woude, 'Fünfzehn Jahre' (1992), p. 26. For a much earlier date, see Rowley, 'Kittim', pp. 92-109; E. Stauffer, 'Der gegenwärtige Stand der Erforschung der in Palästina neu gefundenen hebräischen Handschriften. 19. Zur Frühdatierung des Habakukmidrasch', *TLZ* 76 (1951), cols. 667-74 (674).

341. García Martínez and Van der Woude, *Rollen van de Dode Zee*, II, pp. 221-22.

b. *1QpHab 2.1-6*[342]

(2.1) [פשר הדבר על] הבוגדים[344] עם איש (2) הכזב כי לוא [שמעו דברי[343]]
מורה הצדקה מפי א(3)ל: ועל הבו[גדים בברית] החדשה כיאלוא
(4) האמינו בברית אל [ויחללו[345]] את ש[ם] קודשו:(5) וכן פשר הדבר
[על הבו]גדים לאחרית א[346] (6) הימים:

(2.1) The interpretation of the word: about those who were unfaithful, with[347] the Man of (2) Lies, for they did not listen to the words of the Teacher of Righteousness (who had received them) from the mouth (3) of God. And about those who were unfaithful to the new covenant, for they did not (4) trust the covenant of God, but they profaned his holy name. (5) And likewise is the interpretation of the word about those who will be unfaithful towards the last (6) days.

With reference to Hab. 1.5, or a variant of it,[348] the author says who he views as traitors.

According to this writing, the Man of Lies, who we also met in the *Damascus Document*,[349] will have many followers. They are described as unfaithful, because they do not follow the exegesis of the Teacher of Righteousness (2.1-3). Another group is mentioned, a group of people who did belong to the Qumran Community at some point, but who later distanced themselves from it, which was considered as even worse than not having belonged to it at all (3.3-4).[350] Finally, these groups were expected to grow

342. The text follows Brownlee (M. Burrows and W.H. Brownlee, *The Dead Sea Scrolls of St. Mark's Monastery*. I. *The Isaiah Manuscript and the Habakkuk Commentary* [New Haven: ASOR, 1950]); where a remnant of a letter was still visible, this letter was used as visible, according to Horgan; the additions are from F.A.W. van 't Land and A.S. van der Woude, *De Habakuk-rol van ʿAin Fašḫa: Tekst en vertaling* (Assen: Van Gorcum, 1954).

343. Horgan adds: האמינו בדברי.

344. Brownlee: ובוגדים; Van 't Land and Van der Woude: no ו but ה! (thus also Brownlee, *Midrash Pesher, ad loc.*).

345. Since the imperf. cons. does function in 1QpHab, the form ויחללו (thus Horgan, and Lohse, *Texte aus Qumran, ad loc.*) is preferable. (Van 't Land and Van der Woude has וחללו.)

346. Perhaps this א was written to make another addition to the line impossible: Brownlee, *Midrash Pesher, ad loc.*

347. Dupont-Sommer, 'Commentaires bibliques', *ad loc.*, interprets as 'toward', but the usual preposition for that is ב: Zorell, *Lexicon, s.v.* בגד.

348. There are no 'traitors' in the MT, only in the LXX. See Knibb, *Qumran Community*, pp. 222-23, and in general, Bruce, *Biblical Exegesis*, pp. 12-14.

349. Cf. Carmignac, 'Interprétations', *ad loc.*

350. Cf. CD 20.14-15. Cf. Van der Woude, *Die messianischen Vorstellungen*, p. 36.

in the end times, which were considered to be not too far off.[351] This may be a reference to people who were members of the Qumran Community at the time of edition, but who could not be regarded as actual[352] members (2.5-6).

c. *1QpHab 8.8-13*

(8.8) פשרו על הכוהן הרשע אשר (9) נקרא על שם האמת בתחלת עומדו
וכאשר משל (10) בישראל רם לבו ויעזוב את אל ויבגוד בחוקים בעבור
הון (11): ויגזול ויקבוץ הון אנשי חמס אשר מרדו באל (12) והון עמים
לקח לוסיף עליו עון אשמה ודרכי (13) תועבות פעל בכול נדת טמאה:

(8.8) Its interpretation: about the Wicked Priest, who (9) was counted as belonging to the truth[353] at the beginning of his ministry, but when he ruled (10) in Israel, his heart became proud and he forsook God and became unfaithful to the commandments because of (11) riches. And he stole and accumulated wealth from violent people who rebelled against God, (12) and he took riches of the nations, so that he increased in his sinful iniquity, detestable ways (13) he made in manifold unclean defilement.

According to Hab. 2.5-6,[354] the desire for riches leads to iniquity. It is the Wicked Priest who has fallen victim to this trap. It is generally assumed that a high priest is referred to here.[355] This means we are dealing with someone who was known even before the Qumran Documents were found. There is less unity about the question which high priest is referred to here. We will discuss this pesher according to the Groningen hypothesis—which sees a description here of the succession of high priests—in the first place on the grounds of his attempts to harmonize as many details as possible without doing them injustice.

This hypothesis leads to the conclusion that the priest referred to is Judas Maccabee. Van der Woude assumes that Menelaus could no longer have been regarded as high priest during the Cleansing of the Temple in 164, and that Judas Maccabee had temporarily taken up this task.[356] At the start of his career[357] he was still regarded as an acceptable priest (by the stan-

---

351. Cf. Steudel, 'אחרית הימים', p. 239.
352. For the three groups, see Brownlee, *Midrash Pesher*, pp. 54-56, and Van der Woude, *Die messianischen Vorstellungen*, pp. 34-36.
353. A.S. van der Woude, 'Wicked Priest or Wicked Priests. Reflections on the Identification of the Wicked Priest in the Habakuk Commentary', *JJS* 33 (1982), pp. 349-59 (354); see also Brownlee, *Midrash Pesher*, pp. 134-37.
354. Here too, the text deviates from the MT.
355. Note the word play הכוהן הרשע—הכוהן הראש.
356. A.S. van der Woude, 'Once Again: The Wicked Priests in the *Habakkuk Pesher* from Cave 1 of Qumran', *RevQ* 17 (1996), pp. 375-84 (380-81).
357. For the translation of עמד, see also Brownlee, *Midrash Pesher*, pp. 137-38.

dards of the Qumran Community), but shortly afterwards his desire for riches led to hubris[358] and unfaithfulness toward God. He no longer conformed to God's standards for his servants (8.8-11).[359] What is unusual is that the *Habakkuk Pesher* mentions that he obtained his plunder from violent people who revolted against God—is this the Hellenistic[360] party? —and from foreign nations[361] (Idumeans, Philistines, *et al.*),[362] and that this was still held against him. The latter fits in with the interpretation of Dupont-Sommer (the 'violent people' are the Qumran Community),[363] but otherwise this is a very unusual identification. If it refers to Pharisees, it may not be logical but there is a parallel: in spite of the animosity, the Qumran Community could not endorse the crucifixion of Pharisees.[364] It is unclear what the 'detestable ways' and 'unclean defilement' refer to. Brownlee says that we should not attribute any specific meaning to these terms (8.11-13).[365]

Other hypotheses see Jonathan,[366] Simon,[367] Alexander Janneus,[368] and Hyrcanus II[369] in the Wicked Priest.

---

358. Brownlee, *Midrash Pesher*, *ad loc.* Cf. Ezek. 28.5, although this does not use the same words.

359. Brownlee, *Midrash Pesher*, pp. 135, 138-39, refers to Exod. 18.21, and demonstrates that the Wicked Priest failed on each point. However, this text can hardly be regarded as a standard text: see, e.g., C. Houtman, *Exodus*. II. *Exodus 7.14–19.25* (Commentaar op het Oude Testament; Kampen: Kok, 1989), *ad loc.*

360. Brownlee, *Midrash Pesher*, pp. 140-41, thinks of Samaritans. The interpretation that it refers to Pharisees is also defendable: see Carmignac, 'Interprétations', *ad loc.*

361. Other Hasmoneans also caused hardship for their neighbouring nations! Cf. Knibb, *Qumran Community*, *ad loc.*, about Jonathan; this chapter, 3b, about Simon and Hyrcanus I; Carmignac, 'Interprétations', *ad loc.*, for Alexander Janneus.

362. Van der Woude, 'Wicked Priest', pp. 354-55, and 'Once Again: The Wicked Priests', pp. 380-81, 383.

363. Dupont-Sommer, 'Commentaires bibliques', *ad loc.*

364. Cf. the discussion of 4Q169 3-4 i 7-8.

365. Brownlee, *Midrash Pesher*, p. 142.

366. Knibb, *Qumran Community*, pp. 238-39; Burgmann, *Weitere lösbare Qumranprobleme*, p. 77; Horgan, *Pesharim*, p. 7; T.H. Lim, 'The Wicked Priests of the Groningen Hypothesis', *JBL* 112 (1993), pp. 415-25 (424); E. Puech, 'Jonathan le Prêtre Impie et les débuts de la Communauté de Qumrân. *4QJonathan (4Q523)* et *4QPsAp (4Q448)*', *RevQ* 17 (1996), pp. 241-70 (268-69).

367. Horgan, *Pesharim*, p. 7.

368. Cf. Carmignac, 'Interprétations', p. 106 nn. 10, 14 (p. 107), p. 108 n. 16. I. Fröhlich, 'Le genre littéraire des Pesharim de Qumran', *RevQ* 12 (1986), pp. 383-98 (393): including his sons Aristobulus II and Hyrcanus II.

369. Fl. 76–67 and 63–40. Dupont-Sommer, 'Commentaires bibliques', *ad loc.*

3. *The Antichrist in the Qumran Writings* 201

d. *1QpHab 10.9-13*

(10.9) פשר הדבר על מטיף הכזב אשר התעה רבים (10) לבנות עיר שוו[370]
בדמים ולקים[374] עדה בשקר (11) בעבור[373] כבודה[372] לוגיע[371] רבים בעבודת
שוו ולהרותם[375] (12) במ[ע]שי שקר להיות עמלם לריק בעבור יבואו (13)
למשפטי אש אשר גדפו ויחרפו את בתירי אל:

(10.9) The interpretation of the word: about the Preacher of Lies who led many astray (10) by building a worthless city with blood and by making a community remain in deceit (11) for the sake of their own dignity, to fatigue many in worthless labour and by making them pregnant (12) with deceitful

370. St. abs. (thus Horgan, *Pesharim*, *ad loc.*; Van 't Land and Van der Woude, *Habakuk-rol, ad loc.*; Carmignac, 'Interprétations', *ad loc.*; Knibb, *Qumran Community*, *ad loc.*). Possible, but more difficult thematically: st. cstr. + suff. 3 sg. m. of שוא (thus Brownlee, *Midrash Pesher*, p. 169; Dupont-Sommer, 'Commentaires bibliques', *ad loc.*). See also Qimron, *Hebrew*, §§100.63, 200.18.

371. Prep. + hiphil inf. cstr. of יגע (Qimron, *Hebrew*, §310.145).

372. St. cstr. + suff. 3 sg. fem., referring to עיר or עדה (which is to be preferred in my opinion) (thus Van 't Land and Van der Woude, *Habakuk-rol, ad loc.*; Horgan, *Pesharim*; Brownlee, *Midrash Pesher, ad loc.*; for the last two authors the suffix refers to עיר). Another possibility is st. cstr. + suff. 3 sg. m. (thus F. García Martínez and E.J.C. Tigchelaar, *The Dead Sea Scrolls Study Edition*. I. *1Q1–4Q273* [Leiden: E.J. Brill, 1997], *ad loc.*; cf. Horgan, *Pesharim, ad loc.*). García Martínez and Van der Woude, *Rollen van de Dode Zee*, II, *ad loc.* (and of course the French-speakers) are vaguer. From the author's perspective the difference is probably not of great importance.

373. Thus Van 't Land and Van der Woude; Brownlee: בעבוד.

374. Brownlee: ולקום. Conj. + prep. + hiphil inf. cstr. (cf. Qimron, *Hebrew*, §310.145; the same view is held by Brownlee, *Midrash Pesher, ad loc.*).

375. This form is hard to explain. Four possibilities have been given (apart from conj. + prep. and suff. 3 pl. m.).

1. Hiphil inf. cstr. of ירה ('to instruct'; cf. translation by García Martínez and Van der Woude, *Rollen van de Dode Zee*, II, *ad loc.*). But: *a.* Why did the author not write it out in full (להורותם)? (Brownlee, *Midrash Pesher*, p. 171, suggests lack of space.) *b.* Why was the ה not elided (see Qimron, *Hebrew*, §310.145)? *c.* Why would the author use the root ירה (Brownlee, *Midrash Pesher*, p. 172)?

2. Hiphil inf. cstr. of ראה ('to see'; Van 't Land and Van der Woude, *Habakuk-rol, ad loc.*). But: *a.* Where did the א go? *b.* Why was the ה not elided (cf. 1*b*)?

3. Hiphil inf. cstr. of רוה ('to become drunk'; G. Vermes *apud* Horgan, *Pesharim, ad loc.*). But: *a.* Why was it not written out in full (להורותם) (cf., however, 1*a*)? *b.* Why was the ה not elided? (cf. 1*b*). Admittedly the term would fit in very nicely with מטיף etc.

4. Piel inf. cstr. of הרה ('to be pregnant'; cf. translation by Dupont-Sommer, 'Commentaires bibliques', *ad loc.*; Carmignac, 'Interprétations', *ad loc.*). See also (and for other references) Brownlee, *Midrash Pesher*, pp. 171-72.

works so that their efforts are futile because they (13) are heading for judgment by fire, because[376] they have slandered and outraged the elect of God.

In Hab. 2.12-13, woe is announced over the Chaldean who will build Babel in blood and over the nations whose efforts will turn out to be futile. In the *Habakkuk Pesher* this is applied to the Preacher of Lies,[377] who will lead many astray by his framework of thoughts, which will be accompanied by bloodshed.[378] Unsurprisingly, early researchers have linked this to Epiphanes, who erected the πόλις, acted deceitfully and persecuted the believers.[379] We will, however, start from the general chronological framework of the Qumran Communities in which the persecutions at the time of Antiochus IV still played in the background but were part of history. This would mean that Dupont-Sommer's interpretation also falls outside the accepted chronology, but in the future.[380]

Let us return to the text. Did the leading astray take place first, followed by the building works, or did he lead people astray by way of the building works? We will assume that the competing group existed before the Preacher of Lies did his work,[381] and that he strengthened something that already existed, albeit in a less stable form.[382] This means that he led others astray by continuing the building works. He also started a physical building project.[383] The Preacher of Lies only paid attention to the honour

376. This translation of אשר is also possible and makes the sentence flow much better than 'those who'. (See also Brownlee, *Midrash Pesher, ad loc.*)

377. For the double meaning of מטיף, see n. 126.

378. This may be surprising when keeping the Damascus Document and the Psalm Pesher in mind, but we can also think of אנשי מלחמה in CD 20.13-15. According to Carmignac, 'Interprétations', *ad loc.*, and Knibb, *Qumran Community, ad loc.*, it is possible that the use of בדמים was only determined by the quotation of the text and therefore plays no role in the translation.

379. H.H. Rowley, *The Zadokite Fragments and the Dead Sea Scrolls* (Oxford: Basil Blackwell, 1952), pp. 67, 70; Mertens, *Das Buch Daniel*, p. 77.

380. He refers to the rebuilding of the walls of Jerusalem in 47 by Hyrcanus II, who had been high priest again since 63. See also P. Schäfer, 'Geschiedenis en godsdienst van het Palestijnse Jodendom vanaf Pompejus tot en met de opstand onder Bar Kochba', in A.S. van der Woude (ed.), *Bijbels Handboek. III. Het Nieuwe Testament* (Kampen: Kok, 1987), pp. 17-58 (19-22); M. Stern, 'The Reign of Herod and the Herodian Dynasty', in S. Safrai and M. Stern (eds.), *The Jewish People in the First Century* (CRINT, 1; Assen: Van Gorcum, 1974), pp. 216-307 (216-17).

381. Cf. Brownlee, *Midrash Pesher*, p. 169.

382. הקים can take this meaning: see Job 4.4 (and Kroeze, *Job, ad loc.*); Ps. 89.44 (and Van der Ploeg, *Psalmen*, II, *ad loc.*).

383. This means that Saw (see the discussion of the Damascus Document) was a

of the community[384] and thereby ensured—not that this was the object from the perspective of the Preacher of Lies but rather as a necessary result according to the author[385]—that many[386] made efforts that turned out to be futile (10.9-11). The form ולהרותם is difficult to explain from a grammatical viewpoint, but the point is that the Preacher of Lies initiates his followers into his own viewpoints, which, according to the Qumran Community, will turn out to be futile, because they have turned against the Qumran Community and will therefore be[387] judged by fire (10.11-13).[388]

e. *1QpHab 12.7-9*

(12.7) פשרו הקריה היא ירושלם (8) אשר פעל בה הכוהן הרשע מעשי
תועבות ויטמא את (9) מקדש אל

(12.7) Its interpretation: the city, that is Jerusalem, (8) where the Wicked Priest did wicked things and (9) defiled God's sanctuary.

---

proponent of the building of the walls surrounding Jerusalem, even though this led to problems with the Seleucid general Tryphon (the head of the kings of Greece) and with the Qumran Community, who saw this as lack of faith.

384. Grammatically this is the most probable explanation; thematically it does not make much of a difference whether it was the honour of the Preacher of Lies or that of his group that was at stake.

385. The same is said by Carmignac, 'Interprétations', *ad loc.*

386. This is often a reference to the Qumran Community, but not in this case: Brownlee, *Midrash Pesher*, p. 170.

387. This is a *second* interpretation of יגעו in the quoted text (Hab. 2.13; MT: וייגעו), based on the root נגע (the first was based on יגע, 'to labour'). See also Jer. 51.58, where the two aspects are also in the order of the pesher (Brownlee, *Midrash Pesher, ad loc.*). This may have been a well-known saying: B.N. Wambacq, *Jeremias, Klaagliederen, Baruch, Brief van Jeremias* (Boeken van het Oude Testament; Roermond: Romen, 1957), *ad loc.*

388. An eschatological judgment by fire for people is not mentioned as frequently as we would suspect when reading secondary literature (e.g. K. Nielsen, '"Gud Herren kaldte på ilden til dom". Dommedagsmotivet og dets forskydninger', *DTT* 58 [1995], pp. 3-15): cf. Carmignac, 'Interprétations', p. 110 n. 6 (p. 111); A. Lacocque, *Le Livre de Daniel* (CAT; Neuchâtel: Delachaux et Niestlé, 1976), p. 110. Num. 16.35 (albeit not eschatological); Isa. 30.33 (not eschatological, but the verse played a role in the preparation of several specific eschatological images: see E.J. Young, *The Book of Isaiah*. II. *Chapters 19-39* [Grand Rapids: Eerdmans, 1969]; A. Schoors, *Jesaja* [Boeken van het Oude Testament; Roermond: Romen, 1972], *ad loc.*), and Mal. 3.2-3 (but perhaps here too as cleansing rather than as judging: J.G. Baldwin, *Haggai, Zechariah, Malachi* [TOTC; Leicester; Downers Grove: Inter-Varsity Press, 1972], *ad loc.*) are the most obvious. Outside the Old Testament, see also *1 En.* 90.26; 100.9; 103.8; Mt. 25.41.

Again the text (Hab. 2.17bα) diverts from the Masoretic text.[389] The Wicked Priest referred to here is claimed to be Alexander Janneus. His actions were extremely violent[390] and he was not deemed to be suitable for the task of high priest[391] (12.7-9).[392]

f. *The Antichrist in the* Habakkuk Pesher

The activities of the Man of Lies take place in the religious arena. By not siding with the Teacher of Righteousness he and his group turned away from God (2.1-4). In that sense he can be regarded as lawless.[393] Saw was not alone in his wrongdoings. He led a large group into wrongdoing, and deceit was characteristic of his deeds (10.9-10, 12). Here he acts like a false prophet. The blood in 10.10 can be interpreted as referring to the tyrannical aspect, but whether the word דמים can carry this meaning is debatable.

The text does not claim its author was living in the end times (2.5-6), but we may assume this period was expected to arrive soon; also the judgment of unbelievers was to take place in the near future (10.12-13).

Several details that we found when reading the *Damascus Document* are confirmed here: Saw, the Man of Lies, is a lawless false prophet who places himself opposite the Teacher of Righteousness in a period regarded to be pre-eschatological.

What is new is that according to the Groningen hypothesis, Saw's actions can be dated at the time of high priest Simon,[394] because he is mentioned after Simon[395] in the *Habakkuk Pesher*. This fits in with his general dating at the time of the appearance of the Teacher of Righteousness.

---

389. In 1QpHab 12.1 this passage has been quoted 'correctly', which means that it might be better to speak of a short summary here rather than a quotation. (קרה does occur in Hab. 2.17bβ.)

390. See Josephus, *Ant.* 13.373. For other 'despicable deeds', see Brownlee, *Midrash Pesher*, pp. 206-207.

391. See Josephus, *Ant.* 13.272-373, 380, 383. Van der Woude, 'Wicked Priest', pp. 358-59.

392. The 'old' interpretation considered Menelaus (fl. 172–163): Rowley, *Zadokite Fragments*, pp. 67, 69.

393. Cf. also 1QpHab 5.11-12, without many further details.

394. Fl. 142–135.

395. Van der Woude, 'Wicked Priest', p. 357. The criticism by Lim, 'Wicked Priests', p. 424 n. 36, is unjustified. Since Saw is not categorized as a priest, he should not be placed in that line. The time of his actions probably overlapped with the reigns of Simon (fl. 142–135) and John Hyrcanus I (fl. 135–104). The identification of Burgmann,

3. The Antichrist in the Qumran Writings

We have not discussed all the texts in which the Wicked Priest appears, but only those that lead us to our goal. It is after all not our aim to study the Wicked Priest, but only those elements in intertestamental literature that point towards the Antichrist theme.

While the Wicked Priest is a historical figure (or rather a historical function), his time was considered to be pre-eschatological.[396] The end times were coming.[397] This eschatological man acted like a tyrant (8.9-12), but his motivations were religious (8.10, 12-13). He soon came to hubris (8.10). This way he reached a high degree of sin, but not its apex (8.12). All his actions were despicable (8.12-13; 12.8). Since he was the high priest, there were consequences for the adequate functioning of the Temple (12.13; 10.8-9). We see that the religious and political aspect of the Antichrist clearly meet in the Wicked Priest.

In the *Habakkuk Pesher* we find a double presentation of the pre-eschatological variant of the Antichrist: on the one hand the false prophet Saw and on the other the Wicked Priest who combines religious and political characteristics.

Again we have seen a Hasmonean who is a pre-eschatological type of the Antichrist.[398]

9. War Scroll

a. *Setting*

The main manuscript of the *War Scroll* (1Q33) can palaeographically be dated to the last few years BCE,[399] but other manuscripts are available (4Q493 and 4Q496) that are older and have been written in the first half of the first century CE.[400]

'Antichrist—Antimessias', *passim* (a summary by H. Bietenhard, 'Die Handschriftenfunde vom Toten Meer [Hirbet Qumran] und die Essener-Frage. Die Funde in der Wüste Juda [Eine Orientierung]', *ANRW*, II 19.1 [1979], pp. 704-78 [719 n. 40]), of the Man of Lies with Simon, confirms the dating, although the identification is wrong—the Man of Lies is not of the same social category as the Wicked Priest.

396. Since we recognize that 'historical' and 'pre-eschatological' go together in these texts, a comparison with the man of Ezek. 28, who had made a good start but then fell, is not justified.

397. See 1QpHab 9.6.

398. See also *Pss. Sol.* (Chapter 2, section 9f), and possibly the *Testimonia*.

399. García Martínez and Van der Woude, *Rollen van de Dode Zee*, II, p. 99.

400. 4Q493: M. Baillet, *Qumrân grotte 4. III. 4Q482–4Q520* (DJD, 7; Oxford: Clarendon Press, 1982), p. 50. Materially, 4Q496 offers a complex situation: 4Q505, 4Q506

On the basis of the contents of 1Q33 and the manuscripts from the fourth cave, scholars have decided that the history of its origin is very complicated and probably runs along the following lines. The oldest part, a number of prayers and military operations, is dependent on 1 Maccabees.[401] A first edition made use of data from the book of Daniel and is therefore judged to have taken place after 165.[402] This stage is probably reflected in 4Q491. In Roman times, after 63, a final edition adapted the writing to the 40-year schedule.[403]

I would suggest that the 40-year schedule may indeed stand apart from the rest of the work (and therefore probably be younger). I also believe that a 'realistic' addition took place, in which it was admitted that members of the Qumran Community can die in battle.

Several scholars do not wish to join up 4Q491 and 4Q494 with 1QM, and claim that manuscript 4Q491 contains a different, and older, final edition.[404]

Another possibility is that the latter is not an older stage but a different, related writing.[405] Palaeographically, manuscript 4Q493 can be dated shortly before the Herodian epoch, towards the end of the first half of the first century,[406] which means that the writing must stem from the beginning of the first century.[407] According to Dimant we are dealing with a different revision of the same writing.[408]

---

and 4Q509 belong to the same papyrus, but palaeographically there are great differences. 4Q505 and 4Q509 (recto side) were written around 70–60, 4Q496 (verso side) shortly after that (just before 50), 4Q506 (verso) around the middle of the first century CE: see Baillet, *Qumrân grotte 4*, III, pp. 57-58, 168, 170, 184.

401. This means it was written after 100 (see Chapter 2, section 7a). This reasoning is unusual, since 1 Maccabees has not been found in Qumran and the Maccabees were not especially appreciated there. For a comparison between 1 and 2 Macc. and 1QM, see von der Osten-Sacken, *Gott und Belial*, pp. 68-69.

402. The basic writing is also from after 165, so this date does not give any new clues. About the use of Daniel, see G.K. Beale, *The Use of Daniel in Jewish Apocalyptic Literature and in the Revelation of St. John* (Lanham: University Press of America, 1984), pp. 60-66.

403. García Martínez and Van der Woude, *Rollen van de Dode Zee*, II, pp. 101-103.

404. García Martínez and Van der Woude, *Rollen van de Dode Zee*, II, p. 105.

405. A.S. van der Woude, 'Fünfzehn Jahre Qumranforschung (1974–1988)', *TRu* 55 (1990), pp. 245-307 (256).

406. Baillet, *Qumrân grotte 4*, III, p. 50.

407. García Martínez and Van der Woude, *Rollen van de Dode Zee*, II, pp. 106-107.

408. Dimant, 'Qumran Sectarian Literature', p. 515 n. 149.

3. The Antichrist in the Qumran Writings   207

In my view, 4Q491 and 4Q493 are sufficiently similar to 1QM for us to study them together.[409]

The dating of the final edition is also influenced by the context in which the Roman elements are placed. Roman influence was possible even before the principate,[410] even before 63.[411]

I prefer to opt for a final edition in 60.[412] During that time the straightforward confrontation with the Romans, and the reporting of it, could have led to a more realistic approach, and this date does not clash with the palaeographic data. This does not mean, however, that large portions could not be much older.[413]

Taking all elements into account, it seems that the age of the portions we will study follows the numeric order, from older to younger.[414]

The *War Scroll* is not an apocalypse in the usual sense.[415] Nor is it a purely military tract. What we need to point out here is that in the Hellenistic world, similar military tracts were written by philosophers,[416] that is,

---

409. This is not the case for other writings which are related to 1QM (namely, 4Q285, 4Q471, 11Q14).

410. Against Schürer, Vermes and Black, *History of the Jewish People*, III, p. 403.

411. See J.P.M. van der Ploeg, *Le rouleau de la guerre* (STDJ, 2; Leiden: E.J. Brill, 1959), p. 9. It cannot be stated with absolute certainty that the art of war is of Roman origin: cf. J. Duhaime, 'The War Scroll from Qumran and the Greco-Roman Tactical Treatises', *RevQ* 13 (Mémorial Jean Carmignac; 1988), pp. 133-51 (142), and K.M.T. Atkinson, 'The Historical Setting of the "War of the Sons of Light and the Sons of Darkness"', *BJRL* 40 (1957–58), pp. 272-97 (280-82) (however, her dating is partly based on a completely outdated reconstruction of the historical setting of the Qumran Community; see her pp. 283-88). Hengel, *Judentum und Hellenismus*, pp. 27-32, points out that the military experience the Jews obtained as hired soldiers in Hellenistic armies was of importance.

412. García Martínez and Van der Woude, *Rollen van de Dode Zee*, II, p. 103; A. Dupont-Sommer, 'Règlement de la guerre', in Dupont-Sommer and Philonenko (eds.), *La Bible: Ecrits intertestamentaires*, pp. 185-226 (188).

413. Thus Mertens, *Das Buch Daniel*, p. 25. Also Dimant, 'Qumran Sectarian Literature', pp. 516-17, and J. Carmignac, *La Règle de la Guerre des fils de lumière contre les fils de ténèbres* (Paris: Letouzey et Ané, 1958), p. xiii, for the whole writing. The mention of Kittites from Egypt and Assyria also points to this possibility (*pace* Carmignac, *Règle de la Guerre*, p. 4).

414. Whereby in my view 1.3-5, 11.1-2 and 11.16 belong to the 'basic document' and 15.2-3 and 17.5-6 stem from the period of realistic additions.

415. It might be in an unusual sense: J. Duhaime, 'La règle de la Guerre de Qumrân et l'apocalyptique', *ScEs* 36 (1984), pp. 67-88 (82-87).

416. Duhaime, 'War Scroll', p. 141.

208   *The Antichrist Theme in the Intertestamental Period*

by ideologically oriented people, and not only with those with military-technical interests. This means that the genres cannot really be differentiated: the *War Scroll* is a military tract[417] written by people who knew more about liturgy than military-technical issues and who had an apocalyptic background.

b. *1QM 1.3-5*[418]

(1.3) ואחר המלחמה יעלו משם (4) [... מלך[419]] הכתיים במצרים ובקצו
יצא[420] בחמה גדולה להלחם במלכי הצפון ואפו להשמיד ולהכרית את קרן
(5) ישראל[421]:

(1.3) And after the war they will set out from there (4) against the king of the Kittites in Egypt, and at his moment he will go forth in great anger to wage war with the kings of the North and his fury (will be aimed at[422]) destroying and exterminating the horn of (5) Israel.

According to Dupont-Sommer, the first column of the *War Scroll* contains an introduction, which in lines 3-7 depicts the final battle; this means that המלחמה refers to the first war.[423] According to Yadin, the war with the Kittites in Egypt is part of the second phase, taking place during the first six years of the 40-year war.[424] This would mean that המלחמה refers to the first phase, the war against neighbouring nations, traditional enemies (including the Kittites of Assyria) and the enemies within Israel.[425] Carmignac

417. It gives realistic expectations, unlike allegories etc. Cf. Duhaime, 'War Scroll', pp. 150-51.
418. According to Sukenik, *Dead Sea Scrolls, ad loc.*; to 1QM 1.5 the text of 4Q496 3 was added, and to 1QM 1.4 Baillet's conjecture (according to Baillet, *Qumrân grotte 4*, III, p. 58).
419. According to the reconstruction by Baillet, *Qumrân grotte 4*, III, p. 58, on the basis of 4Q496, and before him by Van der Ploeg, *Rouleau de la guerre, ad loc.*
420. Imperf.
421. This word has been added to with the help of 4Q496 3 i 4: Baillet, *Qumrân grotte 4*, III, p. 58.
422. Nuance of aim.
423. Dupont-Sommer, 'Règlement de la guerre', *ad loc.* (division into paragraphs); Van der Woude, *Die messianischen Vorstellungen*, pp. 119-20.
424. See the overview by Y. Yadin, *The Scroll of the War of the Sons of Light against the Sons of Darkness* (trans. B. Rabin and C. Rabin; Oxford: Oxford University Press, 1962), pp. 36-37. However, Yadin (p. 22) is of the view that the battle with the Kittites is critical and is elaborately described throughout the *War Scroll*. In spite of Yadin's impressive chronological overview there is apparently no chronological order in the writing. For further criticism, see Van der Ploeg, *Rouleau de la guerre*, pp. 20-21.
425. Yadin, *Scroll of the War, ad loc.*

3. *The Antichrist in the Qumran Writings* 209

opts for the first phase as well, but he has this determined by the Semitic nations, and the second phase by the Hammites.[426] The *War Scroll* deviates from the majority of the Qumran writings in the sense that it pays much attention to enemies outside Israel.

Baillet's publication of 4Q496 was crucial to the 'filling in' of the gaps in 1QM (1Q33) and the older commentaries are now out of date on those specific points.

According to the *War Scroll*, the Children of the Light[427] will prepare for war[428] and move from the spiritual desert[429] of Jerusalem to the king of the Kittites in Egypt.[430] The preposition ב[431] may lead to the question whether the king was there by chance[432] or whether the king in question was a Ptolemy,[433] but this question actually places the verse in a historical context, while the author saw these events as future only. All we can say is that this reconstruction lends an undetermined character to the text. This is stated more generally by Carmignac, who says that we should not look for a precise identification because 'Kittites' is a very general reference to 'the enemy'.[434]

426. Carmignac, *Règle de la Guerre*, pp. 7-8.
427. According to B. Jongeling, *Le rouleau de la guerre des manuscrits de Qumrân* (SSN, 4; Assen: Van Gorcum, 1962), *ad loc.*; Carmignac, *Règle de la Guerre*, p. 8; Van der Ploeg, *Rouleau de la guerre, ad loc.* Not the priests, since they provide spiritual leadership; the members will be doing the work: see 1QM 8.
428. Carmignac, *Règle de la Guerre*, p. 8; Yadin, *Scroll of the War, ad loc.*
429. Jongeling, *Rouleau de la guerre*, p. 55.
430. The lacuna also offers the possibility of separating the advance by the Children of the Light from that of the king of the Kittites. This would mean that the second sentence indicates that the king of the Kittites will *enter* Egypt: thus Dupont-Sommer, 'Règlement de la guerre', *ad loc.*; Atkinson, 'Historical Setting', p. 277. It does not make much difference to the rest of the account, which definitely refers to the king of the Kittites. Apart from the arguments mentioned elsewhere, the military initiative of the Children of the Light, which is typical for the Qumran Community, also leads us to opt for the translation suggested here.
431. Yadin, *Scroll of the War, ad loc.*: not 'of Egypt'!
432. Bruce, *Biblical Exegesis*, p. 63: 'leader of the Roman forces in Egypt'.
433. According to Ginsberg, 'Hebrew University Scrolls', p. 20.
434. Carmignac, *Règle de la Guerre*, p. 4. He also claims that 'from Assyria' only refers to the legendary brutality of the Assyrians. Others regard this as an indication—subject to their further interpretation—of the Seleucids (thus Ginsberg, 'Hebrew University Scrolls', p. 20; Rowley, *Zadokite Fragments*, p. 65; for the eastern ambitions of the Seleucids cf. Tarn, *Greeks in Bactria and India*, pp. 187-88, 203, 213-14), or the Roman troops in Syria (thus Bruce, *Biblical Exegesis*, p. 63; Hadas-Lebel, 'L'évolution de l'image de Rome', p. 750).

The king of the Kittites will choose the right moment[435] to advance against the kings of the North. The plural 'kings of the North' is remarkable, because 1QM deviates from Dan. 11.40 here, while it is strikingly similar to it elsewhere, even more so than was assumed by the researchers who were not yet aware of the text of 4Q496.[436] This war of the southern enemies of Israel against its northern enemies is aimed at defeating Israel. According to Van der Ploeg, להלחם ב׳ could mean 'wage war together with', but there are no real linguistic arguments that underpin his theory.[437] The horn of Israel refers to his power in the war against the enemies.[438] We note that the term 'Israel' is always used in a positive sense in the *War Scroll*,[439] whereas it is occasionally used in a negative sense in other Qumran writings.

c. *1QM 11.1-2*

(11.1) ואת גולית הגתי איש גבור חיל (2) הסגרתה ביד דויד עבדכה כיא
בטח בשמכה הגדול ולוא בחרב וחנית כיא לכה המלחמה:

> (11.1) And the Gattite Goliath, a courageous warrior, (2) You delivered him into the hand of your servant David, because he trusted in your great name and not in sword or spear, for the battle is yours.

In the prayers of the high priest who encourages the warriors, other figures are mentioned, including David and Goliath as described in 1 Sam. 17. The same biblical passage is referred to in the first part of 11.1.[440]

The text explains how God delivered Goliath into David's hand, thereby confirming that the battle belongs to God. In other words, the outcome of wars are determined by God.

David is mentioned several times in the Qumran writings, but the theme is not usually elaborated on; Qumran always gave most of its attention to

---

435. Qimron, *Hebrew*, §500.1, gives the translation 'epoch' for קץ in Qumranic Hebrew, but the suggestion by H. Stegemann *apud* J. Licht, 'Time and Eschatology in Apocalyptic Literature and in Qumran', *JJS* 16 (1965), pp. 177-82 (181 n. 12), is also helpful ('significant date which divides two periods' and also 'point of time').

436. See, e.g., Carmignac, *Règle de la Guerre, ad loc.*, but also Beale, *Use of Daniel*, p. 63.

437. Van der Ploeg, *Rouleau de la guerre, ad loc.* (*lhtlhm* must be a printing error).

438. Dhorme, *L'emploi métaphorique*, pp. 39-40.

439. See 1QM 1.10; 2.7; 3.13; 5.1; 12.16; 13.2, 13; 14.4; 15.13; 16.1, 19 (4Q491 11 ii 16); 17.7-8; 18.3, 6.

440. Jongeling, *Rouleau de la guerre*, p. 258.

3. *The Antichrist in the Qumran Writings*   211

the priests.[441] David was hardly ever depicted in an eschatological light in Qumran,[442] but the few 'historical' remarks indicate that this line was kept open. We are here dealing with a reference to David's history in an eschatological context. The same thing occurs in the David Apocryphon.

d. *4QapDavid (4Q373) 1-2 3-6 (= 2Q22 i 1)*[443]

(3) אמות וחצי רמו ושתים [אמות רחבו ...] רמח כארז [...] (4) מגן כמגדל:
הקל ברגל]יו...] (5) המרחיקם שבעה ראסות לא עמד[תי] (6) ולא שניתי
כי שברו יהוה אלהינו: לפי [חרב הכיתיו]:

(3) ...cubits and a half was his height and two cubits his width...a spear like a cedar tree... (4) a shield like a tower. The swift-footed... (5) who removed them. (At a distance of) seven stadia I did not stand... (6) And I did not repeat it, for the Lord our God had broken him. I had defeated him with the sharpness of the sword.

On palaeographic grounds the text must be dated before 75.[444] The use of the Tetragram[445] in the text indicates that it was written before the establishment of the Qumran Community. Apparently the writing was a success,[446] even though only fragments have been preserved of all the extant manuscripts. This means that we do not have the context, but we can say that this psalm is autobiographic.[447]

---

441. K.E. Pomykala, *The Davidic Dynasty Tradition in Early Judaism: Its History and Significance for Messianism* (SBLEJL, 7; Atlanta: Scholars Press, 1995), pp. 212-13. This is made clear by a comparison of *Pss. Sol.* 17 with the situation in Qumran. The differences are linked to the spiritual differences between Pharisees and Essenes. No personal encounter of David with a king of the Kittites is described in the text.

442. CD 7.16, 4QpIsa (4Q161) 8-10 18-19, 4QMidrEschat^a (4Q174) iii 11-13, 4QpGen (4Q252) 1 v 2-4, 4QM B (4Q285) 5 3-4.

443. The text, including the reconstructions, follows E. Schuller, 'A Preliminary Study of 4Q373 and Some Related (?) Fragments', in J. Trebolle Barrera and L. Vegas Montaner (eds.), *Madrid Qumran Congress* (STDJ, 11; Leiden: E.J. Brill; Madrid: Complutense, 1992), pp. 513-30 (519) (4Q373 1-2 3-6), with addition of the legible parts of 4Q372 19 2-4 (Schuller, 'Preliminary Study', pp. 517-19) and of 2Q22 i 1 (M. Baillet, J.T. Milik and R. de Vaux, *Les 'petites grottes' de Qumrân* [DJD, 3; Oxford: Clarendon Press, 1962], p. 81). The MSS are combined into one running text.

444. Schuller, 'Preliminary Study', p. 518. (This is about 4Q373; 2Q22 is much younger: see Baillet, *'Petites grottes'*, p. 81.)

445. 4Q373 1-2 6.

446. Schuller, 'Preliminary Study', p. 525.

447. Schuller, 'Preliminary Study', pp. 524-25.

Even though the number is absent from 4Q373 1-2 3, 'cubits and a half' indicates that this refers to Goliath.[448] The exact wording and the comparisons used here do not refer back to 1 Sam. 17,[449] but the line of thought does. Suddenly the text focuses on David, the light-footed ('he who is light on his feet'). A רס is a stadium (180 metres),[450] so the total is 1,250 metres. Does this distance refer to where David went or where he stood? In view of the many gaps in the manuscript we cannot be certain, but it is possible that the author made use of litotes to indicate that David definitely dared to approach Goliath.[451] Goliath was killed in a single blow, and David did not need to make another attempt. The text then continues with David's later wars with the Philistines.[452]

The theme of David and Goliath occurs more than once, but simply the fact that I am using this unclear text to prove this shows that this theme is not used very much.

e. *1QM 11.16*

(11.16) [בעש]ותכה[454] שפטים בגוג ובכול קהלו [ה]נק[ה]ל[נ]ים ע[ל]י[ו][453]:

(11.16) When You chastise Gog and all his assembly that has gathered around him...

The context is the same as in the previous passage, but here it is Ezek. 38 that is alluded to and that can be used for a reconstruction of the text.[455] If the Kittites are a reference to the Romans, Gog[456] refers to them here. The term קהל, used for the people gathered around Gog, is also used for the religious group.

There is also another Qumran text that is reminiscent of Gog.

---

448. Schuller, 'Preliminary Study', p. 521.
449. Schuller, 'Preliminary Study', pp. 520-21.
450. See Baillet, Milik and de Vaux, *'Petites grottes'*, pp. 187-88, and Herodotus 2.6.
451. Schuller, 'Preliminary Study', p. 522.
452. Schuller, 'Preliminary Study', p. 522.
453. According to the reconstruction by Jongeling, *Rouleau de la guerre, ad loc.*; Carmignac, *Règle de la Guerre, ad loc.*
454. According to the reconstruction by Yadin, *Scroll of the War, ad loc.*; Jongeling, *Rouleau de la guerre, ad loc.*; Van der Ploeg, *Rouleau de la guerre, ad loc.*
455. Jongeling, *Rouleau de la guerre*, pp. 270-71; Carmignac, *Règle de la Guerre, ad loc.*
456. Hadas-Lebel, 'Evolution de l'image de Rome', p. 845.

f. *4QApoc ar (4Q550f) 1*[457]

(1) ארו מן צפונה אתיה[458] באישתא:

(1) Behold, the evil is coming from the North.

This text is from a manuscript that palaeographically dates from the turn of the era. Milik has linked it to the history of Esther, but it does not have much in common with that work.[459]

Since this writing is clearly an Aramaic version of Isa. 14.31-32, it would be tempting to name it 4QtgIsa instead of 4QApoc ar. The replacement of עשן by באישתא does not prevent us from doing that, since even the *Targum Jonathan* does not offer a translation at this point but uses the word פורענא. However, we will remain with 4QApoc ar since the following sentence does not have much in common with Isa. 15.1 and because of the interaction with other texts.

Although the enemy from the north was not yet a prophetic theme in Isa. 14, it did become so in later writings, especially in Jeremiah and to a lesser degree in Ezekiel.[460] This means we can state that the theme occurs here.

Milik refers to a number of texts in the book of Jeremiah[461] for this line. Perhaps the best verse to refer to is Jer. 6.1, because this speaks of evil that is about to come,[462] as indicated by the use of the participle. The original

---

457. According to J.T. Milik, 'Les modèles araméens du livre d'Esther dans la grotte 4 de Qumrân', *RevQ* 15 (Mémorial Jean Starcky, II; 1992), pp. 321-406 (361); for the passage quoted the text is identical with K. Beyer, *Die aramäischen Texte vom Toten Meer samt den Inschriften aus Palästina, dem Testament Levis aus der Kairoer Genisa, der Fastenrolle und den alten talmudischen Zitaten: Ergänzungsband* (Göttingen: Vandenhoeck & Ruprecht, 1994), p. 133.

458. Peal ptc. sg. fem.

459. Milik, 'Modèles araméens', pp. 361-63; F. García Martínez, 'Las fronteras de "lo Bíblico"', *Scripta Theologica* 23 (1991), pp. 759-84 (773-74). The other MSS, which are best named 4Q550a-d, are linked to Esther (4Q550a-c: 4QprotoEst A ar [*olim* 4QprotoEst[a-c] ar]; 4Q550d: 4QprotoEst B ar [*olim* 4QprotEst[d-e] ar]) (García Martínez and van der Woude, *Rollen van de Dode Zee*, II, pp. 441-43). If we were to give consecutive numbers to each of the MSS, what we call 4Q550f would become 4Q550e, but then the link with the original title of 4QprotoEst[f] ar would be lost. García Martínez and van der Woude, *Rollen van de Dode Zee*, II, pp. 442-43, gives a palaeographic date for 4Q550f in the first half of the first century CE; Beyer, *Die aramäischen Texte...Ergänzungsband*, p. 132, however, dates it in 30 BCE.

460. Schoors, *Jesaja, ad loc.*

461. Milik, 'Modèles araméens', pp. 361-62: Jer. 1.14; 4.6; 6.1; 47.2; also in Isa. 14.31-32; Ezek. 26.7; Joel 2.20.

462. B.J. Oosterhoff, *Jeremia. I. Jeremia 1–10* (Commentaar op het Oude Testament; Kampen: Kok, 1990), p. 217; note the occurrence of Zion in Jer. 6.2.

meaning is made clear by Jer. 1.13-14, where a boiling pot is used to announce that God is going to judge by causing foreign nations to invade Israel from the north.[463]

We see that the theme of the enemy from the north occurs in several places in the Qumran documents, but simply the fact that I am using this unclear text to prove it shows that this theme is not very common.

g. *1QM 15.2-3*

(15.2) וכול ע[נ]תידי[464] המלחמה ילכו וחנו נגד מלך הכתיים ונגד כול חיל
(3) בליעל הנועדים עמו ליום [נקמה[466]] בחרב אל[465]:

(15.2) And all who are ready for battle will go and pitch their camps opposite the king of the Kittites and opposite the entire army of (3) Belial, those who gathered around him on a day of revenge by the sword of God.

This passage links in with the contents of the first passage we have studied. It is about the final battle,[467] but only as taken up in these later chapters. This line forms the beginning of the series on the Kittites: the Children of the Light will *pitch their camps opposite* the Kittites.[468] Here the Kittites take up their position at the head of the enemy armies.[469] The Kittites will have a king, but the monarchy is not emphasized because the king is not mentioned in a parallel passage (16.3).[470] With what nation the Kittites should be identified depends on the interpretation of the entire *War Scroll*. In order to best follow the author's thinking we should therefore not look for a specific identification.[471] Relative identification is possible, however, and Van der Ploeg states that this is about the army of Gog.[472]

---

463. Oosterhoff, *Jeremia*, I, pp. 96-98.

464. Jongeling, *Rouleau de la guerre, ad loc.*; Carmignac, *Règle de la Guerre, ad loc.*; Van der Ploeg, *Rouleau de la guerre, ad loc.*, have עתודי. The form used above is more frequent in Biblical Hebrew.

465. This was written as one word in the MS.

466. According to the reconstruction by Jongeling, *Rouleau de la guerre, ad loc.*; Carmignac, *Règle de la Guerre, ad loc.*

467. According to Jongeling, *Rouleau de la guerre, ad loc.*

468. Later on they will also *take up their position opposite* the Kittites and even later *near* them: Yadin, *Scroll of the War, ad loc.*

469. Yadin, *Scroll of the War, ad loc.*; Jongeling, *Rouleau de la guerre, ad loc.*

470. Carmignac, *Règle de la Guerre, ad loc.*

471. J.J. Collins, *The Apocalyptic Imagination: An Introduction to the Jewish Matrix of Christianity* (New York: Crossroad, 1984), p. 129.

472. Van der Ploeg, *Rouleau de la guerre, ad loc.* For a link between the Kittites and

3. *The Antichrist in the Qumran Writings* 215

Belial is not a man but a spiritual being, which is to be identified with Satan.[473]

Eventually God will judge using his sword; in an eschatological context this sword refers to judgment for the nations that oppose God.[474]

h. *1QM 17.5-6*

(17.5) היום מועדו להכניע ולהשפיל שר ממשלת (6) רשעה:

(17.5-6) Today is his appointed time to bring a prince of wicked rule down on his knees and to humiliate him.

This sentence has the same context as the previous passage; it is a description of the final battle.

The term מועד (appointed time) is typical for the Qumran documents. This text points out that God will act in his own time, eliminating his great enemy. The wording seems to suggest that the great enemy is Belial. Moreover, a bit further in the text Michael is mentioned, who is the great opponent of Belial,[475] which is another argument to identify the 'prince of wicked rule' with Belial. However, the elements in this text could also refer to the king of the Kittites.[476]

i. *The Antichrist in the* War Scroll

The *War Scroll* definitely describes an event that will take place in the future and will lead to the end of times, that is, an eschatological event.[477]

Gog, cf. Num. 24.7, 24 LXX (cf. above, Chapter 2, n. [376]) and Beale, *Use of Daniel*, p. 65 n. 95.

473. M.J. Davidson, *Angels at Qumran: A Comparative Study of 1 Enoch 1–36, 72–108 and Sectarian Writings from Qumran* (JSPSup, 11; Sheffield: JSOT Press, 1992), pp. 163-65; Von der Osten-Sacken, *Gott und Belial*, p. 73 (on p. 78 n. 2, however, he does state that the names 'Belial' and 'Satan' were not used interchangeably). Cf. P.J. Kobelski, *Melchizedek and Melchirešaʿ* (CBQMS, 10; Washington: Catholic Biblical Association of America, 1981), p. 79; Milik, '4Q Visions', p. 86; Noack, *Satanás und Sotería*, pp. 32, 39, 44; M. Testuz, *Les idées religieuses du Livre des Jubilés* (Geneva: Droz; Paris: Minard, 1960), p. 82; and above Chapter 2, section 10g (incl. n. 497) and 4g in this Chapter.

474. Schoors, *Jesaja*, p. 203 (re. Isa. 34.6).

475. Jongeling, *Rouleau de la guerre, ad loc.*; Davidson, *Angels at Qumran*, pp. 218-19.

476. Mentioned as a possibility by Van der Ploeg, *Rouleau de la guerre*, p. 177.

477. Beale, *Use of Daniel*, p. 61, thinks 1QM 1 is an eschatological midrash. According to Fishbane, 'Use, Authority and Interpretation', p. 347, the story of David and Goliath is viewed as an 'antitype of future divine deed'.

We should therefore check whether the Antichrist is described as well. In doing this, we must distinguish between the historical Goliath who is mentioned as a model, and the wicked king who is only regarded as future.

While David is at the centre of attention here, we are mainly concerned with Goliath. As we have seen before, the memory of this event was kept alive in eschatological contexts,[478] as indeed it is here.[479]

While the author never describes the king of the Kittites as the main character, this king seems to match our Antichrist definition in several different ways. When checking the characteristics of the figure in 17.5-6 as described by Davidson,[480] it becomes clear in my opinion that it too could be a reference to the king of the Kittites a.k.a. the Antichrist.

As we have seen, the context is eschatological. What we see about the king of the Kittites is that he will act in furious violence against Israel, that is, the true believers (1.4-5), that he will ethically be evil (17.6), that as a man he will work closely with Satan (15.2-3)[481] and thus end up in a final conflict with God (15.3; 17.5). The choice of the right moment indicates a sense of power that leans towards hubris (1.4).

Assuming the identification by Van der Ploeg,[482] we can include Gog in the description of the king of the Kittites. Apart from the animosity between the God who punishes (11.16) and Gog who has wicked ethics (4Q550f 1), nothing concrete is mentioned about him. Therefore, all we can say is that the theme of Gog was known to the Qumran Community.

There are also some critical notes I wish to put forward. We have distinguished Gog, the king from the north, and the Antichrist,[483] but the two themes are closely related and are sometimes even combined into the same historical figure.[484]

There is another problem in the *War Scroll*. On the basis of other writings we would assume that the king of the Kittites comes from the north, but

---

478. See above, Chapter 2, sections 2c, 3c, 5h, 7f, 10g; for 1 Sam. 17 see Chapter 1, section 3b.

479. Cf. Carmignac, *Règle de la Guerre*, p. 157 ('cette victoire de David était devenue comme le symbole du triomphe de Dieu contre les ennemis de son peuple').

480. Davidson, *Angels at Qumran*, p. 219 (elevated position [שׂר], opposition to God, the ethical character of his rule [רשעה]).

481. Van der Ploeg, *Rouleau de la guerre*, p. 164 ('sous l'inspiration de Bélial'); Collins, *Apocalyptic Imagination*, p. 128 ('Belial...has a human counterpart in "the king of the Kittim"').

482. See the discussion of 1QM 15.2-3.

483. Chapter 2, section 9f (n. [376]).

484. It is possible, however, to think of Antiochus IV Epiphanes or of Pompey.

3. *The Antichrist in the Qumran Writings*

we read in 1QM 1.4 that he actually wages war *against* the kings from the north. We could deduce from this that *the* king from the north will wage war against *other* kings in the north, but this is probably too hypothetical. Since the single king is not linked with the Kittites from Assur, it is not possible to establish a link with Antiochus IV Epiphanes as a Seleucid king.

There was room for the Antichrist in the thinking of the author of the *War Scroll*. He was aware of the themes of Gog and the Antichrist, and he used variations on those themes. Since he was not concerned about a detailed description of the opponents he never systematically elaborated on them.

10. Pseudo-Moses

a. *Setting*

We shall be using the text compiled by Ms. Dimant from 4Q385a (4QpsMos^a), 4Q387a (4QpsMos^b), 4Q388a (4QpsMos^c), 4Q389 (4QpsMos^d) and 4Q390 (4QpsMos^e).[485] It would be best to regard the last of these as a separate work.[486] On palaeographic grounds the writing that can be reconstructed from the other manuscripts, 4QpsMos (A), should be dated in 45 at the latest.[487] A setting for the contents of the writing has not yet been provided.

b. *4QpsMos (4Q387a 3 ii 7-8 = 4Q388a 1 ii 3 = 4Q389 1 ii 9)*[488]

4Q387a 3 ii 7-8

(7) בימים (8) ההמה ... גדפן ועשה תעבות:

4Q388a 1 ii 3

(3) ההמה יקום מלך] לגו[ים גדפן ועשה רעות:

4Q389 1 ii 9

(9) י]קום מלך לגוים גדפן [וע]שה רעות:

---

485. Dimant, 'New Light', p. 412.

486. García Martínez and Van der Woude, *Rollen van de Dode Zee*, II, p. 417. This writing, 4QpsMos B, probably originates from Essene circles around the year 150: Dimant, 'New Light', pp. 445-47 (adapted to our reconstruction of the history of the Qumran Community).

487. Strugnell and Dimant, '*4Q Second Ezekiel*', p. 45.

488. Based on the text and numbering by García Martínez and Tigchelaar, *Study Edition*, II, *ad loc.*, but with fewer reconstructional devices.

Synthetic text

בימים ההמה יקום מלך לגוים גדפן ויעשה רעות:

And in those days a king will arise for the nations, a slanderer, and he will do evil things.

In this text, God tells Moses that a ruler will come in the future (an eschatological future?) who will slander him and will not comply to his ethical standards.

The form גדפן is unusual. The possibility of *scriptio defectiva* for גְדְפִין[489] can almost certainly be ruled out. This means this is a noun with ן as an affix (גַּדְפָן), even though this noun formation was generally not productive in Qumran.[490]

c. *The Antichrist in* Pseudo-Moses

This sentence does not tell us very much, and since a discussion with other researchers is not possible as yet, the discussion will be short.

We find in this text an individual evil man who fulfils a political role (מלך), who opposes God (גדפן, [491]יעשה רעות) and who lives in the future, at least from Moses' perspective. This means that the Antichrist theme could play a role.

---

489. Qal ptc. st. abs. pl. m., which would lead to the translation 'for slandering nations'.

490. It was productive in later times, see M. Jastrow, *A Dictionary of the Targumim, the Talmud Babli and Yerushalmi, and the Midrashic* Literature (New York: Choreb; London: Shapiro, Vallentine, 1926), s.v. גדפן (only pl. seems to be usual!); M.H. Segal, *A Grammar of Mishnaic Hebrew* (Oxford: Clarendon Press, 1927), §267; Qimron, *Hebrew*, does not mention this noun formation. For Biblical Hebrew, cf. Joüon, *Grammaire*, §88Me; W. Gesenius, E. Kautzsch and A.E. Cowley, *Hebrew Grammar* (Oxford: Clarendon Press, 2nd edn, 1910), §85u.

491. 4Q387a 1 8 uses the more explicit תעבות (scandalousness).

Chapter 4

THE ANTICHRIST IN THE INTERTESTAMENTAL PERIOD

1. *Theme Development*

a. *General Overview of the Writings*
Psalm 152 is early Hellenistic and tells the story of David's fight with a bear. Because of the eschatological accents the story leans towards the Antichrist theme.

The *Laus Patrum* of Jesus Sirach dates from the year 190. It contains the story of David and Goliath, which takes on an unusual dimension, and we can safely say that this passage already leans towards the idea of an eschatological Antichrist.

We will now look at a number of texts dating from 165 to 150. The Apocryphon of David is of Essene origin and the only thing we can deduce from it is that the story of Goliath was still alive at the time. The oldest passages, which contain a sufficient amount of elements of our definition to allow us to say that they contain an Antichrist theme, are the oldest parts of the *Sibylline Oracles*, even though the information they offer is limited. More information can be found in the metahistorical story of Judith. All characteristics are clearly present, but the form of the story does not immediately point to an eschatological figure. However, the chronological dating of the story indicates that it must be regarded as taking place in a time that follows on from a period of salvation. Taking all the elements into consideration, I believe we may deduce that the author probably consciously worked on the Antichrist theme.

I agree with Bunge that 2 Maccabees should be dated in the year 124. The book does not openly discuss the Antichrist theme, but all the characteristics are present and the book contains so many elements relating to this theme that we must assume that the author was eschatologically aware. *Pseudo-Ezekiel* (4Q386) can be dated shortly after 2 Maccabees. Here too we find many elements of the Antichrist theme, but we also find data that imply that the author did not consciously address the theme. *Wiles of the*

Wicked Woman (4Q184) originated in the third century as a piece of wisdom literature building on biblical data, and the new interpretation of these data played an important role in the development of the view the Qumran Community had of the leader of their opponents.

We have dated the *Damascus Document* to 107, and this is predominantly a relative dating. Because of the many biblical parallels in this text, it is even more 'biblical' than the Peshers. Here the view of the *Wiles of the Wicked Woman* has been fully developed: the Qumran Community lives in a pre-eschatological period and Saw is an Antichrist. Of course the term 'Antichrist' is not used here—it is used in none of the intertestamental writings—but the pseudoprophetic aspect of the Antichrist is abundantly present. Less is being said about Tryphon, but he definitely represents the tyrannical aspect. We see therefore that the full scope of the theme is present in these two figures.

The First Book of Maccabees is comparable to the Second. It is not eschatological, but many elements of the definition are present, and Goliath and Antiochus IV are not only used as historical figures, but also as themes.

The *Testimonia* (4Q175) clearly feature an eschatological Antichrist.

In the first few chapters of *3 Maccabees*, which I would date as early as possible (around 80), we see several elements, but they are limited to the historical arena.

In the *Hymns* we can distinguish an eschatological Antichrist, as in the *Testimonia*, but this time in the figure of a serpent. Saw features again in the *Psalms Pesher* (4Q171).

The *Nahum Pesher* (4Q169) is the earliest document in which we find a royal Hasmonean high priest as a pre-eschatological Antichrist, but we must take account of the fact that the *Habakkuk Pesher*, which was completed slightly later, offers a wider retrospective on a number of royal high priests. Saw too is mentioned again, and together they fill the complete scope of our Antichrist theme.

The *War Scroll* of the Qumran Community is eschatological, and the king of the Kittites could play the role of an Antichrist, but the author is not systematic. The same is true for the *Testament of the Twelve Patriarchs*, which originates from circles linked to the Qumran Community. Again we find many elements of the theme, but for the period in which I would tend to date this writing (not long after Pompey took Jerusalem) the results are meagre. Incidentally, the *Testament of the Twelve Patriarchs* has close links with both the Old and the New Testament. However, we cannot deduce from this that the writing is chronologically close to the New Tes-

4. *The Antichrist in the Intertestamental Period* 221

tament as well, because similar links are also found in *Pseudo-Daniel* (4Q246) which dates from 160.[1]

The *Psalms of Solomon*, a Pharisaic writing, again gives the full scope of the Antichrist theme, in the combination of Aristobulus II (and the other Hasmoneans) and Pompey. Here too, many biblical parallels can be distinguished.

A few elements can be found in *Pseudo-Moses* (4Q387a, 4Q388a, 4Q389), but their number is disappointing, especially in the light of the palaeographic dating of around 45, and it is impossible to give a date of origin for the contents.

In the old additions to the Third Book of *Sibylline Oracles*, a number of violent individuals feature, but we do not gain much clarity.

Not enough research has been carried out into the general meaning of the *Treatise of Shem*, which probably originates from 20 to 25 CE in Alexandria. If our interpretation is correct, the black king of *Tr. Shem* 11.14-18 is a clear picture of the Antichrist.

The *Testament of Moses*, which originates from shortly after 6 CE, from a strict Pharisaic environment, clearly depicts the Antichrist theme.

In the *Aramaic Apocalypse* (4Q550f), which can only be dated palaeographically (to 25 CE), we only find one element, which means we can only say that this element was still active in apocalyptic thinking.[2]

The Second Book of *Enoch* is the last text in this study. I believe this text may be interpreted to contain certain elements of our definition, but no clear and systematic picture of the Antichrist can be found in this writing.

At this stage it is good to point out where the Antichrist is *not* mentioned. The most notable text where the theme is absent is the Mesopotamian writing of Tobit. Furthermore, Wisdom of Solomon, the *Testament of Job* from Egypt, the book of *Baruch* (which is difficult to categorize), the Hasidic writings of *1 Enoch*, the *Apocryphon of Genesis*, and the *Apocryphon of Jubilees*, and lastly the *Rule* and the *Temple Scroll* from Qumran, do not refer to the Antichrist.

Let us now group our data in a more specific way. Unfortunately some repetition cannot be avoided.

---

1. See Van der Woude, ' "Hij zal Zoon" ', pp. 137, 141, 143-44.
2. Here and elsewhere in this text the word 'apocalyptic' takes a broad meaning, namely, a particular, non-prophetic technique, used to reveal something about the essence of life, especially about the end of all things.

b. *The Environments of Origin*

When taken in fully chronological order, the texts do not show a straight-lined development. Let us therefore see if a pattern emerges when we categorize the writings by the environments from which they originate. This approach carries the risk of underestimating mutual links, for instance, between Alexandria and the Holy Land,[3] but it may offer some interesting perspectives.

In Egyptian Apocalyptic literature we actually see a decline in clarity. The Third Book of *Sibylline Oracles* features an individual evil man, even though the details are vague because of the genre. In the *Treatise of Shem* the Antichrist is clearly distinguishable. In *2 Enoch* we see no more than some unconnected elements. The Third Book of Maccabees cannot be included in this category, because it is not apocalyptic even though it is Egyptian. It contains several elements of our definition, but only in a historical perspective.

The pro-Maccabean authors do not give a clear picture of the Antichrist at all. Many characteristics are present, but only an eschatological awareness (2 Maccabees) and an evolution towards (1 Maccabees) the Antichrist theme can be demonstrated, which means that there is some degree of unity.

In the oldest Pharisaic writings (Ps. 152, *Laus Patrum*) an evolution towards more clarity can be demonstrated. Judith proves an important text for the development of the theme, and in the *Psalms of Solomon* and the *Testament of Moses* the theme plays an important role.

With the Essenes, all that can be distinguished is a few unconnected elements (in the *David Apocryphon*).

In the Qumran Documents there is a lot of scope for the Antichrist theme. *Pseudo-Ezekiel* only contains elements of the Antichrist theme, but the *Wiles of the Wicked Woman* paves the way, and in the *Damascus Writing*, the *Psalms Pesher*, the *Nahum Pesher*, and the *Habakkuk Pesher*, the leader of the competing group and the Hasmonean royal high priest are seen as pre-eschatological manifestations of the Antichrist. At the same time there is room for a truly eschatological Antichrist in the *Testimonia*, the *Hymns* and the *War Scroll* (mentioned in declining order of

---

3. See in general M. Smith, 'Pseudepigraphy in the Israelite Literary Tradition', in K. von Fritz (ed.), *Pseudepigrapha*. I. *Pseudopythagorica—Lettres de Platon—Littérature pseudépigraphique juive* (Entretiens sur l'Antiquité Classique, 18; Geneva: Fondation Hardt, 1972), pp. 189-227 (191); Rigaux, *Antéchrist*, pp. 190 ('les idées des Juifs de la terre sainte étaient partagées par leurs congénères de la Diaspora'), 192. Specifically for Alexandria, see Charlesworth, 'Old Testament Pseudepigrapha', p. 22.

clarity). Both the pre-eschatological and the eschatological form of the Antichrist occur in writings of different periods, and it is clearly not true that the theme was eschatologized or actualized at a specific point in time after which the newer form was maintained.

c. *The Audiences*
While studying the texts, I suspected that the difference in clarity and openness regarding the Antichrist could have been determined by whether the authors were writing for their own sects or for a more general audience. It has now become apparent that when categorized by audience, the books fall into nearly the same groups as when categorized by the environments of their authors. The Hasidic (and apocalyptic) writings and those from Qumran were meant for internal use, and the Pharisaic and pro-Maccabean writings were aimed at the whole Jewish nation, even though the Psalms (both the Syrian Psalms and the *Psalms of Solomon*) started off individually and the Egyptian writings were intended to be read by outsiders as well, at least in theory. Only a small number of writings falls into a different group when categorized by audience. The *Testament of Moses* may have been intended for a limited group of Pharisees only, and 1 Maccabees is suitable for general use. To keep matters simple I have classified the Third Book of *Sibylline Oracles* as Egyptian in its entirety.

A notable amount of writings in the first, sectarian group, only contains a few elements. Only two texts—*Testimonia* and *Hymns*—clearly speak of an eschatological Antichrist. A number of important texts feature a pre-eschatological Antichrist (Saw, Tryphon, the royal high priest).

The majority of the texts in the general Jewish group is unclear, but there are some important 'bridging texts': Judith (the first text in which all the elements occur), *Psalms of Solomon* (the first clear apocryphal text, the introduction of Pompey), *Testament of Moses* (an almost systematic theological exposition of an eschatological Antichrist).

The writings in the missionary group are largely unclear. This is due to the genre. The clearest picture of the Antichrist occurs in the *Treatise of Shem*, but here I seem to be on my own, since no other researchers have looked into this as yet. There is a wider base for the oldest parts of the *Sibylline Oracles* (*Sib. Or.* 3.388-92, 608-15). There is no development of any teaching on the Antichrist in *2 Enoch*. There is no pre-eschatological interpretation to speak of in this apocalyptic group, even though the actions of Pompey, which are portrayed as future in *Sib. Or.* 3.470-73, might be regarded as such.

We must therefore conclude that, against our expectations, it is not the sectarian and the apocalyptic writings that are more open about the Antichrist. In fact, the clearest texts about the Antichrist are divided quite evenly over three categories, and a pre-eschatological interpretation is found in the writings of the Qumran Community and in the Pharisaic *Psalms of Solomon*. In both cases the Hasmonean royal high priests are the objects of anger. The Qumran Community adds its great opponent Saw, as well as Tryphon, who was slightly further removed from their community, and the Pharisee adds Pompey. In all three categories an eschatological interpretation can be found: Belial in the *Testimonia*, the king of kings in the *Testament of Moses*, the black king in the *Treatise of Shem*. Secondarily there are also the *Hymns* (with the serpent), Judith (Holophernes), and the Third Book of *Sibylline Oracles* (several figures).

d. *The Chronological Development of the Antichrist Theme*
It should now be possible to give an overview of the development of the image of the Antichrist on the basis of the writings that are most important to this theme.

We find a first clue in the early Hellenistic passage of Ps. 152.4-6. This features a beast (a bear) opposite a messianic[4] figure (i.e. David) in an eschatological context. In what cannot be regarded as a further development but rather as another clue, we find in Sir. 47.4-5 (dating from 190) a first mention of Goliath as a type. These texts originate from Palestine and are Hasidic (and quite Pharisaic).

The first Antichrist theme can be found in *Sib. Or.* 3.388-92 and 608-15. These passages originated in Egypt around 160–150. In them we see the evolution of Antiochus IV Epiphanes into an eschatological individual in a messianic context. In Judith, which is slightly younger and of Pharisaic origin, we see all the elements converge for the first time (even the military and religious aspects converge here!), even though the structure of the story prevents us from concluding that we have found a fully eschatological Antichrist here.

Two texts from the period 150–107 form a kind of interval. 2 Maccabees gives so many clues that we must conclude that some eschatological awareness is present in this historical work. A peculiar situation is found in the new interpretation that the Qumran Community gave to the *Wiles of the*

---

4. We are using the word 'messianic' in quite a general definition here: a person who, in dependence on God, contributes to the salvation of mankind. A passage that is messianic does therefore not necessarily use the term 'Anointed One'.

4. The Antichrist in the Intertestamental Period 225

Wicked Woman. There are objections to the view that the Woman portrays the Antichrist, but we must insist that this text has laid the foundation for the ideas about the Antichrist in the Qumran Community.

This brings us to our six clearest texts: the *Damascus Document*, the *Habakkuk Pesher*, *Testimonia*, *Psalms of Solomon*, *Treatise of Shem* (albeit in an unclear context) and *Testament of Moses*.

The authors of the *Damascus Document* (dated in 107) and of the *Habakkuk Pesher* (final edition only in 60, but with a long history) seem to have believed that they were living in a pre-eschatological time in which Saw, the ideological opponent of the sect (especially as a false prophet), the head of the kings of Greece, Tryphon (especially as a tyrant) and several Hasmonean royal high priests (active both in the religious and the military domain) played the role of the Antichrist. During the same period, the concept of an eschatological Antichrist was present in the Qumran Community. We first find this in the *Testimonia* (4Q175) 21–30. Here the Antichrist features opposite messianic figures, and is active in both the military and the religious domain, under the influence of Satan (Belial).

In the writings of a generation later (64–37), the pre-eschatological Antichrist figures again, this time in Pharisaic circles. The poet of the *Psalms of Solomon* now projected the theme on later Hasmonean royal high priests (especially Aristobulus II), albeit in a completely different spiritual attitude from his chronological predecessors. Pompey[5] now played a more important role—after Goliath and Antiochus IV—in fleshing out the Antichrist theme. Both were tyrannical and evil. Did the Pharisaic poet base his writing on the thinking of the Qumran Community? In view of my conviction that the ideas of Qumran were known in Jerusalem, this is not impossible.[6] Could the author have delved into 2 Maccabees, which was two generations older?[7] Even that is not impossible, since there are many similarities: both an internal and a foreign enemy, the high priest as a tyrant, the action against the Temple undertaken by the foreign enemy, hubris and wickedness by the foreign enemy, the comparison with an animal or beast. Our poet probably used both sources as well as his own creativity to form a new synthesis.

---

5. Here Pompey features opposite Caesar, who granted the Jews many privileges. (cf. Hadas-Lebel, 'L'évolution de l'image de Rome', pp. 787-97). Although both men were ambitious and imperialistic, general history could also have encouraged completely opposite sympathies. A similar situation can be found with Antiochus IV Epiphanes.

6. See above in Chapter 3 n. 2.

7. Even though the Hasmoneans were the successors of the Maccabees, whom the author supported. See above in Chapter 2 n. 192.

Another generation later, in 25–20, we again find a reflection of the Antichrist theme in Egypt, in *Tr. Shem* 11.14-18. Obviously the image of the eschatological black king must have undergone influences from astrological texts. We must also mention other extra-biblical sources: the image of Cambyses, the image of Alexander the Great, the Potter's Oracle.[8]

Yet another generation later, in 6 CE or later, we find a last clear description in *Ass. Mos.* 8. The eschatological king of kings—clearly in the footsteps of Antiochus IV Epiphanes—is both tyrannical and active in the religious arena. The chapter has a messianic context and a link to Satan can be demonstrated. The rigorous Pharisee who was responsible for this writing may have consulted the *Psalms of Solomon* (which originated from his own group) as well as like-minded people in the Qumran Community.

From this we can deduce that a pre-eschatological interpretation of the Antichrist is only found in the middle of the period covered by this research, that is, from 107 to 147. We can also conclude that although the theme was not continually at the centre of attention, it was discussed again and again, at least from the historical actions of Antiochus IV Epiphanes onwards and always with intervals of one generation. I do not wish to read too much into that, but it seems to imply a measure of intensity. Incidentally, one generation after the *Testament of Moses* the theme appears yet again, this time in the New Testament.

Finally I must mention some writings that were written too late to mark a new stage or which are too vague to be of importance to us. *Pseudo-Ezekiel* may contain several interesting elements, especially in view of its date in the second half of the second century, but our theme does not feature very clearly in it. The First Book of Maccabees, from 100, contains many elements, but is too similar to the Second, which is older (from 124). The *Hymns* from Qumran also mention an eschatological Antichrist, but less clearly so than the *Testimonia*. The *Nahum Pesher* speaks evil of a Hasmonean, but since this is closely followed by a discussion of the whole Hasmonean dynasty in the *Nahum Pesher*, the relative importance of the *Nahum Pesher* is small. The *War Scroll* contains many elements of an eschatological Antichrist, but does not provide new insights, and for its period (60) it is not very interesting. This also applies to the *Testament of the Twelve Patriarchs*, which is from nearly the same time. Finally, the oldest additions to the Third Book of *Sibylline Oracles* are too fragmentary to add anything of interest to our theme for the period in which additions were made to the corpus (around 31).

---

8. See Chapter 2, 4b and also n. 191.

e. *Elements of the Definition*
Aside from references to the historical David, the individual aspect of the Antichrist is first found in *Sib. Or.* 3.388-92, 608-15, dating from 160–150. If we leave Nebuchadnezzar in Judith and the Abyss in *Wiles of the Wicked Woman* out of the picture, the link to Satan first appears in the *Damascus Writing*, which dates from 107. The lawlessness first clearly appears in *Psalms of Solomon*, if we leave *Wiles of the Wicked Woman* out of consideration. References to animals or beasts occur from the start. Also the tyrannical and religious aspects are always present, except in very fragmentary passages. If we leave the misleading aspect of *Wiles of the Wicked Woman* out of consideration, the false prophet is really only discussed in Saw. Again the *Wiles of the Wicked Woman* could be taken as a build-up to the interpretation of Saw as the Antichrist. Often there is a messianic context, but not always, and wherever the Antichrist occurs in this context, there is a clear relationship. Hubris occurs often but not always and only from the time of Judith, that is from 150, until the *Psalms of Solomon*, that is, until 47. Balaam does not appear to feature in the passages we have studied. Goliath plays a diminishing but important role and is last mentioned in the *Hymns*, that is, in 60. My attempt, on the basis of the data from the book of Revelation, to keep the themes of the Antichrist and of Gog (the king from the north) separated in the intertestamental writings, proved unsuccessful. This is especially clear in the *Psalms of Solomon* (in relation to Pompey) and in the *War Scroll*, while in the *Aramaic Apocalypse* the theme of Gog simply matches the texts we have looked at. Finally, Antiochus IV Epiphanes does not always feature, but he is referred to during a very long period: from around 160 in *Sib. Or.* 3.388-92, 608-15, through the first two books of Maccabees (while perhaps Tryphon as his successor may be reminiscent of him in the *Damascus Writing*), and finally in the portrayal of the Antichrist in the *Testament of Moses*, the last intertestamental text which is important to our theme.

f. *Uniqueness in Relation to the Old and New Testaments*
With regard to the Pentateuch we have discussed the false prophet. He resurfaced in the intertestamental writings, especially in the figure of Saw.

The possibility that an opponent of David (specifically Goliath) would have developed beyond the historical, was already present in 1 Sam. 17 and was finally realized during the intertestamental period. This is especially clear in the Song of the Lamb,[9] and this provides us with a reliable anchor

---

9. This song is found as an amplification in *Tg. 1 Sam.* 17.43 (to be read with *Tg.*

for our interpretations of Goliath and the bear. The bear became eschatological in Ps. 152 and again in *T. Jud.* 2.4. Goliath became a type in the Laus Patrum and again in the *David Apocryphon* (4Q373), in 1 Macc. 4.30, Jdt. 13.9, 2 Macc. 1.16; 15.30-33, 1 Macc. 7.47 (the motif of the decapitated head), and the *War Scroll* 11.1-2.

Not only the bear, but other animals played a role as well: a serpent in 1QH 11 (*olim* 3).12-18, a lion in the *Nahum Pesher* (4Q169), a dragon in *T. Ash.* 7.3 and *Pss. Sol.* 2,[10] and dragons and serpents in CD 19.22-26.

On the basis of the data on Gog in Rev. 20 I have attempted to keep the Antichrist theme separate from the Gog theme, and this proved to be very difficult. Often the two themes occur in one person, for example, Antiochus IV Epiphanes in Dan. 11 and Pompey in the *Psalms of Solomon*. I remain of the opinion, however, that these are two separate themes, even though the distinction only becomes apparent in the New Testament.[11]

The evil shepherd of Zech. 11.15-17 does not explicitly feature anywhere. We only find an allusion to him in Jdt. 11.19, which is a gigantic compilation of allusions anyway.

Antiochus IV Epiphanes features quite often, and we will return to him later. The link between the tyrannical and the religious occurs in many writings. It even occurs quite regularly in one and the same person, that is, in Holophernes (Judith), Antiochus IV Epiphanes (1 and 2 Maccabees), One of Belial (*Testimonia*), the serpent (*Hymns*), Hasmoneans (*Habakkuk Pesher*, *Psalms of Solomon*), king of the Kittites (*War Scroll*), Pompey (*Psalms of Solomon*), the black king (*Treatise of Shem*), and even in the Opponent (*2 Enoch*). The Antichrist can also be represented by more figures than one. This is most clearly the case in the *Damascus Document* (Saw and Tryphon) the *Habakkuk Pesher* (Saw and the wicked priest), and the *Psalms of Solomon* (Aristobulus II and Pompey). Also in 2 and even 1 Maccabees we must point out that not only Antiochus IV, but also Menelaus and Nicanor carry the theme. We can therefore conclude that the single

---

1 Sam. 23.8). This text should be dated around the turn of the era, but it does fall outside the framework of this study. See Van Staalduine-Sulman, 'Song of the Lamb', pp. 286-91. (The text itself can also be found in A. Sperber, *The Bible in Aramaic Based on Old Manuscripts and Printed Texts*. II. *The Former Prophets According to Targum Jonathan* [Leiden: E.J. Brill, 1959], *ad loc.*)

10. We could perhaps also think of a dragon in the *Wiles of the Wicked Woman* (4Q184), but only via Sir. 25.15.

11. See Strecker, *Die Johannesbriefe*, p. 341 n. 33: the Antichrist is successful, at least for a while, but the king from the north (Gog) is not.

and undivided theme of the Antichrist can be divided into several different, mostly historical, persons. (We see a similar phenomenon in the *Testimonia*, but not about the link between the tyrannical and the religious aspect.) The phenomenon of a *Doppelgestalt* (double figure) does occur, but not very often.

In the intertestamental period, the development of Goliath and the bear is new, as is the introduction of the woman as an image of the Antichrist and the clearly pre-eschatological content of the term in the view that the Qumran Community and the author of the *Psalms of Solomon* had of their own time. The presence of a pre-eschatological Antichrist in the Qumran writings did not prevent the sect from speaking of an eschatological Antichrist[12] as well, although the term was not used at the time. The absence of such a unique term does however raise the question of how concrete this concept was to them.

In any case we can conclude that the topical value of the book of Daniel was the main drive behind the development of the Antichrist theme. Many more details on the Antichrist can be found in the intertestamental period than in the Old Testament, even when considering the fact that many more writings from that period have been preserved. This development can mainly be explained by the historical actions of Antiochus IV Epiphanes, which placed the prophecies of Daniel in the spotlight, but also by their after-effect.

When focusing on the texts from before 100, we must consider:

- that with the topical value of the book of Daniel, an individual, eschatological core of the Antichrist (of false prophet and evil shepherd) also existed elsewhere,
- that even before the actions of Antiochus IV, the Goliath theme had undergone some development (in Ps. 152 and Sirach),
- that in Judith, the great collection of allusions to the Antichrist, Antiochus IV does not play any role (and can certainly not be compared to Holophernes)
- that Antiochus is of course important in 2 Maccabees, but he is assisted by Menelaus and Nicanor,

12. Cf. Van der Woude, *Die messianischen Vorstellungen*, Thesis 1: 'Men dient in het Damaskusgeschrift onderscheid te maken tussen een historische en een eschatologische Leraar der Gerechtigheid.' (In the *Damascus Document* one needs to make a distinction between a historical Teacher of Righteousness and an eschatological one.) In the same way do we need to make a distinction between the historical, pre-eschatological Antichrist and the eschatological Antichrist in the Qumran writings.

- and that in the *Damascus Document* it is especially Saw who is under fire, whereas Tryphon receives less criticism, even though he as Antiochus IV's successor would have been more interesting if Antiochus IV had had an overruling impact on the development of the theme.

Lastly we can conclude that even in the approach of the intertestamental texts the Antichrist is an individual figure, who has strong connections with a messianic figure wherever he occurs.

The lawlessness of 2 Thessalonians is not new to the Antichrist theme. Even when we leave the *Wiles of the Wicked Woman* out of consideration, it clearly features in the Hasmoneans in the *Psalms of Solomon*, which was a well-known writing. An appeal to איש הכזב is therefore not necessary (lies and lawlessness are related, but not synonymous), even though the ideas of the Qumran Community were generally well known.[13]

In Revelation, the Antichrist takes shape in several different figures: beasts and a false prophet. The theme also occurs in 'double figures' in other writings. The purest example of such a *Doppelgestalt* is found in the Damascus Document, where Saw and Tryphon only represent one aspect each of the Antichrist.

With the exception of 2 Maccabees, the term 'beast' is not used very lightly in the intertestamental writings, but there are sufficient references to many more or less concrete animals or beasts. The term 'false prophet' is not used elsewhere, but the portrayal of Saw in the *Damascus Document* and the *Habakkuk Pesher* is more or less that of such a false prophet.

Where we wondered whether there was scope for an individual, eschatological Antichrist in the Epistles of John, the intertestamental texts have clearly proven that it is definitely possible.

Is the picture getting clearer? In order to answer this question, we must take a look at the eschatological variant only, because most of the pre-eschatological realizations are also found in other sources, which means that they leave us with a more precise impression than is justified by their roles as Antichrists. When looking at the eschatological variant only, we see that the intertestamental data are clearer than the Old Testament data, and that the New Testament data are even clearer, even though the intertestamental data admittedly only become really clear when viewed through a definition based on the writings of the Church Fathers. It is only in the latter that the concept is clear and the term 'Antichrist' is used as such.

---

13. Chapter 3 n. 2.

4. *The Antichrist in the Intertestamental Period* 231

Even though the New Testament does use the term in 1 Jn 2.18, 22; 4.3; 2 Jn 7, there is confusion in these verses, because it is not immediately clear whether we are actually dealing with an eschatological individual.

We did not start out with a well-defined definition. Rather, we noted that the term has been used, that the meaning of the term only becomes clear after reading the Church Fathers, and that this meaning, the theme, was definitely present in the intertestamental period.[14]

The Antichrist theme is not the only theme that follows this pattern of clarification. Christology follows a similar pattern and only reaches its full development in the early history of the Church. However, this does not mean that we should regard Christ and Antichrist as opposites in the intertestamental or New Testament texts.

The appeal to the Church Fathers (instead of the Nag Hammadi texts, for instance) may be regarded as taking a confessional viewpoint, but the majority in the Christian Church has followed this path, and, secondly, it should not be a problem that also this study has been written against a specific background, namely, the wish to link in with mainstream Christian tradition.

Overview of Significant Intertestamental and New Testament Data

(330 BCE TO 100 CE)

310	*David and the bear in eschatological perspective* (Ps. 152)
290	
270	
250	
230	
210	
190	*David and Goliath in typical perspective* (Sirach)
170	
	Antiochus IV Epiphanes, angry king (*Sibylline Oracle*)
	Holophernes (Jdt.)
130	
	(Antiochus IV, Menelaus, Nicanor) (2 Maccabees)

---

14. Cf. Ernst, *Die eschatologischen Gegenspieler*, p. xii.

110	Saw (first as Woman?), **Tryphon** (Damacus Document) (Antiochus IV, Goliath, Nicanor) (1 Maccabees) / **One of Belial** (Testimonia)
90	serpent (*Hymns*)
70	Alexander Janneus (*Habakkuk Pesher*) **Hasmoneans** (*Psalms of Solomon*) / king of Kittites (*War Scroll*) **Pompey** (*Psalms of Solomon*)
30	woman (and more?) (*Sibylline Oracles*) black king (*Treatise of Shem*)
10	
10 CE	king of kings (*Assumption of Moses*)
30 CE	opponent (?) (*2 Enoch*)
50 CE	man of lawlessness (2 Thessalonians)
70 CE	
90 CE	**Beast, False Prophet** (Revelation) **Antichrist** (1–2 John)

g. *The Origins of the Antichrist Theme*

The following elements from the Old Testament form the basis of the Antichrist theme:

- the concepts of the good and the wicked prophet
- the history of David and his opponents (bear and Goliath)
- the concepts of the good and the wicked shepherd
- the horn
- the actions of Antiochus IV Epiphanes

The prophet, David and the good shepherd belong to the core of the Old Testament, and the horn is a body part that is often used metaphorically. Antiochus IV Epiphanes, the Hasmoneans and Pompey play a role in the history of Israel itself. It is therefore not necessary to look for origins outside the Old Testament or the history of Israel.

We also need to consider the Gog theme. The origin of Gog has remained unclear. (Is he a historical figure, a Babylonian mythological being, or derived from a Sumeric word?) We note that Zimmerli refers to David, who is also well known and hidden at the same time.[15] This means that the figure of David—as an opponent of the bear and Goliath, as the

---

15. W. Zimmerli, *Ezechiel*, II (BKAT; Neukirchen–Vluyn: Neukirchener Verlag, 1969), p. 947.

good shepherd and as a similar enigma—receives more prominence as one of the bases of the Antichrist theme. This would confirm the existence of a connection with messianism from the very start. There is one more area in which opposition to David can be distinguished: the Hasmoneans had usurped David's throne.[16] Actually, the hope for the restoration of Davidic kingship was never very prominent in the Qumran Community.

Intertestamental innovations can all be traced back to the Old Testament. The beast can equally well be a development of David's bear as of a Babylonian monster. The woman originates from Prov. 7 and related passages. Their pre-eschatological interpretation has proved to be wrong, since their own time did not immediately precede the end times, but the taking shape of an eschatological theme with the help of historical figures is fully within the lines of biblical thinking.

We conclude that all elements can be traced back to the Old Testament (core) and the history of Israel (actualization by idealization), and that at no point does it become necessary to appeal to an Iranian or Babylonian origin. This does not mean, however, that all marginal influence from those areas should be excluded. We have already noted the influence of the image of Cambyses and that of Alexander the Great (who was hardly ever active in Israel), of the Oracle of the Potter and of astrological texts, and undoubtedly there are many other interesting parallels.

2. *Comparisons with Other Figures*

a. *Satan*

In comparing the Antichrist and Satan we must remember that their relationship is predetermined by our definition: 'A man acting under the influence of Satan'. On the basis of this criterion we have seen for several specific figures that they do not qualify as the Antichrist. Mastema in *Jubilees*, Belial in the *Qumran Documents*, and Melkiresha in the *Berakhot* (4Q280) and the *Testament of Amram* (4Q544) cannot be identified with the Antichrist, because a comparison with Satan seems more justified. In contrast to the activities of the Antichrist, those of Satan are not limited to the end times.

Wherever Βελιαρ / בליעל is mentioned in the intertestamental writings, he can be identified with Satan, whilst an identification with the Antichrist is sometimes possible but never necessary.

The relationship between the Antichrist and Satan is not often discussed in the intertestamental writings. In the oldest parts of the Third Book of

---

16. Cf. Van der Woude, *Die messianischen Vorstellungen*, p. 227.

Sibylline Oracles this relationship can only be reconstructed on the basis of a risky inversion of the relationship between the messiah and God. In *Pss. Sol.* 17 a similar situation occurs. In Judith, the relationship between Holophernes and Nebuchadnezzar is comparable to the relationship between the Antichrist and Satan. In the *Testimonia* (4Q175 23) the influence of Satan is clear. In the *Hymns*, the realm of Satan is said to assist the serpent. Both *T. Dan* 5.6 and *T. Gad* 4.7 mention the guidance of Satan, but those verses do not refer to the Antichrist.[17] The same is probably true for *Pseudo-Ezekiel* (4Q386). In *Ass. Mos.* 10.1, the presence of Satan where we would expect the Antichrist indicates a close relationship.

The image of the dragon is used for Satan in Rev. 13.2b, but in *Pss. Sol.* 2.25 and *T. Ash.* 7.3 there is sufficient reason to assume that they refer to the Antichrist (and also to Pompey).

In the *Assumption of Moses* we see more of God's sovereign power than of dependence on Satan, but the recognition of one does not necessarily imply a negation of the other.

In conclusion we can say that maintaining the distinction between the Antichrist and Satan is important in determining which figures qualify for the Antichrist theme, and that there is hardly any further clarification of the relationship between the Antichrist and Satan in the intertestamental writings.

b. *Gog, the King from the North*
The relationship between the Antichrist theme and the Gog theme is rather complicated. On the one hand we see on the basis of Rev. 20.7-9 that the two themes are distinct, on the other hand we see on the basis of Ezek. 38–39 that certain elements from that biblical passage may have had some influence on the Antichrist theme.

In Judith it is unclear at first whether this book is more concerned with the Gog theme than with the Antichrist theme, but a closer look reveals that this doubt is unjustified. In *Pss. Sol.* 17 it is possible to think of Pompey as the king from the north, but *Pss. Sol.* 2 makes clear that Pompey can carry the full scope of the Antichrist theme. On this basis the dragon in *T. Ash.* 7.3 can be identified with the Antichrist instead of the king from the north.

Gog is also mentioned in the Qumran documents. The author of the *War Scroll* is not very systematic, but as we have seen the king of the Kittites it

---

17. The deduction from the Testament of Dan that the Antichrist will come from that tribe is therefore not justified.

can be equated with the Antichrist, even though there are links with Gog as well.

In conclusion we can say that in principle a distinction can be made between the unsuccessful military figure of Gog and the temporarily successful military and religious figure of the Antichrist, and that the themes are interrelated in the intertestamental writings.

c. *Messiah*
When we studied 2 Thessalonians we saw that the Antichrist can be seen as a false god. This aspect is also evident elsewhere. Yet the Antichrist occurs together with Christ in the texts of the Fathers and with messianic figures in the intertestamental texts.

For instance, Ps. 152.4aα has messianic connotations, the *Laus Patrum* has messianic overtones, the messiah in *Sib. Or.* 3.652-56 is not far removed from *Sib. Or.* 3.608-15, and in those verses the βασιλεὺς μέγας has been interpreted as a messianic figure, whereas in my view he is the Antichrist. We see a similar situation in *Pss. Sol.* 17.7-9, but there we are dealing with a divergent aspect of Pompey rather than a wrong interpretation. The Anointed One in *Pss. Sol.* 17.32-43 is not far removed from the Antichrist mentioned earlier in the psalm. In the *Testimonia* (4Q175) the passage that we are concerned with immediately follows three messianic testimonies. In the Hymn that we have looked at, the Antichrist (the serpent) is an opposite to the messiah. In *Sib. Or.* 3.75-77 the messianic figure and the Antichrist can be opposites, but the text is very sibylline.

To the Qumran Community, the Teacher of Righteousness is not the messiah in the strict sense of the word, but he is related to him. In his dependence on God he makes a significant contribution to the salvation of the majority of mankind. Since he is also historical, I use the term 'pre-messianic'. Like the Teacher of Righteousness, the Antichrist is both pre-eschatological (especially Saw as an opposite to the Teacher of Righteousness) and eschatological. In this New Testament perspective we can also state about Jesus Christ that his first coming heralded the *eschaton*, but that we are not yet living in the end times; only his return will be eschatological.

Where the Antichrist can be compared to the messiah in a specific writing (in the *Testimonia* four separate texts have been grouped together), the comparison is usually antithetical. Only in the oldest parts of the Third Book of *Sibylline Oracles* is the Antichrist more a bad copy than an opposite of Christ.

In conclusion we can say that there certainly are links between the Antichrist theme and the expectation of the messiah. However, the two figures do not necessarily occur together and in that sense we can definitely view the Antichrist as an independent figure.

d. *Evil Man, Tyrant, False Prophet*
In this last section I shall attempt to answer some of the questions that have been raised during my research.

Is the Antichrist an evil man? He is and he is not. In an eschatological perspective he is an evil man *par excellence*. For this reason I have not included texts that only describe evil historical men.

Is the Antichrist the same as the Tyrant? The Antichrist is a tyrant, but not every tyrant is the Antichrist, even though a number of tyrannical figures have contributed to the way the Antichrist is portrayed. Antiochus IV and Cambyses are the clearest examples of this phenomenon, but in this study I have only looked at the tyrant in an eschatological perspective.

Is the Antichrist the False Prophet? Even though the Antichrist is definitely portrayed as active in the religious arena, 'false prophet' is hardly a description that would immediately spring to mind. The theme of the false prophet does not seem to occur frequently, not even in non-eschatological perspective, but the deceitful aspect of the Antichrist occurs as early as in the Old Testament.[18]

3. *Evaluation of the Views of Other Researchers*

a. *H. Gunkel*
Gunkel was opposed to the Historical-Critical method and founded the Form-Critical school. However useful and interesting it may be to place Israel against the background of its contemporary religions and cultures—but always as close to home as possible—an appeal to those religions and cultures is not necessary, as we have seen, whereas an understanding of Israel's own history is important to this study.

Gunkel sees a development from contemporary enemies to an eschatological enemy, and I agree. He also sees a shift from protology to eschatology. Obviously, understanding the way global history works is important in apocalyptics, and it is clearly related to protology and eschatology, but in the case of the Antichrist theme we cannot simply jump from the one to the other.

---

18. Contra W.C. Weinrich, 'Antichrist in the Early Church', *Concordia Theological Quarterly* 49 (1985), pp. 135-47 (142).

4. The Antichrist in the Intertestamental Period 237

According to Gunkel, the number 666 in the book of Revelation should be explained as the numeric value of תהום קדמוניה (Tiamat). As we have seen, the number χξς' indicates the opponent of Christ ($\overline{XC}$) who receives authority from Satan (ξ). The number also indicates the fullness of human imperfection.

b. *W. Bousset*

Bousset too was a founder of the Form-Critical school. Unlike Gunkel he preferred to find his sources in Iran instead of Babylon. The same criticism that applies to Gunkel also applies to Bousset. Like Gunkel, he sees in the Antichrist theme an eschatologization of a creation myth, and for this too I refer to my earlier comments on Gunkel's thesis.

Typical for Bousset is the stability axiom. On the basis of the assumption that hardly any development took place around the turn of the millennium, he gathers all his material into one single, extremely varied collection, no matter how much the times and places of origin may vary. In his view, the passing on of oral tradition (*Geheimlehre*) created a straight line from intertestamental literature to the Church Fathers. I agree that an introduction to intertestamental literature is not only useful for Old and New Testament scholars, but also for those who specialize in knowledge of the Church Fathers. Indeed, we have looked at many different sources in this study, but it must be maintained that we cannot simply place a wide variety of sources into one and the same category. In reality people do not live, or indeed write, in a vacuum, and the stability axiom is therefore unrealistic.

Bousset sees a triple Antichrist in the book of Revelation, in Dragon, Beast and False Prophet. Even though the multiple presentation of the Antichrist is not at all problematic, I believe that Bousset is going too far here. He allocates a place to Satan in the Dragon, thereby mixing the images of Antichrist and Satan, which he believes have the same origin: 'The Antichrist legend now seems to me a simple humanization of that old dragon myth.'[19]

c. *R.H. Charles*

Charles's achievements in the area of intertestamental literature are formidable. The main problems with his approach, however, are his preference for the *lectio difficilior* and his rationalism. The *lectio difficilior* rule is good in itself, but should not lead to absurd solutions. Similarly, some

---

19. 'Eine einfache Vermenschlichung jenes alten Drachenmythos scheint mir nun die Sage vom Antichrist zu sein'. Bousset, *Der Antichrist*, p. 93.

measure of rationalism can be good, but to suspect the same amount of rationalism with the authors of the apocalyptic writings is simply asking for problems. Some have criticized him for his focus on the historical background of the texts and on the development of dogmas or theological themes, but I shall not criticize him for this—I even chose to use the same approach.

Charles gives a rather detailed picture of the development of the Antichrist theme, and claims it was completed between 88 and 90 CE. The main ingredients are Antiochus IV (a human opponent of God), later complemented by Pompey, Beliar (a satanic spirit) and Nero. The combination of Antiochus and Beliar is found from 50 CE onwards in Paul's Second Epistle to the Thessalonians and in the book of Revelation. A combination of all this with Nero is found in Rev. 13.18. A combination of Beliar and Nero is found in *Sib. Or.* 3.63-74, which is of a relatively late date.[20] Charles dismisses any influence from elsewhere. To him, Old Testament data, historical events from the intertestamental period and internal Jewish developments suffice, and the term Antichrist is therefore recent, whereas the concept is ancient.

I can agree with most of these general principles, but there are several mistakes in Charles's New Testament exegesis and the interpretation of the *Sibylline Oracles*. For instance, I believe it can be proven that the core of the Antichrist theme is much older. I also believe that the element of the false prophet does not receive sufficient attention in Charles's reconstruction. Thirdly, I do not believe that a fusion with the Beliar tradition took place. (There may have been an influence, but 2 Thess. 2.3 does not prove that.) Fourthly, the first Beast in Rev. 13.1-10 portrays the Antichrist, and, fifthly, Simon Magus and Nero cannot both be introduced in *Sib. Or.* 3.63-74.

d. *B. Rigaux*

Rigaux regards the Antichrist as an individual concept, which has always been very closely linked to collective anti-divine powers throughout the millennia. He believes that influence from outside Israel is not necessary, and that the Antichrist theme developed under the influence of the development of messianism. In the Old Testament the idea was applied to Gog and Antioch IV, and in the intertestamental period Pompey was added. In the Third Book of *Sibylline Oracles* the Antichrist was still mainly collective.

---

20. A problem that does not become apparent in this short summary is that Charles uses the word 'Antichrist' in several different ways.

4. *The Antichrist in the Intertestamental Period* 239

In the New Testament the head of the eschatological enemies was crystallized into an individual,[21] Antichrist, the Man of Lawlessness, on the basis of the book of Daniel.

As we have seen, there are important objections to the wide scope of the theme with Rigaux. This became apparent at an early stage of this study when we were still considering the possibility that we would only find elements of the Antichrist in the intertestamental period, but it is even clearer now we have seen that the theme did indeed exist at that time. Contrary to what Rigaux thinks, the core of an individual eschatological opponent already existed, although admittedly there have been influences from Gog, Antiochus IV and Pompey. The influence of messianism is an interesting thought, in view of the link with David that I believe exists, but I would not go so far as Rigaux when he said: 'Antimessianism corresponds to messaianism.'[22]

e. *D. Flusser*

According to Flusser, the concept of the Antichrist originated in Jewish apocalyptic circles including the Qumran Community. He is a human exponent of satanic evil powers. As an example, Flusser mentions Melkiresha in the *Berakhot* (4Q280) and the *Testament of Amram* (4Q544), and the Son of the Most High in *Pseudo-Daniel* (4Q246). He also attempts to include the Oracle of Hystaspes. Unfortunately I cannot agree with Flusser. In this study we have identified Melkiresha with Satan and the Son of the Most High with the messiah,[23] and the origin and reliability of the text of the Oracle of Hystaspes (which is very limited) are too uncertain to enable us to build any theories on the text.

f. *H. Burgmann*

Burgmann is the researcher who has made the most efforts to find the Antichrist—a human tool in the hands of the evil one—in the Qumran writings. He believes that the concept refers to the Hasmonean Simon, who used violence against the Qumran Community and harmed them theologically by founding the party of the Pharisees. Simon appears in the Qumran Documents as One of Belial (in the *Testimonia* [4Q175]), which is thus the oldest text about the Antichrist), as the Man of Deceit, a Man of Arrogance, Saw,

---

21. Or do we have to speak about a 'corporate personality' (Rigaux, *Saint-Paul*, p. 278)?
22. 'L'antimessianisme répond au messianisme'. Rigaux, *Antéchrist*, p. x.
23. Flusser does have an excuse here: he did not know the whole text.

the mother of the serpent, and the Woman. This historical human opponent had to be an important figure, because he opposed what was perceived as the community of the elect. Thus he became the model for the eschatological Antichrist, who made his way from Qumran into the Epistles of John. There is no Old Testament model, and the theme was linked with Antiochus IV much later.

Burgmann's reconstruction seems far too hypothetical. The link between Simon and the Pharisees is especially unfounded, but also in other aspects his work lacks credibility. In my view the Man of Deceit is not a priest, the mother of the serpent does not play a conceptual role, and the limitation to the Qumran Community and John's Epistle is unjustified.

Finally I must point out that Burgmann is not wrong in all of his conclusions. *Testimonia*, *Wiles of the Wicked Woman* and 1QH 11 (*olim* 3) are important texts. Saw did play a role in the development of the image of the Antichrist, and a link between the Qumran writings and the Epistles of John is not impossible. However, the concentration of all elements into one man—Simon—is wrong.

g. *G.C. Jenks*
Jenks believes the writers of the third century CE all had about the same concept of the Antichrist, and I can agree, but some differences remain. For the period of the Fathers, I have consciously limited my study to texts from mainstream Christianity in which both the theme and the word 'Antichrist' occur.

Jenks prefers to eliminate the Bousset hypothesis, since the Antichrist theme is pre-eminently a Christian theme. Naturally, this is determined, at least in part, by the definition that is used: Jenks assigns more space to the relationship with Jesus Christ than I do. Another difference on the level of definition is the importance of demons. In my definition the Antichrist is human, but Jenks has also looked at demonology, including that of Qumran. In doing so, he runs the risk of paying less attention to the *context* and the *translation* of the (many) texts he has studied.

In general, research into the antecedents of the third century CE Antichrist is not the same as research into the functioning of the theme in the intertestamental period. And lastly, Jenks thinks too highly of the Combat Myth, which does not seem as yet to have been successfully combatted.

h. *L.J. Lietaert Peerbolte*
As we have seen, Lietaert Peerbolte's research parallels that of Jenks in many aspects. The relationship between New Testament and Patristic texts

on the one hand and Jewish intertestamental texts on the other is reversed in my research. To him, the first category is the primary target area with the second as the background, whereas I have them the other way round. Lietaert Peerbolte notes that the elements of the picture of the third-century Antichrist that Jenks reconstructs never occur together and none of them occur everywhere. This requirement seems exaggerated. Like Jenks I too developed a definition, since I believe this to be the only way to determine what exactly I was looking for in the intertestamental period. However, I believe I did not fall into the trap for which Lietaert Peerbolte warns, of trying to fit all my results into a predetermined mould. For the origin of the various elements of the Antichrist theme, Lietaert Peerbolte fixated on the eschatological expectations Christians had for their own days. In my opinion there is more room for a real eschatological expectation, focused on a future that is further ahead than he allowed for. In any case, we should avoid both extremes of being so minimalist that we cannot distinguish our theme anywhere as such, and of being so inclusivist that we see foreshadows of our theme everywhere.

4. *Final Conclusions*

After finding the weak points in the arguments of early researchers of this subject and after forming my own definition on the basis of the earliest group of texts that can provide clarity, namely the Church Fathers, we have seen, contrary to my initial expectations, that the concept of the Antichrist does occur in its fullness in intertestamental literature, that the theme of the Antichrist is linked to that of the messiah (considering the importance of David and his history in the development of the Antichrist theme), and that the theme does not occur more often in esoteric texts than in general or missionary texts.

This conclusion is squarely opposed to that of two other contemporary researchers, Jenks and Lietaert Pierbolte. Naturally this may be cause for concern, but a closer look reveals that they use a much stricter definition as their starting point. Since they include the person of Jesus Christ in their Antichrist definition, it is not surprising that they do not find this theme in the intertestamental period. Moreover, Lietaert Peerbolte pays much more attention to the miraculous works of the Antichrist, which indeed cannot be found in the intertestamental texts. However, the miraculous works mentioned by Cyril of Jerusalem and in Jerome are aimed at deceit, and this is an aspect that is included in my definition. All in all I do believe that my definition is reasonable and that it is therefore right to conclude that the

Antichrist theme was indeed present in the intertestamental period. However, those who demand an Antichrist who is an opponent of Jesus Christ will not agree, and neither will those who prefer to speak of an Antichrist only when the *word* 'Αντίχριστος is used.

Of those who have extensively studied the problem of the Antichrist, Charles is the one I can agree with most, but that does not imply (perhaps even the contrary is true) that I do not criticize any of his conclusions. In the area of the importance of the Old Testament I agree with him. Initially I only studied the Old Testament texts to find out what the distinctives of the intertestamental writings are, but this part of my research appeared to be of importance to the origin of the Antichrist theme.

Do we now know how the Antichrist theme has developed during the intertestamental period? In spite of my efforts, two limitations remain that may still make it possible for the conclusions of my research to disagree with the historical truth: the quality of my sources and the quality of my research. We do not know whether the extant sources reflect mainstream thinking, but we do know that they provide us with the thinking of some theologizing groups. I made all efforts to ensure that my research is independent and complete, as scientific researchers are expected to do.

Many times it became apparent, however, that if I were to make my research *complete*, it would lead nowhere, simply because every result leads to new questions. I would have liked to include the 'literary Jewish-Hellenistic' writings (including Artapanus, Ezekiel Tragicus and Philo of Alexandria) in my research, but theirs is a completely different world.[24] Theoretically, certain parts of the Targums and Talmuds also originated in the intertestamental period, but it is impossible to clearly mark the boundaries, and again this is a wholly different world.

I have also found that a fully *independent* study of each text and every problem is impossible, because I depended on the works of others, as is

---

24. It is my impression that some elements can be found with Philo (see, e.g., *Legum allegoriae* 3.79-80, *De somniis* 2.61-66, 123, 130-32, *De benedictionibus* [*De praemiis*] 93-97a) and I can imagine that he may have hidden his Antichrist expectation as successfully as he hid his Messianic expectations (cf. E.R. Goodenough, *The Politics of Philo Judaeus: Practice and Theory. With a General Bibliography of Philo* [New Haven: Yale University Press, 1938], pp. 25, 115; *pace* R.D. Hecht, 'Philo and Messiah', in J. Neusner *et al.* [eds.], *Judaisms and their Messiahs at the Time of the Christian Era* [Cambridge: Cambridge University Press, 1987], pp. 139-68 [162-63]). In the other 'literary Jewish-Hellenistic' writings I have not noticed anything that deserves a closer look.

4. *The Antichrist in the Intertestamental Period* 243

abundantly clear from the footnotes.[25] I simply had to assume that a scholar who has extensively studied a specific text knows more about the setting and meaning of that text than I do. Perhaps my trust in their knowledge was unjustified in places, but no work can be done without some degree of reliance on others. I hope that this study may form the basis of further research in that same spirit of trust.

---

25. The footnotes do not even give the full picture. I have used the dictionaries more often than would appear from the footnotes. Here I must mention Zorell, *Lexicon*, in the first place. Also my use of A.S. van der Woude (ed.), *Bijbels Handboek* (Kampen: Kok, 1981–87), has not always been indicated. I pay tribute to their works as good basic literature.

BIBLIOGRAPHY

Aalders, G.C., *Ezechiël*. II. *Hfdst. 25–48* (Commentaar op het Oude Testament; Kampen: Kok, 1957).
Abel, F.-M., *Les livres des Maccabées* (Ebib; Paris: Gabalda, 1949).
Alexander, P.S., 'From Poetry to Historiography: The Image of the Hasmoneans in Targum Canticles and the Question of the Targum's Provenance and Date', *JSP* 19 (1999), pp. 103-28.
Alexandre, C., Χρησμοὶ Σιβυλλιακοί (Paris: Didot, 2nd edn, 1869).
Allegro, J.M., 'Further Light on the History of the Qumran Sect', *JBL* 75 (1956), pp. 89-95.
—*Qumrân Cave 4*. I. *4Q158–4Q168* (DJD, 5; Oxford: Clarendon Press, 1968).
—'The Wiles of the Wicked Woman: A Sapiential Work from Qumran's Fourth Cave', *PEQ* 96 (1964), pp. 53-55.
Andersen, F.I., '2 (Slavonic Apocalypse of) Enoch', *OTP*, I, pp. 91-221.
Anderson, H., '3 Maccabees', *OTP*, II, pp. 509-29.
Applebaum, S., 'The Legal Status of the Jewish Communities in the Diaspora', in Safrai and Stern, *Jewish People in the First Century*, pp. 420-62.
Arenhoevel, D., *Die Theokratie nach dem 1. und 2. Makkabäerbuch* (Walberberger Studien der Albertus Magnus-Akademie. Theologische Reihe, 3; Mainz: Grünewald, 1967).
Atkinson, K.M.T., 'The Historical Setting of the "War of the Sons of Light and the Sons of Darkness"', *BJRL* 40 (1957–58), pp. 272-97.
Attridge, H.W., 'Historiography', in Stone (ed.), *Jewish Writings of the Second Temple Period*, pp. 157-84.
Badian, E., 'Carriages', OCD^2, pp. 207-208.
Baillet, M., *Qumrân grotte 4*. III. *4Q482–4Q520* (DJD, 5; Oxford: Clarendon Press, 1982).
Baillet, M., J.T. Milik and R. de Vaux, *Les 'petites grottes' de Qumrân* (DJD, 3; Oxford: Clarendon Press, 1962).
Baldwin, J.G., *1 and 2 Samuel* (TOTC; Leicester; Downers Grove: Inter-Varsity Press, 1988).
—*Haggai, Zechariah, Malachi* (TOTC; Leicester; Downers Grove: Inter-Varsity Press, 1972).
Bar-Kochva, B., *Judas Maccabaeus: The Jewish Struggle against the Seleucids* (Cambridge: Cambridge University Press, 1989).
Barstad, H.M., 'The Understanding of the Prophets in Deuteronomy', *SJOT* 8 (1994), pp. 236-51.
Barta, W., *Untersuchungen zur Göttlichkeit des regierenden Königs: Ritus und Sakralkönigtum in Altägypten nach Zeugnissen der Frühzeit und des Alten Reiches* (Münchner Ägyptologische Studien, 32; Munich: Deutscher Kunstverlag, 1975).
Barthélemy, D., and J.T. Milik, *Qumran Cave I* (DJD, 1; Oxford: Clarendon Press, 1955).
Baumgarten, A.I., *The Flourishing of Jewish Sects in the Maccabean Era: An Interpretation* (JSJSup [*olim* SPB], 55; Leiden: E.J. Brill, 1997).
Baumgarten, J.M., 'On the Nature of the Seductress in *4Q184*', *RevQ* 15 (Mémorial Jean Starcky; 1991), pp. 133-43.

Beale, G.K., *The Use of Daniel in Jewish Apocalyptic Literature and in the Revelation of St. John* (Lanham, MD: University Press of America, 1984).
Becker, J., *Die Testamente der zwölf Patriarchen* (JSHRZ, 3.1; Gütersloh: Gerd Mohn, 1981).
—*Untersuchungen zur Entstehungsgeschichte der Testamente der Zwölf Patriarchen* (AGJU, 8; Leiden: E.J. Brill, 1970).
Beckwith, R.T., 'Daniel 9 and the Date of Messiah's Coming in Essene, Hellenistic, Pharisaic, Zealot and Early Christian Computation', *RevQ* 10 (1979-81), pp. 521-42.
—'The Pre-History and Relationships of the Pharisees, Sadducees and Essenes: A Tentative Reconstruction', *RevQ* 11 (1982), pp. 3-46.
—'The Qumran Calendar and the Sacrifices of the Essenes', *RevQ* 7 (1971), pp. 587-91.
—'The Significance of the Calendar for Interpreting Essene Chronology and Eschatology', *RevQ* 10 (1979-81), pp. 167-202.
Beentjes, P.C., *The Book of Ben Sira in Hebrew: A Text Edition of All Extant Hebrew Manuscripts and a Synopsis of All Parallel Hebrew Ben Sira Texts* (VTSup, 68; Leiden: E.J. Brill, 1997).
Begg, C., 'The David and Goliath Story According to Josephus', *Mus* 112 (1999), pp. 3-20.
Bénétreau, S., *L'épître aux Hébreux*, I (Commentaire Evangélique de la Bible; Vaux-sur-Seine: Edifac, 1989).
Berger, K., *Die griechische Daniel-Diegese: Eine altkirchliche Apokalypse* (SPB, 27; Leiden: E.J. Brill, 1976).
Berkhof, H., *Christus, de zin der geschiedenis* (Nijkerk: Callenbach, 1958).
Bertholet, A., 'Renan', RGG^2, IV, cols. 1983-84.
Betz, O., 'Past Events and Last Events in the Qumran Interpretation of History', in *Proceedings of the Sixth World Congress of Jewish Studies* (Jerusalem: World Union of Jewish Studies, 1977), pp. 27-34.
Bevan, E.R., *The House of Seleucus*, II (London: Edward Arnold, 1902).
Bévenot, H., *Die beiden Makkabäerbücher* (Die Heilige Schrift des Alten Testamentes; Bonn: Hanstein, 1931).
Beyer, K., *Die aramäischen Texte vom Toten Meer samt den Inschriften aus Palästina, dem Testament Levis aus Kairoer Genisa, der Fastenrolle und den alten talmudischen Zitaten* (Göttingen: Vandenhoeck & Ruprecht, 1984).
—*Die aramäischen Texte vom Toten Meer samt den Inschriften aus Palästina, dem Testament Levis aus der Kairoer Genisa, der Fastenrolle und den alten talmudischen Zitaten: Ergänzungsband* (Göttingen: Vandenhoeck & Ruprecht, 1994).
Bickerman, E., *The God of the Maccabees: Studies on the Meaning and Origin of the Maccabean Revolt* (SJLA, 32; Leiden: E.J. Brill, 1979).
Bierling, N., *Giving Goliath his Due: New Archaeological Light on the Philistines* (Grand Rapids: Baker Book House, 1992).
Bietenhard, H., 'Die Handschriftenfunde vom Toten Meer (Hirbet Qumran) und die Essener-Frage. Die Funde in der Wüste Juda (Eine Orientierung)', *ANRW*, II 19.1 (1979), pp. 704-78.
Bimson, J.J., *Redating the Exodus and Conquest* (JSOTSup, 5; Sheffield: Almond Press, 1981).
Bimson, J.J., and J.P. Kane, *New Bible Atlas* (Leicester: Inter-Varsity Press, 1985).
Blass, F., A. Debrunner and F. Rehkopf, *Grammatik des neutestamentlichen Griechisch* (Göttingen: Vandenhoeck & Ruprecht, 16th edn, 1984).
Boerwinkel, F., *Kerk en secte* (The Hague: Boekencentrum, 1953).
Bonwetsch, N., *Das slavische Henochbuch* (Abhandlungen der Königlichen Gesellschaft der

Wissenschaften zu Göttingen. Philologisch-historische Klasse, 1.3; Berlin: Weidmann, 1896).

Borger, R., *Einleitung in die assyrischen Königsinschriften*. I. *Das zweite Jahrtausend v. Chr.* (HO, 1.5.1.1; Leiden: E.J. Brill, 2nd edn, 1964).

Bornhausen, K., 'Troeltsch', RGG^2, V, cols. 1284-87.

Bottéro, J., *Mythes et rites de Babylonie* (Geneva: Slatkine–Champion, 1985).

Böttrich, C., *Weltweisheit, Menschheitsethik, Urkult: Studien zum slavischen Henochbuch* (WUNT, 2.50; Tübingen: J.C.B. Mohr, 1992).

Bousset, W., *Der Antichrist* (Göttingen: Vandenhoeck & Ruprecht, 1895).

—'Die Beziehungen der ältesten jüdischen Sibylle zur chaldäischen Sibylle und einige weitere Beobachtungen über den synkretistischen Charakter der spätjüdischen Literatur', *ZNW* 3 (1902), pp. 23-49.

—*Die Offenbarung Johannis* (KEK; Göttingen: Vandenhoeck & Ruprecht, 5th edn, 1896).

—*Die Offenbarung Johannis* (KEK; Göttingen: Vandenhoeck & Ruprecht, 6th edn, 1906).

Bowman, J., *Samaritanische Probleme: Studien zum Verhältnis von Samaritanertum, Judentum und Urchristentum* (Stuttgart: W. Kohlhammer, 1967).

Boyce, M., 'On the Antiquity of Zoroastrian Apocalyptic', *BSOAS* 47 (1984), pp. 57-75.

Brandenburger, E., 'Himmelfahrt Moses', in *Apokalypsen* (JSHRZ, 5.2; Gütersloh: Gerd Mohn, 1976), pp. 57-84.

Braun, F.-M., 'Les testaments des XII Patriarches et le problème de leur origine', *RB* 67 (1960), pp. 516-49.

Braun, H., 'Vom Erbarmen Gottes über den Gerechten. Zur Theologie der Psalmen Salomos', *ZNW* 43 (1950–51), pp. 1-54.

Brongers, H.A., *I Koningen* (Prediking van het Oude Testament; Nijkerk: Callenbach, 1967).

Broshi, M., 'Hatred—An Essene Religious Principle and its Christian Consequences', in B. Kollmann, W. Reinbold and A. Steudel (eds.), *Antikes Judentum und Frühes Christentum* (Festschrift H. Stegemann; BZNW, 97; Berlin: W. de Gruyter, 1999), pp. 245-52.

Broshi, M., and E. Eshel, 'The Greek King Is Antiochus IV (4QHistorical Text=4Q248)', *JJS* 48 (1997), pp. 120-29.

Brouwer, C., *Wachter en herder: Een exegetische studie over de herder-figuur in het Oude Testament, inzonderheid in de pericopen Zacharia 11 en 13.7-9* (Wageningen: Veenman, 1949).

Brownlee, W.H., *The Midrash Pesher of Habakkuk: Text, Translation, Exposition with an Introduction* (SBLMS, 24; Missoula, MT: Scholars Press, 1979).

—'The Wicked Priest, the Man of Lies, and the Righteous Teacher—the Problem of Identity', *JQR* 73 (1982), pp. 1-37.

Bruce, F.F., *Biblical Exegesis in the Qumran Texts* (Exegetica, 3.1; The Hague: Van Keulen, 1959).

—*Second Thoughts on the Dead Sea Scrolls* (Grand Rapids: Eerdmans, 2nd edn, 1961).

Brütsch, C., *Clarté de l'Apocalypse* (Geneva: Labor et Fides, 5th edn, 1966).

Buchanan, G.W., 'Introduction', in R.H. Charles, *Eschatology: The Doctrine of a Future Life in Israel, in Judaism, and in Christianity. A Critical History* (New York: Schocken Books, 3rd edn, 1963), pp. vii-xxx.

Buis, P., and J. Leclercq, *Le Deutéronome* (SB; Paris: Gabalda, 1963).

Bunge, J.G., 'Der "Gott der Festungen" und der "Liebling der Frauen". Zum Identifizierung der Götter in Dan 11.36-39', *JSJ* 4 (1973), pp. 169-82.

—'Münzen als Mittel politischer Propaganda: Antiochos IV. Epiphanes von Syrien', *Studii Clasice* 16 (1974), pp. 43-52.

—'Untersuchungen zum zweiten Makkabäerbuch. Quellenkritische, literarische, chronologische und historische Untersuchungen zum zweiten Makkabäerbuch als Quelle syrischpalästinensischer Geschichte im 2. Jh. v. Chr.' (dissertation, Bonn, 1971).

Burchard, C., 'Zur armenischen Überlieferung der Testamente der zwölf Patriarchen', in W. Eltester (ed.), *Studien zu den Testamenten der Zwölf Patriarchen* (BZNW, 36; Berlin: Alfred Töpelmann, 1969), pp. 1-29.

Burgmann, H., 'Antichrist—Antimessias: der Makkabäer Simon?', *Judaica* 36 (1980), pp. 152-74.

—'"The Wicked Woman": Der Makkabäer Simon?', *RevQ* 8 (1974), pp. 323-59.

—*Vorgeschichte und Frühgeschichte der essenischen Gemeinden von Qumrân und Damaskus* (ANTJ, 7; Bern: Peter Lang, 1987).

—*Weitere lösbare Qumranprobleme* (Qumranica Mogilanensia, 9; Kraków: Enigma, 1992).

Burkitt, F.C., 'Robert Henry Charles. 1855-1931', *Proceedings of the British Academy* 17 (1931), pp. 437-45.

Burrows, M., *More Light on the Dead Sea Scrolls: New Scrolls and New Interpretations. With Translations of Important Recent Discoveries* (London: Secker & Warburg, 1958).

Burrows, M., and W.H. Brownlee, *The Dead Sea Scrolls of St. Mark's Monastery*. I. *The Isaiah Manuscript and the Habakkuk Commentary* (New Haven: ASOR, 1950).

Busink, T.A., *Der Tempel von Jerusalem: Von Salomo bis Herodes. Eine archäologisch-historische Studie unter Berücksichtigung des westsemitischen Tempelbaus*. II. *Von Ezechiel bis Middot* (Leiden: E.J. Brill, 1980).

Callaway, P.R., *The History of the Qumran Community: An Investigation* (JSPSup, 3; Sheffield: JSOT Press, 1988).

Campbell, J.G., 'Scripture in the Damascus Document 1.1-2.1', *JJS* 44 (1993), pp. 83-99.

Caquot, A., 'Ecrits qoumrâniens', in Dupont-Sommer and Philonenko (eds.), *Ecrits intertestamentaires*, pp. xxx-xliv.

—'La pérennité du sacerdoce', in *Paganisme, judaïsme, christianisme: Influences et affrontements dans le monde antique* (Festschrift M. Simon; Paris: de Boccard, 1978), pp. 109-16.

—'Le messianisme qumrânien', in M. Delcor (ed.), *Qumrân: Sa piété, sa théologie et son milieu* (BETL, 46; Gembloux: Duculot; Leuven: Leuven University Press, 1978), pp. 231-47.

—'Les Hasmonéens, les Romains et Hérode: observations sur *Ps. Sal.* 17', in A. Caquot *et al.* (eds.), *Hellenica et Judaica* (Memorial V. Nikiprowetzky; Leuven: Peeters, 1986), pp. 213-18.

Caquot, A. (ed.), *La littérature intertestamentaire* (Paris: PUF, 1985).

Caquot, A., and P. de Robert, *Les livres de Samuel* (CAT; Geneva: Labor et Fides, 1994).

Carmignac, J., 'Interprétations de Prophètes et de Psaumes', in J. Carmignac (ed.), *Les Textes de Qumrân traduits et annotés*. II. *Règle de la Congrégation—Recueil des Bénédictions—Interprétations de Prophètes et de Psaumes—Document de Damas—Apocryphe de la Genèse—Fragments des grottes 1 et 4* (Paris: Letouzey et Ané, 1963), pp. 43-128.

—*La Règle de la Guerre des fils de lumière contre les fils de ténèbres* (Paris: Letouzey et Ané, 1958).

—'Les esséniens et la Communauté de Qumrân', in A. George and P. Grelot (eds.), *Introduction à la Bible*. III 1. *Au seuil de l'ère chrétienne* (Paris: Desclée, 1976), pp. 142-61.

—'Les Hymnes', in J. Carmignac (ed.), *Les Textes de Qumrân traduits et annotés*. I. *La Règle de la Communauté—La Règle de la Guerre—Les Hymnes* (Paris: Letouzey et Ané, 1961), pp. 127-282.

—'Poème allégorique sur la secte rivale', *RevQ* 5 (1965), pp. 361-74.

Chantraine, P., *Grammaire homérique*. II. *Syntaxe* (Collection de philologie classique, 4; Paris: Klincksieck, 1963).
Charles, R.H., *A Critical and Exegetical Commentary on the Revelation of St. John* (ICC; Edinburgh: T. & T. Clark, 1920).
—*Eschatology: The Doctrine of a Future Life in Israel, in Judaism, and in Christianity: A Critical History* (New York: Schocken Books, 3rd edn, 1963).
—*Studies in the Apocalypse* (Edinburgh: T. & T. Clark, 1913).
—*The Ascension of Isaiah* (London: A. & C. Black, 1900).
—'The Assumption of Moses', *APOT*, II, pp. 407-24.
—'The Testaments of the XII Patriarchs', *APOT*, II, pp. 282-367.
Charles, R.H., and W.R. Morfill, *The Book of the Secrets of Enoch* (Oxford: Clarendon Press, 1896).
Charlesworth, J.H., 'A History of Pseudepigrapha Research: The Re-emerging Importance of the Pseudepigrapha', *ANRW* II 19.1 (1979), pp. 54-88.
—'Die 'Schrift des Sem': Einführung, Text und Übersetzung', *ANRW*, II 20.2 (1987), pp. 951-87.
—'Rylands Syriac ms 44 and a New Addition to the Pseudepigrapha. The Treatise of Shem', *BJRL* 60 (1978), pp. 376-403.
—'The Concept of the Messiah in the Pseudepigrapha', *ANRW*, II 19.1 (1979), pp. 188-218.
—'The Significance of the New Edition of the Old Testament Pseudepigrapha', in Caquot, *Littérature intertestamentaire*, pp. 11-28.
—'Treatise of Shem', *OTP*, I, pp. 473-86.
Charlesworth, J.H., and J.A. Sanders, 'More Psalms of David', *OTP*, II, pp. 609-24.
Chary, T., *Aggée. Zacharie. Malachie* (SB; Paris: Gabalda, 1969).
Chilton, D., *The Days of Vengeance: An Exposition of the Book of Revelation* (Fort Worth: Dominion, 1987).
Collins, J.J., 'Sibylline Oracles', *OTP*, I, pp. 317-472.
—'Some Remaining Traditio-Historical Problems in the Testament of Moses', in Nickelsburg (ed.), *Studies*, pp. 38-43.
—'Testaments', in Stone (ed.), *Jewish Writings of the Second Temple Period*, pp. 325-55.
—*The Apocalyptic Imagination: An Introduction to the Jewish Matrix of Christianity* (New York: Crossroad, 1984).
—'The Date and Provenance of the Testament of Moses', in Nickelsburg (ed.), *Studies*, pp. 15-32.
—'The Development of the Sibylline Tradition', *ANRW*, II 20.1 (1987), pp. 421-59.
—'The Genre Apocalypse in Hellenistic Judaism', in D. Hellholm (ed.), *Apocalypticism in the Mediterranean World and the Near East* (Tübingen: J.C.B. Mohr, 1983), pp. 531-48.
—'The Sibyl and the Potter: Political Propaganda in Ptolemaic Egypt', in L. Bormann, K. del Tredici and A. Standhartinger (eds.), *Religious Propaganda and Missionary Competition in the New Testament World* (Festschrift D. Georgi; NovTSup, 74; Leiden: E.J. Brill, 1994), pp. 57-69.
—'The Sibylline Oracles', in Stone (ed.), *Jewish Writings of the Second Temple Period*, pp. 357-81.
—*The Sibylline Oracles of Egyptian Judaism* (SBLDS, 13; Missoula, MT: Scholars Press, 1974).
—'The *Son of God* Text from Qumran', in M.C. de Boer (ed.), *From Jesus to John: Essays on Jesus and New Testament Christology in Honour of Marinus de Jonge* (JSNTSup, 84; Sheffield: Sheffield Academic Press, 1993).

Coser, L.A., *Greedy Institutions: Patterns of Undivided Commitment* (New York: Free Press; London: Collier Macmillan, 1974).
Cowley, A.E., *Aramaic Papyri of the Fifth Century B.C.* (Oxford: Clarendon Press, 1923).
Craigie, P.C., *The Book of Deuteronomy* (NICOT; Grand Rapids: Eerdmans, 1976).
Cross, F.M., *The Ancient Library of Qumran and Modern Biblical Studies* (Garden City, NY: Doubleday, 2nd edn, 1961).
Dahl, N.A., 'Sigmund Mowinckel. Historian of Religion and Theologian', *SJOT* [2.]2 (1988), pp. 8-22.
Davidson, M.J., *Angels at Qumran: A Comparative Study of 1 Enoch 1–36, 72–108 and Sectarian Writings from Qumran* (JSPSup, 11; Sheffield: JSOT Press, 1992).
Davies, P.R., *Damascus Covenant: An Interpretation of the 'Damascus Document'* (JSOTSup, 25; Sheffield: JSOT Press, 1983).
—'Notes en marge: Reflections on the Publication of DJDJ 5', in Fabry, Lange and Lichtenberger, *Qumranstudien*, pp. 103-109.
De Goeij, M., *De Pseudepigrafen: Psalmen van Salomo, IV Ezra, Martyrium van Jesaja* (Kampen: Kok, *s.d.*).
De Jonge, M., *De toekomstverwachting in de Psalmen van Salomo* (Leiden: E.J. Brill, 1965).
—*Testamenta XII Patriarcharum: Edited According to Cambridge University Library* MS *Ff 1.24 fol. 203a-261b* (PVTG, 1; Leiden: E.J. Brill, 2nd edn, 1970).
—'Testament Issachar als "typisches" Testament. Einige Bemerkungen zu zwei neue übersetzungen der Testamente der Zwölf Patriarchen', in M. de Jonge (ed.), *Studies on the Testaments of the Twelve Patriarchs* (SVTP, 3; Leiden: E.J. Brill, 1975), pp. 291-316.
—*The Testaments of the Twelve Patriarchs: A Critical Edition of the Greek Text* (PVTG, 1.2; Leiden: E.J. Brill, 1978).
—'The Testaments of the Twelve Patriarchs: Central Problems and Essential Viewpoints', *ANRW*, II 20.1 (1987), pp. 359-420.
Delcor, M., *Le livre de Daniel* (SB; Paris: Gabalda, 1971).
—*Les Hymnes de Qumrân (Hodayot): Texte hébreu—introduction—traduction—commentaire* (Paris: Letouzey et Ané, 1962).
—'L'histoire selon le livre de Daniel, notamment au chapitre 11', in van der Woude (ed.), *Book of Daniel*, pp. 365-86.
Denis, A.-M., *Introduction aux pseudépigraphes grecs d'Ancien Testament* (SVTP, 1; Leiden: E.J. Brill, 1970).
Denis, A.-M., and Y. Janssens, *Concordance grecque des pseudépigraphes d'Ancien Testament: Concordance. Corpus des Textes. Indices* (Louvain-la-Neuve: UCL, 1987).
De Romilly, J., *The Rise and Fall of States* (Jerome Lectures, 11; Ann Arbor: University of Michigan Press, 1977).
Descamps, A., 'Le Révérend Père Béda Rigaux', in A. Descamps and A. de Halleux (eds.), *Mélanges bibliques en hommage au R.P. Béda Rigaux* (Gembloux: Duculot, 1970), pp. ix-xxi.
De Vaulx, J., *Les Nombres* (SB; Paris: Gabalda, 1972).
De Vaux, R., *Les institutions de l'Ancien Testament. II. Institutions militaires. Institutions religieuses* (Paris: Cerf, 1960).
Dhorme, E., *L'emploi métaphorique des noms de parties du corps en hébreu et en akkadien* (Paris: Gabalda, 1923).
Díez Merino, L., *Targum de Salmos: Edición Príncipe del* MS. *Villa Amil n. 5 de Alfonso de Zamora* (Bibliotheca Hispana Biblica, 6; Poliglota Complutense. Tradición sefardí de la Biblia Aramea, 4.1; Madrid: Instituto 'Francisco Suárez', 1982).

Dimant, D., '*4Q386* ii-iii. A Prophecy on Hellenistic Kingdoms?', *RevQ* 18 (1998), pp. 511-29.
—'Apocrypha and Pseudepigrapha at Qumran', *DSD* 1 (1994), pp. 151-59.
—'New Light from Qumran on the Jewish Pseudepigrapha—4Q*390*', in Trebolle Barrera and Vegas Montaner (eds.), *Madrid Qumran Congress*, pp. 405-48.
—'Qumran Sectarian Literature', in Stone (ed.), *Jewish Writings of the Second Temple Period*, pp. 483-550.
—'The Qumran Manuscripts. Contents and Significance', in D. Dimant and L.H. Schiffman (eds.), *Time to Prepare the Way in the Wilderness* (STDJ, 16; Leiden: E.J. Brill, 1995), pp. 23-58.
Döbertin, W., *Adolf von Harnack: Theologe, Pädagoge, Wissenschaftspolitiker* (European University Studies, 23.258; New York: Peter Lang, 1985).
Doran, R., 'The Jewish Hellenistic Historians before Josephus', *ANRW*, II 20.1 (1987), pp. 246-97.
Dörrie, H., *Die Stellung der vier Makkabäerbücher im Kanon der griechischen Bibel* (Nachrichten von der Gesellschaft der Wissenschaften zu Göttingen. Philologisch-historische Klasse. Fachgruppe V. Religionswissenschaft. Neue Folge 1.2; Göttingen: Vandenhoeck & Ruprecht, 1937), pp. 45-46, 53.
Dougherty, R.P., *Nabonidus and Belshazzar: A Study of the Closing Events of the Neo-Babylonian Empire* (Yale Oriental Series Researches, 15; New Haven: Yale University Press, 1929).
Drioton, E., and J. Vandier, *L'Egypte: Des origines à la conquête d'Alexandre* (Paris: PUF, 7th edn, 1989).
Duhaime, J., 'Dualistic Reworking in the Scrolls from Qumran', *CBQ* 49 (1987), pp. 32-56.
—'La règle de la Guerre de Qumrân et l'apocalyptique', *ScEs* 36 (1984), pp. 67-88.
—'Relative Deprivation in New Religious Movements and the Qumran Community', *RevQ* 16 (1993), pp. 265-76.
—'The War Scroll from Qumran and the Greco-Roman Tactical Treatises', *RevQ* 13 (Mémorial Jean Carmignac; 1988), pp. 133-51.
Dupont-Sommer, A., 'Commentaires bibliques', in Dupont-Sommer and Philonenko (eds.), *La Bible: Ecrits intertestamentaires*, pp. 333-80.
—' "Le Chef des rois de Yâwân" dans l'*Ecrit de Damas*', *Sem* 5 (1955), pp. 41-57.
—'Le "Commentaire d'Habaccuc" découvert près de la Mer Morte. Traduction et Notes', *RHR* 137.2 (1950), pp. 129-71.
—'Ecrit de Damas', in Dupont-Sommer and Philonenko (eds.), *Ecrits intertestamentaires*, pp. 133-83.
—'Hymnes', in Dupont-Sommer and Philonenko (eds.), *Ecrits intertestamentaires*, pp. 227-99.
—*Les écrits esséniens découverts près de la mer morte* (Paris: Payot, 2nd edn, 1960).
—'Pièges de la femme', in Dupont-Sommer and Philonenko (eds.), *Ecrits intertestamentaires*, pp. 441-51.
—'Règlement de la guerre', in Dupont-Sommer and Philonenko (eds.), *Ecrits intertestamentaires*, pp. 185-226.
—'Testimonia', in Dupont-Sommer and Philonenko (eds.), *Ecrits intertestamentaires*, pp. 413-20.
Dupont-Sommer, A., and M. Philonenko (eds.), *La Bible: Ecrits intertestamentaires* (Bibliothèque de la Pléiade; Paris: Gallimard, 1987).

Eddy, S.K., *The King Is Dead: Studies in the Near Eastern Resistance to Hellenism* (Lincoln: University of Nebraska Press, 1961).
Eisenman, R.H., and J.M. Robinson, *Facsimile Edition of the Dead Sea Scrolls* (Washington: Biblical Archaeology Society, 1991).
Eissfeldt, O., *Einleitung in das Alte Testament* (Tübingen: J.C.B. Mohr, 3rd edn, 1964).
—'Religionsgeschichtliche Schule', *RGG*², IV, cols. 1898–05.
Engel, H., ' "Der Herr ist ein Gott, der Kriege zerschlägt". Zur Frage der griechischen Originalsprache und der Struktur des Buches Judit', in K.-D. Schunck and M. Augustin (eds.), *Goldene Äpfel in silbernen Schalen: Collected Communications to the XIIIth Congress of the International Organization for the Study of the Old Testament* (BEATAJ, 20; Bern: Peter Lang, 1992), pp. 155-68.
Enroth, R., *Youth, Brainwashing, and the Extremist Cults* (Grand Rapids: Zondervan; Exeter: Paternoster Press, 1977).
Enslin, M.S., and S. Zeitlin, *The Book of Judith* (Dropsie University Edition. Jewish Apocryphal Literature, 7; Leiden: E.J. Brill, 1972).
Ernout, A., and F. Thomas, *Syntaxe latine* (Nouvelle collection à l'usage des classes, 38; Paris: Klincksieck, 2nd edn [5th printing], 1972).
Ernst, J., *Die eschatologischen Gegenspieler in den Schriften des Neuen Testaments* (Biblische Untersuchungen, 3; Regensburg: Pustet, 1967).
Eshel, H., 'The Historical Background of the Pesher Interpreting Joshua's Curse on the Rebuilder of Jericho', *RevQ* 15 (1991), pp. 409-20.
Evans, C.A., 'Luke and the Rewritten Bible: Aspects of Lukan Hagiography', in J.H. Charlesworth (ed.), *The Pseudepigrapha and Early Biblical Interpretation* (JSPSup, 14; Sheffield: JSOT Press, 1993), pp. 170-201.
Fabry, H.-J., A. Lange and H. Lichtenberger, *Qumranstudien* (Schriften des Institutum Judaicum Delitzschianum, 4; Göttingen: Vandenhoeck & Ruprecht, 1996).
Fischer, U., *Eschatologie und Jenseitserwartung im hellenistischen Diasporajudentum* (BZNW, 44; Berlin: W. de Gruyter, 1978).
Fishbane, M., 'Use, Authority and Interpretation of Mikra at Qumran', in Mulder and Sysling (eds.), *Mikra*, pp. 339-77.
Fitzmyer, J., ' "4QTestimonia" and the New Testament', *TS* 18 (1957), pp. 513-37.
—'The Contribution of Qumran Aramaic to the Study of the New Testament', in *A Wandering Aramean: Collected Aramaic Essays* (SBLMS, 25; Missoula, MT: Scholars Press, 1979), pp. 85-113.
Flusser, D., 'Hystaspes and John of Patmos', in S. Shaked (ed.), *Irano-Judaica* (Jerusalem: Ben Zvi Institute, 1982), pp. 12-75.
—'Psalms, Hymns and Prayers', in Stone (ed.), *Jewish Writings of the Second Temple Period*, pp. 551-77.
—'The Four Empires in the Fourth Sibyl and in the Book of Daniel', *IOS* 2 (1972), pp. 148-75.
—'The Hubris of the Antichrist in a Fragment from Qumran', *Immanuel* 10 (1980), pp. 31-37.
—'The Parable of the Unjust Steward: Jesus' Criticism of the Essenes', in J.H. Charlesworth (ed.), *Jesus and the Dead Sea Scrolls* (New York: Doubleday, 1992), pp. 176-98.
Foerster, W., and K. Schäferdiek, 'σατανᾶς', *TWNT*, VII, pp. 152-53.
Fontinoy, C., 'Les noms du Diable et leur étymologie', *Acta Iranica* 23 (1984), pp. 157-70.
Friedländer, M., *Der Antichrist in den vorchristlichen jüdischen Quellen* (Göttingen: Vandenhoeck & Ruprecht, 1901).
—'L'Anti-Messie', *REJ* 38 (1899), pp. 14-37.

Friedlieb, J.H., *Die Sibyllinischen Weissagungen: Vollstaendig gesammelt, nach neuer Handschriften-Vergleichung, mit kritischem Commentare und metrischer deutscher Uebersetzung* (Leipzig: Weigel, 1852).
Fröhlich, I., 'Le genre littéraire des Pesharim de Qumran', *RevQ* 12 (1986), pp. 383-98.
Gabrion, H., 'L'interprétation de l'Ecriture à Qumrān', *ANRW*, II 19.1 (1979), pp. 779-848.
García Martínez, F., 'Las fronteras de "lo Bíblico"', *Scripta Theologica* 23 (1991), pp. 759-84.
—*Qumran and Apocalyptic: Studies on the Aramaic Texts from Qumran* (STDJ, 9; Leiden: E.J. Brill, 1992).
García Martínez, F., and E.J.C. Tigchelaar, *The Dead Sea Scrolls Study Edition*. I. *1Q1–4Q273* (Leiden: E.J. Brill, 1997).
—*The Dead Sea Scrolls Study Edition*. II. *4Q274–11Q31* (Leiden: E.J. Brill, 1998).
García Martínez, F., and A.S. van der Woude, 'A "Groningen" Hypothesis of Qumran Origins and Early History', *RevQ* 14 (1990), pp. 521-41.
—*De Rollen van de Dode Zee ingeleid en in het Nederlands vertaald*. I. *Wetsliteratuur en Orderegels, Poëtische teksten* (Kampen: Kok; Tielt: Lannoo, 1994).
—*De Rollen van de Dode Zee ingeleid en in het Nederlands vertaald*. II. *Liturgische teksten, Eschatologische teksten, Exegetische literatuur, Para-bijbelse literatuur en overige geschriften* (Kampen: Kok, 1995).
Gazov-Ginzberg, A.M., 'Double Meaning in a Qumran Work (The Wiles of the Wicked Woman)', *RevQ* 6 (1967), pp. 279-85.
Geffcken, J., *Die Oracula Sibyllina* (GCS, 8; Leipzig: J.C. Hinrichs, 1902).
—'Die Sage vom Antichrist', *Preussische Jahrbücher* 102 (49. Jahrgang; 1900), pp. 385-99.
—*Komposition und Entstehungszeit der Oracula Sibyllina* (TU, 23.1; Leipzig: J.C. Hinrichs, 1902).
Gera, D., and W. Horowitz, 'Antiochus IV in Life and Death: Evidence from the Babylonian Astronomical Diaries', *JAOS* 117 (1997), pp. 240-52.
Gesenius, W., E. Kautzsch and A.E. Cowley, *Hebrew Grammar* (Oxford: Clarendon Press, 2nd edn, 1910).
Gilbert, M., 'Wisdom Literature', in Stone (ed.), *Jewish Writings of the Second Temple Period*, pp. 283-324.
Ginsberg, H.L., 'The Hebrew University Scrolls from the Sectarian Cache', *BASOR* 112 (1948), pp. 19-23.
Ginzberg, L., *An Unknown Jewish Sect* (New York: Jewish Theological Seminary of America, 1976).
Glare, P.G.W. (ed.), *Oxford Latin Dictionary* (Oxford: Clarendon Press, 1982).
Glorie, F., *S. Hieronymi presbyteri commentariorum in Danielem libri III <IV>* (CChr Series Latina, 75A; Turnholti: Brepols, 1964).
Goedicke, H., *Die Stellung des Königs im Alten Reich* (Ägyptologische Abhandlungen, 2; Wiesbaden: Otto Harrassowitz, 1960).
Goldstein, J.A., *II Maccabees* (AB; Garden City, NY: Doubleday, 1983).
—'The Testament of Moses: Its Content, its Origin, and its Attestation in Josephus', in Nickelsburg (ed.), *Studies*, pp. 44-52.
Goodenough, E.R., *Jewish Symbols in the Greco-Roman Period*. VIII. *Pagan Symbols in Apocalyptic Literature*, II (Bollingen Series, 37.8; New York: Pantheon, 1958).
—*The Politics of Philo Judaeus: Practice and Theory. With a General Bibliography of Philo* (New Haven: Yale University Press, 1938).
Gooding, D.W., 'An Approach to the Literary and Textual Problems in the David–Goliath

Story', in D. Barthélemy, D.W. Gooding, J. Lust and E. Tov, *The Story of David and Goliath: Textual and Literary Criticism, Papers of a Joint Research Venture* (OBO, 73; Göttingen: Vandenhoeck & Ruprecht; Fribourg: Editions Universitaires, 1986), pp. 55-86.

Goslinga, C.J., *Het eerste boek Samuël* (Commentaar op het Oude Testament; Kampen: Kok, 1968).

—*Het tweede boek Samuël* (Commentaar op het Oude Testament; Kampen: Kok, 1962).

Gray, G.B., 'The Psalms of Solomon', *APOT*, II, pp. 625-52.

Grosheide, F.W., *Het Heilig Evangelie volgens Mattheus* (Kommentaar op het Nieuwe Testament; Amsterdam: Van Bottenburg, 1922).

Guldentops, G., 'Iulius Firmicus Maternus, *Mathesis* I 6. Filosofische retoriek tussen Oudheid en Middeleeuwen', *Kleio* 29 (1999–2000), pp. 172-86.

Gunderson, L.L., 'The Portrait of Alexander the Great in the Sibylline Oracles', in *Ancient Macedonia*, II (Thessaloniki: Institute for Balkan Studies, 1977), pp. 53-66.

Gunkel, H., 'Duhm', RGG^2, I, cols. 2043-44.

—*Schöpfung und Chaos in Urzeit und Endzeit: Eine religionsgeschichtliche Untersuchung über Gen 1 und Ap Joh 12* (Göttingen: Vandenhoeck & Ruprecht, 1895).

—'Wellhausen', RGG^2, V, cols. 1820-22.

Gutberlet, C., *Das erste Buch der Machabäer* (Alttestamentliche Abhandlungen, 8.3-4; Münster: Aschendorff, 1920).

—*Das zweite Buch der Machabäer* (Alttestamentliche Abhandlungen, 10.3-4; Münster: Aschendorff, 1927).

Haag, E., 'Die Theokratie und der Antijahwe nach 1 Makkabäer 1–2', *TTZ* 109 (2000), pp. 24-37.

—'Jesaja, Assur und der Antijahwe. Literar- und traditionsgeschichtliche Beobachtungen zu Jes 10,5-15', *TTZ* 103 (1994), pp. 18-37.

—*Studien zum Buche Judith: Seine theologische Bedeutung und literarische Eigenart* (Trierer Theologische Studien, 16; Trier: Paulinus, 1963).

Hadas, M., *The Third and Fourth Books of Maccabees* (Dropsie College Edition. Jewish Apocryphal Literature; New York: Ktav, 1953).

Hadas-Lebel, M., 'L'évolution de l'image de Rome auprès des Juifs en deux siècles de relations judéo-romaines -164 à +70', *ANRW*, II 20.2 (1987), pp. 715-856.

Hall, R.G., 'Epispasm and the Dating of Ancient Jewish Writings', *JSP* 2 (1988), pp. 71-86.

Halperin, D.J., 'Crucifixion, the Nahum Pesher, and the Rabbinic Penalty of Strangulation', *JJS* 32 (1981), pp. 32-46.

Halpern, A., 'Erasing History: The Minimalist Assault on Ancient Israel', in V.P. Long (ed.), *Israel's Past in Present Research: Essays on Ancient Israelite Historiography* (Sources for Biblical and Theological Studies, 7; Winona Lake, IN: Eisenbrauns, 1999), pp. 415-26 (original edition of this article 1995).

Hamp, V., *Der Begriff 'Wort' in den aramäischen Bibelübersetzungen: Ein exegetischer Beitrag zur Hypostasen-Frage und zur Geschichte der Logos-Spekulationen* (Munich: Neuer Filser-Verlag, 1938).

Harrison, R.K., *Introduction to the Old Testament: With a comprehensive review of Old Testament Studies and a Special Supplement on the Apocrypha* (Grand Rapids: Eerdmans, 1969).

Hecht, R.D., 'Philo and Messiah', in J. Neusner *et al.* (eds.), *Judaisms and their Messiahs at the Time of the Christian Era* (Cambridge: Cambridge University Press, 1987), pp. 139-68.

Heinen, H., 'The Syrian–Egyptian Wars and the New Kingdoms of Asia Minor', *CAH* (1984), pp. 412-45.

Hengel, M., 'Anonymität, Pseudepigraphie und "Literarische Fälschung" in der jüdisch-hellenistischen Literatur', in K. von Fritz (ed.), *Pseudepigrapha*. I. *Pseudopythagorica— Lettres de Platon—Littérature pseudépigraphique juive* (Entretiens sur l'Antiquité Classique, 18; Geneva: Fondation Hardt, 1972), pp. 229-329.

—*Judentum und Hellenismus: Studien zu ihrer Begegnung unter besonderer Berücksichtigung Palästinas bis zur Mitte des 2. Jh. v. Chr.* (WUNT, 10; Tübingen: J.C.B. Mohr, 1st edn, 1969).

Hepp, V., *De Antichrist* (Kampen: Kok, 1st edn, 1919).

Herr, M.D., 'The Calendar', in Safrai and Stern (eds.), *Jewish People in the First Century*, pp. 834-64.

Hobbs, T.R., *A Time for War: A Study of Warfare in the Old Testament* (Old Testament Studies, 3; Wilmington, DE: Michael Glazier, 1989).

Hoftijzer, J., *The Function and Use of the Imperfect Forms with Nun Paragogicum in Classical Hebrew* (SSN, 21; Assen: Van Gorcum, 1985).

Hollander, H.W., *Joseph as an Ethical Model* (SVTP, 6; Leiden; Leiden: E.J. Brill, 1981).

Hollander, H.W., and M. de Jonge, *The Testaments of the Twelve Patriarchs: A Commentary* (SVTP, 8; Leiden: E.J. Brill, 1985).

Holm-Nielsen, S., *Die Psalmen Salomos* (JSHRZ, 4.2; Gütersloh: Gerd Mohn, 1977).

—*Hodayot, Psalms from Qumran* (ATDan, 2; Aarhus: Universitetsforlaget, 1960).

Horgan, M.P., *Pesharim: Qumran Interpretations of Biblical Books* (CBQMS, 8; Washington: Catholic Biblical Association, 1979).

Houtman, C., *Exodus*. II. *Exodus 7.14–19.25* (Commentaar op het Oude Testament; Kampen: Kok, 1989).

Hultgård, A., *L'eschatologie des Testaments des Douze Patriarches*. I. *Interprétation des textes* (Acta Universitatis Upsaliensis. Historia Religionum, 6; Stockholm: Almqvist & Wiksell, 1977).

—*L'eschatologie des Testaments des Douze Patriarches*. II. *Composition de l'ouvrage, textes et traductions* (Acta Universitatis Upsaliensis. Historia Religionum, 7; Stockholm: Almqvist & Wiksell, 1982).

Humbert, J., *Syntaxe grecque* (Tradition de l'humanisme, 8; Paris: Klincksieck, 3rd edn, 1960).

Humbert, P., 'Démesure et chute dans l'Ancien Testament', in maqqél shâqédh, *la branche d'amandier* (Festschrift W. Vischer; Montpellier: Causse, Graille, Castelnau, 1960), pp. 63-82.

Huppenbauer, H.W., 'Belial in den Qumrantexten', *TZ* 15 (1959), pp. 81-89.

—*Der Mensch zwischen zwei Welten: Der Dualismus der Texte von Qumrân (Höhle I) und der Damaskusfragmente. Ein Beitrag zur Vorgeschichte des Evangeliums* (ATANT, 34; Zürich: Zwingli Verlag, 1959).

Hyldahl, N., 'The Maccabean Rebellion and the Question of "Hellenization"', in P. Bilde *et al.* (eds.), *Religion and Religious Practice in the Seleucid Kingdom* (Studies in Hellenistic Civilization, 1; Aarhus: University Press, 1990), pp. 188-203.

Jagersma, H., '"…Veertig dagen en veertig nachten …"', *NedTTs* 28 (1974), pp. 1-15.

Jansen, H.L., *Die Politik Antiochos' des IV*. (Skrifter Norske Videnskaps-Akademi Oslo. II. Historisk-Filosofiske Klasse, 1942, 3; Oslo: Dybwad, 1943).

Jastrow, M., *A Dictionary of the Targumim, the Talmud Babli and Yerushalmi, and the Midrashic Literature* (New York: Choreb; London: Shapiro, Vallentine, 1926).

Jeanmaire, H., *Dionysos: Histoire du culte de Bacchus. L'orgiasme dans l'antiquité et les temps modernes. Origines du théâtre en Grèce. Orphisme et mystique dionysiaque. Evolution du dionysisme après Alexandre* (Paris: Payot, 1951).

Bibliography 255

Jeremias, G., *Der Lehrer der Gerechtigkeit* (SUNT, 2; Göttingen: Vandenhoeck & Ruprecht, 1963).
John, W., 'Quinctilius 27. P. Quinctilius Varus', PW, XXIV, cols. 907-84.
Jongeling, B., *Le rouleau de la guerre des manuscrits de Qumrân* (SSN, 4; Assen: Van Gorcum, 1962).
Jope, E.M., 'Vehicles and Harness', in C. Singer *et al.* (eds.), *A History of Technology. II. The Mediterranean Civilizations and the Middle Ages* c. 700 B.C. to c. A.D. 1500 (Oxford: Clarendon Press, 1956).
Joüon, P., *Grammaire de l'hébreu biblique* (Rome: Institut Biblique Pontifical, corr. edn, 1965).
Jull, A.J.T., D.J. Donahue, M. Broshi and E. Tov, 'Radiocarbon Dating of Scrolls and Linen Fragments from the Judean Desert', *Radiocarbon* 37 (1995), pp. 11-19.
Kapera, Z.J., 'Hans Burgmann 1914–1992', in H. Burgmann, *Weitere lösbare Qumranprobleme* (Qumranica Mogilanensia, 9; Cracow: Enigma, 1992), pp. 167-73.
Kasher, R., 'The Interpretation of Scripture in Rabbinic Literature', in Mulder and Sysling (eds.), *Mikra*, pp. 547-94.
Kee, H.C., 'Testaments of the Twelve Patriarchs', *OTP*, I, pp. 775-828.
Kellermann, D., 'Die Geschichte von David und Goliath im Lichte der Endokrinologie', *ZAW* 102 (1990), pp. 344-57.
Kippenberg, H.G., '"Dann wird der Orient herrschen und der Okzident dienen". Zur Begründung eines gesamtvorderasiatischen Standpunktes im Kampf gegen Rom', in N.W. Bolz and W. Hübener (eds.), *Spiegel und Gleichnis* (Festschrift J. Taubes; Würzburg: Königshausen & Neumann, 1983), pp. 40-48.
—*Garizim und Synagoge: Traditionsgeschichtliche Untersuchungen zur samaritanischen Religion der aramäischen Periode* (Religionsgeschichtliche Versuche und Vorarbeiten, 30; Berlin: W. de Gruyter, 1971).
Kittel, B.P., *The Hymns of Qumran: Translation and Commentary* (SBLDS, 50; Chico, CA: Scholars Press, 1981).
Klatt, W., *Hermann Gunkel: Zu seiner Theologie der Religionsgeschichte und zur Entstehung der formgeschichtlichen Methode* (FRLANT, 100; Göttingen: Vandenhoeck & Ruprecht, 1969).
Klauck, H.-J., *Der erste Johannesbrief* (EKKNT; Zürich: Benziger; Neukirchen–Vluyn: Neukirchener Verlag, 1991).
Klein, R.W., *1 Samuel* (WBC; Waco, TX: Word Books, 1983).
Knibb, M.A., *The Qumran Community* (Cambridge Commentary on Writings of the Jewish and Christian World 200 BC to AD 200, 2; Cambridge: Cambridge University Press, 1987).
Kobelski, P.J., *Melchizedek and Melchireša'* (CBQMS, 10; Washington: Catholic Biblical Association of America, 1981).
Koch, K., 'Die Entstehung der Heilandserwartung in Israel und ihre kanonische Rezeption', in H.M. Niemann *et al.* (eds.), *Nachdenken über Israel, Bibel und Theologie* (Festschrift K.-D. Schunck; BEATAJ, 37; Frankfurt am Main: Peter Lang, 1994), pp. 235-50.
—'Sabbatsstruktur der Geschichte. Die sogenannte Zehn-Wochen-Apokalypse (I Hen 93, 1-10; 91, 11-17) und das Ringen um die alttestamentliche Chronologie im späten Israelitentum', *ZAW* 95 (1983), pp. 403-40.
Koehler, L., and W. Baumgartner, *Lexicon in Veteris Testamenti libros* (Leiden: E.J. Brill, 2nd edn, 1958).
Koekkoek, H.G., *De geheimen van de offers* (Alphen aan den Rijn: Licht des Levens, 1986).
Koenen, L., 'Die Prophezeiungen des "Töpfers"', *Zeitschrift für Papyrologie und Epigraphik* 2 (1968), pp. 178-209.

Kolenkow, A., and J.J. Collins, 'Testaments', in R.A. Kraft and G.W.E. Nickelsburg (eds.), *Early Judaism and its Modern Interpreters* (The Bible and Its Modern Interpreters, 2; Atlanta: Scholars Press; Philadelphia: Fortress Press, 1986), pp. 259-85.

König, F., *Zarathustras Jenseitsvorstellungen und das Alte Testament* (Wien: Herder, 1964).

Koorevaar, H.J., 'God of men (iemand), Satan of een tegenstander', in G.W. Lorein (ed.), *Naar een nieuwe bijbelvertaling?* (Leiden: Groen, 1994), pp. 88-100.

Kosmala, H., *Hebräer—Essener—Christen* (Leiden: E.J. Brill, 1959).

Kroeze, J.H., *Het Boek Jozua* (Commentaar op het Oude Testament; Kampen: Kok, 1968).

—*Job* (Commentaar op het Oude Testament; Kampen: Kok, 1961).

Kuhn, K.G., 'Die beiden Messias Aarons und Israels', *NTS* I (1954–55), pp. 168-79.

Kümmel, W.G., *Das Neue Testament: Geschichte der Erforschung seiner Probleme* (Freiburg: Alber, 1958).

Kuyper, A., 'Locus de Consummatione Saeculi', in *Dictaten Dogmatiek*, V (Kampen: Kok, 2nd edn, 1910).

Kvalbein, H., 'The Wonders of the End-Time. Metaphoric language in 4Q521 and the interpretation of Matthew 11.5 par', *JSP* 18 (1998), pp. 87-110.

Laato, A., *Josiah and David Redivivus: The Historical Josiah and the Messianic Expectations of Exilic and Postexilic Times* (ConBOT, 33; Stockholm: Almqvist & Wiksell, 1992).

Labat, R., *Le poème babylonien de la création* (Paris: Adrien-Maisonneuve, 1935).

Labuschagne, C.J., *Deuteronomium*, II (Prediking van het Oude Testament; Nijkerk: Callenbach, 1990).

Lacocque, A., *Le Livre de Daniel* (CAT; Neuchâtel: Delachaux et Niestlé, 1976).

Lagrange, M.-J., *Le Judaïsme avant Jésus-Christ* (Ebib; Paris: Gabalda, 2nd edn, 1931).

Lamarche, P., *Zacharia IX–XIV: Structure littéraire et messianisme* (Ebib; Paris: Gabalda, 1961).

Lanchester, H.C.O., 'The Sibylline Oracles', *APOT*, II, pp. 368-406.

Lannert, B., *Die Wiederentdeckung der neutestamentlichen Eschatologie durch Johannes Weiss* (Tübingen: Francke, 1989).

Laperrousaz, E.-M., 'Le Testament de Moïse (généralement appelé "Assomption de Moïse"). Traduction avec introduction et notes', *Sem* 19 (1970), pp. i-xx, 1-140.

LaSor, W.S., 'Interpretation and Infallibility: Lessons from the Dead Sea Scrolls', in C.A. Evans and W.F. Stinespring (eds.), *Early Jewish and Christian Exegesis* (Mem. W.H. Brownlee; Scholars Press Homage Series; Atlanta: Scholars Press, 1987), pp. 123-37.

Lattey, C., 'The Messianic Expectation in "the Assumption of Moses"', *CBQ* 4 (1942), pp. 9-21.

Lebram, J.C.H., 'König Antiochus im Buch Daniel', *VT* 25 (1975), pp. 737-72.

Lee, T.R., *Studies in the Form of Sirach 44–50* (SBLDS, 75; Atlanta: Scholars Press, 1986).

Lemche, N.P., "חפשי in 1 Sam. XVII 25', *VT* 24 (1974), pp. 373-74.

Lewy, H., 'The Babylonian Background of the Kay Kâûs Legend', *ArOr* 17.2 (1949), pp. 28-109.

Licht, J., 'Taxo or the Apocalyptic Doctrine of Vengeance', *JJS* 12 (1961), pp. 95-103.

—'Time and Eschatology in Apocalyptic Literature and in Qumran', *JJS* 16 (1965), pp. 177-82.

Liddell, H.G., and R. Scott (eds.), *A Greek–English Lexicon* (Oxford: Clarendon Press, 9th edn, 1940).

Lietaert Peerbolte, L.J., *The Antecedents of Antichrist: A Traditio-Historical Study of the Earliest Christian Views on Eschatological Opponents* (JSJSup [*olim* SPB], 49; Leiden: E.J. Brill, 1996).

Lim, T.H., 'The "Psalms of Joshua" (4Q379 fr. 22 col. 2): A Reconsideration of its Text', *JJS* 44 (1993), pp. 309-12.
—'The Wicked Priests of the Groningen Hypothesis', *JBL* 112 (1993), pp. 415-25.
Littmann, E., 'De Lagarde', *RGG*², III, cols. 1452-53.
Lobel, E., and C.H. Roberts, *The Oxyrhynchus Papyri*. XII (Greek–Roman Memoirs, 31; London: Egypt Exploration Society, 1954).
Lohse, E., *Die Texte aus Qumran: Hebräisch und Deutsch* (Darmstadt: Wissenschaftliche Buchgesellschaft, 2nd edn, 1971).
Lorein, G.W., '4Q448: Een gebed tegen Jonathan de Makkabeeër', *NedTTs* 53 (1999), pp. 265-73.
—'Some Aspects of the Life and Death of Antiochus IV Epiphanes. A New Presentation of Old Viewpoints', *Ancient Society* 31 (2001), pp. 157-71.
—'The Antichrist in the Fathers and their Exegetical Basis', *SacEr* 412 (2003), pp. 115-60.
Lübbe, J., 'A Reinterpretation of 4Q Testimonia', *RevQ* 12 (1986), pp. 187-97.
Lüdemann, G., and M. Schröder, *Die Religionsgeschichtliche Schule in Göttingen* (Göttingen: Vandenhoeck & Ruprecht, 1987).
Maarsingh, B., *Ezechiël*, III (Prediking van het Oude Testament; Nijkerk: Callenbach, 1991).
Maes, A., 'Le costume phénicien des stèles d'Umm el-'Amed', in E. Lipiński (ed.), *Studia Phoenicia*. XI. *Phoenicia and the Bible* (Orientalia Lovaniensia Analecta, 44; Leuven: Oriëntalistiek; Peeters, 1991), pp. 209-30.
Maggiorotti, D., 'La datazione del Testamento di Mose', *Henoch* 15 (1993), pp. 235-62.
Maier, G., *Mensch und freier Wille: Nach den jüdischen Religionsparteien zwischen Ben Sira und Paulus* (WUNT, 12; Tübingen: J.C.B. Mohr, 1971).
Manson, T.W., 'Charles, Robert Henry', in L.G.W. Legg (ed.), *The Dictionary of National Biography 1931–1940* (London: Oxford University Press–Cumberlege, 1949), pp. 169-70.
Mansoor, M., *The Thanksgiving Hymns* (STDJ, 3; Leiden: E.J. Brill, 1961).
Marcus, R., *Flavius Josephus*. VII. *Jewish Antiquities, Books XII–XIV* (LCL, 365; Cambridge, MA: Harvard University Press; London: Heinemann, 1933).
Martin, W.R., *The Kingdom of the Cults* (Minneapolis: Bethany Fellowship, 3rd edn, 1977).
McCarter, P.K., Jr, *I Samuel* (AB; Garden City, NY: Doubleday, 1980).
Mertens, A., *Das Buch Daniel im Lichte der Texte vom Toten Meer* (SBM, 12; Würzburg: Echter Verlag, Stuttgart: KBW, 1971).
Meyer, A., 'Weiss', *RGG*², V, col. 1811.
—'Wrede', *RGG*², V, col. 2025.
Milik, J.T., '4Q Visions de 'Amram et une citation d'Origène', *RB* 79 (1972), pp. 77-97.
—*Dix ans de découvertes dans le désert de Juda* (Paris: Cerf, 1957).
—'Les modèles araméens du livre d'Esther dans la grotte 4 de Qumrân', *RevQ* 15 (Mémorial Jean Starcky, II; 1992), pp. 321-406.
—'*Milkî-ṣedeq* et *Milkî-reša'* dans les anciens écrits juifs et chrétiens', *JJS* 23 (1972), pp. 95-144.
—'"Prière de Nabonide" et autres écrits d'un cycle de Daniel', *RB* 63 (1956), pp. 407-15.
—*Ten Years of Discovery in the Wilderness of Judea* (trans. J. Strugnell; SBT, 26; London: SCM Press, 1959).
Miller, A., *Das Buch Judit* (Die Heilige Schrift des Alten Testamentes; Bonn: Hanstein, 1940).
Mingana, A., 'Some Early Judaeo-Christian Documents in the John Rylands Library', *BJRL* 4 (1917–18), pp. 59-118.
Momigliano, A., 'La portata storica dei vaticini sul settimo Re nel terzo libro degli Oracoli Sibillini', in *Forma Futuri* (Festschrift M. Pellegrino; Turin: Erasmo, 1975), pp. 1077-84.

Moore, C.A., *Judith* (AB; Garden City, NY: Doubleday, 1985).
Moore, R.D., 'Personification of the Seduction of Evil: "The Wiles of the Wicked Woman"', *RevQ* 10 (1981), pp. 505-19.
Mørkholm, O., *Studies in the Coinage of Antiochus IV of Syria* (Historisk-filosofiske Meddelelser Kongelige Danske Videnskabernes Selskab, 43.3; Copenhagen: Munksgaard, 1963).
Mounce, R.H., *The Book of Revelation* (NICNT; Grand Rapids: Eerdmans, 1977).
Mulder, M.J., and H. Sysling (eds.), *Mikra* (CRINT, 2.1; Assen: Van Gorcum; Philadelphia: Fortress Press, 1988).
Mulert, H., 'Eichhorn', RGG^2, II, col. 46.
Nelis, J.T., *I Makkabeeën* (Boeken van het Oude Testament; Roermond: Romen, 1972).
—*II Makkabeeën* (Boeken van het Oude Testament; Bussum: Romen, 1975).
—*Daniël* (Boeken van het Oude Testament; Maaseik: Romen, 1954).
Newsom, C., '4Q378 and 4Q379: An Apocryphon of Joshua', in Fabry, Lange and Lichtenberger, *Qumranstudien*, pp. 35-85.
—'The 'Psalms of Joshua' from Qumran Cave 4', *JJS* 39 (1988), pp. 56-73.
Nickelsburg, G.W.E., 'An Antiochan Date for the Testament of Moses', in Nickelsburg (ed.), *Studies*, pp. 33-37.
—'Stories of Biblical and Early Post-Biblical Times', in Stone (ed.), *Jewish Writings of the Second Temple Period*, pp. 33-87.
Nickelsburg, G.W.E. (ed.), *Studies on the Testament of Moses: Seminar Papers* (SBLSCS, 4; Cambridge: SBL, 1973).
Nielsen, K., '"Gud Herren kaldte på ilden til dom". Dommedagsmotivet og dets forskydninger', *DTT* 58 (1995), pp. 3-15.
Nikiprowetzky, V., 'La sibylle juive et le 'Troisième Livre' des "pseudo-Oracles Sibyllins" depuis Charles Alexandre', *ANRW*, II 20.1 (1987), pp. 460-542.
—*La Troisième Sibylle* (Etudes Juives, 9; The Hague: Mouton, 1970).
—'Oracles sibyllins', in Dupont-Sommer and Philonenko (eds.), *Ecrits intertestamentaires*, pp. 1035-140.
Nikolainen, A.T., *Der Auferstehungsglauben in der Bibel und ihrer Umwelt. I. Religionsgeschichtlicher Teil* (Annales academiae scientiarum Fennicae, B 49.3; Helsinki: Academia scientiarum Fennica, 1944).
Noack, B., 'Satanás und Sotería: Untersuchungen zur neutestamentlichen Dämonologie' (dissertation, Aarhus; Copenhagen: Gads, 1948).
Noort, E., 'JHWH und das Böse. Bemerkungen zu einer Verhältnisbestimmung', *OTS* 23 (1984), pp. 120-36.
—'Toekomstverwachting in het Oude Testament—enkele aspecten', in H. Baarlink, W.S. Duvekot and A. Geense (eds.), *Vervulling en voleinding* (Kampen: Kok, 1984), pp. 13-29.
Noth, M., 'Die fünf syrisch überlieferten apokryphen Psalmen', *ZAW* 48 (1930), pp. 1-23.
Nuchelmans, J., 'Aetolische bond', in Nuchelmans *et al.* (eds.), *Woordenboek der Oudheid*. I (Bussum: Romen, 1976), cols. 68-69.
'Obituary. Archdeacon Charles. A Great Apocalyptic Scholar', *The Times* (2 February 1931), p. 14.
O'Dell, J., 'The Religious Background of the Psalms of Solomon (Re-evaluated in the Light of the Qumran Texts)', *RevQ* 3 (1961-62), pp. 241-57.
Oosterhoff, B.J., *Jeremia*. I. *Jeremia 1-10* (Commentaar op het Oude Testament; Kampen: Kok, 1990).

Osswald, E., 'Zur Hermeneutik des Habakuk-Kommentars', *ZAW* 68 (1956), pp. 243-56.
Pagels, E., 'The Social History of Satan, the "Intimate Enemy": A Preliminary Sketch', *HTR* 84 (1991), pp. 105-28.
Palumbo, A.E., Jr, 'A New Interpretation of the Nahum Commentary', *Folia Orientalia* 29 (1992–93), pp. 153-62.
Pardee, D., 'A Restudy of the Commentary on Psalm 37 from Qumran Cave 4 (Discoveries in the Judaean Desert of Jordan, vol. V n° 171)', *RevQ* 8 (1973), pp. 163-94.
Paul, A., 'Le troisième livre des Macchabées', *ANRW*, II 20.1 (1987), pp. 298-336.
Paulus, W., *Marduk Urtyp Christi?* (Or, 29; Rome: PIB, 1928).
Pearson, B.A., 'Jewish Sources in Gnostic Literature', in Stone (ed.), *Jewish Writings of the Second Temple Period*, pp. 443-81.
Peretti, A., *La Sibilla babilonese nella propaganda ellenistica* (Biblioteca di cultura, 21; Florence: Nuova Italia, 1943).
Péter-Contesse, R., 'Main, pied, paume? Les noms des extrémités des membres (כף, רגל, יד) en Hébreu et en Araméen biblique', *RB* 105 (1998), pp. 481-91.
Pezhumkattil, A., 'Husband–Wife Relationship in the Wisdom Literature', *Bible Bhashyam* 20 (1994), pp. 69-87.
Philonenko, M., 'Essénisme et misogynie', *CRAIBL* (1982), pp. 339-53.
—'La cosmogonie du "livre des secrets d'Hénoch"', in P. Derchain (ed.), *Religions en Egypte Hellénistique et Romaine* (Paris: PUF, 1969), pp. 109-16.
—*Les interpolations chrétiennes des Testaments des Douze Patriarches et les Manuscrits de Qoumrân* (Cahiers de la RHPR, 35; Paris: PUF, 1960).
—'Livre des secrets d'Hénoch', in Dupont-Sommer and Philonenko (eds.), *Ecrits intertestamentaires*, pp. 1165-1223.
—'L'origine essénienne des cinq Psaumes syriaques de David', *Sem* 9 (1959).
—'Pseudépigraphes de l'Ancien Testament', in Dupont-Sommer and Philonenko (eds.), *Ecrits intertestamentaires*, pp. lix-cxlvi.
—'Testaments des Douze Patriarches', in Dupont-Sommer and Philonenko (eds.), *Ecrits intertestamentaires*, pp. 811-944.
Pines, S., 'Eschatology and the Concept of Time in the Slavonic Book of Enoch', in R.J.Z. Werblowsky and C.J. Bleeker (eds.), *Types of Redemption* (Studies in the History of Religions [NumenSup], 18; Leiden: E.J. Brill, 1970), pp. 72-87.
Pomykala, K.E., *The Davidic Dynasty Tradition in Early Judaism: Its History and Significance for Messianism* (SBLEJL, 7; Atlanta: Scholars Press, 1995).
Ponthot, J., 'In memoriam Béda Rigaux', *RTL* 13 (1982), pp. 256-60.
Poulssen, N., *Judith* (Boeken van het Oude Testament; Roermond: Romen, 1969).
Priest, J., 'Testament of Moses', *OTP*, I, pp. 919-34.
Prigent, P., *L'Apocalypse de Saint Jean* (CNT; Genève: Labor et Fides, 2nd edn, 1988).
—'Psaumes de Salomon', in Dupont-Sommer and Philonenko (eds.), *Ecrits intertestamentaires*, pp. 945-92.
Provan, I.W., 'Ideologies, Literary and Critical: Reflections on Recent Writing on the History of Israel', *JBL* 114 (1995), pp. 585-86.
Puech, E., 'Jonathan le Prêtre Impie et les débuts de la Communauté de Qumrân. *4QJonathan (4Q523) et 4QPsAp (4Q448)*', *RevQ* 17 (1996), pp. 241-70.
—*La croyance des Esséniens en la vie future: immortalité, résurrection, vie éternelle? Histoire d'une croyance dans le judaïsme ancien. I. Les données qumraniennes et classiques* (Ebib, NS 22; Paris: Gabalda, 1993).

—'Messianism, Resurrection, and Eschatology at Qumran and in the New Testament', in E. Ulrich and J. Vanderkam (eds.), *The Community of the Renewed Covenant* (Christianity and Judaism in Antiquity Series, 10; Notre Dame: University Press, 1994).

—'Quelques aspects de la restauration du Rouleau des Hymnes (1QH)', *JJS* 39 (1988), pp. 38-55.

Qimron, E., *The Hebrew of the Dead Sea Scrolls* (HSS, 29; Atlanta: Scholars Press, 1986).

—'The Text of CDC', in M. Broshi (ed.), *The Damascus Document Reconsidered* (Jerusalem: Israel Exploration Society; Israel Museum, 1992).

Rabin, C., *The Zadokite Documents* (Oxford: Clarendon Press, 2nd edn, 1958).

Rahlfs, A., *Septuaginta: Id est Vetus Testamentum Graece iuxta LXX interpretes*, I (Stuttgart: Privilegierte Württembergische Bibelanstalt, 1935).

—*Septuaginta. Id est Vetus Testamentum Graece iuxta LXX interpretes*. II. *Libri poetici et prophetici* (Stuttgart: Privilegierte Württembergische Bibelanstalt [1935]).

Reicke, B., 'Die Taʿāmire-Schriften und die Damaskus-Fragmente', *ST* 2 (1948), pp. 45-70.

Reitzenstein, R., *Die hellenistischen Mysterienreligionen nach ihren Grundgedanken und Nachwirkungen* (Leipzig: Teubner, 3rd edn, 1927).

Ridderbos, J., *De kleine Profeten*. II. *Van Obadja to Zefanja* (Korte Verklaring; Kampen: Kok, 2nd edn, 1949).

—*De kleine Profeten*. III. *Haggai, Zacharia, Maleachi* (Korte Verklaring; Kampen: Kok, 2nd edn, 1952).

—*De Psalmen*. II. *Psalm 42–106* (Commentaar op het Oude Testament; Kampen: Kok, 1958).

—*Het boek Deuteronomium*. II. *Hoofdstuk 16.18–34.12* (Korte Verklaring; Kampen: Kok, 1951).

Rigaux, B., *L'Antéchrist et l'Opposition au Royaume Messianique dans l'Ancien et le Nouveau Testament* (Universitas Catholica Lovaniensis. Dissertationes ad gradum magistri in Facultate Theologica consequendum conscriptae, 2.24; Gembloux: Duculot; Paris: Gabalda, 1932).

—*Saint-Paul: Les épîtres aux Thessaloniciens* (Ebib; Paris: Gabalda; Gembloux: Duculot, 1956).

Rofé, A., 'The Battle of David and Goliath: Folklore, Theology, Eschatology', in J. Neusner *et al.* (eds.), *Judaic Perspectives on Ancient Israel* (Philadelphia: Fortress Press, 1987), pp. 117-51.

Rowley, H.H., 'The Internal Dating of the Dead Sea Scrolls', *ETL* 28 (1952), pp. 257-76.

—'The Kittim and the Dead Sea Scrolls', *PEQ* 88 (1956), pp. 92-109.

—*The Relevance of Apocalyptic: A Study of Jewish and Christian Apocalypses from Daniel to the Revelation* (London: Lutterworth, 3rd edn, 1963).

—'The Teacher of Righteousness and the Dead Sea Scrolls', *BJRL* 40 (1957–58), pp. 114-46.

—*The Zadokite Fragments and the Dead Sea Scrolls* (Oxford: Basil Blackwell, 1952).

Rubinstein, A., 'Observations on the Slavonic Book of Enoch', *JJS* 13 (1961), pp. 1-21.

Rudolph, W., *Haggai—Sacharja 1–8—Sacharja 9–14—Maleachi* (KAT; Gütersloh: Gerd Mohn, 1976).

Russell, D.S., *The Method and Message of Jewish Apocalyptic: 200 BC–AD 100* (OTL; London: SCM Press, 1964).

Rüterswörden, U., 'Das Böse in der deuteronomischen Schultheologie', in T. Veijola (ed.), *Das Deuteronomium und seine Querbeziehungen* (Schriften der Finnischen Exegetischen Gesellschaft, 62; Helsinki: Finnische Exegetische Gesellschaft; Göttingen: Vandenhoeck & Ruprecht, 1996), pp. 223-41.

Rzach, A., *Kritische Studien zu den Sibyllinischen Orakeln* (Denkschriften der kaiserlichen Akademie der Wissenschaften. Philosophisch-historische Classe, 38.4; Vienna: Tempsky, 1890).

—Χρησμοὶ Σιβυλλιακοί—*Oracula Sibyllina* (Vienna and Prague: Tempsky; Leipzig: Freytag, 1891).

Sacchi, P., *L'apocalittica giudaica e la sua storia* (Biblioteca di cultura religiosa, 55; Brescia: Paideia, 1990).

Sachs, A.J., and D.J. Wiseman, 'A Babylonian King List of the Hellenistic Period', *Iraq* 16 (1954), pp. 202-12.

Safrai, S., and M. Stern (eds.), *The Jewish People in the First Century* (CRINT, 1; Assen: Van Gorcum, 1974).

Saggs, H.F.W., *The Encounter with the Divine in Mesopotamia and Israel* (Jordan Lectures 1976; London: Athlone Press, 1978).

Sánchez Mielgo, G., 'Perspectivas eclesiológicas en la primera carta de Juan', *Escritos del Vedat* 4 (1974), pp. 9-64.

Schäfer, P., 'Geschiedenis en godsdienst van het Palestijnse Jodendom vanaf Pompejus tot en met de opstand onder Bar Kochba', in Van der Woude (ed.), *Bijbels Handboek*, III, pp. 17-58.

Schmid, J., 'Charles', LTK^2, II, cols. 1030-31.

Schoors, A., *Jesaja* (Boeken van het Oude Testament; Roermond: Romen, 1972).

Schouten, D., 'Sycophant', in J. Nuchelmans *et al.* (eds.), *Woordenboek der Oudheid*, III (*s.l.*: Romen, 1986), col. 2885.

Schuller, E., 'A Preliminary Study of 4Q373 and Some Related (?) Fragments', in Trebolle Barrera and Vegas Montaner (eds.), *Madrid Qumran Congress*, pp. 513-30.

Schunck, K.-D., *1. Makkabäerbuch* (JSHRZ, 1.4; Gütersloh: Gerd Mohn, 1980).

—*Die Quellen des I. und II. Makkabäerbuches* (dissertation, Greifswald; Halle: Niemeyer, 1954).

Schüpphaus, J., *Die Psalmen Salomos: Ein Zeugnis Jerusalemer Theologie und Frömmigkeit in der Mitte des vorchristlichen Jahrhunderts* (ALGHJ, 7; Leiden: E.J. Brill, 1977).

Schürer, E., G. Vermes and M. Black, *The History of the Jewish People in the Age of Jesus Christ (175 B.C.–A.D. 135)* (Edinburgh: T. & T. Clark, 2nd edn, 1973–87).

Segal, M.H., *A Grammar of Mishnaic Hebrew* (Oxford: Clarendon Press, 1927).

Skehan, P.W., and A.A. Di Lella, *The Wisdom of Ben Sira* (AB; New York: Doubleday, 1987).

Smith, M., '4Q391. 4QpapPseudo-Ezekiel^e', in M. Broshi *et al.*, *Qumran Cave 4*. XIV. *Parabiblical Texts, Part 2* (DJD, 19; Oxford: Clarendon Press, 1995), pp. 153-93.

Smith, M., 'Pseudepigraphy in the Israelite Literary Tradition', in K. von Fritz (ed.), *Pseudepigrapha. I. Pseudopythagorica—Lettres de Platon—Littérature pseudépigraphique juive* (Entretiens sur l'Antiquité Classique, 18; Geneva: Fondation Hardt, 1972), pp. 189-227.

Smith Margoliouth, J.P., *A Compendious Syriac Dictionary* (Oxford: Clarendon Press, 1903).

Sperber, A., *The Bible in Aramaic Based on Old Manuscripts and Printed Texts*. II. *The Former Prophets According to Targum Jonathan* (Leiden: E.J. Brill, 1959).

Stauffer, E., 'Der gegenwärtige Stand der Erforschung der in Palästina neu gefundenen hebräischen Handschriften. 19. Zur Frühdatierung des Habakukmidrasch', *TLZ* 76 (1951), cols. 667-74.

Stegemann, H., 'Some remarks to *1QSa*, to *1QSb*, and to Qumran Messianism', *RevQ* 17 (1996), pp. 479-505.

Stephan, H., 'Ritschl', *RGG*², IV, cols. 2043-46.
Stern, M., 'The Reign of Herod and the Herodian Dynasty', in Safrai and Stern (eds.), *Jewish People in the First Century*, pp. 216-307.
Steudel, A., 'אחרית הימים in the Texts from Qumran', *RevQ* 16 (1993), pp. 225-46.
—*Der Midrasch zur Eschatologie aus der Qumrangemeinde (4QmidrEschat*ᵃ,ᵇ*): Materielle Rekonstruktion, Textbestand, Gattung und traditionsgeschichtliche Einordnung des durch 4Q171 ('Florilegium') und 4Q177 ('Catena A') repräsentierten Werkes aus den Qumranfunden* (STDJ, 13; Leiden: E.J. Brill, 1994).
Stoebe, H.-J., *Das erste Buch Samuelis* (KAT; Gütersloh: Gerd Mohn, 1973).
Stone, M.E., 'Apocalyptic Literature', in Stone (ed.), *Jewish Writings of the Second Temple Period*, pp. 383-441.
Stone, M.E. (ed.), *Jewish Writings of the Second Temple Period* (CRINT, 2.2; Assen: Van Gorcum; Philadelphia: Fortress Press, 1984).
Strecker, G., 'Der Antichrist. Zum religionsgeschichtlichen Hintergrund von 1 Joh 2, 18.22; 4, 3 und 2 Joh 7', in T. Baarda, A. Hilhorst, G.P. Luttikhuizen and A.S. van der Woude (eds.), *Text and Testimony* (Festschrift A.F.J. Klijn; Kampen: Kok, 1988), pp. 247-54.
—*Die Johannesbriefe* (KEK; Göttingen: Vandenhoeck & Ruprecht, 1989).
Strobel, A., 'Weltenjahr, grosse Konjunktion und Messiasstern. Ein themageschichtlicher Überblick', *ANRW*, II 20.2 (1987), pp. 988-1187.
Strugnell, J., 'Notes en marge du volume V des "Discoveries in the Judaean Desert of Jordan"', *RevQ* 7 (1970), pp. 163-276.
Strugnell, J., and D. Dimant, '4Q Second Ezekiel', *RevQ* 13 (1988), pp. 45-58.
Sukenik, E.L., *The Dead Sea Scrolls of the Hebrew University* (Jerusalem: Magnes Press, 1955).
Tarn, W.W., *The Greeks in Bactria and India* (Cambridge: Cambridge University Press, 2nd edn, 1951).
Tcherikover, V.A., 'The Third Book of Maccabees as a Historical Source of Augustus' Time', in A. Fuks and I. Halpern (eds.), *Studies in History* (ScrHier, 7; Jerusalem: Magnes Press, 1961), pp. 1-26.
Tedesche, S., and S. Zeitlin, *The First Book of Maccabees* (Dropsie College Edition. Jewish Apocryphal Literature; New York: Harper, 1950).
—*The Second Book of Maccabees* (Dropsie College Edition. Jewish Apocryphal Literature; New York: Harper, 1954).
Testuz, M., *Les idées religieuses du Livre des Jubilés* (Geneva: Droz; Paris: Minard, 1960).
Thissen, H.-J., '"Apocalypse Now!", Anmerkungen zum *Lamm des Bokchoris*', in W. Clarysse, A. Schoors and H. Willems (eds.), *Egyptian Religion in the Last Thousand Years* (Memorial J. Quaegebeur; Orientalia Lovaniensia Analecta, 84–85; Leuven: Peeters; Oosterse Studies, 1998), pp. 1043-53.
Thorion, Y., 'Die Syntax der Präposition B in der Qumranliteratur', *RevQ* 12 (1985), pp. 17-63.
Tidiman, B., *Le livre de Zacharie* (Commentaire Evangélique de la Bible; Vaux-sur-Seine: Edifac, 1996).
Torm, F., 'Die Psychologie der Pseudonymität im Hinblick auf die Literatur des Urchristentums (1932)', in N. Brox (ed.), Pseudepigraphie *in der heidnischen und jüdisch–christlichen Antike* (Darmstadt: Wissenschaftliche Buchgesellschaft, 1977), pp. 111-48.
Trafton, J.L., *The Syriac Version of the Psalms of Solomon: A Critical Evaluation* (SBLSCS, 11; Atlanta: Scholars Press, 1985).
Trebolle Barrera, J., and L. Vegas Montaner (eds.), *The Madrid Qumran Congress* (STDJ, 11; Leiden: E.J. Brill; Madrid: Complutense, 1992).

Tromp, J., *Assumption of Moses: A Critical Edition with Commentary* (SVTP, 10; Leiden: E.J. Brill, 1993).
—'The Formation of the Third Book of Maccabees', *Henoch* 17 (1995), pp. 311-28.
Turcan, R., *Firmicus Maternus: L'erreur des religions païennes* (Collections des Universités de France...Budé; Paris: Belles Lettres, 1982).
Turdeanu, E., *Apocryphes slaves et roumains de l'Ancien Testament* (SVTP, 5; Leiden: E.J. Brill, 1981).
Ulrich, E.C., Jr, *The Qumran Text of Samuel and Josephus* (HSM, 19; Missoula, MT: Scholars Press, 1978).
Ulrichsen, J.H., *Die Grundschrift der Testamente der Zwölf Patriarchen: Eine Untersuchung zu Umfang, Inhalt und Eigenart der ursprünglichen Schrift* (Acta Universitatis Upsaliensis. Historia Religionum, 10; Stockholm: Almquist & Wiksell, 1991).
Ungnad, A., *Syrische Grammatik* (Clavis linguarum Semiticarum, 7; Munich: Beck, 1913).
Väänänen, V., *Introduction au latin vulgaire* (Bibliothèque française et romane. A. Manuels et études linguistiques, 6; Paris: Klincksieck, 3rd edn, 1981).
Vaillant, A., *Le livre des secrets d'Hénoch: Texte slave et traduction française* (Textes publiés par l'Institut d'Etudes slaves, 4; Paris: Institut d'Etudes slaves, 1952).
Vanacker, G., *De Religieuze Sekten: Religie, waanzin of bedrog?* (Kapellen: DNB-Pelckmans, 1986).
Van Bruggen, J., *Wie maakte de bijbel? Over afsluiting en gezag van het Oude en Nieuwe Testament* (Kampen: Kok, 1986).
Van den Born, A., *Wijsheid van Jezus Sirach (Ecclesiasticus)* (Boeken van het Oude Testament; Roermond: Romen, 1968).
Van der Kooij, A., 'The Story of David and Goliath: The Early History of its Text', *ETL* 68 (1992), pp. 118-31.
Van der Lingen, A., *David en Saul in I Samuel 16–II Samuel 5: Verhalen in politiek en religie* (dissertation, Groningen; The Hague: Boekencentrum, 1983).
Vanderostyne, M., 'Hulpverleners sterven aan de lopende band', *De Standaard* (26 April 1996), p. 27.
Van der Ploeg, J.P.M., *Le rouleau de la guerre* (STDJ, 2; Leiden: E.J. Brill, 1959).
—*Psalmen*. II. *Psalm 76 t/m 150* (Boeken van het Oude Testament; Roermond: Romen, 1975).
—*Vondsten in de woestijn van Juda: De rollen van de Dode Zee* (Aula, 447), Utrecht: Spectrum, 1957).
Van der Westhuizen, M.J., *De Antichrist in het Nieuwe Testament* (Amsterdam: Van Bottenburg, 1916).
Van der Woude, A.S., 'Die fünf syrischen Psalmen (einschliesslich Psalm 151)' in *Poetische Schriften* (JSHRZ, 4.1; Gütersloh: Gerd Mohn, 1974), pp. 29-47.
—*Die messianischen Vorstellungen der Gemeinde von Qumrân* (SSN, 3; Assen: Van Gorcum, 1957).
—'Fakten contra Phantasien: die Bedeutung der Rollen vom Toten Meer für die Bibelwissenschaft und die Kunde des Frühjudentums', in F. García Martínez and E. Noort (eds.), *Perspectives in the Study of the Old Testament and Early Judaism* (Festschrift A.S. van der Woude; VTSup, 73; Leiden: E.J. Brill, 1998), pp. 249-71.
—'Fifty Years of Qumran Research', in P.W. Flint and J.C. VanderKam (eds.), *The Dead Sea Scrolls after Fifty Years: A Comprehensive Assessment*, I (Leiden: E.J. Brill, 1998), pp. 1-45.
—'Fünfzehn Jahre Qumranforschung (1974–1988)', *TRu* 55 (1990), pp. 245-307.
—'Fünfzehn Jahre Qumranforschung (1974–1988)', *TRu* 57 (1992), pp. 1-57, 225-53.

—'Geschiedenis en godsdienst van het Palestijnse Jodendom vanaf Alexander de Grote tot aan de komst van de Romeinen', in Van der Woude, *Bijbels Handboek*, IIB, pp. 5-89.

—'"Hij zal Zoon des Allerhoogsten genoemd worden..."', in J.A. Hofman and D. Jorissen (eds.), *Hoogten en diepten* (Festschrift A.A. Spijkerboer; Kampen: Kok, 1993), pp. 137-44.

—'Melchisedek als himmlische Erlösergestalt in den neugefundenen eschatologischen Midraschim aus Qumran-Höhle XI', *OTS* 14 (1965), pp. 354-73.

—*Micha* (Prediking van het Oude Testament; Nijkerk: Callenbach, 1976).

—'Nabloeiers en uitlopers: apocriefen, pseudepigrafen en Dode-Zeerollen', in T.C. Vriezen, *De literatuur van Oud-Israël* (Wassenaar: Servire, 4th edn, 1973), pp. 307-80, 408-33.

—'Once Again: The Wicked Priests in the *Habakkuk Pesher* from Cave 1 of Qumran', *RevQ* 17 (1996), pp. 375-84.

—*The Book of Daniel in the Light of New Findings* (BETL, 106; Leuven: Leuven University Press; Peeters, 1993).

—'Wicked Priest or Wicked Priests. Reflections on the Identification of the Wicked Priest in the Habakuk Commentary', *JJS* 33 (1982), pp. 349-59.

—'Wisdom at Qumran', in J. Day *et al.* (eds.), *Wisdom in ancient Israel* (Festschrift J.A. Emerton; Cambridge: Cambridge University Press, 1995), pp. 244-56.

—*Zacharia* (Prediking van het Oude Testament; Nijkerk: Callenbach, 1984).

Van der Woude, A.S. (ed.), *Bijbels Handboek* (Kampen: Kok, 1981–87).

Van Deuren, J., 'Het beeld van Pompeius bij Dio Cassius in vergelijking met de Pompeius-Vita van Plutarchus' (licentiate's thesis, Leuven, 1977).

Van Gelderen, C., *De Boeken der Koningen*. II. *1 Koningen 12–22 en 2 Koningen 1–4* (Korte Verklaring; Kampen: Kok, 1936).

—*Het boek Hosea* (ed. W.H. Gispen; Commentaar op het Oude Testament; Kampen: Kok, 1953).

Van Henten, J.W., 'Antiochus IV as a Typhonic Figure in Daniel 7', in Van der Woude (ed.), *Book of Daniel*, pp. 223-43.

Van Hoonacker, A., *Les douze Petits Prophètes* (SB; Paris: Gabalda, 1908).

Van Leeuwen, C., *Hosea* (Prediking van het Oude Testament; Nijkerk: Callenbach, 1968).

Van Ooteghem, J., *Pompée le Grand, bâtisseur d'Empire* (Mémoires de l'Académie Royale de Belgique. Classe des lettres et des sciences morales et politiques, 49; Brussels: Palais des Académies, 1954).

Van Staalduine-Sulman, E., 'The Aramaic Song of the Lamb', in J.C. de Moor and W.G.E. Watson (eds.), *Verse in Ancient Near Eastern Prose* (AOAT, 42; Kevelaer: Butzon & Bercker; Neukirchen–Vluyn: Neukirchener Verlag, 1993), pp. 265-92.

Van 't Land, F.A.W., and A.S. van der Woude, *De Habakuk-rol van ʿAin Fašḫa: Tekst en vertaling* (Assen: Van Gorcum, 1954).

Van Zyl, A.H., *I Samuël*, II (Prediking van het Oude Testament; Nijkerk: Callenbach, 1989).

Vattioni, F., *Ecclesiastico: Testo ebraico con apparato critico e versioni greca, latina e siriaca* (Naples: Istituto orientale, 1968).

Vegas Montaner, L., 'Some Features of the Hebrew Verbal Syntax in the Qumran Hodayot', in Trebolle Barrera and Vegas Montaner (eds.), *Madrid Qumran Congress*, pp. 273-86.

Vergote, J., and G. Bartelink, 'Alexandrië', in J. Nuchelmans *et al.* (eds.), *Woordenboek der Oudheid*, I (Bussum: Romen, 1976), cols. 115-21.

Verheule, A.F., *Wilhelm Bousset: Leben und Werk. Ein theologiegeschichtlicher Versuch* (Amsterdam: Bolland, 1973).

Vermes, G., 'Methodology in the Study of Jewish Literature in the Graeco-Roman Period', *JJS* 36 (1985), pp. 145-58.
—*The Dead Sea Scrolls in English* (London: Penguin Books, 3rd edn, 1987).
Viteau, J., *Les Psaumes de Salomon: Introduction, texte grec et traduction* (Documents pour l'étude de la Bible; Paris: Letouzey et Ané, 1911).
Von der Osten-Sacken, P., *Gott und Belial: Traditionsgeschichtliche Untersuchungen zum Dualismus in den Texten aus Qumran* (SUNT, 6; Göttingen: Vandenhoeck & Ruprecht, 1969).
Von Nordheim, E., *Die Lehre der Alten*. I. *Das Testament als Gliedgattung im Judentum der Hellenistisch-Römischen Zeit* (ALGHJ, 18; Leiden: E.J. Brill, 1980).
Von Soden, Hans, Freiherr, 'Von Harnack', RGG^2, II, cols. 1633-36.
Von Soden, Wolfram, Freiherr, *Einführung in die Altorientalistik* (Orientalistische Einführungen in Gegenstand, Ergebnisse und Perspektiven der Einzelgebiete; Darmstadt: Wissenschaftliche Buchgesellschaft, 1985).
Von Stuckrad, K., *Das Ringen um die Astrologie: Jüdische und christliche Beiträge zum antiken Zeitverständnis* (Religionsgeschichtliche Versuche und Vorarbeiten, 49; Berlin: W. de Gruyter, 2000).
Vouga, F., *Die Johannesbriefe* (HNT; Tübingen: J.C.B. Mohr, 1990).
Vriezen, T.C., *Hoofdlijnen der theologie van het Oude Testament* (Wageningen: Veenman, 3rd edn, 1966).
Vriezen, T.C., and A.S. van der Woude, *Oudisraëlitische en vroegjoodse literatuur* (Ontwerpen, 1; Kampen: Kok, 10th edn, 2000).
Wallis, G., 'Hermann Gunkel. Zum 100. Geburtstag am 23. Mai 1962', in G. Wallis (ed.), *Mein Freund hatte einen Weinberg, Aufsätze und Vorträge zum Alten Testament* (BEATAJ, 23; Frankfurt: Peter Lang, 1994), pp. 241-53.
Waltke, B.K., 'The Samaritan Pentateuch and the Text of the Old Testament', in J.B. Payne (ed.), *New Perspectives on the Old Testament* (Evangelical Theological Society Supplementary Volumes. Symposium Series, 3; Waco, TX: Word Books, 1970), pp. 212-39.
Waltke, B.K., and M. O'Connor, *An Introduction to Biblical Hebrew Syntax* (Winona Lake, IN: Eisenbrauns, 1990).
Wambacq, B.N., *Jeremias, Klaagliederen, Baruch, Brief van Jeremias* (Boeken van het Oude Testament; Roermond: Romen, 1957).
Weinfeld, M., *The Organizational Pattern and the Penal Code of the Qumran Sect: A Comparison with Guilds and Religious Associations of the Hellenistic–Roman Period* (NTOA, 2; Fribourg: Editions Universitaires; Göttingen: Vandenhoeck & Ruprecht, 1986).
Weinrich, W.C., 'Antichrist in the Early Church', *Concordia Theological Quarterly* 49 (1985), pp. 135-47.
Wénin, A., 'David roi, de Goliath à Bethsabée. La figure de David dans les livres de Samuel', in L. Desrousseaux and J. Vermeylen (eds.), *Figures de David à travers la Bible*: *XVIIe congrès de l'ACFEB* (LD, 177; Paris: Cerf, 1999), pp. 75-112.
Widengren, G., *Religionsphänomenologie* (Berlin: W. de Gruyter, 1969).
Will, E., *Histoire politique du monde hellénistique*. II. *Des avènements d'Antiochos III et de Philippe V à la fin des Lagides* (Nancy: Presses Universitaire, 2nd edn, 1982).
Williams, D.S., '*3 Maccabees*: A Defense of Diaspora Judaism?', *JSP* 13 (1995), pp. 17-29.
Wood, M., 'Pesher Habakkuk and the Targum of Jonathan ben Uzziel', *JSP* 19 (1999), pp. 129-46.
Wright, R.B., 'Psalms of Solomon', *OTP*, II, pp. 639-70.

Yadin, Y., *The Scroll of the War of the Sons of Light against the Sons of Darkness* (trans. B. Rabin and C. Rabin; Oxford: Oxford University Press, 1962).
Yamauchi, E.M., *Persia and the Bible* (Grand Rapids: Baker Book House, 1990).
—'The Current State of Old Testament Historiography', in A.R. Millard, J.K. Hoffmeier and D.W. Baker (eds.), *Faith, Tradition, and History: Old Testament Historiography in its Near Eastern Context* (Winona Lake, IN: Eisenbrauns, 1994), pp. 1-36.
Yarbro Collins, A., 'Composition and Redaction of the Testament of Moses 10', *HTR* 69 (1976), pp. 179-86.
Young, E.J., *The Book of Isaiah.* II. *Chapters 19 to 39* (Grand Rapids: Eerdmans, 1969).
—*The Prophecy of Daniel* (Grand Rapids: Eerdmans, 1949).
Zenger, E., *Das Buch Judit* (JSHRZ, 1.6; Gütersloh: Gerd Mohn, 1981).
Zimmerli, W., *Ezechiel*, II (BKAT; Neukirchen–Vluyn: Neukirchener Verlag, 1969).
Zimmermann, J., *Messianische Texte aus Qumran: Königliche, priesterliche und prophetische Messiasvorstellungen in den Schriftfunden von Qumran* (WUNT, 2.104; Tübingen: J.C.B. Mohr, 1998).
Zorell, F., *Lexicon Hebraicum et Aramaicum Veteris Testamenti* (Roma: PIB, repr., 1968).

INDEXES

INDEX OF REFERENCES

OLD TESTAMENT

Genesis		13.2-3	30	17.16-19	33
30.40	169	13.3-4	30	17.20-24	34
49.5	182	13.4-5	30	17.25-31	34
		13.6	30	17.26	36, 48
Exodus		18.18-19	181	17.32-40	34
3.5	101	18.21-22	30	17.32	61
11.7	61	19.14	59, 164,	17.41-47	35
14.21	72		166, 167	17.43	36
18.21	200	21.23	196	17.44	36
20.4	146	27.17	167	17.46	36
		32.33	171	17.48-49	35, 190
Leviticus		32.35	177	17.50-51	35
3–4	48	33.8-11	181	17.51-53	35
15.18	81			17.51	63
		Joshua		17.54	35
Numbers		5.15	101	17.55-58	36
12.6	30	6.26	22, 181	23.8	228
12.14	81	10.21	61		
16.35	203			*2 Samuel*	
23.22	155	*1 Samuel*		7.16	96
24.7	104, 215	2.10	48	21.19	32
24.8	155	14	80		
24.15-17	181	16.13	33	*1 Kings*	
24.24	215	17	31, 41, 44,	16.33-34	182
			64, 75,	18.40	31
Deuteronomy			105, 120,		
1.26	173		210, 212,	*1 Chronicles*	
2.13-14	177		216, 227	20.5	32
2.14	173	17.1-3	32		
4.19	73	17.4-10	33	*Job*	
5.28-29	181	17.9	36	4.4	202
13	40, 41	17.11	33	11.17	155
13.1-6	30	17.12-15	33	12.24	166, 167

Job (cont.)		152.4	44, 45,	14.29	189
22.25	155		120, 235	14.31-32	213
26.6	188	152.5	46	15.1	213
26.12	72	152.6	46, 120	24.17	169
38.16	187, 190	153	44	24.18	169
40.19	159	153.2	45	27.1	8
41.22	72	153.5	45	28	170
		154	44	28.10	169
Psalms		155	44	28.13	170
6.10	190			28.14	170
29.1-2	91	Proverbs		30.7	8
37.7	174	2.7	172	30.10	167
37.35-36	174	7	159, 163,	30.33	203
65.8	72		233	34.6	215
67.30	91	7.5	159	40.12	72
68.19	117	7.9	159	47.8-9	129
68.30	91	7.12	159	51.15	72
68.31	8	7.15	159	56.10	61
74	8	7.23	159	57.15	84
75.12	91	7.25	159		
76.12	91	8.22	159	Jeremiah	
87.4	8			1.13-14	214
89	151	Ecclesiastes		1.14	213
89.10	72	7.26	163	4.6	213
89.23	151			6.1	213
89.44	202	Isaiah		6.2	213
91.5	190	1	91	14.12	174
94.17	156	1.2-3	91	31.25	72
95.4	155	2.17	167	47.2	213
96.7-8	91	9.5-6	56	51.58	203
107.18	189	9.5	190, 191	52.29	58
107.23	188, 189	10.5-19	67		
107.27	189	10.26	72	Ezekiel	
107.40	166, 167	11	112	5.13	174
110	22	11.1-10	56	13	172
110.1	22	11.1-5	98	13.10	172
151-155	44	11.4	98	16	163
151	44	11.6-8	48	23	163
151.1	44	11.8	112	26.7	213
151.6-7	44	11.9-10	98	28	205
152	44, 46,	14	75, 76,	28.5	200
	120, 124,		213	29	8
	219, 222,	14.6	75	30	152
	228, 229,	14.11	75	30.1-19	151
	231	14.12	75	30.13	151
152.1	46	14.13-14	73, 75, 91	30.16	151
152.2	46	14.16	75	32	8
152.4-6	44, 224	14.19	99	37.16	104

Index of References

37.19	104	2.12-13	202	*Wisdom of Solomon*	
38–39	104, 234	2.13	203	16.29	119
38	212	2.17	204		
		3	197	*Ecclesiasticus (Sirach)*	
Daniel		3.6	164, 166	25.15	160, 228
3.4	113			44–49	47
3.7	113	*Zechariah*		47.2-11	47
4	73	9.9-10	39	47.2	48
7	8, 10, 103	11	41, 42, 64	47.4-5	47, 224
7.11	190	11.4-17	39	47.4	47, 48
7.26	192	11.4-14	37, 38	47.5	47, 48
8	103	11.4-5	38	49.14-16	47
8.10	73	11.7	38		
8.25	190, 192	11.8-14	38	*1 Maccabees*	
11	228	11.13	39	1–2	82
11.21	51	11.15-17	37, 38, 41,	1.15	140
11.22-23	51		64, 228	1.21-24	78
11.25-28	77	11.15-16	38	1.24	77, 78, 82
11.31	121	11.16	62	1.25-28	78
11.33	140	12.10–13.1	39	1.32	140
11.40	210	13.7-9	38, 39	1.41-43	78, 82
11.45	190, 192			1.41	76, 78, 79
		Malachi		1.42	78, 79
Hosea		3.2-3	203	1.43	78, 79
1–3	163			1.47	141
4.16	166	Apocrypha		1.48	140
5.11	169	*Judith*		2.62	82
6.10	182	2.1-3	58	2.70	80
9.1-6	151	2.1-2	64	3–4	79
9.2	152	2.1	58, 64	3.24	79
9.6	151	2.2	58	3.31-36	79
		2.3	58	3.37	79
Joel		3.8	59, 64	4.28	79, 80
2.20	213	3.9	64	4.30	79, 82,
		5.5	61		228
Micah		5.13	61	4.52	79
2.6	168, 170	6.9	60, 64	7	194
2.11	172	8.1	63	7.1	81
		10.21	62	7.34-35	80, 82
Nahum		11.16	64	7.34	80
1.1	151	11.19	61, 64,	7.35	80
2.12-13	194		228	7.39-47	74
		13.9	62, 64	7.43	81
Habakkuk		14.10	73	7.47	80, 82,
1–2	197	16.5-10	63		228
1.5	198	16.6	62-64	7.50	81
2.5-6	198	16.21-25	64	10.10-11	176, 183
2.5	197			12.25-37	176

1 Maccabees (cont)		1.29	66	9.4	75		
12.36-37	183	2.7	66	9.5	72, 75		
13.10	183	2.16-18	66	9.7-12	70, 192		
13.49-51	184	3–15	65, 70	9.7	71, 72, 75		
13.51	74	4.25	68, 75	9.8	71, 75		
13.52	183	4.27-28	68	9.9	71, 72, 75		
14.7	184	5	96	9.10	71, 75, 91, 103		
14.37	183	5.11-17	68				
15.28-29	184	5.11-14	75	9.11	71, 72, 75		
16	22	5.11	68, 69	9.12	71, 72		
16.2-3	184	5.12	68, 69	9.19	67		
16.15-16	184	5.13	68, 69	11.16-21	79		
		5.14	68, 69	11.22-33	80		
2 Maccabees		5.15-16	75	11.22-26	80		
1.1-10	65, 70	5.15	69, 75	11.27-33	80		
1.10–2.18	65, 66, 70	5.16	69	15.3-5	74		
1.10-18	66	5.17	69, 75	15.3	75		
1.10	66	5.21	72	15.4-5	75		
1.14	67	5.24	140	15.30-33	73, 75, 228		
1.15-16	66, 75	6.4	139				
1.15	66	6.7	140	15.30	73, 74		
1.16	66, 75, 228	7.36	75	15.31	73, 74		
		8.17	75	15.32	73, 74		
1.18–2.15	66	9	75	15.33	73, 74		
1.27	66	9.2	75				

NEW TESTAMENT

Matthew		*Acts*		1.13	117
3.7	189	9.2	166	9.27	102
5.17	111				
24.7	147	*2 Corinthians*		*1 John*	
24.15	121, 141	6.15	5	2.18	231
24.22	152			2.22	178, 231
25.41	203	*Ephesians*		4.3	231
27.9-10	39	4.8	116		
				2 John	
Mark		*2 Thessalonians*		7	178, 231
13.8	147	2.1-12	29		
13.14	141	2.3	238	*Revelation*	
		2.8	190	5.9	113
Luke		3.16	117	7.9	113
1.17	117			11.7	13
2.11	95	*1 Timothy*		13	14, 29, 186
10.19	112	2.5	117		
				13.1-10	238
John		*Hebrews*		13.1	120
14.27	117	1.4-8	117	13.2	234

Index of References

13.11-17	13	16.13	13	20–22	121		
13.11-14	13	17	14	20	228		
13.13-15	89	17.12-17	13	20.2	123		
13.16-17	13	17.17	192	20.7-9	234		
13.16	89, 92	19.20	13, 123, 190	20.10	13, 123		
13.18	13, 238						

OTHER ANCIENT REFERENCES

Pseudepigrapha		2.26	85, 86, 89	8.3	137-39		
1 Enoch		2.27	85, 86	8.4	137-39		
10.4	111	2.28	85-87, 89	8.5	137, 138, 141		
10.7	56	2.29	85-87, 89, 92, 103, 140				
10.17–11.2	56			9–10	135		
45	45			10.1	142, 234		
48.6	45	2.30	87	10.8	135		
49.2	45	2.31-33	88	11	135		
51.3	45	3.1	85, 86, 89	12	135		
53.6	45						
55.4	45	*Assumption of Moses*		*Jubilees*			
90.26	203	1	135	15.33	140		
91-104	135	2–6	135				
91.12-14	56	3.1	136, 139	*Psalms of Solomon*			
100.9	203	5–6	134	1	90, 91		
103.8	159, 203	5	134	1.1-2	91		
		6–7	134	1.2	92		
2 Enoch		6	134, 135	1.3-4	91		
42.1	190	6.1	136, 138, 139	1.5-8	90, 91		
70.3-10	143			1.5-6	92, 103		
70.5-7	145	6.7	137	1.5	91, 103		
70.5	145, 146	6.8-9	138	1.6	91, 92, 171		
70.6	145	6.8	139				
70.7	145	6.9	139	1.7-8	92, 103		
70.10	147	7–10	134	1.7	91, 92, 101		
		7	134, 135, 138	1.8	91, 92, 101, 103		
3 Maccabees		7.3-4	136				
1–2	88	7.5	136	2	90, 98, 100, 105, 121, 124, 228, 234		
1.1–3.1	83	7.6-10	136				
2.1-23	84	8–9	134				
2.2-3	84	8	135, 136, 141, 196, 226	2.1-3	98, 99, 119, 171		
2.2	84, 88, 89						
2.3	84, 89			2.1	98-100, 102, 103		
2.24–3.1	85, 86	8.1-2	139				
2.24	86	8.1	136, 137, 142	2.2-3	101		
2.25-29	85, 86			2.2	98, 99, 103		
2.25-26	86	8.2	137, 139				
2.25	85, 86, 88, 89	8.3-5	139				

Psalms of Solomon (cont.)		17.11-12	103		123, 125,
2.3	98, 99, 103	17.11	93, 94, 96, 103	3.63	128, 238 15
2.4-9	101	17.12	93, 95, 96	3.75-77	125, 128, 129
2.9	98, 99, 101, 103	17.13	93, 95, 96, 103	3.75	128
2.10	101	17.14	93, 95-97, 102, 103	3.77	128
2.11-14	101			3.78-81	129
2.14	101	17.15	93, 95, 97, 103	3.97-349	49
2.15-18	101			3.338-392	50
2.19-23	101	17.17	97	3.350-380	125
2.19	101	17.20	93-95, 97, 103	3.365-366	127
2.24-29	98, 99			3.365	127
2.24	98, 99, 101, 103	17.21-23	98	3.366	127
		17.22	95, 98, 106	3.381-400	49
2.25-27	119			3.388-400	57
2.25	98, 99, 101, 103, 120, 171, 234	17.23-43	106	3.388-392	76, 142, 223, 224, 227
		17.23	93-95, 98, 102, 103, 106		
				3.388	56
2.26-29	102	17.24	106	3.389	51
2.26-27	103	17.25	106	3.390-391	56
2.26	99, 100, 190, 192	17.26	94, 106	3.390	50, 56, 89
		17.27-28	106	3.392	56
2.27	99, 100, 103	17.29	106	3.401-488	125
		17.30	102, 106	3.434-435	126
2.28-29	103	17.31	98	3.435	126
2.28	99, 100	17.32-43	98, 235	3.470-473	126, 223
2.29	99-101, 103	17.32	93-96, 98, 106	3.470-472	129
				3.470	126
15.6	92	17.34	106	3.489-829	49
15.9	90, 92, 103	17.35	93-95, 98, 102, 106	3.608-615	52, 77, 142, 223, 224, 227, 235
17	90, 93, 95, 102, 104-106, 112, 196, 211, 234	17.37	106		
		17.39-41	106		
		17.40-41	106	3.610	52, 53
		17.42	106	3.611-615	57
		17.43	106	3.612-613	56
				3.613	53
17.5-6	93, 94	*Sibylline Oracles*		3.615	53
17.5	93-96, 103	1	125	3.616-618	54
		2	125	3.652-656	54, 105, 235
17.6	93, 94, 96, 103	3	5, 17, 49, 57, 125, 129		
				3.652	56
17.7-9	96, 235			3.653-654	56
17.7	93	3.1-92	125	3.655-656	56
17.11-15	93, 94, 171	3.62	128	3.655	55
		3.63-76	17	3.776	49
17.11-13	102	3.63-74	13, 15,	4.107	127

Index of References

Testament of Asher	
1.8	122
3.2	122
7.2-3	118, 120
7.2	111, 118, 119
7.3	118-20, 190, 228, 234

Testament of Benjamin	
3.2-5	122
3.3	122
3.4	122
3.8	122
6.1	122
6.7	122
7.1	122
7.2	122
9.1	111
11.4	45

Testament of Dan	
1.7	122
4.7–5.1	118
4.7	122
5.1	122
5.3	116
5.4	111, 115
5.6	111, 113-15, 121, 234
5.7-9	115
5.10-11	113, 123
5.10	114, 115, 122, 123
5.11	114, 116, 117, 122
5.12-13	116
6.1-4	113
6.1	114, 115, 123
6.2	114, 115, 117
6.3-4	123
6.3	114, 115
6.4	114, 115
7.3	111

Testament of Gad	
1.3	113
4.7–5.1	117, 121
4.7	117, 234
5.1	117, 118
8.2	111

Testament of Issachar	
6.1	111, 122
7.7	122

Testament of Joseph	
7.4	122
20.2	122

Testament of Judah	
2.1	120
2.4	112, 113, 120, 228
18.1	111
19.4	123
25.3	112, 113, 122, 123

Testament of Levi	
3.3	122
8.4-7	111
8.11-15	111
14.1	111
16.1-2	110-12
16.1	110, 121
16.2	110, 111, 121
16.3-4	111
16.3	111
16.8	112
16.9-10	111
16.13	112
18	121
18.12	110-12, 122, 123
19.1	122

Testament of Naphtali	
2.6	122
4.1	111

Testament of Reuben	
2.2	122
4.7	122
4.11	122
6.3	122

Testament of Simeon	
2.7	123
5.3	122
5.4	111
6.6	112

Testament of Zebulun	
9.5	111
9.8	112, 122
10.3	113

Treatise of Shem	
11	131
11.2-9	131
11.10-13	131
11.14-18	130, 221, 226
11.14-15	131
11.14	130, 131
11.15	130, 131
11.16-17	131
11.16	130, 131
11.17	130, 131
11.18	130, 131, 190, 192
12.1	131

Qumran
1QH	
11	240
11.9-10	191
11.12-18	187, 228
11.12-13	189
11.12	187, 188, 189
11.13	187, 188
11.14-15	189
11.14	187, 188
11.15	187, 188, 190
11.16-17	190
11.16	187, 188
11.17	188, 189, 190
11.18	188, 190

1QS		1.3-7	208	3-4 i 2-8	193
2.8	159	1.3-5	207, 208	3-4 i 2-3	195
4.13	159	1.3	208	3-4 i 2	193
		1.4-5	216	3-4 i 3	193
1QpHab		1.4	208, 216, 217	3-4 i 5-6	196
2.1-6	198			3-4 i 5	193
2.1-4	204	1.5	208	3-4 i 6-8	96, 196
2.1-3	1982.1 198	1.10	210	3-4 i 6	193
		2.7	210	3-4 i 7-8	200
2.2	160, 198	3.13	210	3-4 i 7	158, 193, 194
2.3	198	5.1	210		
2.4	198	8	209	3-4 i 8	193, 194
2.5-6	199, 204	11.1-2	228, 207, 210	3-4 ii 2	197
2.5	198			3-4 ii 9	196
2.6	198	11.1	210	3-4 iii 4-5	196
3.3-4	198	11.2	210		
5.11-12	204	11.16	207, 212, 216	*4Q171 (4QpPs)*	
8.8-13	199, 200			i 18–ii 1	173
8.8-11	200	12.1	116	i 18-19	174, 178
8.8	199	12.4	116	i 18	160, 173, 175
8.9-12	205	12.16	210		
8.9	199	13.2	210	i 19	158, 173, 174, 175
8.10	199, 205	13.13	210		
8.11	199	14.4	210	ii 1	174
8.12-13	205	15.2-3	207, 214, 216		
8.12	199			*4Q174 (4QMidrEschata)*	
8.13	199	15.2	214	iii 11-13	211
9.6	205	15.3	214, 216		
10.8-9	205	15.13	210	*4Q175 (4QTest)*	
10.9-13	192, 201	16.1	210	21–30	179, 180, 197, 225
10.9-11	203	16.3	214		
10.9-10	204	16.19	210	21	180, 181
10.9	160	17.4-5	190	22–23	182
10.10-11	159	17.5-6	207, 214	22	180, 181
10.10	201, 204	17.5	216	23–24	182
10.11-13	203	17.6	216	23	180, 181, 185, 234
10.11	201	17.7-8	210		
10.12-13	204	18.3	210	24–30	183
10.12	201, 204	18.6	210	24–25	185
10.13	159, 202			24	180, 181
12.1	204	*2Q22*		25	180, 181, 183
12.7-9	203, 204	i 1	211		
12.7	203			26–28	185
12.8	203, 205	*4Q161 (4QpIsa)*		26	180, 181
12.9	203	8-10	211	27	181
12.13	205	18-19	211	28	181
				29	181, 185
1Q33 (1QM)		*4Q169 (4QpNah)*		30	181
1	215	1.7-8	139		

Index of References

4Q184 (4QWWW)		1-2 3-6	211	1.11-20	178
Frag. 1		1-2 3	211, 212	1.11-18	164, 192
1-2	160	1-2 4	211	1.11-14	166
1	154, 156, 158, 160	1-2 5	211	1.11	164, 165
		1-2 6	211	1.12	164, 177
2	154, 156, 158			1.13	164
		4Q379		1.14-16	167
3	155, 156, 158	22 ii	179	1.14	158, 160, 164, 174, 178
4	155, 156, 162	22 ii 7-15	180		
		4Q386 (4QpsEzek)		1.15-16	178
5-6	158	1 i 1-2	150	1.15	164, 174, 175
5	155, 156, 158	1 ii 3-6	150		
		1 ii 3-4	151	1.16	164, 165, 170
6	155, 156	1 ii 4-5	151		
7-8	159	1 ii 5	152	1.17-18	167
7	155, 156	1 ii 6	151	1.17	164, 165, 177
8-9	160	1 iii 6	151		
8	155, 156, 158	1 iii	151	1.18	158, 164, 165, 175
9	155, 157				
10	155, 157	*4Q387a (4QpsMos)*		1.20-21	22
11	155, 157, 158, 160	1 8	218	4.9-10	168
		3 ii 7-8	217	4.12-20	168, 177
12	155, 157, 162	3 ii 7	217	4.12-13	169
				4.13-16	174
13	155, 157, 158, 162	*4Q388a (4QpsMos)*		4.13	168, 169
		1 ii 3	217	4.14	168, 169, 182
14	155, 157				
15	157, 162	*4Q389 (4QpsMos)*		4.15-19	169
16	157	1 ii 9	217	4.15-18	169
17	156, 157, 158, 162			4.15	168
		4Q491		4.16	168
		11 ii 16	210	4.17	168
4Q252 (4QpGen)				4.18-19	169
1 v 2-4	211	*4Q496*		4.18	168
		3	208	4.19-20	170, 174
4Q285 (4QM B)		3 i 4	208	4.19	160, 168, 175, 178
5 3-4	211				
		4Q525		4.20	168-70
4Q339		2 ii	163	19–20	165
1–2	103			19.15–20.34	170, 173
		4Q550f (4QApoc ar)		19.15-32	170
4Q372		1	216	19.22-26	170, 177, 228
1 10	163	1.1	213		
19 2-4	211			19.22-24	171, 172
		CD		19.22-23	178
4Q373 (4QapDavid)		1–8	165	19.22	170
1-2 2	33				

CD (cont.)		20.13	170, 172	Targum 2 Samuel	
19.23	170	20.14-15	198	23.8	45
19.24-26	175	20.14	158, 172		
19.24-25	172	20.15	160, 172, 175	Targum Isaiah	
19.24	170, 178			42.1	45
19.25-26	172	20.22-24	171	43.10	45
19.25	170, 174, 178	20.25-26	171		
		20.26-34	171	Papyri	
19.26	170, 172, 174	20.26-27	171	Papyrus Oxyrhynchus	
19.32–20.1	170	Targums		22. 2332.30-31	51
20.13-22	170	Targum 1 Samuel			
20.13-15	172, 177, 202	17.43	227		
		23.8	228		

OTHER CLASSICAL AND ANCIENT WRITINGS

Athanasius		Cyril of Jerusalem		Jerome	
Apologia contra Arianos		Λόγοι κατηχητικοί		*Ad Algasiam*	
409D2	28	15.12	28	11.8	28
Oratio I contra Arianos		Firmicus Maternus		*De Antichristo in*	
13A10	28	*De errore profanarum*		*Danielem*	
25B7	28	*religionum*		11.21 IV 62-65	153
		22.4	27	11.21 IV 82-83	28
Vita Antonii monachi				11.31 IV 178-179	28
69.2	28	Herodotus			
		2.25-33	51	John of Damascus	
Augustine		3.16	76	*Expositio fidei*	
De civitate Dei		3.25	76	99.14-15	28
20.19.30-33	28	3.29	76		
		3.30-31	76		
Enarrationes in Psalmos		3.30	76	Josephus	
9.27.11	28	3.33	76	*Antiquities of the Jews*	
		3.66	76	12.228-229	22
Cassius Dio		5.16	67	12.235	22
42.5.5	102			12.240-241	22
		Hippolytus		12.247	77
Chrysostom		*De Antichristo*		12.256	139
In epistulam II ad Thessa-		6	28	13.181-183	176
lonicenses homilia III		15	28	13.228	184
530A	28	57	28	13.236-241	184
				13.254-258	184
Cicero		Irenaeus		13.272-373	204
Pro Flacco		*Adversus haereses*		13.276	184
67	101	5.25.1	28	13.299	184
				13.307-309	184

13.314-318	184	*Commentariorum series*		Tertullian	
13.373	204	*XLVII*		*De praescriptione*	
13.376	195	96.1.25-97.1.2	28	*haereticorum*	
13.377-379	195, 196			4.5	28
13.379	97	Philo			
13.380	139, 204	*Legum Allegoriae*		Theodore of Mopsuestia	
13.383	97, 196, 204	3.79-80	242	*In epistulam ad Thessalonicenses II*	
14.21	97	*De Somniis*		2.3-4 51 II.2-4	28
14.59	100	2.61-66	242	2.3-4 52 II.1-3	28
14.72	101	2.123	242	2.8 56 I.13	28
14.74	101	2.130-132	242		
14.77-78	101			Theodoret of Cyrrhus	
14.79	96	Plutarch		*Interpretatio in quatuor-decim epistolas S. Pauli*	
17.295	139	*Vitae Pompeius*		664A-B	28
		13.7-9	101		
The Jewish War		39.3	96	Victorinus of Pettau	
1.34	140	45.5	96	*Commentarii in Apoca-lypsin editio Victorini*	
1.145	100	76.4–79.5	102	12.3	27
1.147	100	77	102	12.7-9	27
1.149	100	78.4	102		
		80.2	102	Virgil	
Lactantius		80.3	102	*Aeneid*	
De morte persecutorum				4.384	159
33-35	73	Polybius			
33.6-8	73	*Histories*		*Eclogues*	
33.11	73	5.34.3	86	4.6	132
34	73	5.34.10	86		
35.3	73	5.35.6	86	*Georgics*	
		5.87.3	86	2.474	132
Livy					
42.29.5	54	Polycarp		Xenophon	
42.29.7	54	*Epistle of Polycarp*		*Memorabilia*	
		7.1	27	2.1.21-33	162
Origen				2.1.22	162
Contra Celsum		Strabo		2.1.23	162
6.45.13-19	28	16.2.26	102	2.1.30	162
6.46.3	28				

INDEX OF AUTHORS

Aalders, G.C. 151, 172
Abel, F.-M. 68, 71, 77, 78, 81, 184
Alexander, P.S. 76
Alexandre, C. 128
Allegro, J.M. 154, 160, 162, 173, 180,
  181, 193, 195
Andersen, F.I. 143, 144, 146, 147
Anderson, H. 83, 87
Applebaum, S. 87
Arenhoevel, D. 66, 70, 75, 76, 81
Atkinson, K.M.T. 207, 209
Attridge, H.W. 65, 77

Badian, E. 72
Baillet, M. 205, 206, 208, 209, 211, 212
Baldwin, J.G. 36, 203
Bar-Kochva, B. 79
Barstad, H.M. 30
Barta, W. 60
Bartelink, G. 87
Barthélemy, D. 187
Baumgarten, A.I. 108, 176
Baumgarten, J.M. 162
Baumgartner, W. 190
Beale, G.K. 206, 210, 215
Becker, J. 107-10, 114, 116, 117, 122,
  124
Beckwith, R.T. 47, 57, 90, 109, 111, 136,
  149, 162
Begg, C. 37
Beentjes, P.C. 47
Bénétreau, S. 112, 117
Berger, K. 121
Berkhof, H. 104
Bertholet, A. 2
Betz, O. 190
Bevan, E.R. 72
Bévenot, H. 71, 74
Beyer, K. 140, 213

Bickerman, E. 70, 102
Bierling, N. 33
Bietenhard, H. 205
Bimson, J.J. 41, 100
Black, M. 179, 185, 186, 207
Boerwinkel, F. 148
Bonwetsch, N. 143
Borger, R. 138
Bornhausen, K. 2
Bottéro, J. 7
Böttrich, C. 143, 144, 146
Bousset, W. 1-8, 10, 24, 25, 27, 29, 50,
  103, 121, 129, 237, 240
Bowman, J. 104
Boyce, M. 5
Brandenburger, E. 134-36, 138
Braun, F.-M. 108, 109
Braun, H. 105
Brongers, H.A. 182
Broshi, M. 70, 149, 164, 197
Brouwer, C. 38, 39
Brownlee, W.H. 23, 166, 174, 175, 185,
  198-204
Bruce, F.F. 139, 192, 195, 196, 198, 209
Brütsch, C. 31
Buchanan, G.W. 11
Buis, P. 31, 41
Bunge, J.G. 65-70, 73, 75, 83, 219
Burchard, C. 109
Burgmann, H. 20-23, 26, 154, 160, 161,
  165, 173, 178, 180, 183-86, 189,
  191, 200, 204, 239, 240
Burkitt, F.C. 11, 12
Burrows, M. 188, 194, 198
Busink, T.A. 100

Callaway, P.R. 23, 165-68, 173, 175, 186,
  191
Campbell, J.G. 165, 167, 170-72

Caquot, A. 12, 32, 35, 95, 109, 143, 144, 188, 191
Carmignac, J. 149, 154-63, 189-91, 195, 196, 198, 200-203, 207, 209, 210, 212, 214, 216
Chantraine, P. 52
Charles, R.H. 1, 10-15, 24, 25, 29, 108, 110-12, 114, 116-19, 121, 122, 133, 134, 136-39, 143, 145, 237, 238, 242
Charlesworth, J.H. 11, 12, 19, 44, 89, 97, 130-33, 222
Chary, T. 38, 39
Chilton, D. 31
Collins, J.J. 49, 51, 53-55, 57, 106, 108, 109, 125, 127-29, 133-36, 138, 140, 143, 144, 146, 152, 214, 216
Coser, L.A. 148
Cowley, A.E. 51, 218
Craigie, P.C. 30, 167, 177
Cross, F.M. 23, 183, 184

Dahl, N.A. 3
Davidson, M.J. 215, 216
Davies, P.R. 158, 165, 166, 169, 170, 173
De Goeij, M. 91, 94
De Jonge, M. 89, 94, 96, 98, 103, 105-107, 109-11, 113, 115-19, 122
Delcor, M. 73, 188-91
Denis, A.-M. 89, 90, 122, 134, 142
De Robert, P. 32, 35
Descamps, A. 16
De Romilly, J. 37
De Vaulx, J. 103, 104
De Vaux, R. 35, 59, 211, 212
Dhorme, E. 48, 210
Díez Merino, L. 151
Di Lella, A.A. 47, 48
Dimant, D. 150-54, 163, 175, 186, 206, 207, 217
Döbertin, W. 3
Donahue, D.J. 164, 197
Doran, R. 74, 80
Dörrie, H. 84
Dougherty, R.P. 76
Drioton, E. 151, 152
Duhaime, J. 19, 149, 207, 208
Dupont-Sommer, A. 110, 153, 161-63, 168, 171, 172, 174, 175, 182, 186, 188, 192, 195, 196, 198, 200-202, 207, 208

Eddy, S.K. 50-52, 68
Eichhorn, A. 2
Eisenman, R.H. 150
Eissfeldt, O. 2, 3, 41, 42, 109
Engel, H. 57
Enroth, R. 148
Enslin, M.S. 59, 60, 63
Ernout, A. 138
Ernst, J. 5, 14, 15, 231
Eshel, E. 70
Eshel, H. 179, 180, 183-85
Evans, C.A. 117

Fischer, U. 142-44, 146
Fishbane, M. 193, 215
Fitzmyer, J. 21, 180
Flusser, D. 20, 21, 44, 50, 65, 149, 152, 239
Foerster, W. 175
Fontinoy, C. 6
Friedländer, M. 10, 11
Friedlieb, J.H. 53
Fröhlich, I. 200

Gabrion, H. 149, 193
García Martínez, F. 149, 150, 152, 153, 165, 179, 180, 186, 187, 191, 193, 194, 197, 201, 205-207, 213, 217
Gazov-Ginsberg, A.M. 154, 163
Geffcken, J. 7, 15, 50, 52, 126
Gera, D. 80
Gesenius, W. 218
Gilbert, M. 46
Ginsberg, H.L. 18, 209
Ginzberg, L. 165, 169, 170
Glare, P.G.W. 137
Glorie, F. 153
Goedicke, H. 60
Goldstein, J.A. 67, 68, 75, 80, 81, 135
Goodenough, E.R. 130, 242
Gooding, D.W. 32
Goslinga, C.J. 32-36, 96
Gray, G.B. 90, 91, 93, 94, 96, 97, 100-102

Grosheide, F.W. 111
Guldentops, G. 27
Gunderson, L.L. 50-52
Gunkel, H. 2, 3, 5, 7-10, 25, 103, 236, 237
Gutberlet, C. 73, 78, 81

Haag, E. 57, 59-61, 63, 64, 77, 82
Hadas, M. 83, 85-88
Hadas-Lebel, M. 51, 103, 131, 209, 212
Hall, R.G. 140
Halperin, D.J. 195
Halpern, B. 41
Hamp, V. 140
Harrison, R.K. 41, 46, 49, 57, 65, 77
Hecht, R.D. 242
Heinen, H. 88
Hengel, M. 84, 85, 88, 106, 107, 109, 140, 144, 207
Hepp, V. 8, 25
Herr, M.D. 131
Hobbs, T.R. 34
Hoftijzer, J. 168
Hollander, H.W. 47, 107, 108, 111, 113, 115-19, 122
Holm-Nielsen, S. 93, 94, 98-103, 167, 187-91
Horgan, M.P. 193, 195-98, 200, 201
Horowitz, W. 80
Houtman, C. 200
Hultgård, A. 108-20, 122, 124
Humbert, J. 58, 95
Humbert, P. 37
Huppenbauer, H.W. 19, 166, 169, 171, 175
Hyldahl, N. 77

Jagersma, H. 33
Jansen, H.L. 121
Janssens, Y. 122
Jastrow, M. 218
Jeanmaire, H. 88
Jenks, G.C. 23, 24, 26, 240, 241
Jeremias, G. 187
John, W. 135
Jongeling, B. 209, 210, 212, 214, 215
Jope, E.M. 72

Joüon, P. 48, 97, 99, 155, 156, 172, 193, 218
Jull, A.J.T. 164, 197

Kane, J.P. 100
Kapera, Z.J. 21
Kasher, R. 167
Kautzsch, E. 218
Kee, H.C. 108, 109, 111, 118-20
Kellermann, D. 33, 35
Kippenberg, H.G. 55, 104
Kittel, B.P. 154, 189
Klatt, W. 3, 8
Klauck, H.-J. 27
Klein, R.W. 32, 33
Knibb, M.A. 165, 166, 168, 169, 173, 175, 189, 190, 192, 195, 196, 198, 200-202
Kobelski, P.J. 215
Koch, K. 56, 119
Koehler, L. 190
Koekkoek, H.G. 100, 101
Koenen, L. 51
Kolenkow, A. 106, 108, 109, 133
König, F. 5, 11
Koorevaar, H.J. 124
Kosmala, H. 112
Kroeze, J.H. 182, 188, 202
Kuhn, K.G. 108
Kümmel, W.G. 11
Kuyper, A. 159
Kvalbein, H. 149

Laato, A. 39
Labat, R. 7
Labuschagne, C.J. 30
Lacocque, A. 203
Lagrange, M.-J. 9, 136
Lamarche, P. 38, 39
Lanchester, H.C.O. 15, 53, 55, 127
Lannert, B. 2
Laperrousaz, E.-M. 133, 134, 136-42
LaSor, W.S. 149
Lattey, C. 135
Lebram, J.C.H. 51, 76
Leclercq, J. 31, 41
Lee, T.R. 48
Lemche, N.P. 34

Index of Authors

Lewy, H, 76
Licht, J. 134, 136, 210
Lietaert Peerbolte, L.J. 24-26, 41, 125, 186, 240, 241
Lim, T.H. 180, 183, 200, 204
Littman, E. 3
Lobel, E. 51
Lohse, E. 164, 168, 172, 187-89, 198
Lorein, G.W. 26, 28-30, 50, 60, 66, 69, 72, 76, 77, 79, 82, 89, 103, 140, 141, 149, 152, 176, 179
Lowe, E.A. 136
Lübbe, J. 183
Lüdemann, G. 2-4, 7

Maarsingh, B. 104
Maes, A. 101
Maggiorotti, D. 134-36, 142
Maier, G. 89, 90, 97, 102
Manson, T.W. 11, 12
Mansoor, M. 187, 188, 190, 191
Marcus, R. 196
Margoliouth, J.P.S. 45
Martin, W.R. 149
McCarter, P.K. Jr. 32-36
Mertens, A. 22, 197, 202, 207
Meyer, A. 2
Milik, J.T. 19-21, 183, 187, 211-13, 215
Miller, A. 59, 61-63
Mingana, A. 130
Momigliano, A. 53-55, 127
Moore, C.A. 58-63
Moore, R.D. 153, 157-61
Morfill, W.R. 143
Mørkholm, O. 67, 73
Mounce, R.H. 104
Mulert, H. 2

Nelis, J.T. 66-68, 70, 71, 74, 77, 79-82, 121, 140, 183
Newsom, C. 179-82, 184
Nickelsburg, G.W.E. 57, 83, 134, 135
Nielsen, K. 203
Nikiprowetzky, V. 49-56, 95, 122, 123, 125, 127, 128
Nikolainen, A.T. 7
Noack, B. 107, 112, 113, 115, 122, 123, 142, 175, 215
Noort, E. 123, 190

Noth, M. 44-46
Nuchelmans, J. 126

O'Connor, M. 100, 168, 173
O'Dell, J. 89
Oosterhoff, B.J. 213, 214
Osswald, E. 192

Pagels, E. 123
Palumbo, A.E. Jr. 194
Pardee, D. 174
Paul, A. 83-88
Paulus, W. 7, 10
Pearson, B.A. 143
Peretti, A. 54, 55, 127
Péter-Contesse, R. 74
Pezhumkattil, A. 162, 163
Philonenko, M. 46, 49, 89, 108-13, 115-19, 123, 142-46, 161, 162
Pines, S. 144
Pomykala, K.E. 211
Ponthot, J. 16
Poulssen, N. 57, 59-64
Priest, J. 138
Prigent, P. 87, 93, 94, 96, 97, 100, 102
Provan, I.W. 41
Puech, E. 152, 177, 179, 187, 200

Qimron, E. 150, 155, 157, 164, 180, 201, 210, 218

Rabin, C. 165-67, 178
Rahlfs, A. 90, 94
Reicke, B. 171
Reitzenstein, R. 10
Ridderbos, J. 37-40, 151, 156, 171, 172
Rigaux, B. 1, 15-18, 25, 27, 39, 40, 222, 238, 239
Roberts, C.H. 51
Robinson, J.M. 150
Rofé, A. 31, 36
Rowley, H.H. 11, 22, 123, 129, 139, 194, 195, 197, 202, 204, 209
Rubinstein, A. 144
Rudolph, W. 38, 39
Russell, D.S. 11, 103, 105
Ruterswörden, U. 30
Rzach, A. 50, 52-54, 126, 128

Sacchi, P. 19, 108, 118, 122, 123, 142-44, 146
Sachs, A.J. 79
Saggs, H.F.W. 8, 9
Sánchez Mielgo, G. 31
Sanders, J.A. 44
Schäfer, P. 202
Schaferdiek, K. 175
Schmid, J. 11
Schoors, A. 170, 203, 213, 215
Schouten, D. 118
Schroder, M. 2-4, 7
Schuller, E. 211, 212
Schunck, K.-D. 65, 78, 80
Schüpphaus, J. 90, 95-103, 105
Schürer, E. 179, 185, 186, 207
Segal, M.H. 218
Sievers, J. 184
Skehan, P.W. 47, 48
Smith, M. 150, 222
Sperber, A. 228
Stauffer, E. 197
Stegemann, H. 186, 187, 210
Stephan, H. 3
Stern, M. 202
Steudel, A. 165, 173, 174, 177, 199
Stoebe, H.-J. 32-36
Stone, M.E. 143, 144
Strecker, G. 21, 103, 228
Strobel, A. 131, 132
Strugnell, J. 150, 153, 154, 156-58, 161, 162, 173, 180, 193, 217
Sukenik, E.L. 187, 208

Tarn, W.W. 52, 209
Tcherikover, V.A. 83-87
Tedesche, S. 67, 78
Testuz, M. 215
Thissen, H.-J. 51
Thomas, F. 138
Thorion, Y. 181
Tidiman, B. 37, 41
Tigchelaar, E.J.C. 150, 201, 217
Torm, F. 49
Tov, E. 164, 197
Trafton, J.L. 90, 91, 93, 96, 99
Troeltsch, E. 2
Tromp, J. 88, 133-42

Turcan, R. 27
Turdeanu, E. 142

Ulrich, E.C. Jr. 33
Ulrichsen, J.H. 107-109
Ungnad, A. 45

Väänänen, V. 137, 138
Vaillant, A. 142-46
Vanacker, G. 149
Van Bruggen, J. 104
Van den Born, A. 47
Van der Kooij, A. 32
Van der Lingen, A. 35
Vanderostyne, M. 159
Van der Ploeg, J.P.M. 18, 189, 190, 202, 207-10, 212, 214-16
Van der Westhuizen, M.J. 1, 27
Van der Woude, A.S. 19-21, 23, 25, 37-39, 42, 44, 47, 57, 65, 68, 77, 89, 108-12, 114, 115, 121-23, 135, 143, 144, 149, 152-54, 160, 162, 163, 165, 170, 172, 173, 176, 177, 180, 182, 185-88, 190-94, 197-201, 204-208, 213, 217, 221, 229, 233, 243
Van Deuren, J. 102
Vandier, J. 151, 152
Van Gelderen, C. 166, 169, 170, 181
Van Henten, J.W. 51
Van Hoonacker, A. 38
Van Leeuwen, C. 152, 182
Van Ooteghem, J. 96, 100, 101, 104
Van Staalduine-Sulman, E. 31, 37, 46, 228
Van 't Land, F.A.W. 198, 201
Van Zyl, A.H. 32-35
Vattioni, F. 47
Vegas Montaner, L. 188
Vergote, J. 87
Verheule, A.F. 2-5, 7, 8
Vermes, G. 21, 107, 109, 179, 183, 185, 186, 189, 201, 207
Viteau, J. 89, 90, 92-101, 103, 105
Von der Osten-Sacken, P. 19, 206, 215
Von Nordheim, E. 107, 115, 118, 133-35
Von Soden, H. Freiherr 3
Von Soden, W. Freiherr 60

Index of Authors

Von Stuckrad, K. 129, 130, 132, 133
Vouga, F. 27
Vriezen, T.C. 47, 56, 57, 65, 77, 89, 108, 143, 190

Wallis, G. 7
Waltke, B.K. 100, 104, 168, 173
Wambacq, B.N. 203
Weinfeld, M. 149
Weinrich, W.C. 236
Weiss, J. 2
Wénin, A. 34, 36
Widengren, G. 9
Will, E. 54, 84, 126, 127, 176, 194, 195
Williams, D.S. 83
Wiseman, D.J. 79

Wood, M. 174
Wrede, W. 2
Wright, R.B. 89-91, 94, 95, 99, 100, 103

Yadin, Y. 208, 209, 212, 214
Yamauchi, E. 41, 76
Yarbro Collins, A. 135
Young, E.J. 73, 170, 203

Zeitlin, S. 59, 60, 63, 67, 78
Zenger, E. 58-60, 63, 64
Zimmerli, W. 232
Zimmermann, J. 29, 180, 182, 184
Zorell, F. 32, 38, 48, 113, 155, 158, 164, 176, 189, 195, 198, 243

JOURNAL FOR THE STUDY OF THE PSEUDEPIGRAPHA
SUPPLEMENT SERIES

1   John R. Levison, *Portraits of Adam in Early Judaism: From Sirach to 2 Baruch*
2   Per Bilde, *Flavius Josephus between Jerusalem and Rome: His Life, his Works, and their Importance*
3   Philip R. Callaway, *The History of the Qumran Community: An Investigation*
4   Tom W. Willet, *Eschatology in the Theodicies of 2 Baruch and 4 Ezra*
5   James R. Mueller, *The Five Fragments of the Apocryphon of Ezekiel: A Critical Study*
6   Robert G. Hall, *Revealed Histories: Techniques for Ancient Jewish and Christian Historiography*
7   George J. Brooke (ed.), *Temple Scroll Studies: Papers Presented at the International Symposium on the Temple Scroll (Manchester, 1987)*
8   Lawrence H. Schiffman (ed.), *Archaeology and History in the Dead Sea Scrolls: The New York University Conference in Memory of Yigael Yadin*
9   John J. Collins and James H. Charlesworth (eds.), *Mysteries and Revelations: Apocalyptic Studies since the Uppsala Colloquium*
10 Shemaryahu Talmon (ed.), *Jewish Civilization in the Hellenistic-Roman Period*
11 Maxwell J. Davidson, *Angels at Qumran: A Comparative Study of 1 Enoch 1–36, 72–108 and Sectarian Writings from Qumran*
12 David Bryan, *Cosmos, Chaos and the Kosher Mentality*
13 Gordon M. Zerbe, *Non-Retaliation in Early Jewish and New Testament Texts: Ethical Themes in Social Contexts*
14 James H. Charlesworth and Craig A. Evans (eds.), *The Pseudepigrapha and Early Biblical Interpretation*
15 Michael Owen Wise, *Thunder in Gemini, and Other Essays on the History, Language and Literature of Second Temple Palestine*
16 Randall D. Chesnutt, *From Death to Life: Conversion in Joseph and Aseneth*
17 Edith McEwan Humphrey, *The Ladies and the Cities: Transformation and Apocalyptic Identity in Joseph and Aseneth, 4 Ezra, the Apocalypse and The Shepherd of Hermas*
18 Jonathan Knight, *Disciples of the Beloved One: The Christology, Social Setting and Theological Context of the Ascension of Isaiah*
19 Ida Fröhlich, *Time and Times and Half a Time: Historical Consciousness in the Jewish Literature of the Persian and Hellenistic Eras*
20 Paolo Sacchi, *Jewish Apocalyptic and Its History*
21 Isaiah M. Gafni, *Land, Center and Diaspora: Jewish Constructs in Late Antiquity*
22 James H. Charlesworth, *Critical Reflections on the Odes of Solomon, Volume 1: Literary Setting, Textual Studies, Gnosticism, the Dead Sea Scrolls and the Gospel of John*
23 Samuel Cheon, *The Exodus Story in the Wisdom of Solomon: A Study in Biblical Interpretation*

24 Doron Mendels, *Identity, Religion and Historiography: Studies in Hellenistic History*
25 Michael Chyutin, *The New Jerusalem Scroll from Qumran: A Comprehensive Reconstruction*
26 Stanley E. Porter & Craig A. Evans (eds.), *The Scrolls and the Scriptures: Qumran Fifty Years After*
27 Gerbern S. Oegema, *The Anointed and his People: Messianic Expectations from the Maccabees to Bar Kochba*
28 Phillip B. Munoa, III, *Four Powers in Heaven: The Interpretation of Daniel 7 in the Testament of Abraham*
29 James S. McLaren, *Turbulent Times? Josephus and Scholarship on Judaea in the First Century* CE
30 Nikos Kokkinos, *The Herodian Dynasty: Origins, Role in Society and Eclipse*
31 Siân Jones and Sarah Pearce (eds.), *Jewish Local Patriotism and Self-Identification in the Graeco-Roman Period*
32 Steve Mason (ed.), *Understanding Josephus: Seven Perspectives*
33 Craig A. Evans (ed.), *The Interpretation of Scripture in Early Judaism and Christianity: Studies in Language and Tradition*
34 Paulson Pulikottil, *Transmission of Biblical Texts in Qumran: The Case of the Large Isaiah Scroll (1QIsa^a)*
35 Gregory L. Doudna, *4Q Pesher Nahum: A Critical Edition*
36 Magen Broshi, *Bread, Wine, Walls and Scrolls*
37 Bruce N. Fisk, *Do You Not Remember? Exegetical Appropriations of Biblical Narrative in Pseudo-Philo*
38 Timothy H. Lim, Hector MacQueen and Calum Carmichael (eds.), *On Scrolls, Artefacts and Intellectual Property*
39 Lorenzo DiTommaso, *A Bibliography of Pseudepigrapha Research 1850–1999*
42 Mark F. Whittiers, *The Epistle of Second Baruch: A Study in Form and Message*
43 Christopher Rowland and John Barton (eds.), *Apocalyptic in History and Tradition*
44 G.W. Lorein, *The Antichrist Theme in the Intertestamental Period*